University of California Press, one of the most distinguished university presses in the United States, enriches lives around the world by advancing scholarship in the humanities, social sciences, and natural sciences. Its activities are supported by the UC Press Foundation and by philanthropic contributions from individuals and institutions. For more information, visit www.ucpress.edu.

University of California Press
Berkeley and Los Angeles, California

University of California Press, Ltd.
London, England

Also published as *Vins et Vignerons du Sud-Ouest*.
Éditions du Rouergue.
Parc Saint-Joseph - BP 3522 - 12035 Rodez Cedex 9
Tel.: 05-65-77-73-70   Fax: 05-65-77-73-71
www.lerouergue.com

Library of Congress Cataloging-in-Publication Data

Strang, Paul.
   South-west France : the wines and winemakers / Paul Strang ; photographs by Jason Shenai.
      p.   cm.
   Issued simultaneously in French titled : Vins et vignerons du Sud-Ouest.
   Includes bibliographical references and index.
   ISBN 978-0-520-25941-6 (cloth : alk. paper)
   1. Wine and wine making—France, Southwest. 2. Vineyards—France, Southwest. I. Shenai, Jason. II. Title.
TP553.S76 2009
641.2'20944—dc22   2008055515

Manufactured in China
18 17 16 15 14 13 12 11 10 09
10 9 8 7 6 5 4 3 2 1

The paper used in this publication meets the minimum requirements of ANSI/NISO Z39.48-1992 (R 1997) (*Permanence of Paper*).

SOUTH-WEST
FRANCE

For Caroline and Christopher

Paul Strang

PHOTOGRAPHS BY
Jason Shenai

SOUTH-WEST FRANCE

THE WINES AND WINEMAKERS

UNIVERSITY OF CALIFORNIA PRESS
BERKELEY   LOS ANGELES   LONDON

CONTENTS

NOTES ON VISITING THE VINEYARDS AND USING THIS BOOK

Location

Each chapter opens with a map of a wine region, and the entry for each producer is keyed to a number indicating the vineyard's location on the map. Most of the large wine-growing areas have signposts directing the way to individual properties, but it is recommended that visitors travel with detailed maps.

Contact

To avoid disappointment, and also as a courtesy to growers, particularly smaller ones who cannot be expected to stay in their cellars in anticipation of potential visitors, arrange a rendezvous in advance whenever possible.

Telephone and fax numbers and email addresses are supplied when available, but these can change. Those listed were accurate at the time of publication.

Visits

Visits to growers may be made at any time during normal business hours on weekdays (avoid lunchtime, which is usually between 12:00 and 2:00 p.m.). *Caves Coopératives* are generally closed on Saturday afternoon, Sunday and public holidays. Private growers prefer to keep Sunday free, but appointments may be made for any time on Saturday. Although many growers speak English, you may learn more if you can speak to them in French.

Visits are free and there is no obligation to make a purchase. But if a grower pays you more than cursory attention or gives up a lot of his or her time, you might do the courtesy of buying at least a bottle or two. Easy-to-carry, prepackaged cartons of three different wines are often available.

Wine quality

Wines described are given a quality rating of up to three stars. Absence of a star does not necessarily indicate a poor wine, merely one which is not as good as those with stars. Stars usually reflect general opinion as well as the author's own predilection, unless otherwise indicated.

Ratings are valid only within the chapter in which they appear. Thus, a one-star rating in a region well known for the high quality of its wines may be the equivalent of a three-star rating in a much more modest area, and vice versa. Readers may find it more useful to compare wines within a single area than compare the same wines with those of another appellation. No attempt is made to create league tables or to establish hierarchies, Parker-style.

Price

Wine prices change, so no figures are supplied. However, so that readers will have a general idea of the price of each grower's wines, levels are indicated in ascending order from A to D plus. Wines have been divided into the following ranges, based on prices at the time of publication; prices are those charged at the cellar, including TVA:

A: less than 6€ ($8)
B: between 6 and 12€ ($8–$16)
C: between 12 and 20€ ($16–$26)
D: above 20€ ($26)

Every effort has been made to verify these categories, but prices change, not only because of economic fluctuations, but also because a grower may become more fashionable or ambitious, or both.

Pardon my French

The English language is somewhat short on technical vocabulary. Readers will find the text peppered with French words for which there is no adequate translation. A glossary is provided for readers unfamiliar with French wine-speak.

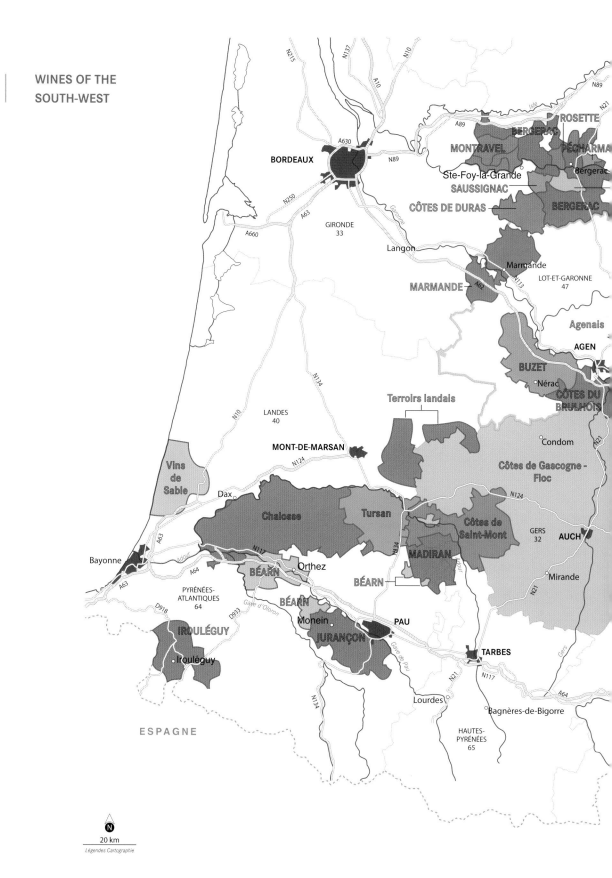

WINES OF THE
SOUTH-WEST

ROSETTE
BERGERAC
MONTRAVEL
PÉCHARMA
Ste-Foy-la-Grande
SAUSSIGNAC
CÔTES DE DURAS
BERGERAC
Bergerac

Langon
Marmande
LOT-ET-GARONNE
47
MARMANDE

GIRONDE
33

Agenais
AGEN
BUZET
Nérac
CÔTES DU
BRULHOIS

Terroirs landais
Condom
MONT-DE-MARSAN
Côtes de Gascogne -
Floc

LANDES
40

Vins
de
Sable
Dax
Chalosse
Tursan
Côtes de
Saint-Mont
GERS
32
AUCH

MADIRAN
Mirande

Bayonne
BÉARN
Orthez
BÉARN

PYRÉNÉES-
ATLANTIQUES
64
BÉARN
Monein
IROULÉGUY
JURANÇON
PAU
Irouléguy
TARBES

ESPAGNE
Lourdes
Bagnères-de-Bigorre

HAUTES-
PYRÉNÉES
65

N
20 km
Légendes Cartographie

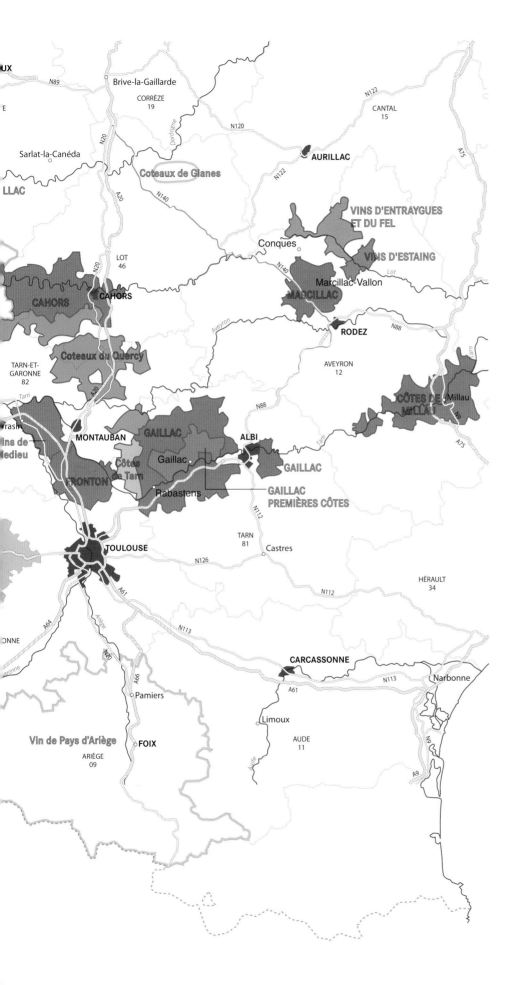

INTRODUCTION

The wines and winemakers described in this book come from an area roughly between the *massif central* and the Pyrenees, a part of France well known to Anglo-Saxons, much loved and visited by them, many of whom have chosen to live there permanently. The wines themselves, however, are little seen outside the region of their production. The purpose of this book is to bring to the attention of wine lovers all over the world the considerable quality and distinctiveness of these wines. Every part of the South-West without exception produces wines of character, made by idiosyncratic growers who are motivated by a passion for their profession. The South-West is still a celebration of the diversity of the vine. At a time when the world market is dominated by a handful of internationally grown grape varieties, it is refreshing to know that other varieties, grown only in the South-West, produce wines which are like no other. The South-West is at the opposite pole from globalization, which may explain why the big players in the wine business (with a few honourable exceptions) have been reluctant to come to grips with it. These pages may help the wine lover to explore and to exercise personal judgment and to cultivate a taste for wines which only now are coming into their own.

We wine drinkers are on the whole an unadventurous lot. We take a great deal of persuading to try a wine which is not familiar to us, so we stick to *sauvignon*, *chardonnay*, *cabernet* and so on. The French, overlooking the diversity of wine styles produced in their own country, are as lazy as the rest of us. Notwithstanding the blandishments of the wine magazines and the efforts of so-called pundits to encourage adventure, the average French wine buyer is more likely to invest for a special occasion in a bottle of third-rate Bordeaux or an indifferent Burgundy than a first-class wine from a 'lesser' region. Despite the emergence of exciting new wines from the South-West, it would be rare indeed to find any of those wines in the average restaurant of northern provincial France.

In the anglophone world the enjoyment of wine was once limited to the relatively rich. Perhaps because wine was a relative luxury, our forebears tended to buy the guarantee of a good claret name or a burgundy grower with a good reputation, for fear that the unknown might spoil an important social occasion. But in the last decade or so, wine has become a more inclusive drink: many people agree with Brillat-Savarin that 'a day without wine is a day without sunshine'; good wine can be had for little money, and the reputations of once supreme wine-growing areas have come under challenge from the New World, where drinkers are now more willing to try the unknown. Whereas in France very little wine from any other country is to be found on a supermarket shelf (0.2 percent of all wines stocked, according to a recent survey), in the United States and Britain wines from elsewhere far outnumber those from the French wine regions in similar outlets.

Despite an occasional willingness to experiment, wines from the South-West of France have yet to make the headway they deserve. It is difficult to find Gaillac or Cahors on a supermarket shelf—other than the cheapest generic examples, which do little to encourage further investigation of the region. Because of a general perception that the public will pay no more than a basic price for a wine from the

South-West, the better ones are rarely seen in anglophone countries. Professional buyers will tell you that they cannot sell these wines because they are too tough, tannic or austere. This is just not true; there are plenty of soft, fruity wines for immediate drinking. In any case, the same buyers seem to have no difficulty selling wines from other parts of the world which are just as tough, just as tannic or just as austere as, say, madiran. Again it is said that the wines take time to mature, but so do comparable wines from California or Australia; then too, there are many wines which can be drunk in the year following the vintage. The most feeble reason for not marketing these wines is that the trade is there to give the customers what they want, not to educate them; but how can consumers decide whether they want a wine if they cannot try it out?

The holdings of vineyards in the South-West are, with a few exceptions, tiny compared with those in other wine-growing areas. This means that the quantities of wine available from any given property are not going to be big enough to stock uniformly the shelves of ever-growing supermarkets with ever-increasing numbers of stores. These outlets buy only from the bulk dealers and from the larger *coopératives*, some of which (Producteurs Plaimont and Jurançon, for example) are excellent. For the average consumer this means that his knowledge of wines from the South-West is going to be based on a small handful of big producers who cannot offer the full range of choice let alone character which the different appellations can offer. His best bet lies with other importers, the better chains and independent merchants, who have the human and financial resources as well as the passion to investigate the vineyards in depth and to offer a real choice from among the many excellent wines which are available.

Some vineyards are as small as four hectares or even less, while few are more than 30. Most are small family concerns without the money to pay for outside promotional help. Stands at important wine shows like Vinexpo or Vinisud are expensive, and, although some growers may club together to share a stand, the cost, usually well over £1,000 ($1,490), often outweighs the benefits. A *vigneron*'s best bet may be to get noticed favourably by French specialist magazines or the *Guide Hachette,* for example, where a good review or mark will spark interest from restaurants and wine merchants, which then filters through to the consumer. Medals at trade competitions are another way a grower can get known, because the French pay a deal of attention, too much in fact, to medals. But little attention is paid by wine magazines in other countries to success of this sort in France.

The wines of South-West France reflect the supreme beauty and variety of its landscapes and microclimates, as well as the passionate devotion of its winemakers, for whom the production of wine is not just a way of making a living but a way of life. They offer a range of choice and style unequalled by any other region, and their quality is much higher than their prices would indicate. I hope that readers will help these fine growers achieve the success they so fully deserve, as well as make for themselves discoveries which transform their wine experience.

A WINE WITHOUT A PAST IS A WINE WITHOUT A FUTURE

BORDEAUX VERSUS THE HAUT-PAYS

Until the 17th century, Bordeaux was not known as a region of quality wines in its own right. The local growers had not yet prepared or irrigated their local *terroir,* nor had they mastered any but the most elementary skills of wine-making. But, as the most important port on the Atlantic seaboard, Bordeaux was able to control the comings and goings of the limitless quantities of wine made in the hinterland, which was called the *haut-pays*. The vineyards of Cahors, Gaillac, Moissac and Bergerac in particular sent most of their production downstream by horse-drawn barge to Bordeaux for export to the north of Europe, England, the Low Countries and the Ile de France.

When the wines reached Bordeaux, some were bought by the Bordelais merchants to stretch their own pale and insipid wines before the resulting blends were shipped overseas. The rest were reloaded onto seagoing vessels and sold under the name of their region of origin. The export of wines from Bordeaux was given a big shot in the arm when Henry II of England married Eleanor of Aquitaine in 1152, thereby bringing Bordeaux into the English sphere of influence and a direct trading relationship. England became one of the thirstiest and most knowledgeable markets for French wine. It still is.

The Bordelais merchants were unscrupulous operators. They charged exorbitant tolls for the passage of wine through the city; and because their own wine was so poor and would not last longer than a few months, they needed to ensure that it left port before any of the wines of the *haut-pays*. From the 14th century onwards the latter were not allowed beyond the Bordeaux quays until Christmas Day. This not only gave the Bordelais first pick of the customers but also enabled them to appropriate markets which the growers upstream had assiduously cultivated for their own exports.

Eventually Bordeaux began to reinvest some of the profits it made in the drainage and improvement of its own marshy suburbs, thus laying the basis for its modern quality production. The development in England of coffeehouse society in the late 17th century, coupled with the progressive economic prosperity of England over the next hundred years, led to a call for an increase in quality of imported wine. Bordeaux itself became increasingly able to meet this demand through the gradual growth of the pattern of wine châteaux, which endures to the present day. Moreover, English importers had discovered the virtues of new clean oak barrels, which ensured better travel and longer life for the wines they bought, and the development of the glass bottle and the cork stopper increased immeasurably the keeping potential of wine.

As the quality of Bordeaux wines increased, the city should have needed to rely less and less on the restrictive practices it had imposed on its up-country neighbours. But old habits die hard: the tolls continued to be exacted, and even the delay in the passage of wines until after the New Year continued until the eve of the Revolution, when *Le Grand Privilège* (as the priority rights of Bordeaux were known) was eventually abolished.

ROME, THE CHURCH AND GRAPES

The vineyards of the *haut-pays* have a long and distinguished history. As the Romans spread westwards from Languedoc and gradually conquered the whole of Gaul, first Gaillac, then Moissac and Cahors established themselves as distinctive wine regions. Today the source of the wines' originality is invariably the variety of grape used in each area, which is more often than not exclusive to the South-West and just as frequently unknown further afield. Universally grown varieties have, it is true, been introduced, the *cabernets*, *merlot* and *sauvignon* for example, but beyond the satellite vineyards of Bordeaux they have not been allowed to supplant the local specialities.

Many of these grape varieties came from south of the Pyrenees, the reason lying in the historical importance of the shrine of Saint-Jacques-de-Compostelle, today called Santiago. It was believed that here lay the forgotten tomb of Saint James the Greater, Spain's adopted apostle, who, according to the claims of the Church, had been washed up on the Atlantic coast in a giant seashell (hence *coquilles Saint-Jacques*). This holy site gradually became a point of pilgrimage of considerable importance. In 1189 Pope Alexander III decreed the town a Holy City, putting it on a par with Jerusalem and Rome. A trickle of pilgrims became a flood. The problem for those living north of the Pyrenees was to cross that mountain range, and in practical terms the only three routes all lay close to the Atlantic Ocean in what is now the French Basque country. The South-West of France gradually became a funnel through which the pious poured on their way to Spain from all over northern Europe. Today it seems hard to find a village in the region which does not claim to lie on one of the historic routes to Saint-Jacques-de-Compostelle.

The growing numbers of pilgrims spawned the creation of important monasteries and abbeys all over the South-West, among whose functions was the giving of hospitality, shelter and sustenance to the faithful. These included Conques (Aveyron), Marcilhac-sur-Célé (Lot), Madiran (Hautes-Pyrénées), Gaillac (Tarn), Lacommande (Jurançon), and Saint-Mont and Éauze (Gers). Both of these last-named were directly controlled by the Abbey of Cluny in Burgundy, from which the route to Compostelle lay over the Massif Central through Conques. These religious foundations developed a kind of network of communication and cultural exchange, becoming in effect a chain of stopovers for the pilgrims.

The traffic to Compostelle was two-way. It is not surprising that pilgrims returning from Spain should have brought with them the grapes and vines they had found on the far side of the Pyrenees. It is almost certainly in this way that the grapes now particular to the South-West became generally cultivated there, and probably also how others such as *cabernet*, *merlot* and *sauvignon* spread northwards via the Atlantic corridor to Bordeaux and the Loire Valley.

Until the second half of the 20th century, viticulture in the South-West pursued its own course, independent of the development of the wine trade in the rest of France. The South-West for long had but the poorest of communications with the rest of France; even today the *département* of Gers has no railways except a local train from Auch to Toulouse. This freedom from outside influence has perhaps helped the South-West to retain its idiosyncratic wines and grape varieties, despite their lack of fame.

THE PHYLLOXERA DISASTER

As the 19th century recedes into history, it is all too easy to forget that the vineyards of the South-West were almost completely wiped out. It was in fact in a greenhouse in Hammersmith, London, that the modern history of the South-West really began. There, for the first time in Europe, an aphid was discovered which would destroy almost the whole of the vineyards of France within a quarter of a century. Fat but tiny, it measured less than a millimetre and could multiply its population twelvefold in a year. It first appeared in the eastern United States. It is particularly fond of vine leaves, feeding on the juice and going down to the roots of the plant, on which it produces nodules which end up killing the vines. Returning to the surface in search of more nourishment, it spreads its devastation.

Soon after its discovery in England, the killer aphid was found near Tarascon in the Rhone Valley. It spread rapidly in the south of France and in 1866 it was seen for the first time in the Bordelais. Within a space of 16 years, nearly 98% of the vineyards of the Gironde were infested. It reached Cahors in 1877, and during the following decades it infiltrated the whole of the South-West. It was appropriately christened *Phylloxera vastatrix.*

The phylloxera tragedy was more keenly felt in the South-West than any-where else, because so much of the land was given over to vines. Over the years the South-West had become the most intensive wine-producing area in the world: indeed Bordeaux and the rest of the South-West, considered together, *were* the vineyard of the civilised world. Vines grew everywhere there, and even in the less favourable regions they represented a crop of real financial importance to the peasant-farmers.

The effects of the phylloxera were so profound that it would take nearly a century for the South-West to recover from them. It had caused the gradual depopulation of some rural areas, especially on the limestone plateaux (*causses*) where nothing but the vines would grow. Entire communities were abandoned. The new generation left to try and find work elsewhere. Some went to Paris, others emigrated.

The situation was aggravated by the general economic decline which followed the social upheavals and creation of the Third Republic in the 1880's. Few *vignerons* were in a position to replant their vineyards with new stock immune to the disease. This involved grafting the traditional French grape varieties on American rootstocks, an impossible expense for the ordinary peasant-farmer. Nevertheless, the amount of land under vine diminished only gradually because the reaction of most growers was to replant, but with ungrafted stock. These fell victim to the disease almost immediately. The already shrinking rural population was further decreased by the loss of life in the First World War, the economic and psychological aftermath of which did nothing to help restore a feeling of confidence.

A BELATED RECOVERY

In France, the demand for cheap wine on the part of the fast-growing proletariat of Northern France was met largely by plonk from the Midi, where unrestricted yields from inferior grape varieties produced limitless quantities of weak, thin wines, often beefed up with tougher stuff from North Africa. But in the middle of the 20th century, growing prosperity led to a demand for wines of better quality at affordable prices. The wines of Bordeaux were not, however, within the means of all purses. Other factors contributed to a renaissance. The coming of independence to Muslim Algeria cut off the supply of wines to the Languedoc, and a number of the North African growers came back to France, bringing with them a spirit of innovation and the desire to experiment with new techniques not always compatible with the ideas of the indigenous French growers. The European Commission offered generous subsidies to those willing to plant quality grape varieties in substitution for the inferior ones planted in the wake of phylloxera.

But it was above all the limitless enthusiasm of a small number of local growers, sometimes working with, sometimes against, a new, younger, better educated generation, which brought about the reconstruction of the vineyards of the South-West. The story of this rebirth is truly a modern romance.

THE WINES OF
THE HILL COUNTRY

MARCILLAC AND THE LOT GORGES

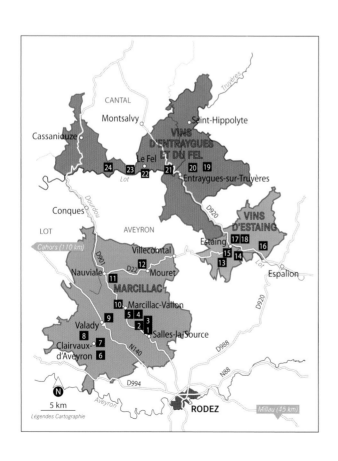

CANTAL

Montsalvy

Saint-Hippolyte

Cassaniouze

VINS D'ENTRAYGUES ET DU FEL

Le Fel

24 23 22 21 20 19

Lot

Entraygues-sur-Truyères

Truyères

Conques

Dourdou

D920

VINS D'ESTAING

LOT

AVEYRON

Estaing 17 18

16

Cahors (110 km)

Villecomtal

15 14

13

D901

D22

Mouret

Lot

Espalion

Nauviale

11

MARCILLAC

D920

10 Marcillac-Vallon

5 4 3

Valady

9

2 1

Salles-la-Source

8

Clairvaux-
d'Aveyron

7

6

N140

D988

Aveyron

D994

N88

RODEZ

Millau (45 km)

N

5 km

Légendes Cartographie

MARCILLAC

AREA OF AOC: selected parcels covering 161 hectares in the communes of Marcillac-Vallon, Balsac, Clairvaux, Goutrens, Mouret, Nauviale, Pruines, Salles-la-Source, Saint-Cyprien-sur-Dourdou, Saint-Christophe-Vallon and Valady.

Red and rosé wines only. Average production 8000 hectolitres.

GRAPE VARIETIES: fer servadou (mansois) minimum 90%; cabernet sauvignon, cabernet franc and merlot also permitted but hardly used.

MINIMUM ALCOHOL CONTENT: 10% by volume. If chaptalization permitted, maximum alcoholic degree is 13%. Variations possible by derogation issued by the authorities.

MAXIMUM YIELD: 50 hl/ha.

MINIMUM PLANTING DENSITY: 4000 plants per hectare except on the terraces.

PRUNING: guyot (single or double).

Lo vin lo cal beure Wine should be drunk
lo matin tot pur neat in the morning,
à miègjour sans aiga without water at midday,
e lo ser tal que lo Bou Dius and in evening just as the Good Lord
l'a donat! gave it to us!
  (Old Aveyron Proverb)

THE WINES OF AVEYRON

Built on a hill, the city of Rodez is the county town of Aveyron, France's fifth largest yet one of its least known *départements*. Its rugged Gothic cathedral dominates the old quarter of the city, trying in vain to draw under its mountainous skirts the rapidly expanding sprawl of suburbs so typical of modern French development.

Aveyron corresponds roughly with the old French province called Rouergue, meaning literally 'red earth'. Until recently it was almost cut off from the culture and commerce of the rest of France; the mountains of the Auvergne to the north,

the Cévennes to the east, the inhospitable *causses* to the south and unnavigable rivers running through impenetrable gorges to the west denied the Ruthénois (as the inhabitants of Rodez are called) the commercial advantages of their neighbours in the Lot to the west and the Tarn to the south.

Although over 2000 feet above sea level, Rodez suffered pestilence and plague from the earliest times. The water supplies of the city were largely polluted, so wine was regarded as an acceptable substitute, even as a medicine. The hospitals and convents needed a regular supply of it. Where today supermarkets and warehouses, blocks of flats and factories make up the suburbs of Rodez, vineyards once grew until they were destroyed by the phylloxera. The climate was far from ideal, however, and some of the sheltered valleys to the north-west of the town, where the temperature is often a good 10 degrees Fahrenheit higher than in the city, offered much better conditions for the vine. The founding clerics of the Abbey of Conques had been quick to spot this; moreover, since Conques was a staging post on one of the main routes to Saint-Jacques-de-Compostelle, there was a need for a good supply of wine. The monks are thought to have come from Burgundy in the 9th century and to have brought with them the wine-making skills which they had learnt there. Their influence on the developments of the Aveyron vineyards was ongoing as well as pioneering.

MARCILLAC

Conques is close by the river Dourdou, which flows downstream into the Lot. Upstream from Conques is the town of Marcillac, and near here two streams join together. One, called Créneau, rises just north of Rodez in the Causse de Comtal, where it spurts from the rock just above the pretty village of Salles-la-Source; the other runs parallel a few miles away to the west and is called the Ady, which gives its name to the village of Valady, today the home of the Marcillac *Coopérative*. The two valleys are steep-sided and covered with the local red earth and a generous dose of chalky pebbles washed down from the *causses*.

The *terroir* was described in this way by an Aveyronnais poet in a letter to her friend George Sand:

> The soil is fiery red. The rocks and the land are of the same colour, the topsoil merely a crumbling of the stone. Rain, frost and sun have shaped these hillsides, man coming in his turn to profit from the result of these erosions; he has built walls on the slopes, bringing to the tops of the hillsides soil brought from lower down; on these terraces he has planted vines and created miniature fields. This landscape should be seen at sunset in summer, when it is of incomparable magnificence; the earth and the red rocks take on an extraordinary powerful colouring.

The vineyards are sheltered from the cruel winter winds of the Auvergne, and particularly those areas which face south and west enjoy an almost Mediterranean climate. This small river network is called Le Vallon, and the wine which is made there bears the name of the local town, Marcillac.

The reputation of the Vallon's microclimate had certainly spread to Rodez by the late Middle Ages. Extensive vineyards were planted by the hospices and convents of the city between the villages of Valady and Clairvaux. Many villages bear witness to this day to the scale of medieval wine-making, having kept their entrance gates and fortifications.There are still whole streets of houses with their characteristic Gothic arches carved out of the local red sandstone, which glow like coals in the evening sun. There are solid but pretty romanesque churches too, such as at Clairvaux, which is clearly modelled on Conques itself, evidence of a once healthy attendance at worship.

VIGNOBLES SECONDAIRES

The emergence of a rich bourgeoisie in Rodez gave further impetus to the expansion of the Marcillac vineyards. The more prosperous local merchants began to plant their own vines and to build country houses in the middle of them. Many of these attractive *maisons de maître* not only survive but have been restored by today's generation of successful businessmen spawned by the recent commercial expansion of Rodez. It has once again become socially *de rigueur* to have a *maison secondaire* among the vines, although today it is perhaps the climate rather than the grapes which are the attraction. In times gone by whole families would spend the summer in their country homes until the vintage was over. In the villages some medieval houses still stand among the now abandoned terraces of vines, many given over to ducks and hens. The whole of the medieval centre of Clairvaux is derelict; I met an elderly lady walking her dog in the silent streets, and she told me that the imposing houses all around had vast underground cellars where the wines of Marcillac were once stored. Their architectural detail is impressive; even the dungheaps for the cattle had roofs made from the local scallop-shaped slates.

The bourgeois *vignerons* usually employed a full-time manager to run their vineyards. These stewards acted as foremen and were a buffer between the *patron* and his vineyard workers. They had their own trade association, which spurred competition between rival vineyards, thus introducing an element of quality into the wine-making. Where once wine had been merely a beverage, a substitute for water, growers now began to vie with each other to produce wine which was better than their neighbours'. So the quality of the wines of the Vallon rose.

The local historian Alexis Monteil, writing just after the Revolution, described the village of Marcillac in a manner that still sounds familiar today:

> This place is languid in the spring, but brilliant in the autumn. During that season, the inhabitants of Rodez, owners of virtually all the vines in the area, come with their families for the harvest. Most are middle-class and well off. They are not prepared to forgo any of the benefits of town life, so bring with them a large quantity of equipment and food. As they pass you on the road, you might think they were going off somewhere to found a new colony.

Vintage time must have been more than usually frenetic in those heady days of Marcillac's golden age. The whole community was engaged in the wine harvest, because there was no other local crop than the vine. The jobless from Rodez walked from the city to the Vallon to be hired for the duration, and accounts of the local labour markets recalled the novels of Thomas Hardy. When the harvest was all over, the Ruthénois packed up and went home; only the stewards were left to deal with the continuing evolution of the wine, racking it every six weeks or so, so that it could be sold in the spring before work began on the next year's vintage. The money would be needed to finance the next *vendange* and to give the absentee *patron* a return on his investment.

It is hard to believe today that this sparsely populated countryside was once home to eight thousand people, much of whose lives was devoted to hewing out the sides of the hills, building retaining walls for the vines against erosion by the rains, or otherwise banking up the plants to prevent their being washed down the hillsides. In such a landscape the terraces could not be reached by plough or oxen: all work had to be done by hand. The stones and earth washed down in storms had to be carried back uphill in baskets on the backs of men, some of whom had living quarters in primitive huts in the hills to which their womenfolk would bring their midday meal.

In those days the terraces were sometimes wide enough to take six or seven rows of vines, and there would be a stone wall seven or eight feet high before the next terrace, with a stairway built into it to give access to the next level.

EVERYTHING CHANGES

This industry disappeared almost overnight with the advent of the phylloxera. The rich citizens of Rodez abandoned their country homes, thousands of country dwellers were left destitute, and the once thickly populated valleys began emptying of people, some drifting to find employment in the big cities, others emigrating. The story is a familiar one in the South-West, but in Marcillac it was to have a different ending.

Beneath the hills adjoining the valley of the Lot lay deep seams of coal. Exploitation started in the middle of the 19th century. The mining town of Decazeville became a magnet for those who had lost their livelihoods to the phylloxera. Conditions in the mines recall those described by Zola in *Germinal*. Squalor was everywhere; crime and riots were frequent and the suffering labour force found their only solace in alcohol, which Vallon was on hand to supply. No sooner had the phylloxera emptied the vineyards, than replanting began. Some growers who had taken jobs in the mines eked out their wretched living by going back to their old homes by the light of their miners' lamps at night and on Sundays. New, grafted and therefore immune vines were planted—not on the high terraces where the best wine had come from in the old days, but on the ground lower down the slopes, which was easier to cultivate. The accent switched from quality to bulk; mass production of cheap and cheerful wine was taken over by the peasants, who picked up ownership of the abandoned vineyards for a song. But in one respect Marcillac succeeded where Cahors had failed: the traditional grape variety, the *mansois*, grafted well and was easy to propagate. Although the thoroughbred juice from it was blended with that of inferior varieties, the distinctive grape of the region survived. This made the later renaissance of Marcillac easier to bring about.

DOWN AND OUT

The thirsty coal miners kept the peasant-growers in the Vallon going for as long as the numbers in the mines kept up. The loss of life in the First World War caused a sharp fall in the male population, and the Second was followed by a general drift to the cities, further reducing the numbers working in the mines. The decline in Marcillac was well under way just when other vineyards in the South-West were beginning to come out of their doldrums. The death knell finally sounded when the Decazeville mines were closed in 1962. Conditions had become too dangerous to work them, and the quality of the coal had fallen to the point where further production was uneconomical.

The area planted in vines fell dramatically from 873 hectares in 1956 to 23 in 1966. The growers, drastically reduced in numbers, were faced with the task of finding new markets. The most imaginative realized that they needed to seek a unified image for the wine, even if this meant sinking their individual identities. So there came about the first tentative move towards a *coopérative*. Nine growers joined together and in an old barn pooled their wine and their resources to make a marcillac which would become the style for the future. In their first year they made just 80 hectolitres between them. To enhance the name of marcillac, and to help them obtain a better name for their wines, they applied for VDQS status in 1966; when this was granted in 1968, the formation of a real *cave coopérative* followed immediately. The efforts of the pioneers and the other growers who have since come on the scene earned full AOC status in 1990. Today the entire vineyard is still only about 180 hectares in extent, compared with the 2000 hectares in the days of Alexis Monteil.

THE *MANSOIS* GRAPE

The 'new' marcillac was to represent a return to the pre-phylloxera standards of quality. The grant of VDQS status enabled the growers, if they so wished, to add some *cabernet* or *merlot* to their wines, but no one I have spoken to has taken advantage of this allowance. For the growers, marcillac meant the *mansois* grape and nothing else. The variety seems not to be grown outside South-West France, where it crops up regionally disguised under various names. We shall find it in Gaillac under the name *braucol*, in Gascony and the Béarn as *pinenc*, while its general name in *occitan* is *fer servadou* or *fer* for short. *Mansois* is derived from the local patois name s*aoumensès*.

In the Vallon, the grape is not just grown: it *is* the wine. In practice virtually nothing else goes into marcillac, which is the only appellation which adopts the grape not just as its principal variety, but virtually as a unique variety. At the *cave coopérative* I was told that less than 3% of the grapes which come in are *cabernet* or *merlot*. The *mansois* is sometimes said to be related to the *cabernet franc*, and certainly the two grapes share the same grassy sappiness and have a distinctive flavour of soft red fruits, currants, raspberries and sometimes blackcurrants. There are often spicy overtones too. It is this very unusual grape, married to the equally unusual local soil that has a great deal of iron in it, which gives marcillac its unmistakable *goût du terroir*. It is one of those few wines which can be picked out even by a beginner at a blind tasting. Its colour is dark, but clear and bright, shot through with violet lights. The fruits are balanced by tannins which are full but not aggressive.The wine matures quickly, and though it will last four to six years if well made and from a good vintage, even the best *cuvées* do not improve much after that, despite claims made by some of the growers. Most marcillac is drunk during the two years following the vintage.

Research by INRA (L'Institut National de la Recherche Agronomique) and L'Institut des Produits de la Vigne has shown that the wine of Marcillac is very rich in catechins and procyanidols, which inhibit the thickening of the blood and so help to limit the incidence of heart disease. The research was prompted by the pharmacist in the town of Marcillac, who did a paper on the subject for his academic degree. So you know what prescription you are likely to get over the counter of his shop.

THE PRINCIPAL GROWERS OF MARCILLAC

▌LA CAVE COOPÉRATIVE DES VIGNERONS DU VALLON
12330 Valady
Tel: 05-65-72-70-21 Fax: 05-65-72-68-39
Email: valady@groupe-unicor.com
www.vigneronsduvallon.com

The *coopérative* has about 60 members, whose wines are of a standard more than worthy of its founding fathers. It accounts for about two-thirds of the total production of marcillac. The enterprise is about the same size as one of the larger Bordeaux châteaux and can therefore be run on artisanal rather than industrial lines. The *coopérative* is forever trying to improve standards, and will not hesitate to reject members' produce if it is not of sufficient quality: *'La cave n'est pas une poubelle'*, they say.

The grapes are destalked, as recommended for all wines of the appellation. They are then fermented in stainless steel for fifteen days. Picking takes place normally in October, by which time there can be a distinct chill in the air. Sometimes the must has to be heated to make fermentation start, especially if the harvest is late. The problem is not so much to keep the temperature down but up, so water-cooling is not needed.

There are two basic red *cuvées,* the **Tradition** (*A) and the **Cuvée Réservée** (*A), the difference in quality being attributable to the standard of raw material provided by the various members. These wines are thoroughly typical of the appellation and very good value, though perhaps not having quite the character or distinctiveness of the wines made by some of the independents. There is a single-property wine called **Domaine de Ladrecht** (*A) which has a certain style about it. The property belongs to the vice-president of the *cave,* Jean-Marc Gombert. A supposedly superior *cuvée* called **Saveur du Rougier** (*A) is made from grapes deriving from some of the best parcels on the higher ground. I cannot help thinking that the oaked *cuvée* **Fût de Chêne** (B) is a mistake, not because of my general wariness about new barrels, but because the effort is wasted on a wine which is essentially best drunk young on its fruit. There is a nice **rosé** (*A) and good bulk wine to take away either in the *cave*'s cubitainers or in one's own *bidons*.

▌DOMAINE DU CROS
Philippe Teulier
12390 Goutrens
Tel: 05-65-72-71-77 Fax: 05-65-72-68-80
Email: pteulier@wanadoo.fr
www.domaine-du-cros.com

Leaving eastwards from the small village of Goutrens, you are on a plateau of parklike pastureland and have no hint of the visual surprise in store. Round a bend in the road, the landscape is suddenly transformed as the Vallon comes into view several hundred feet below you. Where for miles there had been nothing but cattle, now there is nothing but vine terraces, some planted, others still abandoned. The views across to the other side and along the valley to the north are stupendous, especially in the late afternoon sunshine. The green vegetation is in sharp contrast to the purplish red soil, called locally *rougier*.

Nowadays, where the terraces have been replanted, the rows of vines are set far enough apart to enable small tractors to pass between them, but the harvest still has to be done by hand. Yields are low. On the gentler slopes, terracing can sometimes be dispensed with altogether, but generally speaking the quality is not as good, partly because there is a lower proportion of schist in the soil than higher up the hillsides. The lower ground is also more at risk from spring frosts.

In the shock of arriving at the edge of the valley, it is easy to miss Teulier's domaine, which is set high up into a hillside, almost at the upper limit of vine growing. His father started in 1982 with only one hectare, but today Philippe has 25 hectares of vines, which make him the biggest independent grower. Teulier profits from the steepness of the slopes to make the maximum use of gravity. Destemming and pressing are done on the top floor of the *chais,* and the juice goes into the *cuves* on the next level down. When fermentation is finished the wine goes down another storey to the *cave,* where the old *foudres* are. Thus sideways and upwards pumping are more or less eliminated, and in turn disturbance to the wine is reduced. Vinification is in stainless steel for 15 to 20 days at a highish temperature of 30/32 degrees Celsius. The malolactic fermentation is done in the *foudres.*

Philippe has always made two red *cuvées,* his basic wine being called **Lo Sang del Païs** (the blood of the countryside) (***A). Made from his younger vines, it represents two-thirds of his production, all of it mansois. This wine displays a typical character, more so perhaps than his **Cuvée Vieilles Vignes** (***B), which however is a little more sophisticated, enjoying 18 months' ageing in the old *foudres* after 25 days' vinification. This second wine is less grassy but rounder and more supple and comes from grapes produced from centenarian vines.

Philippe never used to make an oaked wine, but temptation has got the better of him, and his **Cuvée Vieilles Vignes en Barriques** (*B) is one

of the few wines from this appellation which really does need keeping. It is given an unusually high *cuvaison* of five weeks. The oak is handled well but, as with the *coopérative*'s efforts in wood, it seems a rather pointless exercise. No doubt he is responding to market demand, but the typicity of marcillac is not there, as he himself admits; *'Ici, on sort du terroir'* ('At this point you lose the *terroir*').

Philippe has also ventured into making white wine: a **dry sémillon** (**A) given just a little barrel ageing, with delicious but delicate fruit; and a sweetish version (**A) from the same grape also aged in the barrel, deliciously light and elegant. These wines do not of course qualify for appellation status: there is no such thing as white marcillac.

▍ LE VIEUX PORCHE

Jean-Luc Matha

Bruéjouls, 12330 Marcillac

Tel: 05-65-72-63-29 Fax: 05-65-72-70-43

Email: jl.matha@wanadoo.fr

Matha and Teulier are very good friends, but they are totally different. Teulier is quiet and reflective, though with a good sense of humour, while Matha is ebullient, with a mischievous twinkle in the eye. Their wines are equally good. Together they have devised their own personal system of *pigeage*, which simulates as far as possible the breaking up of the *marc* by feet through the ingenious use of wooden sticks.

Vines have been in the Matha family for generations, but his father moved to Rodez to get a job so as to support the family. Jean-Luc always wanted to look after the vines, so when he grew up, he joined the *coopérative,* but that didn't satisfy him. He wanted to make the wine as well as grow the grapes. Today he has a dozen or so hectares, which he will proudly show you round if you are prepared for a hair-raising tour in his 4x4. He will enthusiastically describe the hard work of wine-making in a *terroir* like Marcillac, and will hope you will believe him when he tells you that in the old day a *vigneron* would consume up to 15 litres of wine per day. Certainly you will appreciate the extreme gradients as he charges up the impossibly steep slopes, pausing perhaps to show you a nasty insect called a *cigarier*—a beetle which wraps itself up like a cigar in a curled vineleaf—at work on one of his beloved plants.

He maintains his stock by what is called *sélection massale*, i.e. grafting individually from specially chosen vinestocks, rather than reproducing from one clone. Matha makes his wine in a similar way to Teulier, though with even longer vinification. His two *cuvées* are raised in old *barriques* for the same length of time as Teulier's, but Matha does not use new barrels at all. That said, he has one old barrel which will hold no less than 1735 litres.

Comparison with Teulier's wines does an injustice, because they are equally excellent. The **Cuvée Normale,** which is sometimes called **Cuvée Laüris** (***A), though occasionally a little less exuberant than Teulier's, is perhaps the most characteristically 'marcillac' of all. The **Cuvée Spéciale** (***A), sometimes called **Cuvée Peïrafi** (meaning 'little stones'), is darker and perhaps a shade richer. Matha says it will last 10 to 15 years, but why keep it that long?

Jean-Luc also makes some *vins de Table*, a white called **Sève de Caldebrit** (A**), deliciously fresh and beckoning, and a very blackcurrant **Lo Grabel** (*A), which apparently means 'dandelions'. And don't forget the AOC **rosé** (**A).

▌DOMAINE DES COSTES ROUGES

Claudine Costes

Combret, 12330 Nauviale

Tel: 05-65-72-83-85

www.domaine-des-costes-rouges.fr

Claudine Costes's father used to make wine to sell *en vrac* to the Decazeville miners, but when the mines were closed, he started to bottle his wine himself, abandoning the use of the *jurançon noir* grape and concentrating on better quality. Today they only grow *mansois,* of course. This policy has been continued by Claudine and her partner Eric Vinas, and their wines have greatly improved in recent years. Their **Cuvée Tradition** (**A), for example, has 12.5 degrees alcohol, compared with 10.9 ten years previously, which suggests lower yields in the vineyard and much riper fruit. Their prestige wine is called **Clos de la Ferrière** (**B) and is made from the oldest wines on their 4.5-hectare vineyard. The vines themselves are a little way away from the domaine itself, which faces north. The grapes are grown round the corner of the Combret hill, where they can enjoy the best of the afternoon sun. The soil is very red, with lots of iron in it, but surprisingly this does not harden the style of the wine, which manages surprising softness.

As is the custom of many of the smaller growers, the wine here is fermented in open-topped barrels, the length of the *cuvaison* being about 15 days, depending on the year. There is no filtering of the wine. After racking, the wine is transferred to old casks in the middle of the winter, after the malolactic fermentation is over, and bottled six months later.

A further reason to visit these improving producers is that they run a delightful *ferme auberge* with delicious country-style cooking. Booking is essential.

▌DOMAINE LAURENS

Michel and Gilbert Laurens

7 Avenue de la Tour, 12330 Clairvaux

Tel: 05-65-72-69-37 Fax: 05-65-72-76-74

Email: info@domaine-laurens.com

www.domaine-laurens.com

Michel Laurens is president of the *syndicat* of marcillac growers, and his family have been winemakers in Marcillac for many generations, though only more recently independent of the *coopérative*. They have expanded the size of their vineyard from 3.5 to 21 hectares, mostly in the immediate vicinity of the village of Clairvaux, and they organize guided tours of the village as well as group tastings of their own wines, explaining how they are made. Private visits are of course also possible.

No criticism is implied, but the wines of this property are 'commercial' in the sense that some of the extreme curranty character of Marcillac seems to have been toned down with the object of making a wine which appeals to the general rather than the specialized taste. There is a **rosé** (*A), with an attractive bouquet of raspberries, round and at the same time crisp in the mouth and fairly long on the finish. The basic **Marcillac Rouge** (*A) shows black rather than red fruits with spices and sometimes peony flowers. Full on the palate, it is fresh and supple. A wine from their oldest vines, **Château de Flars** (*B), is given some time in new wood, but is again fruity and spicy and the wood a shade too prominent.

The Laurens are also distillers. They make *eaux-de-vie* from plums and also from gentian, which grows on the slopes of the Aubrac and Cantal hills. There are also two ratafias, one red, the other pink, somewhat in the style of Pineau de Charente or Floc de Gascogne, in that they are made from a blend of unfermented grape juice and *eau-de-vie*.

■ **DOMAINE DU MIOULA**
Bernard Angles
12330 Salles-la-Source
Tel: 05-65-71-83-69 Mobile: 06-08-95-15-60
Email: basgroupe@wanadoo.fr
www.marcillac.net

Post-phylloxera tradition has it that marcillac producers are all country-growers. Bernard Angles reverts to an earlier tradition, that of the well-to-do bourgeois from Rodez who wants nothing more than to have his own Marcillac vineyard where he can make the best possible marcillac.

The present house at Mioula is clearly of fairly recent construction, but the domaine claims an old history. Until the Revolution it was listed as belonging to part-time monks of the cathedral at Rodez. The word *mioula* means 'middle' in patois, indicating that the property was in the middle of vines. Bernard Angles claims that some of the vines at Mioula survived the phylloxera and did not need to be replanted on American rootstocks.

The property is not easy to find; you must follow the signs to the little church of Saint-Austremoine and continue a further two kilometres or so along a small lane which seems to lead nowhere. About seven hectares of vines are surrounded by Bernard's lavishly appointed home which lacks no amenity; there is not only a swimming pool for the family, but also a separate one for his hunting dogs. As may be expected, no expense has been spared in creating the *chais,* which has all state-of-the-art equipment including thermoregulation.

Having no previous experience of wine-making, Bernard called in Patrice Lescarret, whom we shall meet again in Gaillac. Patrice is consultant-cum-oenologist at Mioula. Bernard told me that Patrice would have liked to buy the property himself. With the wine-making in such inspired hands, Bernard is sure to make waves in Marcillac. His first vintage was 2001 and he has already achieved *coup de coeur* status in the *Guide Hachette.*

Bernard has kept some old *jurançon noir* vines, which he puts into a *vin de table* called **Le Ballon** (*A) together with 70% mansois. This is a very acceptable everyday quaffing wine, uncomplicated and thirst-quenching. He says it sells like hot cakes. There are two AOC marcillac wines: the basic **Domaine du Mioula** (**B), which has good grip and structure as well as the expected marcillac fruit; and the **Terre d'Angles** (***B), from vines which are 30 years old and more. Lescarret manages to preserve the authentic marcillac style, while giving these wines his own unmistakeable personal stamp. Or is it that the vines here are not on the *rougier,* like those listed above, but on a more chalky soil of the type found on the *causse* which begins just above the skyline?

OTHER MARCILLAC GROWERS

■ FRANCIS COSTES

La Baronnie, 12330 Mouret

Tel: 05-65-69-83-05

■ PHILIPPE CROIZAT

Saint-Austremoine, 12330 Salles-la-Source

Tel: 05-65-71-82-13

■ MICHEL DURAND

Le Monteil, 12330 Salles-la Source

Tel: 05-65-71-80-96

■ CHRISTIAN GERVAS

Limagne, 12330 Salles-la-Source

Tel: 05-65-71-74-33

■ JOËL GRADELS

Domaine de La Carolie, 12330 Marcillac

Tel: 05-65-71-74-13

■ JEAN-MARIE REVEL

Mernac, 12330 Salles-la-Source

Tel: 05-65-71-76-01

Revel's wines are quite probably like the mar-
cillacs his grandfather made—rich and earthy.

ENTRAYGUES ET LE FEL

AREA OF PRODUCTION: selected parcels covering 22 hectares in the communes of Entraygues-sur-Truyère, Le Fel, Campouriez, Florentin-la-Capelle, Golinhac, Saint-Hippolyte (Aveyron), Cassaniouze and Vieillevie (Cantal).

GRAPE VARIETIES:

REDS AND ROSÉS: fer servadou, cabernet franc, cabernet sauvignon, gamay, jurançon noir, merlot, mouyssaguès, négret de Banhars and pinot noir.

WHITES: chenin, mauzac.

ANNUAL PRODUCTION: 1000 hectolitres, of which 60% red, 20% rosé and 20% white.

DISTRIBUTION: 75% locally, otherwise to restaurants and cavistes in Paris.

The town of Entraygues is about an hour's drive from Marcillac. It stands at the confluence of the rivers Lot and Truyère and its name means 'Entre Eaux', rather like Entre Deux Mers. The Truyère rises in the granite mountains of the Cantal, whereas the Lot is born on the limestone *causses* to the south-east. Entraygues is therefore something of a frontier post with the Auvergne, which, rather than Bordeaux, was traditionally the main market for its wines. The *vendange* here is late, and the climate relatively cool, so the wines are not high in alcohol, never reaching more than 12.5 degrees, usually less. The dryness of the whites and the minerality of the reds give them a vivacity which is strikingly attractive, as refreshing as the mountain streams which water the vineyards.

Le Fel is the name given to a tract of hill country to the north-west of the town and is reached by winding country lanes which snake their way up the hillsides. It projects a narrow ridge parallel with the Lot Valley, and the slopes running down from it to the river produce exclusively red and rosé wine, the soil being schistose and until recently not thought rich enough for white grapes. The terracing is even more dramatic than at Marcillac, with just the occasional row of vines here and there clinging to the sides of the mountain. One grower told me that you had virtually to rope yourself to the vines in order to pick the grapes as the sinuous river

Lot curves its way through gorges hundreds of feet below. The vine terraces vary in altitude between 250 and 450 metres above sea level.

These once magnificent vineyards are today but a shadow of their former selves. They extended at one time to over 1000 hectares, and there was scarcely a corner of the south-facing slopes that was not planted with vines. Traces of these extensive terraces still remain, alas bare of vines. As recently as 1982 Le Fel could boast no growers at all, except for a handful of farmers making wine for their own consumption. Then a businessman from Aurillac, Auguste Abeil, seized by the beauty of the site, decided to plant some new vines. This entailed a huge amount of work, in which he was joined by the Mousset family and one Roger Lalo. It was young Mousset, then only 23 years old, who became the leading light in the rebuilding of the Fel vineyard, which was officially blessed by the parish priest of Entraygues on May 24, 1988. Today, there are still only three small producers making wine commercially at Le Fel: Abeil, Mousset and the daughter and son-in-law of a former grower at Vieillevie, some kilometres further along the steep hillside above the river. The soil is composed entirely of the local red schist, sometimes mixed in with chunky rock.

The other three growers in this mini-appellation are to be found on the outskirts of Entraygues itself on much lower and more easily cultivated ground, where wines of all colours can be made. The soil here is based on granite, which ensures retention of moisture, so the white wines are the most successful. They are usually from pure *chenin blanc*, probably not quite the same grape as is grown in the Loire Valley but a near relative. Here it produces perfumed wines of a pale yellow shot with gold. When young, the wines often suggest grilled almonds, green apples and gunflint. They develop complexity with the years, eventually emitting aromas of beeswax, honey and citronella.

Although there are but six growers, they have an active *syndicat* to promote the wines, currently led by Mousset. The total area under vine is barely 22 hectares, just nine of which are at Le Fel, and the remainder round the town of Entraygues itself. Total production averages 1000 hectolitres a year, about a seventh of the production of Marcillac, which is small enough. The wines are seldom seen outside the area of production, except in a few restaurants and wine shops in Paris and Toulouse. There has been talk over the years of a merger between Entraygues and Marcillac, but nothing has come of it. Perhaps because of its small size, Entraygues is moving towards AOC status on its own, having been hitherto a VDQS; its best argument for promotion is to prevent its being smothered in the threatened shakeup of the French appellation system.

PRODUCERS OF ENTRAYGUES WINES

■ LES BUIS

Jean-Marc Viguier
12140 Entraygues
Tel: 05-65-44-50-45 Fax: 05-65-48-62-72

Jean-Marc explains that, much as he would like to expand his domaine, the present restrictions on planting, aimed at reducing the European wine glut, will not let him. He cannot make enough even to fulfil the local demand, let alone bother with trying to market it outside the region of production. This explains why the wine of Entraygues is rarely to be found beyond the boundaries of the Aveyron and Cantal *départements*.

With just seven hectares, Jean-Marc is the largest grower. His vines are on your right as you come down the hill into town from the north. The family is an old local one and his father kept cows and goats as well as making wine, but Jean-Marc now devotes his attention exclusively to wine.

Viguier has nearly half his vineyard in white grapes, the wines from which are given a long cold fermentation before being bottled the March following the vintage. The **Cuvée Spéciale** (**A) is quite singular. Viguier claims that this wine often has a bouquet of quince and ground almonds. The fruit is noticeably well developed. Viguier says his wines keep remarkably well, and he disagrees with those commentators who suggest that Entraygues wine should be drunk as young as possible.

The **basic red** (*A) used to be made from a bewildering cocktail of grapes, including *gamay*,

jurançon noir, *cabernet franc* and quite a lot of a local grape called *négret*. Little is known about that variety, except that it used to be called *moissaguès*, suggesting that it might have come from Moissac. Nowadays, however, it seems that Viguier has kept only the mansois and cabernet franc. This red is the wine from which he draws off his **rosé** (*A). Both red and pink are less grassy than Marcillac, easy to drink and not unlike a *vin nouveau*. The **Cuvée Spéciale** (**B) is a much more impressive affair, and does need some ageing. It is half *mansois* and half *cabernet franc*, and thus much more closely related to marcillac than to his basic red. It is given some ageing in old barrels.

■ DOMAINE DE MÉJANASSÈRE

Véronique and Frédéric Forveille
12140 Entraygues
Tel and fax: 05-65-44-54-76
www.domaine-de-mejanassere.fr

This very attractive old-style Aveyronnais farm, tucked away in the hills on the road to Laguiole, has been in the Forveille family for many generations, and it includes a small vineyard. The wine is difficult to find except at the Forveilles' table, for they also run a much reputed *ferme-auberge* specializing in authentic country food from home-produced ingredients. At their superb site, looking over the vines on their precipitous slopes to the romantic valley beyond, the wines seem to acquire an extra quality, especially when accompanying the delicious country cooking, whether homemade ter-rines or spit-roasted suckling pigs. Occasionally the Forveilles have some to spare for local wine shops and *épiceries*. Over half the total production is of red wine, but the **white** (**A), 100% *chenin blanc* grown on granite soil, is especially good, and in sun-shine years like 2003 and 2005 easily earns ***, showing remarkably ripe fruit and a hint of richness which might develop with age an almost Vouvray-like reminder of the grape variety. It is well worth looking out for.

◼ FRANÇOIS AVALLON
Coteaux de Saint-Georges, 12140 Entraygues
Tel: 05-65-48-61-65 Fax: 05-65-48-63-78

In the early days of this tiny appellation, the Avallon family were one of its leading lights. Such is the improvement in the competition that today Avallon finds it hard to keep up. Nevertheless, his white **Cuvée Spéciale** (**A) can hold its own with the best.

◼ LAURENT AND OLIVIER MOUSSET
Cassos, 12140 Le Fel
Tel and fax: 05-65-44-52-35

The Mousset family farm had no vines until Laurent rented three hectares of them on the pre-cipitous slopes of Le Fel, just along the road from Madame Albespy's popular *auberge*. He is a cousin of Viguier, whose father gave him much help and encouragement in his early years. Nowadays Mous-set, profiting from the official exemption on replant-ing given to young growers, has added two hectares of his own, so his five hectares put him, relatively speaking, in the big league in this micro-appellation. He has built his own terracing for his vines, all *man-sois* and *cabernet franc*. He has constructed the vineyard so that the rows are wide enough to allow the smallest of tractors to pass, but the harvesting is done by hand. In this he is helped by his father and his brother, who has taken over the rest of the

family farm, as well as by any friends whose arms he can twist.

Laurent had the misfortune to start with three difficult years, but by 1995 he was well into the swing and now he produces really good-quality wines. His **rosé** (***A) is perhaps the best of all Aveyron pink wines, often with a marked almondy character. The **basic red** (***A) is also excellent. The **oak-aged version** (**A/B) has lovely mineral-ity from the schist. Then there is the version called **La Pauca** (***B), which has rather more complex-ity. The name comes from *pauc*, the name of the old measure of wine traditional to the region. The cabernet franc is given some ageing in old barrels, the mansois is aged *en cuve*. Laurent makes this as a joint project with locally born Philippe Gard, who is nowadays a winemaker at La Coume del Mas in Banyuls, and who transports his *égrappoir* and *table vibrante* up from the south for the occa-sion. The wine manages to achieve unusual power,

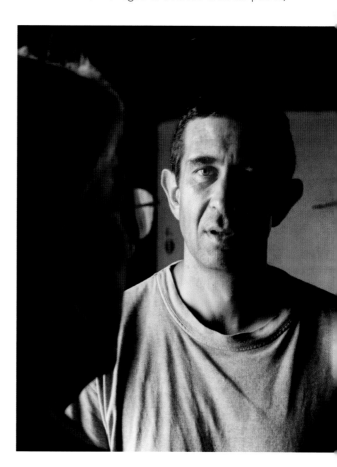

while retaining the finesse of the basic red. It also stresses the fruit and avoids the taste of the barrel. The idea was to make just 3000 bottles as an experiment rather than a commercial project, but the wine has caught on so well that Laurent and Philippe will be hard put to keep to their original idealism. Their first vintage was the lovely 2005, a wine that will last well.

Laurent has now planted 60 ares with *chenin blanc* to see if he can give the lie to the accepted wisdom that the schist at Le Fel does not suit the grape. It should have come on stream in 2008. He has the right to plant a little more, but needs to find the land.

ALSO AT LE FEL

◼ LES TERRASSES DU HAUT-MINDIC
Annie and Auguste Abeil
12140 Enguiales
Tel: 05-65-44-58-35 Fax: 05-65-48-65-62

Only two hectares, all on precipitous schist. Note the smooth **Cuvée Valérie** (**A) with its aromas of wildflowers. Raised in old barrels, the wine is surprisingly light and without oaky flavours. 10% *pinot noir*, the rest *mansois* and *cabernet franc* equally.

◼ LES TERRASSES DE LA VIDALIE
Isabelle and Serge Broha
15120 Vieillevie
Tel and fax: 04-71-49-96-98
Mobile: 06-83-25-15-97
Email: serge.broha@wanadoo.fr

The two hectares of vines are supplemented by the fabrication of splendid prize-winning goat cheeses. The wines include a 100% *chenin blanc,* aromatic and flinty. The reds are notably curranty, from 80% *mansois*, the other grapes being *cabernet franc* and the local *négret* a.k.a *mouyssaguès*.

ESTAING

AREA OF VDQS: selected parcels covering 19 hectares in the commune of Estaing, Coubisou and Sébrazac.

Red, white and rosé wines.
PERMITTED GRAPE VARIETIES:
REDS AND ROSÉS: fer servadou, gamay noir à jus blanc, abouriou (gamay Saint-Laurent), jurançon noir, merlot noir, cabernet franc, cabernet sauvignon, mouyssaguès (négret).
WHITES: chenin blanc, mauzac.
ANNUAL PRODUCTION: 650 hectolitres.

If the appellation of Entraygues is tiny, that of Estaing, another VDQS, needs a magnifying glass: it is the smallest in France. The 18 growers have but 14 hectares of vines between them, compared with about 1000 before the First World War. Today the annual production rarely exceeds 50,000 bottles a year. Nevertheless, the records go back 600 years according to the archives of the small mountain monastery of Cabrespine.

Founded by the monks of Conques, the vineyards of Estaing, a little further up the valley of the Lot from Entraygues, are dotted round the eponymous town. The castle, built by a one-time bishop of Rodez, dominates a cluster of quaint slated buildings. The river is spanned by an especially handsome Gothic bridge which connects the town with the road to Marcillac. Everything about Estaing is picturesque bar the seemingly endless convoys of container-lorries grinding their laborious way from Rodez to Aurillac and back.

PRODUCERS OF ESTAING WINES

■ CAVE SCV LES VIGNERONS D'OLT
Zone Artisanale La Fage, 12190 Estaing
Tel and fax: 05-65-44-04-42
Email: cave.vigneronsdolt@wanadoo.fr

70% of the production is in the hands of this little *coopérative*. There are usually **two reds** (*A), light and fruity, one raised in barrels, the other not. The former is largely *gamay*, with some backing from the local *négret* and another curiosity called *pinotous d'Estaing*, whose origins are equally obscure. The wine, from grapes grown largely on schistose soil, is good with charcuterie, and some of it is drawn off the skins to make an attractive **rosé** (*A), which is perhaps the best product here. The oaked wine is from *cabernet sauvignon* and *mansois* and is a trifle more serious. A minority production of white, **Cuvée de l'Amiral** (*A), is 85% *chenin blanc*. It is bone dry and needs to be served quite cold.

■ DOMAINE LES TERRASSES DE VINNAC
Françoise and Michel Alaux
La Frayssinette, 12190 Estaing
Tel and fax: 05-65-48-05-17

Perhaps the best red estaing comes from this grower. It is a polycultural farm, wine being only one of the crops. The vineyards, up a winding road leading from the north bank of the river, barely cover one hectare, so Michel limits himself to red and rosé wines. He has *gamay* and *mansois*, and also a little *pinotous* and *mauzac*, the latter contributing an apple character to his **rosé** (*A). The **red** (**A) is made from grapes which are not destalked, and is stored in the 150-year-old cellar in fine old *barriques* of 550 litres each. In the bad old days before the grant of VDQS, the family also made a *vin de table* from vines grown down in the valley, but the vines were of inferior varieties and had to be dug up under the rules of the appellation.

■ LA PONSARDERIE
Monique Fages
12190 Estaing
Tel: 05-65-44-06-84

Monique Fages' farm is two or three hairpin bends up the hill from Michel Alaux, and her speciality is her **white** (**A) from *chenin blanc* and a little *mauzac*. She is the only independent grower to make white estaing. Monique has two hectares of vines, and she almost joined the *coopérative,* but she had some old customers whom she wanted to go on dealing with herself, so she has remained independent. She also makes some **red** (*A) from 60% *gamay* and 40% *mansois*. For her **rosé** (*A) she adds a little *jurançon noir* to give colour. The grapes are destalked in the vineyard before a short cuvaison of seven days, after which the wine is put into barrel for the malolactic fermentation. I asked her about the age of the barrels and she looked at me as if I were stupid. Of course they were old. 'New ones would give an acrid taste to the wine, wouldn't they?'

OTHER GROWERS AT ESTAING

■ DOMAINE DES COTEAUX DE MAJORAC
Raymond Nayrolles
12190 Estaing
Tel and fax: 05-65-44-70-41

■ BEAUREGARD
Nelly Guernier
12190 Sébrazac
Tel: 05-65-44-73-72

■ CHÂTEAU DE BEAUREGARD
André Couailhac
Les Camps, 12190 Sébrazac
Tel: 05-65-44-74-98

CÔTES DE MILLAU

AREA OF VDQS: selected parcels covering 48 hectares in 17 communes in the *département* of Aveyron: Aguessac, Broquiès, Castelnau-Pégayrols, Compeyre, Compreignac, Creissels, La Cresse, Millau, Montjau, Mostuéjouls, Paulhe, Peyreleau, Rivière-sur-Tarn, Saint-Georges-de-Luzençon, Saint-Rome-de-Tarn, Le Truel and Viala-du-Tarn

Red, white and rosé wines.
GRAPE VARIETIES:
REDS: gamay and syrah, each of which must be 30% of the grower's red wine vineyard.
Also permitted: cabernet sauvignon (max. 20%), fer servadou and duras.
ROSÉS: gamay (at least 50%), syrah, cabernet sauvignon, fer servadou, duras.
WHITES: chenin, mauzac.
All wines must contain at least two grape varieties.
MINIMUM ALCOHOL CONTENT: at least 11% for the reds, 10.5 for the whites and rosés.
PLANTING DENSITY: 4500 plants per hectare; 45 hectares of vines.
MAXIMUM YIELD: 60 hl/ha.
ANNUAL PRODUCTION: 1980 hectolitres.

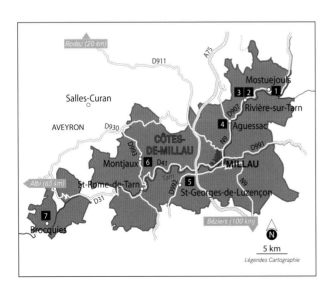

The town of Millau is at the centre of what was once an extensive wine-making region of quality, extending over 15,000 hectares, a rather larger area than the whole of present-day Bergerac. Standing guard over the entry to the famous gorges of the river Tarn is the ruined citadel of Compeyre, a wine-warehouse town where the fissures in the rocks, as at Roquefort farther downstream, guaranteed the passage of cooling air to the cellars stacked to the roof with barrels. The entrances to some of these natural caves can still be seen, giving the abandoned town the appearance of a giant Gruyère cheese.

The vineyards once extended from Peyreleau in the east, frontier town to the gorges, as far downstream as Connac, away to the west of Millau. They must have looked like those of Switzerland today, with thousands of almond trees decking the vines in spring with their white blossoms. The grape variety most commonly used was probably the *abouriou*, still to be found in the vineyards of Marmande. It was called in Millau *gamay Saint Laurent,* but be warned that nobody in this part of France is serious about the historical identification of their grape varieties. One of the Avignon popes, anxious to escape from the mosquitoes that were then the scourge of that town, was frequently entertained by one of his cardinals, a native of the village of Mostuéjouls in the Tarn valley. Naturally the papal entourage took back to Avignon a good supply of the Millau wine; the grape was thenceforth known as *gamay du pape*.

When the fortress of Compeyre, bitterly fought over during the wars of religion, was finally demolished by Richelieu, this initiated the decline of the Millau vineyards, which nevertheless managed to cling on until the arrival of the phylloxera. Local folklore maintains that the cellar owners of the time used to throw wild parties at which the local wines would be used to wash down dried and salted sardines nicknamed 'gendarmes', roquefort cheese stiffened with local *eau-de-vie*, and *fouace*, a local cake, all of which were calculated to dry out the tastebuds of even the thirstiest drinker. Ribald songs and the most unlikely tales would accompany these gatherings, which would last the whole of a Sunday evening, while the womenfolk prayed piously in church that their men would not come home too drunk.

After the phylloxera, the vineyards were replanted as at Marcillac with inferior stocks, and the choicest slopes were abandoned. Competition from the Midi was exacerbated by the requisitoning of all the local horses in the First World War, the depopulation of the region afterwards, and the loss of life in battle, which meant that even those who survived the war returned to find their vines overgrown with brambles and weeds. It needed only the frosts of 1956 to deliver the *coup de grâce*.

The local Chamber of Agriculture stepped in and encouraged that the vineyards be rebuilt with quality grapes. As at Marcillac, the best hope for restoring the reputation of the area was the creation of a *coopérative*. Founded in 1980, it is still small, but under the pioneering direction of Louis Valès and later of Alain Montrozier, it has prospered and today is making good wines which are an excellent value for the money. Production has no doubt been spurred on by the development of tourism in the Tarn gorges and the completion of the A9 motorway over the famous bridge by Norman Foster.

There are also a handful of independent growers, based on the terraces rising above the river Tarn on either side of Millau. Their wines can be bought at the door as well as found in local shops and restaurants.

PRODUCERS OF CÔTES DE MILLAU

▌CAVE DES VIGNERONS DES GORGES DU TARN

Alain Montrozier

Rue du Colombier, 12520Aguessac

Tel: 05-65-59-84-11 Fax: 05-65-59-17-90

Email: scvcotes-demillau@wanadoo.fr

This good *Cave* makes a full range of wines of all three colours (*A). The *Cave* controls three-quarters of the production and makes wine of very good quality. The basic traditional red is called **Seigneurs de Peyreviel** (**A), while the *gamay*-based **Domaine des Mille Pierres** (*A) and the lightly oaked **Maître des Sampettes** (*A) show well the variety and potential of this area. AOC cannot be far away? Needless to say, there is also a *cuvée* named after the famous Viaduct.

▌DOMAINE DE BOURJAC

Olivier Toulouse

Le Bourg, 112480 Broquiès

Tel: 05-65-99-48-17 Fax: 05-65-99-47-31

Note particularly the **reds** (*A), including a *cuvée* from old vines and a *tête de cuvée* aged in oak. Broquiès is an attractive riverside village, noted for its wild orchids in the late spring.

▌DOMAINE DE LA CARDABELLE

Jean Meljac

Les Salles, 12640 Riviére-sur-Tarn

Tel: 05-65-59-85-78

Good country **red** (*A)

▌DOMAINE BERTAU

Eddi Bertau

Candas, 12490 Montjaux

Tel and fax: 05-65-58-18-56

▌DOMAINE DU TRESCOL-POTTIER

Dominique and Isabelle Pottier

Craissac, 12100 Saint-Georges-de-Luzençon

Tel and fax: 05-65-62-38-73

▌DOMAINE DU VIEUX NOYER

Bernard Portalier

Boyne, 12640 Rivière-sur-Tarn

Tel and fax: 05-65-62-64-57

A basic blend of *syrah, gamay* and *cabernet* (**A) is to be preferred to its oaked brother from the same grapes; simpler and less pretentious.

▌BRUNO LAFAYSSE

12640 Rivière-sur-Tarn

Tel: 05-65-59-77-22

VINS DE PAYS DE L'AVEYRON

A *syndicat* of growers gathers together a small band of makers of *vins de pays* in the Aveyron.

ALEXANDRE CORJON
Rue du Château
12270 Najac

Over on the far western edge of the *département*, under the walls of the ruined château of Najac, Alexandre Corjon makes a *cabernet*-based *vin de pays* in his diminutive vineyard, on a site which once, before the phylloxera, produced wine of considerable quality. Corjon was brought up in Burgundy so can claim to know a thing or two about wine-making. Nowadays he is retired but says it is better to grow old in a vineyard rather than a hospice, 'even the hospices de Beaune'. His production of 3000 bottles or so under the name **Les Terrasses des Consuls** (*A/B) is certainly good enough for the excellent local hostelries, and Corjon claims it could be as good as anything made in Gaillac, for example.

RAYMOND TOURNIER
Les Vignes Grandes
12270 Mazerolles
Tel: 09-60-00-55-66

Just two or three kilometres away, up on the *causse* but still overlooking the village of Najac, Raymond Tournier at **Les Vignes Grandes** (*A) makes a very different *vin de pays* based on *gamay*, less characteristic of the South-West perhaps but very drinkable all the same.

Back in the traditional wine-making areas, there are some other growers worthy of interest to the intrepid:

PATRICK ROLS
Le Colombier
12320 Conques
Tel: 06-27-80-27-09

FRÉDÉRIC VASSAL
Le Claux
12500 Saint-Côme d'Olt
Tel: 05-65-48-17-66

ALAIN FALGUIÈRES
Domaine de l'Albinie
12330 Salles-la-Source
Tel: 05-65-67-02-69

And near to Villefranche-de-Rouergue, once an important wine-growing centre but now alas almost bereft of vines:

SANDRA LEMOINE
Pleyjean
12200 Martiel
Tel: 05-65-19-46-57

COTEAUX DE GLANES

LES VIGNERONS DU HAUT-QUERCY
46130 Glanes
Tel and fax: 05-65-38-62-69

In the hills above Bretenoux in the Lot, the village of Glanes is home to a group of eight growers who have formed a small *coopérative* which makes a very attractive *vin de pays* (**A). There are no steep gorges here, the beautifully gentle countryside being shared by vines, walnut and peach trees. Vines take priority on the best parcels, those which face south-west on a soil composed of clay and sandstone.

Here lives the appropriately named Monsieur Quercy, one of the growers, who, because of his strategic position just behind the *cave*, gets the job of showing most of the visitors round. Like his seven colleagues, he displays a plaque at the entrance to his house indicating his name and membership in the *coopérative*. They will all receive you and sell you the *coopérative*'s wine. The enterprise is democratic, without a manager or any other labour. The members share all the work, even the bottling, for which a rota is pinned up in the cellars. The paperwork is done by the members' wives. The growers' names are Bernard Blin, Bruno Canet, Laurent Cérou, Jacques Ferrand, Maison Frégeat, Gilbert Lapauze, Maison Quercy, and Bernard Sirieys, and a map showing where they can be found is posted in the village.

The production is small: the members have only 32 hectares between them, and they limit the yield to 50 hl/ha. The permitted maximum is 70, but they prefer to concentrate on quality, under-standing that although their fellow-countrymen drink less these days, they drink better than their forebears. The overall vineyard is planted with 45% *merlot*, 40% *gamay* and 15% *ségalin*. This last is a grape which was conceived specially for them by Bordeaux nurserymen, and is a cross between the old varieties of *jurançon noir* and *portugais bleu*, both once common in the region. *Ségalin* gives the wine a typicity, an element of rusticity and depth of colour. It is also resistant to *coulure* and rot, to both of which *merlot* is prone. In the old days, wine was made in this district based on *fer*, but this grape has been abandoned.

All three present grape varieties are early-maturing, and the wine is quick to develop. It suggests a softened version of Marcillac, with the same summer fruits and hints of raspberries, but with less grassiness and softer tannins. It is hardly surprising that the *cave* has won strings of medals for it. The growers claim that 70% of their production is sold to local customers, the rest to the restaurants, shops and hotels of the region.

The **rosé** (**A), which represents 20% of the total production, is 85% *gamay* and 15% *ségalin*, deep-coloured, remarkably fruity and with a nice acidity which raises it above the ordinary. The **Cuvée Tradition** (**A) has lots of red fruit on the nose and, after an attacking entry on the palate, develops spices and more fruit, black rather than red. The **Cuvée des Fondateurs** (**B), their top wine which is all *merlot* and constitutes but 5% of the total output, is richer and fatter. All the wines here are aged *en cuve*.

VIN PAILLÉ DE CORRÈZE

There was once an old-fashioned country café tucked away in the hills above Beaulieu-sur-Dordogne in a tiny village called Queyssac-les-Vignes. It was called 'Le Vin Paillé'. This was also the name of the apéritif they served there, almost to the exclusion of anything else: a deep brownish wine, with a bouquet of walnuts, apricots, orange peel and spices. It was quite sweet and had a slightly madeira-like taste through having oxidized slightly. It was purely local, made in small quantities by small growers to add a modest income to their earnings from strawberries, tobacco and walnuts. It was marketed mainly at the country fairs within the immediate neighbourhood, mainly Beaulieu and Meyssac. It was good with desserts as well as an apéritif.

According to an old-timer, the grapes in those days were harvested at the normal time and not allowed to over-ripen on the plant. They were taken under cover and laid on a bed of straw in a warm but ventilated barn or attic for several weeks. During this period they shrivelled, the juice having largely evaporated; but what was left was very sweet. The raisin-like grapes were then pressed, fermented for two months or so during the cool of the winter, and then stored in tanks or barrels for a couple of years. Evaporation over this time caused a slightly oxidized character.

When the café at Queyssac eventually closed, the *vin paillé* might have disappeared, but there were still local farmers making the wine for their own if not for the public's consumption. Perhaps it was inevitable that some of them would get together to commercialize it once again. Their first step in this direction was the creation in 1997 of a local *syndicat* of growers. Today there are 22 members, and a *mini-coopérative* has also been formed combining the efforts of four more growers.

Partly because of the restrictions on planting, and partly because of the very low yields, the production of *vin paillé* is still very modest, though set to double to 25,000 bottles (50 centilitre size) in the next two or three years as new vines come on stream. The *syndicat* of growers is certainly highly motivated and looks sure to make permanent the revival of this vinous curiosity.

The growers mentioned below are all *C.

PRODUCERS OF *VIN PAILLÉ* DE CORRÈZE

JEAN MAGE
Chirac, 19200 Brivezac
Tel: 05-55-91-52-30

The president of the *syndicat* is Jean Mage, whose farm is at Brivezac just east off the main road north out of Beaulieu. His father had kept the tradition of *vin paillé* alive and at one time had no fewer than 30 grape varieties with which he was experimenting on his 3.5 hectares of land. He finally settled for two: *chardonnay* and *cabernet sauvignon*.

This marked a bold departure from tradition. In the old days, the grapes used were mostly from hybrid varieties planted as much as a hundred years ago in the wake of the phylloxera epidemic. Monsieur Mage Junior explained that the French wine authorities, on whom the growers ultimately depend for formal recognition, did not allow these hybrids to be planted anymore. The result is that today most of the production of *vin paillé* derives from noble grape varieties. These are cultivated quite high off the ground, so as to avoid the effect of spring frosts and to ensure minimum spoilage of fruit.

The wine can be made from black as well as white grapes. The difference in colour is quite small, because the wine is made like a white wine, drawn off the skins immediately and given a long cold fermentation. Mage uses barrels for ageing his wines, some new, some old. Undoubtedly the wood adds some complexity and there is a bit of flavour of the oak itself.

JEAN-LOUIS ROCHE
Queyssac Bas, 19120 Queyssac-les-Vignes
Tel: 05-55-91-05-21

Jean-Louis Roche, whose vines are at Queyssac itself, is another who is trying his luck with oak barrels. Jean-Louis, who has a brand new *chais,* also makes a *vin de noix*, another old country speciality, beefed up with *eau-de-vie*. There is nothing old-fashioned about Jean-Louis, however, who will be still bursting with energy even after a day's work in the vineyards.

DOMINIQUE SOLEILLET
Laval, 19120 Nonards
Tel: 05-55-91-50-01

Dominique Soleillet and his father will be keen to show you their immaculate vineyard, replanted with *cabernet franc* and some *chardonnay* in 1999. They would love to have more than their present couple of hectares, but the ban on new planting of vines restricts them. Their wines are sold largely to local wine-merchants as well as to customers at the door. In the neighbourhood, *vin paillé* is still the favoured ceremonial drink at family gatherings, New Year's Eve and other formal occasions. In the old days, it was also given to nursing mothers as a medicine.

JEAN AUGEAT
Farges, 19120 Puy d'Arnac
Tel: 05-55-91-53-21

A more purely artisanal style marks the wines of Jean Augeat, whose vines are hidden in the middle of nowhere beyond the village of Puy d'Arnac. Jean has not only both *cabernets* and some *chardonnay* but a little old *folle blanche* as well. Instead of laying the grapes out on straw, he, like many other makers, uses ventilated wooden trays. He insists that the grapes must never be artificially heated, although some growers are said in the past to have hastened the process of *séchage* by using their prune ovens. Jean presses his grapes when they reach a potential alcohol level of 20 or 21 degrees. Fermentation continues until there are actually 15 or 16 degrees in the wine, leaving a balance of residual unfermented sugar. The ultimate yield is tiny, about 10 hectolitres from a hectare of vines.

ANTOINE TRONCHE
Tillet, 19120 Queyssac-les-Vignes
Tel: 05-55-91-01-96

As you would expect in such a deeply rural community, some farmers eschew the modern grape varieties and don't wish to know about new oak barrels. They also keep to old-fashioned straw and consider the wooden trays an abomination. Such is Antoine Tronche, another Queyssac grower, who gives the impression of being shy about his perpetuation of the old traditions. Tasting Tronche's wine immediately revealed the difference between the old and new schools of producers. The *nouvelle vague*, with their fashionable grapes, their wooden trays, and above all their tendency to top up the barrels and *cuves* as the wine oxidizes during its ageing, are making wines more akin to traditional sweet wines, a sort of unfortified *vin doux naturel*. Tronche, however, is still making the kind of wine which used to be poured in the old café at Queyssac, with its suggestion of walnuts and more than a touch of *rancio*.

OTHER CORRÈZE GROWERS

ANDRÉ ARNAUD
La Plancas, 19120 Beaulieu

CHRISTIAN BARRIÈRE
Le Bourg, 19500 Saint Julien Maumont

CHRISTOPHE CHASTANET
Mas Vidal, 19120 Bilhac

MME MARIE-CLAUDE CID
Mirande, 19120 Queyssac-les-Vignes

JEAN-MICHEL DELMAS
Le Bourg, 19500 Saint Julien Maumont

DANIEL GAUBERT
Le Bourg, 19120 Queyssac-les-Vignes

JEAN GAUBERT
Croix du Battut, 19120 Queyssac-les-Vignes

MME LAURENCE LAUBAT
Ferrance, 19500 Branceilles

GEORGES LEYMAT
Le Portail, 19500 Branceilles

JACQUES LEYMAT
Le Clos, 19500 Branceilles

DANIEL MOULÈNE
Le Mastral, 19120 Sioniac

JEAN MOULÈNE
La Gardelle,19500 Saint Julien Maumont

PIERRE PERRINET
La Bourdie, 19500 Branceilles

JOËL SOURSAC
Le Pilou, 19120 Queyssac-les-Vignes

ALBERT TAURISSON
Gandalat, 19120 Sioniac

CHRISTIAN TRONCHE
Tillet, 19120 Queyssac-les-Vignes

GÉRARD TRONCHE
La Coste, 19500 Saillac

GAEC VITALAIT (M. BONNEVAL)
Louradour, 19120 La Chapelle aux Saints

ERIC VLOGMAN
Le Mortier, 19500 Branceilles

OTHER WINES FROM THE CORRÈZE

At Branceilles, one of the *vin paillé* villages, there is a small *coopérative*, **Cave Coopérative de Branceilles** (Tel: 55-84-09-01), under the direction of a Monsieur Perrinet, making a quaffable red wine called **Mille et Une Pierres** (*A). This is much in the same style as the Coteaux de Glanes, with a pronounced *merlot* character.

Farther north, another *vin de pays* comes from Voutezac, where Christian Chauffier at **Domaine de Mégénie** (Tel: 05-55-25-83-95) makes an attractive red (*A), which is often to be found at the Paris brasserie Thoumieux, between the Invalides and the Eiffel Tower. It matches well the country character of the cooking there, which is also derived from the Corrèze.

THE WINES
OF CAHORS
AND THE CAUSSES

CAHORS

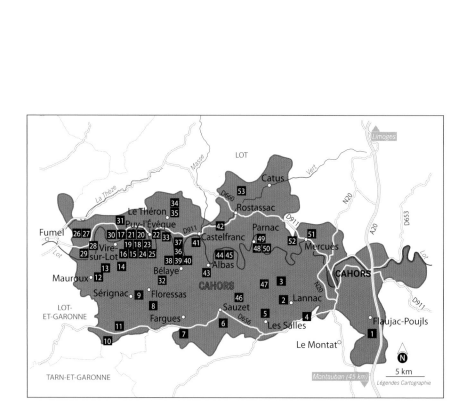

LOT

Catus

53

Rostassac

34
35
Le Théron
31
Puy-l'Évêque
42
Castelfranc
Parnac
51
49
52
Mercuès

Fumel
26 27
30 17 21 20 22 33
28 Vire- 19 18 23 37 41
sur-Lot 16 15 24 25 36
29
38 39 40
44 45
Albas
43

Mauroux 12
13
14
CAHORS
47
3
CAHORS

Sérignac 9 Floressas
8
Sauzet
46
2 Lannac

Fargues
5
Les Salles
4

11
6
Le Montat
1
Flaujac-Poujls

10

LOT-
ET-GARONNE

TARN-ET-GARONNE

Montauban (45 km)

N

5 km

Légendes Cartographie

AREA OF AOC: selected parcels covering 4404 hectares

CANTON OF CAHORS: communes of Cahors, Lamagdelaine, Mercuès, Pradines, Arcambal and Trespoux-Rassiels.

CANTON OF CATUS: communes of Catus, Crayssac, Labastide-le-Vert, Nuzéjouls, Pontcirq and Saint-Médard-Catus.

CANTON DE LALBENQUE: communes of Cieurac and Flaujac-Poujols.

CANTON OF LUZECH: communes of Albas, Anglars-Juillac, Belaye, Caillac, Cambayrac, Carnac-Rouffiac, Castelfranc, Douelle, Luzech, Parnac, Saint-Vincent-Rive-d'Olt, Sauzet and Villesèque.

CANTON OF MONTCUQ: communes of Bagat-en-Quercy, Le Boulvé, Fargues, Saint-Matré and Saux.

CANTON OF PUY-L'ÉVÊQUE: communes of Duravel, Floressas, Grézels, Lacapelle-Cabanac, Lagardelle, Mauroux, Pescadoires, Prayssac, Puy-l'Évêque, Sérignac, Soturac, Touzac and Vire-sur-Lot.

Red wines only from malbec (aka auxerrois and cot noir), minimum 70%, and tannat and merlot (maximum singly or together 30%). Average production 250,000 hectolitres.

MINIMUM ALCOHOL CONTENT: 10.5% by volume; maximum 13%, subject to derogation.

MAXIMUM YIELD: 50 hl/ha; minimum density of plantation 4000 plants/ha; distance between rows max. 2.5 metres, between plants 0.9 to 1.3 metres. Dispensation until 2010 for vines planted before 1992.

Vines may be planted either *en gobelet* or on wire. Concentration techniques forbidden during vinification.

OLD MAN RIVER

Today the Lot is a tranquil, idyllic, slow-moving river of great beauty. But there are old folk still living who will tell you that it was once a busy commercial highway. Before the advent of the phylloxera, thousands of barrels of wine went down the river every year to Bordeaux, so the boatmen—called in French *gabarriers* after the flat-bottomed *gabarres* they piloted—were very important people. A forebear of the Jouffreau family, whom we will meet later, ran an *auberge* on the banks of the river expressly to feed and water the oarsmen. These tough men needed great strength and courage: it was quite normal for 30 or so of them to be drowned every year and many tons of merchandise to be lost to the river-bed. There is a chapel just outside Luzech where, each September just before the wine harvest, the faithful would gather to pray to the Virgin for the safe return of the boatmen from Bordeaux. Legend has it that one of them, believing himself about to drown in the river, promised God to restore the chapel if He would save the man's life. The man was saved and he kept his promise.

ALL THE WORLD LOVED CAHORS

The story of riverside life is but one aspect of the fascinating history of the wine trade in the Lot. Another has been already touched on, the love-hate relationship between the Bordelais and the wine-makers upstream. In the case of Cahors this has left an indelible mark on the style of the local wine. It was the English who christened the wine of Cahors as 'black', though this, as will be seen, was, and to this day remains, an unfair and unfortunate tag. By the first half of the fourteenth century, over half the wine being shipped out of Bordeaux came from the vineyards of Quercy, the province of which Cahors was the capital. Such was its reputation that in the French merchant navy officers were provided with cahors, while other ranks had to make do with graves or mere bordeaux. Exports were not confined to England. Russia was an important market because the Orthodox Church favoured cahors as a *vin de messe*. The French too have always admired cahors. The Avignon

Pope John XII was a native of the Lot and had cahors vines planted at the papal vineyards in the Rhône Valley. François I engaged a grower from Cahors to plant the royal vinery at Fontainebleau.

The stranglehold of Bordeaux over the wines of Cahors lasted until the Revolution. Cahors emerged perhaps more wounded from this long ordeal than other wine-growing areas. The arsenal of weapons which the Bordeaux merchants had used against Cahors had a depressing and discouraging effect on its growers, who were often constrained to sacrifice their wines at a cruelly low price to speculators only too well aware of their value and importance. A dealer from Luzech in the heart of the Cahors vineyards, issued a public warning as early as 1750 in which he predicted with the accuracy of a prophet the need to put in place controls in order to maintain basic quality: 'Although the wines of Cahors are apparently able to maintain their reputation, they are nevertheless on the point of losing it in the French American colonies and overseas lands, unless immediate steps are taken to prevent the discredit which could easily overwhelm this province: it will be totally wiped out if it loses its only resource, namely its vines, because it has practically no other crops such as those upon which other regions can rely for a living.'

THE 'BLACK' LABEL

The classic account of the style of wines being made in the Lot before the phylloxera is that of André Jullien, who wrote in 1816: 'Three kinds of red wines are made in this area: those which are called black because of the intensity of their colour, those which are called full-bodied red wines, and finally pink wines. The first are normally used only for blending, the second are good table-wines, and the third are ordinary wines, some better than others, which are the everyday drink of the local inhabitants.

'The black wines are made with grapes coming from the plant which is called in the area "auxerrois"; they combine a very deep colour, a good flavour and plenty of "guts". They are not really suitable for everyday use; but they are very useful for adding colour, body and strength to feeble wines, and they survive transportation well.'

Then Monsieur Jullien comes to the point about the 'black wines'. He says: 'They make a point of baking a proportion of [the grapes] in the oven, or bringing to the boil the whole of the vintage before it is put into barrel for its natural fermentation. . . . The first-mentioned process removes from the must quite a lot of the water content of the wines, and encourages a more active fermentation in which the colouring agents dissolve perfectly. The merchants who trade in these wines do not stop here: they blend with the must of the auxerrois a distillation at a strength of some 29 degrees a kind of liquor which they add in the proportion of one-fifth, one-quarter, or even one-third, according to the quality [sic] that they wish to produce'.

Doctor Guyot, the first great expert on the pruning of vines, wrote in the 1850s confirming the earlier account of Jullien, and put in perspective the roles of the unfortunate growers and wine-makers, whose lack of organization in those days put them at the mercy of counterfeit dealers: 'The table wines, much better than the black wines, are excellent and very clean, without too much alcohol.'

Thus the table wines of Cahors never corresponded with the description of the so-called 'black' wines. Cahors has lived for hundreds of years branded with the epithet 'black', when the wines which were indeed 'black' were never drunk as table wines on their own at all. The problem is compounded today by the recent decision of the local promotional authorities to re-brand cahors as 'black wine'. Not only is it untrue of most Cahors wines even today, but it is historically false and perhaps more likely to put off buyers than attract them. History will tell whether the local syndicate of growers is shooting itself in the foot or not.

THE CAHORS STYLE: THE *AUXERROIS* GRAPE aka *MALBEC*

The typicity of cahors derives from a combination of *terroir*, the climate and above all the principal grape variety. The *auxerrois* is known variously elsewhere as *malbec* or *pressac* in Bordeaux, and *cot* in other parts of the South-West. Nobody knows how the name *auxerrois* came into usage. Some have suggested that there is a link with the city of Auxerre, the birthplace of a one-time bishop of Cahors. Others have suggested the grape variety of the same name common in Alsace, but that is a white grape. The most superficially attractive explanation is that *auxerrois* is a corruption of *Haute-Serre*, the name of a very old vineyard to the south-east of Cahors. Perhaps because of the newly fashionable *malbec* wines from Argentina, there is a tendency to switch in Cahors from the name *auxerrois* to *malbec*.

Whatever the origin of its name, the fame of cahors rests on the *auxerrois*. It gives a deep-coloured juice, with rich tannins. Its aromas suggest cherries, damson plums and soft black fruits, particularly when young. It can then be quite astringent unless vinified for early drinking. With age the wine darkens, and its suppleness gradually acquires structure as the phenols add complexity and length. The wine develops another dimension of aromas, sometimes violets or licorice, and with increasing maturity, the forest floor, game, leather and even truffles. The *auxerrois* is fairly low-yielding, sometimes lacking in acidity, and its weakness is its susceptibility to the disease called *coulure,* in which, particularly following a cold spring, the grapes fail to swell and eventually drop off the plant. It produces wines with firm tannins, needing time to resolve them. The best wines benefit from being cellared. The half-Atlantic, half-Mediterranean climate of the region gives perfect conditions for the grape, which is of a more southern style than Bordeaux, while providing a perfect accompaniment to the famous cooking of the South-West. It is impossible to imagine cahors without its *auxerrois*, even if these days some wine-makers legitimately add some *merlot* to soften the perceived roughness of some of the wines. Others add some *tannat* to boost alcoholic potential, which can be a problem with the *auxerrois*.

THE *TERROIRS*

The *auxerrois* grape lends an overall umbrella of distinctiveness to all cahors, but in reality there are many different *terroirs*, all producing variations on the *auxerrois* theme.

The river Lot winds its way through a high limestone plateau called *causse*. The whole area was once below the sea. When the waters receded, they left behind a bed of fossilized fish, now the limestone *causse*. Later, the upheavals which caused the Pyrenees and the Alps to push from out of the centre of the earth cracked the *causse*, and rivers found their way through the gaps, the gradual erosion of which has created the present network of river valleys. Today, therefore, there is the limestone plateau, and through it the alluvial river valley rising in three terraces towards the hills on either side. Occasionally subsidiary valleys lead off, and the slopes of these are called the *coteaux*. It might be expected that the styles of wine produced from the three *terroirs* would vary from one to the other, but it is difficult to generalize about this; the unifying character of the *auxerrois* often makes it difficult to distinguish between wines grown on the different soils, and even vines grown on the same type of soil can produce subtly different results.

CAHORS AND THE PHYLLOXERA

The middle of the 19th century had seen a rapid and unexpected rise in the fortunes of Cahors. The region profited from the spread of a disease common throughout France called 'oidium' which managed to leave Cahors untouched. This sudden and much-needed stroke of luck created a surge in demand for cahors, which was sadly rather short-lived. Soon it was reversed by competition from the wines of the Midi. The coming of the railways enabled the growers in Languedoc to undercut Cahors in the markets of the north. But even the fierce threat from the South was like a flea-bite compared with the disaster of the phylloxera. The first areas to be hit were those on the *causse*. In this shallower and poorer soil, the vine roots were unable to penetrate as deeply into the ground as those in the valley, and were therefore easier for the aphid to attack. The vines on the higher ground were immediately wiped out. At first the valley producers thought they would be spared, but eventually the whole vineyard was ruined, only a few parcels here and there surviving.

Some growers reacted, as in other wine-growing areas of the South-West, by trying the most outlandish and unscientific of remedies, reminiscent of the most bizarre practices of witch-doctors. Others tackled the problem by replanting more of the same grape varieties, only to find that these lasted but a few years in the face of the disease; some of these plants never even reached maturity. At least wine-making did not die out, because those who decided to replace the *auxerrois* with other kinds of vine made wine of some sort, though most of it was worse than *ordinaire*.

As the replacement of dead stocks with more of the same had failed, many growers took to planting American varieties, but all were unsatisfactory. The

Cahors wine-makers finally followed the example of other vineyards by grafting their traditional *auxerrois* vines onto American rootstocks which were immune to the disease. This was a success in almost every other area where it was tried. In Cahors it failed.

WHY DID CAHORS NOT REVIVE AFTER THE PHYLLOXERA?

The rootstock (*porte-greffe*) most widely used in the southern half of France, called *rupestris,* was the obvious choice for Cahors to adopt. However, *rupestris* proved too vigorous for the *auxerrois* graft; it accented the vulnerability of *auxerrois* to *coulure*. Grafting, as a process, was by then fully proven as the only valid way of fighting phylloxera, so more and more growers applied it to other inferior grape varieties. Wine-making was also kept alive by experimentation with Franco-American hybrid vines rather than grafting, although the results could not compare with the old-fashioned pre-phylloxera cahors based on pure unblended *auxerrois*.

Meanwhile, the replanting of the mass-producing rival vineyards of Langue-doc had been an enormous success. Worse still, in the 1930's bulk quantities of wine began to be produced in Algeria, and much of it, contrary to received wisdom, was good wine from grapes such as *carignan, grenache* and *cinsault*. The North African wines not only were useful to the Midi to boost the quality and alcoholic content of their own rather poor stuff, but were exported direct to Nantes and Rouen in tankers, feeding some of the markets which a hundred years before had been the exclusive hunting ground for cahors.

SIGNS OF REVIVAL

The terrible frosts of 1956 and 1957 might have been expected to put an end to the wines of Cahors forever. In 1958 real cahors represented a bare 1% of the total production of the Lot Valley. But it is strange how, throughout history, those with the inspiration or calling to defy adversity manage to keep the flame of their faith alive. Cahors was lucky to have a handful of these.

Their first task, in the face of the widespread fraud and adulteration which cahors suffered in the early years of the 20th century, and of the drop in quality which the adoption of inferior vine-stocks had brought about, was to obtain the protection of the law for the name and standards of production of real cahors. A band of the faithful had already obtained recognition for the name in some tentative legislation of the 1920's. In 1929 they created the *Syndicat de Défense de l'Appellation d'Origine Cahors*, but such was the low point from which they started that not even their enthusiasm was able to make their voices heard in Paris when the first of the AOCs were created in 1935.

After a pause imposed by the Second World War, the movement gathered strength again. The *cave coopérative* of Parnac, one of the big players in the later revival, was created in 1947. The grant of VDQS status in 1951 defined the geographical limits of the appellation, and these were carried over into the grant of full AOC status in 1971 for selected parcels in 45 communes stretching almost from

Fumel in the west upstream to a point some 10 kilometres or so east of the town of Cahors.

Legal protection was secure. But now there was the difficult task of re-introducing the *auxerrois* grape into an area where it had been largely abandoned by most of the growers and virtually discredited. Here the newborn *coopérative* played a vital role in identifying better *porte-greffes* than the old ones which had not worked for the *auxerrois*. New stocks were found which were not only suitable for the grape variety but minimized the risk of the *coulure* disease. The harder problem was to rebuild the morale and confidence of the growers.

Ironically, it was Bordeaux that came to the rescue. A Monsieur Mallambic, a grower near Blaye in the Gironde and a fanatical devotee of the *malbec* grape (as it was called there), worked with the *coopérative* to produce new grafts, which were then planted in an experimental vineyard near Luzech in the Lot Valley. Local growers were taken on a trip to Blaye to see for themselves the thriving plantations of M. Mallambic.

New clones were produced on ground next to the Parnac *coopérative*, and from these much of the replanted Cahors vineyard has been developed. A continuous public relations exercise was needed to sustain the interest of the local producers over this period. The new Cahors pioneers, encouraged by the authorities in Paris, who were anxious to bury Cahors' reputation for the production of 'black' wines, decided to introduce up to 30% *merlot* and/or *tannat* into their wines, so creating the basis of the *encépagement* permitted under the AOC rules in 1971.

THE GOLD RUSH

At the beginning of the 1960's, Cahors was for once in luck. The revival of interest in quality wine and the buzz of excitement caused by new research coincided with the beginning of the French economic revival called *les Trentes Glorieuses*, the glorious thirty years. There was suddenly a demand for better-quality table wines which a wider public could afford. The growers in the Lot were caught off guard because their meagre production was nowhere near enough to satisfy the sudden demand. They responded with a programme of massive over-planting, over-production and over-pricing. A serious, if temporary, crisis arose in 1971, when many growers decided to celebrate the grant of AOC status by jacking up the price of the wines. The market didn't comply. There were then three poor vintages in a row, the growers were left with stocks of second-rate wine, and the price fell sharply again.

Since the heyday of the '70's, life has not been easy for the average grower in Cahors. The majority have not been able to secure for their wines a better price than they got for their poor wine in the bad old days. Cahors has never regained the standing in export markets which it enjoyed pre-phylloxera, though in France itself it has maintained its prestige if not its place in the market. Many of the smaller producers who flocked to the *coopérative* as an outlet for small crops of grapes which they were unable to vinify themselves, have left to set up on their own. Some have been successful, others not. Some older growers have seen their sons train at college or university, returning home as adults ready not merely to grow grapes but to make the wine too. There has nevertheless been a drop of 20% in the number of vineyards since 1987.

THE STRUGGLES OF THE ARTISAN GROWERS

The 1970's boom saw the emergence of powerful *négociants* who bought up the crop of many small growers, made wine and marketed it at knock-down prices, sometimes blending the wine with goodness-knows-what. Fifty years ago there was only one important *négociant*, the house of Reutenauer, which is today enjoying a revival but was at that time overtaken by the likes of the Rigals, the Vigouroux, the Castels and the Delgoulets. Some of these have turned *vignerons* themselves, creating relatively large estates whose wines of course get priority in the marketing efforts of their makers. Other growers, such as Alain-Dominique Perrin, the Verhaeghe brothers, the Pelvillain family and François Pelissié, have gone in the reverse direction, becoming *négociants* after having started out as growers. In this situation, the peasant-farmer-*vigneron* is obliged to stand by and watch as the big players in the appellation are able to command up to 70 euros a bottle for their premium wines, while he is lucky to get one euro a litre for his wine *en vrac*, even though AOC.

IMAGE

A problem which is shared by big and small alike is that there is no longer any generally accepted image of cahors today. There are the traditional artisans trying to perpetuate the style of cahors as it was understood in the past; there are the young Turks making wines, albeit in small quantities, of an international style, relying often on overripe fruit, high concentration, over-extraction and the prodigal use of new oak barrels; there are those who are making a kind of *cahors nouveau* (a travesty); and then there are the hundreds of tiny growers, for some of whom the grape is just another crop so that all they are concerned about is getting the going rate for their raw material. This confusion of purpose was made worse by the decision of the Cahors growers to secede from the *Comité Inter-professionnel des Vins du Sud-Ouest,* an umbrella organization which existed to promote all the wines of the South-West. The latter has reconstituted itself as the *Comité du Bassin du Sud-Ouest,* and Cahors has rejoined. It remains to be seen with what result.

CASHING IN ON THE NAME

In these circumstances, Cahors became a somewhat unhappy appellation. Bad feeling was exacerbated by the arrival on the scene of 'outsiders' from other areas and walks of life. Alain Senderens, the famous Paris chef, burnt his fingers badly when he overspent himself on the acquisition and equipping of Château de Gautoul; likewise, the Americans Stephen and Sherry Schechter seem to have failed in trying to make Château Pech de Jammes viable, even though Georges Vigouroux made the wine and handled the French distribution. Vigouroux and his son Bertrand have, however, been able to strengthen his portfolio by taking on wine-making for the Queen of Denmark (a former *coopérateur* at Château de Caïx) and by acquiring a controlling stake in the Château Léret-Monpezat owned by his brother-in-law. Vigouroux is also the owner in his own right of Château de Haute-Serre and the flagship Château de Mercuès, the latter dominating symbolically the Cahors vineyards from its heights on the *causse*. Vigouroux also has a large retail shop/showroom/*chais* at the southern end of the Cahors bypass called 'Atrium', and it has several branches elsewhere in the Lot. It is here that he sells his own wines and those he represents as *négociant*.

Alain-Dominique Perrin is undoubtedly the most famous of the 'outsiders', having bought the run-down Château de Lagrézette in 1980 and spared no expense in refurbishing the château and vineyard. Many people in Cahors thought that, with all his business experience as managing director of Cartier, he would be the saviour of the local economy, and he certainly provided abundant proof of his undoubted talent for self-promotion. His misfortune was not to understand that the precepts of big business were not always compatible with the syndicalist philosophy of the locals. Having more or less told them that, until he came along, they were making bad wine, he finally upset them badly by backing plans for declassifying parts of the land which had enjoyed AOC status since the beginning.

Then there is Philippe Lejeune, a computer software magnate from northern France and recent purchaser of Château de Chambert.

The Rigals are another of the big *négociant* families, owners of three important domaines, Château Saint Didier at Parnac, Le Prieuré de Cénac and Château de Grézels. They used to have an important wine-dealing business but are now concentrating exclusively on their own vineyards. The Bordeaux firm of Castel too has an important stake in Cahors, though so far does not own any vineyards themselves.

There have been several moves to establish a *Cru Classé* hierarchy of Cahors growers. Perrin led an early attempt in this direction, establishing Les Seigneurs Cahors in the early 1990's along with invited rich colleagues for whom the entry fee was the equivalent of £3000 sterling. This effort has rather withered on the vine; some members have left, while some of the others are no longer in the vanguard of Cahors fashion.

LA CHARTE DE QUALITÉ

Another effort at promoting better growers above others was based on the notion that some parts of the appellation enjoy a superior *terroir*. An idea of Pascal Verhaeghe at Château du Cèdre led to the establishment of a *Charte de Qualité*, to which those having vines in the privileged areas could aspire. The award of *charte* status is rigorously demanding. The candidate wines go before a jury, made up of growers, *négociants*, oenologists, technical experts, restaurateurs, gastronomic critics, sommeliers and even some consumers; every jury member receives specific training. Meanwhile, the *Syndicat de Défense* goes round and verifies the conditions in each relevant parcel of vines, and an analysis is made of the wines one year after the harvest, checking volatile acidity, intensity of colour and extraction. The jury then determines how many of the wines (there are no minima or maxima) qualify for the *charte* for the previous year. The winners not only may but must label their bottles with the sign *'Charte de Qualité'*, using labels available only from the *syndicat*.

All this sounds admirable in theory, but what happens in practice is that growers prepare special *cuvées* to present for the *charte,* usually over-concentrated, over-extracted and over-oaked, believing all too correctly that this is the style of wine which is going to attract the attention of the kind of jury described above. For the 2002 vintage, 22 wines were chosen, of which all but two were predictably of this style.

OAK RULES OKAY

This raises the vexed question of oak barrels. We have seen that the use of new casks goes back to the 17th century, but what is generally not realized is that before being filled with wine, the barrels were thoroughly cleaned out to get rid of the aromas and taste of new wood. The great virtue of the barrel was that while it preserved the wine in a relatively air-tight way, there was just enough oxygen entering through the pores of the wood and the staves to mature the wine slowly but gently. From the 1980's onwards, however, a predilection for the smell and taste of the wood itself has infiltrated the wine market, largely under the impetus of the New World via Bordeaux. Nowadays there is a perception that if a wine is not aged in barrels, it is somehow old-fashioned. Emmanuel Duquoc in his book referred to below says that it is difficult today to produce a great cahors unless it has been matured in oak. This is in stark contrast with the opinion of another writer, José Baudel, who, writing in 1977, maintained, 'There is something artificial in all this; wine becomes no longer the exclusive product of the grape, but that of the grape-plus-wood. Can cahors reach the heights without oak? Undoubtedly yes. A 1975 cahors can laugh at oak. It is sufficiently rich in itself without needing this extra addition, which on the contrary can add excessive hardness.' Baudel was one of the prime movers in the renaissance of Cahors, and wrote with more authority than many of today's pundits.

The truth, as often, lies somewhere in the middle. The great clarets and the burgundies of the past did not need the taste of new oak to make them great. The New World style of wine so prevalent today often sees its fruit and elegance drowned by the taste of floorboards. But there is also no doubt that oak barrels (usually when they have already been used once or more) can add richness and complexity, provided that the wine is given time to mature and throw off the bouquet and flavours of the wood. It takes a master winemaker to achieve the right balance, and a patient consumer to do the rest. There are too many growers today who believe that all you have to do to make a *Cuvée Prestige* is to leave it in wood for a year or more, and hey presto! Cahors wines always did take some time to mature, so they will generally improve with age whether they have been raised in casks or not. On the other hand, many of the finest cahors are still raised otherwise than in new oak.

Of the 200 or so growers who make and bottle their own wines, most will raise only a small percentage of their production in barrels, partly because of the expense and partly because their customers don't always like the result. At Domaine de Maison Neuve, for example, Mme Delmouly told me she reckoned that 85% of her customers did not want her to oak her wines. On the other hand, most growers worry that they will not be taken seriously if they cannot offer visitors a *Cuvée* This-or-That aged in barrels, and even Mme Delmouly is experimenting with five new *barriques*. For most growers, their top oaked wine in the 'modern cahors' style is usually only a small proportion, less than 10% of their total production. Chez Perrin, however, it is hard to find anything that has not been *boisé*.

CAHORS GRAND CRU

The move to create a more developed hierarchy of Cahors than the *Charte de Qualité* has run into rough water. A commission under the joint presidency of Jean-Marie Sigaud and Alain-Dominique Perrin promoted plans for a revision of the area of the appellation established more than 50 years previously. Many vineyards on the *premières terrasses*, those closest to the river, would be excluded. Admittedly, there are properties there which produce less than first-class wine, but there are others, including those of some of the oldest Cahors families, which have always made very good wine. The idea was supported by many who saw that the image of Cahors might be improved if the AOC rules were tightened so as to improve sharply the quality of wines entitled to the cahors name, but they had bargained without the suspicion of others (rightly or wrongly) that the scheme was a ruse to promote the powerful. Even more resented was the idea that a country *vigneron* in the Lot would sacrifice land which had been in the family for generations in exchange for some terrain elsewhere, where he would have to wait five years or so after replant-ing before he could make any wine. The plan was voted down, much to Perrin's chagrin, by a narrow majority of the locals. In a fit of pique, which he may later have regretted, he resigned from all his posts in the Cahors establishment and even threatened to withdraw his Château de Lagrézette from the appellation altogether. The scheme has been shelved but not abandoned. Meanwhile Perrin, safe on the second and third *terrasses*, is still making AOC wine.

Another problem for Cahors arises from the exclusive predilection of the French wine critics for wines which correspond with the heavyweights from else-where in the world. It seems to be forgotten that, if a wine is to be sold as cahors, then it must taste like cahors, and that means it must promote the distinguishing characteristics of the *auxerrois* grape. How depressing it is therefore to read in the *Guide des Vins de Cahors* by Emmanuel Duquoc (Castelnaud la Chapelle: L'Hydre Editions, 2003): 'During blind tastings of top bordeaux, madiran and cahors wines, professionals have been incapable of picking out the cahors. This happens regu-larly. This means that in one respect tannat, auxerrois and cabernet sauvignon offer similar characteristics of taste. This is great news, for it means that cahors has quietly joined the company of the great, while for the most part keeping its prices down.'

'Great news'? What would one say of a chef whose beef was indistinguishable from his lamb? Can there be a better definition of standardization? If professionals could not pick out the cahors, they couldn't by the same token pick out the madiran or the bordeaux either, which is hardly a compliment to any of them.

However, wines of this style are still in a minority, even if they get all the media attention and dominate restaurant wine lists. It is worth noting that in the 2002 vintage, the 22 wines qualifying for the *Charte de Qualité* derived from only 45 hectares in all, as compared with a total area of 4300 under vine in the AOC—barely a tenth of one percent. There are still plenty of cahors to be found which the professionals ought to be able to pick out as cahors in a blind tasting.

THE RANGE OF CONTEMPORARY PRODUCTION

In attempting a survey of today's producers, it is as well to begin with some of those whose families kept Cahors alive through the difficult hundred years between the phylloxera and the revival of the 1960's. It must be remembered that, even if some of them, usually through a younger generation, have coveted *Charte de Qualité* recognition, without them cahors as a wine would be no more than a name in the history books; it would have vanished without a trace.

RECOMMENDED INDEPENDENT GROWERS

■ **CLOS DE GAMOT**
Martine and Maryse Jouffreau
and Yves Hermann-Jouffreau
46220 Prayssac
Tel: 05-65-22-40-26 Fax: 05-65-22-45-44
Email: closdegamot@orange.fr

The 10 hectares of Clos de Gamot are on the third and best of the river terraces. The soil is gravelly on the surface, with large round and polished stones that have washed down the river valley over the centuries. The grapes are all *auxerrois*, some of them 120 years old, replanted immediately after the phylloxera, others a mere 40. The Jouffreau family have been making wine here since 1610. They managed to recover quickly after the phylloxera, after identifying a hybrid called *herbemont* upon which they could graft *auxerrois* plants and which worked where the more usual *porte-greffes* had failed.

In 1947, Jean Jouffreau, then only 19 years old, was entrusted by his father with the vinification. In addition, he started bottling the wines of Gamot, including those which remained unsold because of the war. In this only five other growers followed his example. He was also an indefatigable salesman. His first big customer was the Hotel Terminus at Cahors, whose restaurant, Le Balandre, is still buying Gamot to this day.

Jean worked tirelessly with trusted colleagues first for the grant of VDQS status in 1951 and then for full appellation in 1971. In this he and his friends were helped a great deal by President Pompidou, who lived not far away and who had been intro-

duced to Gamot wine at the Élysée. Paris was not the only seat of government where the wine was appreciated; it reached the White House also.

Jean never compromised on his wine. Tastings *en famille* with his wife, two daughters, Martine and Maryse, and his son-in-law, Yves Hermann, were a ritual much like morning prayers, a tradition which is still continued today. Throughout his life the style of **Clos de Gamot** (***B) remained the same, authentic, deep, fruity, long-lasting, and abundantly satisfying. It was never, as some have claimed, austere and over-tannic, though it needed time to show off its best and to develop its famous bouquet. Jean generally made just the one *cuvée,* although from 1985 onwards, but only in exceptionally good years, he made a special wine from the **vignes centenaires** (***B) planted just after the phylloxera. Jean was not interested in new oak barrels. Nor did he venture into the untraditional, although quite surprisingly he would have liked to have been allowed to plant a little *cabernet sauvignon* to blend with his *auxerrois*. But he had only 10 hectares of vines, at least until he bought the romantic Château du Cayrou a few kilometres downstream. He snatched this from under the nose of a deeply disappointed underbidder, who, it is said, never forgave him. Jean never borrowed a penny for this deal, raising the money largely by a giant auction at Christie's in London of old vintages of Gamot going back to the 1880's. Gossips challenged the authenticity of these wines, but they were genuine and magnificent, as I can testify, having led a tasting of them in London a few years later.

Jean died in 1996, but not before the family had created yet another vineyard high up in the hills near Castelfranc. Here on just a hectare of almost vertical slope, *auxerrois* cuttings from Gamot have been planted to produce a wine of exceptional promise called **Clos Saint Jean** (*** C). The wine is still in its early stages and it is sad that Jean did not live to see its development. There was no 2003 harvest because the plants were ravaged by a horde of wild boar, and in 2004 it was the turn of deer to deprive the Jouffreaus of their precious crop. But the 2001 vintage, produced in tiny quantities, is quite simply magnificent, with a long life ahead assured, and as the vines age, the wine can only get better still. Commercialization of this *cuvée* has been delayed until recently while the vines mature properly.

Jean has been succeeded by his two daughters, Martine and Maryse, ably guided by Martine's husband Yves, a fine oenologist trained by Jean. The family keeps the benchmark style of Gamot virtually unchanged, though they are now producing in addition an easier-to-drink **Cuvée Jouffreau** (**A), as well as a dry **white vin de pays** (*A) based on *sémillon* and *sauvignon*. The wines of **Château du Cayrou** (**B), where the *auxerrois* is softened by *merlot*, are slightly lighter in style and develop a little earlier, but there is still a clear family resemblance.

The Jouffreau wines give the lie to the idea that a great cahors must be raised in new oak. The wines are aged in old Burgundian type *foudres*, but never in virgin barrels.

■ CLOS LA COUTALE
Philippe Bernède
46700 Vire-sur-Lot
Tel: 05-65-36-51-43
Email: info@coutale.com

This property has belonged to the Bernède family since just before the Revolution. They have been winning medals since 1894 (Paris Concours Général). Philippe Bernède runs a modern enterprise which includes stainless steel *cuves* with temperature control. He uses new wood for a small quantity of wine which he markets as his **Cuvée Prestige** (*B); otherwise he uses old barrels. Along with the Jouffreau family he is among the old-timers in not having gone over in part at least to an oaky style of cahors. His mainstream wine, called simply **Clos la Coutale** (**A), is in the same mould as Gamot, though quicker-maturing. Its great virtue is that it is easy to drink.

Today the average age of the vines is about 30 years, which explains the roundness and charm of the wines. They seem to mature quite quickly and are lighter in style than many, though they can also age well. The colour is usually dark but limpid, and sometimes the nose is quite toasty. Chewy and well built, they have plenty of body and maybe a touch of liquorice. The finish is always long and silky and the wine nicely balanced. Coutale often excels in years when others disappoint. It is extremely popular, often to be found in restaurants, and an excellent value for the money.

Bernède produces from time to time a white *vin de pays* which he calls **Valmy** (*A) after the famous victory of the revolutionary armies, in which no fewer than three Bernède brothers participated.

■ CHÂTEAU PINERAIE

Jean-Luc Burc

Leygues, 46700 Puy-l'Évêque

Tel: 05-65-30-82-07 Fax: 05-65-21-39-65

Email: chateaupineraie@wanadoo.fr

www.chateaupineraie.com

The Burc family claim to have been exploiting this domaine since 1456, but Jean-Luc has taken over from his father relatively recently. During the dark years of the 1930's the Burcs managed to find a market for their wines *en vrac* in Paris, but nowadays the accent is on domaine-bottling. The 40 hectares of this estate make it one of the most important in the region. The family have never bothered much with the *tannat* grape, but they are fans of the *auxerrois,* which constitutes 90% of the vineyard. Some of the vines are a few kilometres away, up on the *causse*.

Jean-Luc was one of the first to experiment seriously with oak in 1996, and today the flagship wine, called **L'Authentique**—a misnomer—is not authentic at all but one of the leading wines of the new wave of Cahors growers (C). The wood is prominent on the nose of the young wines, which can show hazelnuts, coffee, a touch of smoke and animal characteristics. On the palate the fruit tends to a good balance with complimentary acidity. The structure is firm and powerful.

But the more traditional wine of this property should not be overlooked. Much lighter in colour, the bouquet too is easier, with red fruits and jam.

The palate is soft, well balanced and with good fruit, and the tannins are easy and round. It is marketed simply as **Château Pineraie** (**A).

■ CLOS TRIGUEDINA

Jean-Luc Baldès

46700 Vire-sur-Lot

Tel: 05-65-21-30-81 Fax: 05-65-21-39-28

Email: contact@jlbaldes.com

www.jlbaldes.com

Jean-Luc, one of the most respected of all cahors producers, can claim for his family nearly 200 years of wine production at this, one of the oldest of all Cahors estates. His 40 hectares enjoy a particularly mild micro-climate which enabled them to survive for the most part the killer frosts of 1956. This accounts for the age of some of the oldest vines in the vineyard, which is planted with 70% *auxerrois*, 20% *merlot* and 10% *tannat*.

Jean-Luc is so traditional that he is producing a wine which he calls **The New Black Wine of Cahors** (*C). This is his version of the infamous style of yesteryear. I would be more enthusiastic about his adventurousness if it were not for the fact that the so-called 'black' wine should be forgotten rather than commemorated. The epithet has done more to prevent cahors from impacting on the export market than any other factor. Jean-Luc proceeds according to the old recipe by heating the wine to reduce it, but he refrains from adding more alcohol to it as they did sometimes in the old days. Try it by all means as an experiment, but I for one am glad he only makes 5000 bottles a year of it.

More to the point are the two mainstream red table wines from his property. These are the wines which have earned him the universal respect of his colleagues. **Clos Triguedina** (**C), though not his top wine, needs to be cellared a long time. Ruby but shot through with darker tints, it gives the impression of being chewy, grainy almost, and the nose takes time to develop in the glass. The fruit is massive and the tannins substantial. For once, the oak is fine, because it is well regulated, and indeed the whole structure of the wine calls out for it.

Prince Probus (***D) is his famous *tête de cuvée*, named after a Roman emperor who lifted a ban on planting vines imposed by one of his less liberal predecessors. It has served as a model for many newcomers to Cahors. It is wonderfully consistent, one vintage being difficult to pick out from another. It is dense and dark to look at, with oak that is prominent on the nose, balancing black fruits, damsons and cherries, and in the mouth the wine has a tremendous structure. Of its style, the wine remains a benchmark. Seven years later, the 1998 could hardly be bettered anywhere in the appellation.

Not to be overlooked are a delicious white *moëlleux vin de pays* called **Vin de Lune** (**C) made from *chenin blanc*, fermented and raised in barrels, and a range of easy-to-drink wines made from younger vines and sold under the name of **Château Labrande** (*B).

■ **CHÂTEAU EUGÉNIE**
La Famille Couture
Rivière-Haute, 46140 Albas
Tel: 05-65-30-73-51 Fax: 05-65-20-19-81
Email: couture@chateaueugenie.com

Jean and Claude Couture each have sons who are professionally qualified oenologists, and they have gradually taken over the reins at this property with the approval of their parents, introducing, as might be expected, innovative styles and techniques to the wine-making. Three of the 32 hectares are being cultivated experimentally under biodynamic rules, and a small part of the estate is given over to the *Charte de Qualité*. New barrels have always been part of the armoury of this family, but nowadays all the wines see more or less new oak. In the past 50 years, this domaine has seen a transition from the traditional to the avant-garde.

The vines are on slopes to the south of Albas and are very largely, though not entirely, planted with *auxerrois*. The first wine is called **Cuvée Réservée des Tsars** (*B) and comes from young vines on the second and third *terrasses* of the left bank of the river. Fruit and wood mingle on the nose, and on the palate there is good concentration. Next in line comes **Cuvée Réservée de l'Aïeul** (*B), darker and less polished than the foregoing and 100% *auxerrois*. The oak is quite pronounced and the wine clearly needs time, especially in a 'keeping' year such as 2000. The top wine, called **Haute Collection** (*C), is very much *nouvelle vague* and the wine which the family enters for the *Charte*. The impression of sweetness, which comes from the vanillin flavours in the wood, is balanced by good acidity as a rule, and if you like this style, then this is a pretty good example.

■ **CHÂTEAU LA CAMINADE**
La Famille Ressès
Parnac, 46140 Luzech
Tel: 05-65-30-73-05 Fax: 05-65-20-17-04
Email: resses@wanadoo.fr
www.chateau-caminade.com

Architecturally this is one of the prettiest and most interesting of all the Cahors properties, its external covered galleries at first-floor level being typical of the Quercy style. A former presbytery, it was seemingly used secretly for christenings during the Revolution. The Ressès have been making wine here for five generations, but it was only in the 1950's that Léonce Ressès started to extend the vineyard beyond its then four hectares. He was until then mainly a cheese-maker, but he devoted all his spare profits to expanding the area of the vineyard until it reached its present size of over 35 hectares. He was a founder-member of the *Syndicat de Défense* and defender of the faith. Today his two sons have taken over respectively in vineyard and *chais* and they combine the old traditions with new technology. They will still not start picking until physical tasting of the grapes has proved to them that the pips crunch and the juice stains, whatever the scientific analysis may tell them. Production has always been divided between the oaked and unoaked, and today the basic wine of the property remains unoaked and is called simply **Château La Caminade** (**B/C); it is unusually light in texture and weight, leaning towards a *primeur* style and not really typical. The other two wines go to the other extreme. **La Commandery** (*B) has been well known as a name in Cahors for many years. It has been getting darker and darker in colour and there are jammy fruits on the nose when you can get beyond the wood, the evidence of which has become more intrusive as the years have gone by. If this wine has to be kept a few years, even more so is the case with the 'top' wine, **Esprit** (D), which is one of the most extreme of all the international-style wines today being made in Cahors. Enough said, really.

From time to time, this property releases wines under other names (e.g. Peyrouse) for early drinking and at A price levels.

■ **CHÂTEAU LA REYNE**
Jean-Claude and Johan Vidal
Leygues, 46700 Puy-l'Évêque
Tel: 05-65-30-82-53 Fax: 05-65-21-39-83

Johan Vidal is an extraordinary young wine-maker who has perhaps created more waves than any other in Cahors, at least in recent years. Born into a family steeped in Cahors tradition, and which made wines of excellent quality, though little noted in the press and media, Johan shocked his family by taking over a small parcel of vines when he was yet a teenager and doing a *vendange verte* on it. 'Infanticide', claimed Grandfather. Iconoclast though he was, he took care to learn from some of the most famous of wine-makers working in the modern school, gradually improving his techniques, which he modelled on such as those of Pascal Verhaeghe.

Those not in tune with the new school can easily content themselves with the basic wine called **Le Tradition** (**A), a continuation of the old family style of this property and an exceptional value for

the money. Nor can the next wine, **Le Prestige** (*B), be called otherwise; it is already a younger relative of the top wines, with its inky colour, an alcoholic nose infused with wood and extremely soft palate. This an apt preparation for the top wines of the property, **L'Excellence** (C) and **Vent d'Ange** (D), which some people may find lacking cahors typicity, tending as they do to the blockbusting style of the New World. You either hate it or love it.

■ **CHÂTEAU DE BOVILA**
Négociants Reutenauer
46800 Fargues
Tel: 05-65-35-26-47
www.reutenauer.fr

CHÂTEAU DE ROUFFIAC
46700 Puy-l'Évêque
(same telephone and website)

Olivier Pieron and his brother, formerly businessmen in the field of heating engineering, are now in charge of these two properties, which belong to the *négociants* Reutenauer. The wines from the two estates could hardly be more different, and, contrary to received opinion, the wines of Bovila, on the *causse* above the left bank of the river, are lighter and more approachable than those of Rouffiac.

Bovila, a vineyard which was created in 1971 and which used to make rather heavy chocolatey wines, has been transformed under its new ownership. On 20 hectares of very chalky clay, the Pierons profit from the rules of the appellation to have their full 30% entitlement to *merlot*. Their first wine, called simply **Château de Bovila** (**A), is very attractive indeed, soft, fruity and characterful, while a lightly oaked version is called **Prieuré de Bovila** (**B), aged in barrels none of which are new.

The wines from Rouffiac, where the vineyard is a rather smaller 6.6 hectares, are altogether more ambitious. The vineyard has 10% *tannat*, 80% *auxerrois* and only 10% *merlot*, all planted on third-terrace land, which has quartzy minerals mixed in with the clay, rather than the chalk of Bovila. The wines are deeper coloured, more structured and more powerful than those of Bovila. The first of them, called **La Grange** (*A), is quite dry and rather austere in its youth, needing plenty of time for the tannins to soften and for the wine to come together. **La Passion** (*B) is the same wine given a little oak ageing, while **L'Exception** (D) is clearly aspiring to the *nouvelle vague* style.

DOMAINE DES BATELIERS
Charles Burc
46700 Puy-l'Évêque
Tel: 05-65-21-30-63 Fax: 05-65-21-31-07
Email: charles.burc@terre-net.fr

As the name of the property suggests, it is close by the river on the left bank almost opposite the hill town of Puy-l'Évêque, evoking the days when the wines of Cahors were shipped downstream in flat-bottomed boats to Bordeaux. The wines from here are often to be found on the wine lists of local restaurants, partly because they seem made to flatter good cooking rather than fight with it, and also because the wines age well without being tough or difficult at any stage of their life.

The property goes back many years, and the growers seem to eschew today's fashion for highly concentrated and extracted wines, favouring aromatic fruit, harmony, elegance and finesse above brute force. These are wines which recall the style of previous generations without in any way replicating their faults. Needless to say they are aged, as they always used to be, in old *foudres,* though there have been recent ventures into a 100% *auxerrois* raised in barrels. There is only one traditional *cuvée* and it bears the name **Domaine des Bateliers** (**A). It never fails to give pleasure. The wine ages well, developing a softness and subtlety which call for a second bottle. Old vintages turn up from time to time in the local restaurants and should be tried without fail.

CHÂTEAU PAILLAS
Germain Lescombes
46700 Floressas
Tel: 05-65-36-58-28 Fax: 05-65-24-61-30
Email: info@paillas.com
www.paillas.com

From his 27 hectares of vines, Lescombes has for many years been making one of the best-known and most popular of all cahors wines. He makes just the one *cuvée,* **Château Paillas** (**A)—no flirtation with the *Charte* here, not even the use of any new wood—and its hallmarks are ease of drinking, freshness of style and good fruit. As well as 82% *auxerrois*, Lescombes has planted *merlot* and just a little *tannat* to give grip.

One of the virtues of this wine is that it is quick to mature, and indeed it is one of the few cahors which is just as good drunk young as cellared for any length of time, although in top vintages such as 2000 it will age well too. Ten years in bottle in fine years brings out a richness and complexity which is quite unexpected. Typically the colour will be a deep garnet colour, absolutely brilliant and limpid, the bouquet offering a cocktail of fruits, varying according to the vintage. The wine is soft on the palate and gives an impression of sweetness. The finish is as rich in fruit and flavour as the wine was on the palate.

The snobbery of the wine world is such that some experts would probably dismiss this wine as being too 'simple', just as highbrow critics dismiss Tschaikowsky because his tunes were so good—but then who minds about that?

CHÂTEAU LES IFS
Jean-Paul Buri
46220 Pescadoires
Tel: 05-65-22-44-53 Fax: 05-65-30-68-52
Email: chateau.lesifs@wanadoo.fr

After it had been destroyed in the frosts of 1956, Buri replanted his vineyard in 1977. He won a

Macon medal for his 1990 vintage and today offers one of the best value-for-money cahors of all. Sold under the château name, **Château les Ifs** (**A), the wine has a good structure and good fruit, often suggesting cherries. Buri's *chais* may be simple—he prefers small concrete *cuves* to stainless steel for his vinification—but the welcome is as warm as the wine is attractive.

There is also a **Prestige** (*B) wine for hardly any more money, but you need to be a lover of new oak barrels to appreciate it. If you are, it is a bargain. It has all the hallmarks of the traditional style, good structure, soft tannins and a long fruity finish.

▮ CHÂTEAU DE GAUDOU
René Durou
46700 Vire-sur-Lot
Tel: 05-65-36-52-93 Fax: 05-65-36-53-60
Email: info@chateaudegaudou.com
www.chateaudegaudou.com

René's father has in his time been mayor of Vire as well as one of its leading growers. Until cahors was reborn in the 1960's, the Durou family grew crops other than grapes, lavender for example, which they sold to dealers in Grasse. They also had cattle. Today, however, they concentrate entirely on their 30-hectare vineyard on the best terraces of the left bank of the river.

René has been responsible for introducing modern techniques of *élevage* to Gaudou, notably the use of new oak barrels in which he ages his prestige wine **Renaissance** (**C). This is notable for its big structure and long fruity finish.

In the vineyard the contemporary practices of leaving the weeds between the rows, exposing the grapes to the sun and the *vendanges vertes* in the summer are all virtuously practised, and, though the crop is harvested by machine, the grapes are hand-selected before going into the press. The wines here have always had plenty of body and are sometimes agreeably peppery, and these characteristics have been carried over into the new wines,

including **Grande Lignée** (**B), which bridges the ancient and modern styles.

In their respective categories, the wines here are a fair value for the money.

▮ CHÂTEAU DU CÈDRE
Pascal and Jean-Marc Verhaeghe
46700 Vire-sur-Lot
Tel: 05-65-36-53-87 Fax: 05-65-24-64-36
Email: contact@chateauducedre.com
www.chateauducedre.com

The Verhaeghes' grandfather settled in the area before the First World War and became a day-worker in the vines. He married a farmer's daughter and together they moved into Le Cèdre in 1956. Charles, Pascal and Jean-Marc's father, gradually exchanged lands to build up the area under vine. Meanwhile he taught himself the *métier*. He ended up with 13 hectares, although there were some more vines from which he made *vin de table*. The domaine now covers 25 hectares, of which half are on a mixture of chalk and clay where the roots of the vines can reach deep into the subsoil with ease, the other half are on pebbles, red with iron on the surface and composed of flinty clay below.

Pascal didn't get the bug until he was 21. He went to Burgundy to do a *stage*, then worked at Saintsbury Vineyards in California. He returned to Cahors when his father retired, but it was not until 1997 that he took over the winemaking. Le Cèdre had been making good enough wine, but the domaine was a bit *fatigué*. Pascal and his brother adopted a neo-organic philosophy, reduced the yields, and gradually increased the percentage of *auxerrois*, though some *merlot* and *tannat* have been retained. Today they find themselves the most highly rated of modern-style Cahors growers. The brothers' basic precept is a respect for the grapes. Pascal says he started with too much over-extraction. He now does less *pigeage* with much less pressure on the fruit. He likes *microbullage*, which he says stabilises the balance between the polyphenols and the tannins. The grapes get four to six weeks' *cuvaison*. The 'malo' is usually done in the barrel and the top wines are aged on their lees. The wines are not filtered, nor are the top wines fined.

Of the three reds, the traditional is confusingly called **Le Cèdre Prestige** (***C). The *assemblage*, which includes 5% each of *merlot* and *tannat*, is made before vinification and the wine is matured in a mixture of old and new wood. This is one of the most admired and successful of all cahors today. Even though it is the *entrée-de-gamme* wine of the property, it is often more praised by critics than the more ambitious wines. For **Le Cèdre** (*D), Pascal usually ages the wine in all-new wood these days, though he used sometimes to prefer a mixture of new and partly new. The *tête de cuvée*, which is called **GC** (*D+), comes from parcels where the yield is only 18 hl/ha. The wine invariably is placed in brand-new barrels for its two fermentations. If I am thought churlish in giving these two much-admired top wines less than three stars, it is because of their hefty oak character, which betrays the *terroir*, depriving the wines of much of their cahors typicity. Many enthusiasts would gladly award the wines four stars.

The Verhaeghes produce also tiny quantities of a delicious, pure *viognier vin de pays* called **Le Cèdre Blanc** (**B), lovely as an apéritif. Three-quarters of the juice is fermented in barrels, the rest given a preliminary cold maceration before being vinified in tanks. It is matured for nine months on its lees, with *bâtonnage* twice a week. There is another dry **white vin de table** (**B), a crisp and refreshing blend of equal quantities of *sémillon* and *sauvignon*, with just a touch of *muscadelle*.

Pascal found it difficult to sell his wine at first, so he built up an export trade, mainly to Quebec, Germany, Belgium and Japan. Like Perrin, he has turned to trading *en négoce*, to diversify his financial risks. No doubt he will take care not to allow Le Cèdre to be dumbed down by becoming a brand name.

▄ CHÂTEAU CROZE DE PYS

René and Jean Roche
46700 Vire-sur-Lot
Tel: 05-65-21-30-13 Fax: 05-65-30-83-76
Email: chateau-croze-de-pys@wanadoo.fr
www.chateaucrozedepys.com

René Roche's family had been making wine in the Cahors region for many generations since 1773, but it was only in 1966 that he acquired what is now this quality château. The vines are not all at Vire; some are at Belaye, others at nearby Puy-l'Évêque and others still at Duravel. There are 60 hectares in all and they are today looked after by René's son Jean, who took over the reins in 1987. It is largely due to him that the property has acquired its present-day reputation.

Auxerrois contributes 80% of the *assemblage* of the **Tradition** (**B), a very fine example of the traditional cahors style, gentle, fruity, well-balanced and soft in tannins. The **Prestige** (**B) is aged in wood, but the barrels are a mix of new, one-year- and two-year-old casks, so that the taste of the wood itself is avoided, the ageing giving just that little bit of extra complexity to the wine. Here the malbec content is increasd to 90%, the rest being merlot. Besides the AOC wines, a small quantity of *vin de pays* is made here.

This is an excellent property in terms of value for money, and a safe haven for those wishing to avoid the New World style.

▄ CHÂTEAU HAUT-MONPLAISIR

Cathy and Daniel Fournié
Monplaisir, 46700 Lacapelle-Cabanac
Tel: 05-65-24-64-78 Fax: 05-65-24-68-90
Email: chateau.hautmonplaisir@wanadoo.fr

Cathy took over from her parents in the late 1990's and has made impressive strides in improving the wines from this property. Her parents were doubtful, to say the least, but she and Daniel started doing all the 'in' things: leaving the weeds between the rows, disbudding in the spring and removing surplus vegetation in the summer. They bought a few new barrels too.

Pascal Verhaeghe lives just down the hill in the valley, and persuaded Cathy to allow him to sell some of the Haut-Monplaisir wines as part of his venture into being a *négociant.* Cathy and Daniel were quick to profit from Pascal's offer to give them technical advice as well as a market. Now they have gone totally independent and are bottling all their own wines. With a large cellar of new casks and an insistence on low yields, they are making a range of excellent wines, some in the old style, some in the new. All are good because the Fourniés aim to benefit from the oak without giving the wine the taste of it.

The basic traditional wine, called simply **Château Haut-Monplaisir** (**A), is all that it should be, with good flavours of soft black fruits. In their next wine, **Prestige** (**B), there is some oak certainly but it is well integrated, the wine dominated often by floral perfumes carrying on to the palate, with good concentration and a long finish. In their top wine, **Pur Plaisir** (**C), the school of Verhaeghe shows through, the wine being made in open *demi-muids* and then aged in them; this is a wine which needs ageing but acquires considerable complexity in the process.

■ **CHÂTEAU FAMAEY**
SCEA Luyckx–Van Antwerpen
Les Inganels, 46700 Puy-l'Évêque
Tel: 05-65-30-59-42 Fax: 05-65-30-50-53
Email: chateau.famaey@wanadoo.fr
www.chateaufamaey.fr

Maarten Luyckx, a man from Flanders whose father was a dealer in the wine trade in Belgium, gives the lie to those who say how difficult it is to export the wines of Cahors. Maarten manages to sell between 80 and 90% of his output overseas, to his home country of course, but also to Canada, Mexico, Japan and Taiwan, as well as the more tra-

ditional market in Holland. The present partnership took over this property, formerly known as La Fontaine, in 1998. They are near neighbours of Jean-Luc Baldès at Triguedina. The vines are on the second and third terraces and go back at least 20 years, some of them more than 50. The range of wines, made as naturally as possible, start with a **vin de pays rosé** (**A) from pure *auxerrois*, something original in itself, fresh and fruity and very quaffable as well as being an extraordinary value. This wine is drawn off the grapes which go into a **red vin de pays** (*A), a wine to be enjoyed on its fruit while it is young.

There is a range of three AOC wines. First, there is a **Tradition** (*A), an attractive, unpretentious and good-value wine in which the *auxerrois* is blended with 20% *merlot*. A lightly oaked **Fût de Chêne** (**B), nearly all *auxerrois*, with just 10% *tannat*, is a firm, full-bodied wine aged for 14 months in barrels some of which are new, some already used once. The top wine is called **Cuvée X** (*C) and is raised in entirely new wood, which shows. Oak fanciers will no doubt relish the good value as well as the richness of this wine.

■ **DOMAINE LA BÉRENGERAIE**
La Famille Bérenger
Coteaux de Cournou, 46700 Grézels
Tel and fax: 05-65-31-94-59
Email: berengeraie@wanadoo.fr

Sylvie and André Bérenger bought the property in the 1970's, and they replanted the vineyard with *auxerrois* mostly, and just a little *merlot.* Their eight hectares have now grown to 23, most of which face south-east, thus benefitting from the morning sun which dries off the dew. Production is as ecologically sound as can be; artificial weedkillers are banned, and fertilisers are made only from a mix of chicken manure, seaweed and peat. 'Ladybirds are the best insecticides', and they are credited on the bottle labels. Harvesting is by hand, and *remontages* are done every six hours to increase

for this reason they favour well-ripened fruit, which has enabled them to reverse a previous tendency in favour of chaptalization. The wines are as attractive drunk young as they are when aged. A third wine, called **Les Quatre Chambrées** (***B), comes from vines grown on a particularly iron-rich soil and the wine has corresponding minerality and vivacity.

Although the bulk of the production would please the traditionalists, Maurin has a foot in the *Charte de Qualité* camp with his **Gorgée de Mathis Bacchus** (**C), a wine named after their son and which they first produced in 2000. Vanilla from the wood dominates the bouquet when the wine is young, hiding black fruit and spices. Good length suggests long life. A fair example of this style for those who like it and have the patience and the storage facilities to allow it to show its best.

■ DOMAINE D'HOMS
Roger Thierry and Daniel Cauzit
46800 Saux
Tel: 05-65-24-93-12 Fax: 05-65-24-96-78
Email: scea.domaine.dhoms@wanadoo.fr
www.domainedhoms-cahors.fr

This is a partnership between a retired octogenarian and a young grower. Until they met, Cauzit sold the wine from his four hectares on the *causse* at Saux *en vrac*. Meanwhile, Thierry was in love with this property but had no idea what to do about the 30 hectares of vines that went with it. So his neighbour Cauzit came to the rescue and ever since they have worked together to produce one of the most admired of *causse*-grown Cahors wines. Moreover, they have the rare distinction of winning *Charte de Qualité* status without the use of new wooden barrels. Their cahors are all produced from 100% *auxerrois*.

Since their first vintage in 1993, much money has been invested and steady improvement made in the quality of the product. The wines are characterized by their dark, dense colour. They take time to develop their fine bouquet, and tend to close up after their first year or two in bottle. When they come round, they show powerful aromatic fruit,

the wines' suppleness; the wines are not filtered, and fining is by real egg-whites, derived from the family's free-range hens.

Sylvie and André have an oenologist son, Maurin, and a daughter, Juline, and nowadays it is the younger generation, with their respective spouses, who are the locomotives behind the growing reputation of this domaine. Maurin is the young secretary general of both the *Syndicat de Défense* and of the *Comité Interprofessionnel des Vins de Cahors*, in which offices he steers a middle path between the various and often conflicting schools and commercial interests of Cahors production.

The two 'traditional' wines (although Maurin eschews use of the word 'tradition') are named after him and his sister, and neither is aged in oak. **Cuvée Juline** (**A) has just a touch of *merlot*, whereas **Cuvée Maurin** (**A) is all *auxerrois* and therefore just a touch more macho. The Bérengers seek above all to avoid the development of bitter tannins, and high concentration and fairly tough tannins which need time to round themselves out. They are for those who have the possibility of storage, because most of this wine is going to be drunk up in local restaurants long before it is ready.

There are three *cuvées*: a **Tradition** (**A), the **Charte de Qualité** (**B/C) and an oaked so-called *haut-de-gamme* version of the same wine, **Chevaliers d'Homs de Favols,** which is not half as good (*C).

The vineyard is on the very edge of the Cahors appellation, and there are some *auxerrois* and *merlot* vines just over the border into Lot-et-Garonne. Cauzit makes an attractive **Rosé d'Agenais** (**A) from them, and it must of course be marketed as a *vin de pays*.

DOMAINE DE MAISON NEUVE

Delmouly et Fils
GAEC de Maison Neuve
46800 Le Boulvé
Tel: 05-65-31-95-76 Fax: 05-65-31-93-80
Email: domainemaisonneuve@wanadoo.fr
www.domainemaisonneuve.com

The younger generation seems to be in charge here, although Maman is a gracious and enthusiastic host while her son is busy in the vineyards. The tasting room is like a minstrels' gallery overlooking the *chais de vinification,* with comfortable armchairs making a welcome change from the usual stand-up bar. Conversation may be punctuated with atmospheric shouts from below as the *remontage* pumps are changed over from one tank to another.

Production is typical in so many ways of the average smaller independent cahors producer. About half of their 25-hectare vineyard is given over to grapes destined for *vin de table*, while the other half produces AOC cahors. Some of the latter is sold off *en négoce*, but the best wine is reserved for domaine-bottling and direct sale. The *négociants*, Madame told me, want wine which is essentially fruity and early maturing, but the wine which the family bottle themselves is altogether bigger, more

structured and capable of good development over a period of years, without being excessively tannic or austere.

They make only one wine for direct sale, **Domaine de Maison Neuve** (**A), from 80% *auxerrois* and 20% *merlot*. The vineyards, which have been in the same family since 1900, are unusually neither on the terraces of the Lot Valley, nor on the *causse* above, but on the *coteaux* in between. They face south, benefitting to the full from the drying *vent d'autan* in autumn, and are on a slightly chalky clay soil, which has more iron than usual in it. The wines thus combine fruitiness with a good backbone.

The vines are planted at a regulation density of 4000 per hectare, but the Delmoulys are gradually increasing this to an eventual 6000. The wines are never chaptalized, reaching the minimum alcoholic strength acceptable in the market of 12 degrees without any difficulty, something which more glitzy growers do not always achieve without the help of added sugar.

Vinification is traditional at a temperature of about 28 degrees, and the frequency of *remontage* has been stepped up. The steel tanks enjoy good temperature control. The wines are aged in old cement *cuves*.

This is an astonishingly good domaine, but one word of warning: It is not to be confused with the super-star Cosse-Maisonneuve domaine (see next entry). Confusing too that wines from enterprises with such similar names should exemplify all that is best in traditional and new-wave production.

DOMAINE COSSE-MAISONNEUVE

Mathieu Cosse and Catherine Maisonneuve
Les Clots, 46800 Fargues
Tel: 06-78-79-57-10 or 05-65-24-22-36
Fax: 05-65-24-22-37
Email: laquets.maisonneuve@wanadoo.fr
www.leslaquets.com

Mathieu and Catherine could be described as the post-modernists of Cahors. It is as if they have been through all the excessive oaking, over-extraction and blockbusting of so many of their colleagues and come out the other side. A comparison between their very first vintages and later ones shows this pilgrim's progress very clearly. Their aim is to produce wines which combine concentration of fruit with finesse and elegance, and which avoid extraction of the tannins from the pips. The *élevage* in wood is long, but never more than 30% of the barrels are new; and here the boast that they seek to avoid the taste of *jus de planche*, so often the vain hope of less talented winemakers, is truly justified.

Neither Mathieu nor Catherine had previous experience in winemaking. They were enthusiasts who met on a training course. Catherine dropped out because she formed the view that the best wine-makers don't need diplomas. This is not arrogance on her part; it would be hard to imagine anyone more humble in the face of the problems to be tackled by every wine-maker.

They started in 1999 by buying five hectares of vineyard on the *causse* above the south side of the river, near Fargues. It is from here that Les Laquets, perhaps their best-known wine, comes. Two years later they acquired more vineyards on the north side of the river up in the hills behind Prayssac, a domaine which used to be called Le Patrounet. This is today their headquarters and *chais.* They now have 20 hectares all told of AOC vineyard planted almost entirely with *auxerrois*, and another four hectares of Coteaux du Quercy VDQS land also on the *causse* near Saux. They do not buy new vines from the local clones, but reproduce their own by *sélection massale*.

Mathieu, with his rugby player's build, and Catherine, petite and charming, could hardly be more different, but they are united in a determination to go in the direction of *biodynamie*. They believe that chemicals tend to promote disease rather than prevent or cure it; only the minimum of sulphur is ever used. The soil is worked by hand rather than machine, and the grapes are hand-picked. Yields are on the low side, 35–40 hl/ha.

From vineyards on the third terrace come two wines. The *entrée-de-gamme* **Le Combal** (**B) shows off the fruity style of the domaine perfectly. Although the wine nowadays spends 18 months in the barrel, there is absolutely no evidence of that on the nose or palate. The counterpart of this wine is called **Le Petit Sid** (***B), which has perhaps a more traditional *auxerrois* style, with plenty of cherries and damsons; it is a chewy wine with a long finish. **Les Laquets** (***D), the *causse* wine, has a bigger structure and more tannins, the latter being soft rather than aggressive. The finesse of the wine shows on the long and complex finish. Finally, **Le Sid** (***D), which is allowed just a touch each of *merlot* and *tannat*, comes from Le Patrounet and from soil which contains a deal of iron (a lump of the local rock the size of a melon is almost too heavy to carry). The wine has layers of floral and scented flavours (peony), with especially complex fruits—raspberries and myrtles, for example. The wine is aged in barrels for nearly two years, and one-third of the wood is new, the other two-thirds having been used to make one wine. But the oaking is amazingly discreet, largely because the casks have been given only gentle toasting.

Matthieu Cosse has taken over a leading role in the development of a large vineyard near Avignon. It is hoped this will not distract him too much from his activities in Cahors.

▨ CLOS D'UN JOUR
Véronique and Stéphane Azémar
46700 Duravel
Tel and fax: 05-65-36-56-01
Email: s.azemar@wanadoo.fr

Architectural and archaeological students respectively, with no experience whatsoever of the wine world, Véronique and Stéphane found themselves at Cahors looking for an outdoor life and change from the rat-race in Paris. That was in 1999 and already they are the toast of the appellation. They were lucky enough, with family support, to buy what was once called Le Domaine du Port at Duravel while properties were still affordable.

While not officially 'bio', they work the soil meticulously and ban weedkillers. Spraying is kept to a minimum and yields are low. Their basic wine, if 'basic' is the right word for it, **Clos d'un Jour** (**A), is named after the property. It shows good concentration and spice on the nose, good fruit on the palate with a fleshy structure, fine tannins and a good finish. An astonishing bargain. Their more ambitious wine, **Un Jour** (**B), is wholly *auxerrois* and raised in wood. Torrefaction and fruit are the most obvious characteristics, as well as the oak, which needs time to bring the wine round.

This is clearly a property with a bright future, in the hands of such natural wine-makers.

◼ CHÂTEAU LATUC

Jean-François and Geneviève Meyan
46700 Mauroux
Tel: 05-65-36-58-63 Fax: 05-65-24-61-57
Email: info@latuc.com
www.latuc.com

When Jean-François, a Belgian by origin, was 13 years old, his father opened and allowed him to taste a bottle of Médoc. From then on Jean-François knew that his life was going to be in the world of wine. He trained as an agro-chemist and then went to work in Alsace, where he established many connections which he has maintained to this day. His ambition was always to have his own vineyard, one which was of a viable size but affordable. Cahors fitted the bill well.

In 2001 he bought this property from an English couple who had established a name for Latuc over a period of years, partly enabling Anglo-Saxons in exchange for a down payment to secure the right to 20–25 cases of wine a year from 'their' row of vines over a two-year period. Meyan has been at pains to continue this arrangement. It helps his cash-flow and represents about 60% of his turnover. Meyan is also fortunate in his excellent command of the English language.

His predecessors had been particularly successful because they had established a style of cahors which was easier to drink than most and matured relatively early, without sacrificing typicity. This too the Meyans have continued as a matter of policy, despite criticism in some quarters that the wine lacks weight. In 2002 he gave his *auxerrois* a relatively short 15 days *en cuve.* The fact that he has no shortage of customers speaks for the success of his strategy. He plans nevertheless to increase the percentage of *auxerrois* in his reds from the minimum 70% to 80%, and this may give the wines more backbone. Indeed, his 2004 red is all *auxerrois*.

The vineyard is up on the *causse* at the western extremity of the appellation. It seems particularly vulnerable to freak weather, suffering badly from frost in 2002 and only narrowly missing hailstorms which demolished most of the vines in the commune. Of his 15 or so hectares, Meyan devotes about three to making a **vin rosé** (*A), very popular with summer visitors. This he sells as a *vin de pays* of course, because the AOC extends only to red wines. Meyan also makes another *vin de pays* from **Cabernet Franc** (*A), a very attractive wine in the style of a Coteaux du Quercy but with a deal of curranty fruit flavours. Then there is some *sémillon* and *chardonnay,* from which Meyan makes a white wine; in 2003, the extraordinary heat wave enabled him to make an exceptionally fine *moëlleux* from blending these two grapes, a wine which he called **Présence** (**C). Only about 1700 bottles were made, though Jean-François plans to make the wine again in years when there is plenty of hot sun in the autumn.

But of course the red AOC wines are the mainstay of his production. Like many other small growers he makes a so-called **Tradition** (**A), vinified and aged in tanks, and a **Prestige** (*B), for which he harvests the grapes by hand and which he ages in oak, a quarter of which is new. Both wines are attractive and represent excellent value.

fee aromas on the nose hide the underlying cherry character. It is high in alcohol for a pure *auxerrois* wine, huge on the palate and with massive tannins.

The **Cuvée Particulière** (*B) is less indebted to new wood, though it lacks the concentration of the top wine, while the wine simply called **Château Lamartine** (***B) allows its fruit and flowery character to show themselves through the much diminished level of oak.

Gayraud has been known to say that he is making wines for those whose homes do not have a cellar. That is quite optimistic. Great cahors always needed time, and his, which have the potential of greatness, are no exception.

■ **DOMAINE DE CAUSE**
Martine and Serge Costes
Cavagnac, 46700 Soturac
Tel: 05-65-36-41-96 Fax: 05-65-36-41-95
Email: domainedecause@wanadoo.fr

On the slopes above Lamartine, Martine and Serge Costes make *vins de pays,* both red and rosé, under the name **Bouquet de Cavagnac** (*A), the latter being especially charming and a good example of the kind of wine now being made in the region to meet the public demand for pink wines. It is pure *auxerrois*. There are four AOC cahors, each representing a particular parcel of vines; grapes from one parcel are not blended with those from another, and the Costes family manages to make four quite different styles of Cahors from them. The **Tradition** (*A) has some *merlot* as well as *auxerrois*; it is a fruity wine, ruby in colour with violet flashes and round and supple on the palate. It can be drunk young. **El Domeni** (**B), meaning *Le Domaine*, is quite different in character, dark in colour with loads of blackberries and blackcurrants. It is raised in tanks without the benefit of wood, and shows off well the character of pure *auxerrois*.

La Lande Cavagnac (**B) is oak-aged and enjoys 15% *tannat* in addition to the *auxerrois*, the wood adding vanilla flavours and giving the wine fullness on the palate as well as a long and silky

■ **CHÂTEAU LAMARTINE**
Brigitte and Alain Gayraud
46700 Soturac
Tel: 05-65-36-54-14 Fax: 05-65-24-65-31
Email: chateau-lamartine@wanadoo.fr
www.cahorslamartine.com

Gayraud's vines are almost at the western limit of the Cahors appellation, lying in the hills behind the village of Soturac and enjoying a wonderfully sunny exposure which ensures early maturity of the crop. The Gayrauds are an old Cahors family and have long enjoyed a reputation for making some of the longest-lasting wines of the area. Today, their 'top' wine, **Expression** (**D), made exclusively from low-yielding *auxerrois* and given a long maceration of 35 days as well as ageing in all-new barrels, is, as might be expected, emblematic of its style; its colour when young is dark, approaching the dreaded 'black', and the vanilla and toasted cof-

finish. The top wine, **Notre Dame des Champs** (**C), is named after a fine statue which rules over the vines. It is pure *auxerrois*. This wine is powerful but elegant at the same time. The oak-aged wines are hand-harvested and not filtered.

■ CHÂTEAU LES CROISILLE

Cécile and Bernard Croisille
Fages, 46140 Luzech
Tel and fax: 05-65-30-70-33
Mobile: 06-72-31-02-71
Email: contact@chateaulescroisille.fr.st
www.membres.lycos.fr/chateaucroisille

Bernard's family had been polycultural farmers for many generations some 15 kilometres north of their present domaine. Cécile had never been too keen on farming, but when they went to Parnac in 1989 to help with the *vendange*, they were offered 13 hectares of vines to rent. Not having a *chais*, they sent their grapes to the *coopérative*, but they couldn't make a living from their vines alone. To make ends meet, they planted cereals, farmed sheep, sold vine stakes, which they cut from trees themselves, and went into partnership with Domaine de Fages to produce their wine.

Then they learned that their present home, only a few yards from where they were then living, was up for sale. They grabbed the chance and restored it themselves, doing their own masonry and carpentry. It is set among some of the loveliest scenery in Cahors, and nearby are splendid views overlooking the Lot valley. Spurred on by their success as builders, the Croisilles, aided and abetted by their children, then built their own *chais* and started to make their own wine independently of Domaine de Fages. Though still burdened with debt, they have not looked back, and today are among the up and coming stars of Cahors.

They have 12 hectares under vine, though there is some land waiting to be planted with white grapes experimentally, against the day when there may be a white cahors AOC. Eighty-five percent of the present vineyard is devoted to *auxerrois*, the

remainder to *merlot,* all of which goes into their first wine, called simply **Château les Croisille** (**A). From a yield of 50 hectolitres to the hectare, the wine is given 15 to 18 days' *cuvaison* and is aged in stainless steel for a year or so before bottling. Their 2002 was beautifully clear and limpid in the glass, fragrant with the perfume of fruits in *eau-de-vie*, cherries and damsons. An absolute bargain too.

Their **Noble Cuvée** (**B) was until 2001 their top wine. One hundred percent *auxerrois* and from old vines to boot, it is from a slightly lower yield and given 20 to 25 days' *cuvaison*. This wine is raised in oak barrels for 12 to 18 months. It is much darker than the first wine, and the fruits are here black rather than red. The oak is noticeable, with vanilla on the nose, but not aggressive. The fruit is allowed to shine through, with strong suggestions of prunes. There is good acidity too, and the tannins are well rounded. It would be a pity to drink this wine young, because it will obviously improve no end for five years or more after the vintage.

The top wine, and one which gained *Charte de Qualité* status for the 2001 vintage, is called **Divin Croisille** (*C). The yield is low, 25 to 30 hectolitres per hectare, and the vines are worked and harvested by hand. The *cuvaison* is long, with frequent *pigeage*. This *cuvée* is of course raised in oak, rather more noticeably than one might have wished, but the technique is good all the same. The wood yields caramel and spices on the bouquet, along with blackcurrants and violets. On the palate the wine has plenty of flesh, and it is full and long on the finish. The oak also lends an impression of sweetness to the abundant fruit.

The style which marks the Croisille wines is nicely balanced between the heavyweights of the *nouvelle vague* and Bernard's own leaning towards elegance and finesse as well as power. Bernard is clearly ambitious; although he says he doesn't mind if he fails to achieve *Charte de Qualité* status every year, the look in his eye suggests that he would be bitterly disappointed if he didn't.

■ **CHÂTEAU DE LAGRÉZETTE**

Marie-Thérèse and Alain-Dominique Perrin

46140 Caillac

Tel: 05-65-20-07-42 Fax: 05-65-20-06-95

Email: lagrezette-adpsa@club-internet.fr

www.chateaulagrezette.tm.fr

The property and, it is claimed, the vineyard have a long history, going back to the 16th century when the château was the home of rich Cahors bankers. Marie-Thérèse and Alain-Dominique Perrin, he at one time managing director of Cartier, bought it in 1980 and have restored the whole estate to a degree of incredible splendour and without sparing expense. The château is classé 'monument historique', which may help with the upkeep. French presidents and English prime ministers number among the houseguests.

The vineyard, planted with 77% *auxerrois*, 21% *merlot* and just 2% *tannat* on the second and third terraces of the valley, extends over 60 hectares and, like the château, is meticulously maintained. The nowadays common practices of *enherbement, vendanges verts, effeuillage* and *éclaircissage* are carried out by hand, as is the harvest, which is then hand-sorted before the grapes are destalked and crushed.

In the early years of their wine-making careers, the Perrins sent their grapes to the *coopérative* at Parnac, with varying degrees of success. Today the wines are made and aged in a magnificently equipped underground *chais* built into the hillside beside the château. It measures 55 metres by 19. Its three levels allow all the operations to be carried out by gravity, minimizing the use of pump and piping. Vinification, preceded in all cases by four days of cold maceration at a temperature of 12 degrees, is in stainless steel, with sophisticated temperature control, except that the top *cuvée,* Le Pigeonnier, is fermented in a special 75-hectolitre *foudre.* The malolactic fermentation of all the wines is carried out in barrels, and all the wines are raised to a greater or lesser extent in oak in conditions where humidity and temperature are naturally constant.

Everything here is copybook, overseen by flying *oenologue* Michel Rolland, whose stamp on the wines is clear. Approval by Robert Parker is almost a foregone conclusion.

Lowest in the hierarchy of production is the **Moulin de Lagrézette** (*B), made from the youngest vines on the estate, which date back on average to 1994. Even this wine—70% *auxerrois* and 30% *merlot*—is raised in barrels (nine months in used Saury *barriques*). Though it will age, it can also be drunk young, and the price is fair. Annual production is about 70,000 bottles, about 28% of the output of the domaine.

The **Chevaliers de Lagrézette** (*C) is next in the pecking order. It is generally from 85% *auxerrois*, and aged for 12 months in used Saury barrels. Christian Schiassi, the sales director, calls this 'the second wine' of the château, and he sells about 80,000 bottles of it a year, roughly a third of the property's total production. It is still within the reach of most pockets.

The wine which M. Schiassi calls the 'first' wine is dubbed simply **Château de Lagrézette** (*C) and derives usually from 80% *auxerrois*, 17% *merlot* and 3% *tannat*. The vines go back to the replanting of the vineyard by the Perrins. As with the last two wines, the grapes are fermented at 30 degrees Celsius, followed by long maceration at 28 degrees, with daily *remontage*. But this wine is given its malolactic fermentation in new Saury barrels in which it is then aged for 18 months. Production runs at about 80,000 bottles, again one-third of the total.

For the two top wines we arrive in the Cartier stratosphere. **Cuvée Dame Honneur** (D+) is made from about 91% *auxerrois*, the rest *merlot*, and is aged for two years in new Saury barrels. The Perrins make about ten to eleven thousand numbered bottles of this wine a year. The top wine, the famous **Le Pigeonnier** (D++), is pure *auxerrois* and, following its fermentation in the special Seguin Moreau *foudre*, is aged for 28 months in new Saury barrels. Production is limited to about six to seven thousand bottles a year.

It is not hard to see that, starting with the high concentration deriving from late-picked fruit, the Lagrézette process produces wines of very high extraction, and the *élevage* ensures what the French call *un boisé somptueux.* Perrin regards himself as being at the forefront of the *nouvelle vague* of Cahors, his wines being far removed, he says, 'from the gross tannins and the crudeness of their predecessors'. Some people, including the author, might beg to differ, finding in at least the three top wines an impossible level of over-extraction, emphasized by the monstrous rather than sumptuous *élevage* in new wood. These wines have far more tannins than their 'predecessors', a roughness which will need many, many years to smooth out, and the taste of floorboards which may never disappear. If this is the style of *nouvelle vague* cahors, then it is a denial of the typicity of cahors as an appellation, and of the concept of *terroir* itself, because the wines of Lagrézette are indistinguishable from so many other wines made all over the world in this exaggerated, anonymous and unsympathetic style. Such blockbusters may win medals and *coups de coeurs* all over the place because they hit between the eyes tasters who are looking for just that to happen to them. But for those who seek a wine to accompany and to complement fine cooking, which ought to be the object of any wine-producer, Lagrézette wines and others of the same school are lacking in charm, elegance and finesse. This is not the way to win cahors badly needed friends, but it is the road down which too many young Turks in Cahors are going.

Enough said of the wines of Lagrézette itself. The property was until recently also the scene of the making of almost twice as much *vin de négoce.* Perrin bought in fruit from selected growers 'apt to produce grapes of totally first class quality', he said. Under Rolland's direction, the resulting wines were intended to 'constitute a benchmark in quality, seducing the caring consumer, one who is demanding and interested in authentic *vins de terroir'.* Perrin has, however, sold this side of his wine activities, and there is a question mark over its continuity.

◾ CROIX DU MAYNE
François Pélissié
46140 Castelfranc
Tel: 05-65-36-29-44
Email: cvgso@cvgso-cdso.fr

As well as looking after his small four-hectare vineyard on the left bank of the Lot opposite Castelfranc, Pélissié has an important business *en négoce*, *La Compagnie des Vins du Grand Sud-Ouest*, which has achieved a big turnover in the supermarkets of France. His own wine is available only from supermarkets; to find out where the nearest place to you is where you could buy his wine, just ring him up and he'll tell you.

The vineyard may be small, but the wine called simply **Croix du Mayne** (*A) is respectable and sometimes rather more than that. It is well made, though the bouquet is not its strongest point. But it is soft and more-ish on the palate and goes well with the local cuisine.

Since 2000, Pélissié has, not surprisingly, cast his eyes in the direction of the *Charte de Qualité*. Burnt rubber and tar do not sound attractive as a description of a bouquet, but experts nod approvingly when they find them. Well, here they are sometimes, with good blackcurrants on the palate. Powerful tannins and a long finish suggest a wine which will age well.

OTHER GOOD GROWERS

■ CHÂTEAU ARMANDIÈRE
Bernard Bouyssou
46140 Parnac
Tel: 05-65-36-75-97 Fax: 05-65-36-02-23
Email: chateau @armandiere.com

■ CHÂTEAU CAMP D'AURIOL
Jérôme Souques
46140 Luzech
Tel: 05-65-20-12-90 Fax: 05-65-30-72-88
Email: campauriol@wanadoo.fr

■ CHÂTEAU LE BRÉZÉGUET
M. and Mme Longueteau
46800 Saux
Tel: 05-65-93-17-24 Fax: 05-65-24-23-95

■ CHÂTEAU CANTELAUZE
Laurent Nominel
46700 Duravel
Tel and fax: 05-65-20-11-84
Email: nominel@aol.com
www.cantelauze.com

■ CHÂTEAU COUILLAC
Viviane Couaillac
La Séoune, 46140 Sauzet
Tel: 05-65-36-90-82 Fax: 05-65-36-96-41
Email: franckpasbeau@wanadoo.fr

■ CHÂTEAU LA COUSTARELLE
Michel and Nadin Cassot
46220 Prayssac
Tel: 05-65-22-40-10 Fax: 05-65-30-62-46
Email: chateaulacoustarelle@wanadoo.fr

■ DOMAINE DE DECAS
Gérard Decas
Lannac, 46090 Trespoux-Rassiels
Tel and fax: 05-65-35-37-74
Mobile: 06-74-56-48-85

■ DOMAINE DE LA GARDE
Jean-Jacques Bousquet
Le Mazut, 46090 Labastide-Marnhac
Tel and fax: 05-65-21-06-59

■ DOMAINE DU GARINET
Mike and Sue Spring
46800 Le Boulvé
Tel: 05-65-32-96-43 Fax: 05-65-31-96-43
Email: mike.spring@worldonline.fr
Note also a nice *sauvignon vin de pays.*

■ CHÂTEAU GAUTOUL
Eric Swenden
46700 Puy-l'Évêque
Tel: 05-65-30-84-17 Fax: 05-65-30-85-17
Email: gautoul@gautoul.com
www.gautoul.com

■ CHÂTEAU LES GRAUZILS
Philippe Pontié
Gamot 46220 Prayssac
Tel: 05-65-30-62-44 Fax: 05-65-22-46-09
www.chateau-les-grauzils.com

■ CHÂTEAU DE GRÉZELS
Christophe and David Rigal
46140 Parnac
Tel: 05-65-30-70-10 Fax: 05-65-20-16-24
Email: rigal@crdl.fr
www.rigal.fr

■ CHÂTEAU DE HAUTE-SERRE
CFA Georges Vigouroux
Sieurac, 46230 Lalbenque
Tel: 05-65-20-80-20 Fax: 05-65-20-80-21
Email: vigouroux@g-vigouroux.fr
www.g-vigouroux.fr

■ CHÂTEAU LES HAUTS D'AGLAN
Isabelle Rey-Auriat
46700 Soturac
Tel: 05-65-36-52-24
Email: isabelle.auriat@terre-net.fr

■ **DOMAINE DE LAVAUR**
Claude and Yves Delpech
46700 Soturac
Tel: 05-65-36-56-30 Fax: 05-65-36-57-67
Email: domaine.de.lavaur@orange.fr

■ **MANOIR DU ROUERGOU**
Chantal Crenne
46150 Saint-Médard
Tel and fax: 05-65-21-42-59
Email: manoir.rouergou@wanadoo.fr

■ **CHÂTEAU DE MERCUÈS**
Georges Vigouroux
46090 Mercuès
Tel: 05-65-20-80-20 Fax: 05-65-20-80-21
Email: vigouroux@g-vigouroux.fr
www.g-vigouroux.fr

■ **CHÂTEAU NOZIÈRES**
Maradenne-Guitard
'Bru', 46700 Vire-sur-Lot
Tel: 05-65-36-52-73 Fax: 05-65-36-50-62

■ **CHÂTEAU PLAT FAISANT**
Serge Bessières
Les Roques, 46140 Saint-Vincent-Rive-d'Olt
Tel: 05-65-30-76-38 Fax: 05-65-30-76-10
Email: chateauplatfaisan@wanadoo.fr

■ **CHÂTEAU DU PORT AND CHÂTEAU DE CÉNAC**
Pelvillain Frères
46140 Albas
Tel: 05-65-30-52-97 Fax: 05-65-30-75-67
Email: albasdistribution@wanadoo.fr

■ **PRIEURÉ DE CÉNAC**
Christophe and David Rigal
46140 Parnac
Tel: 05-65-30-70-10 Fax: 05-65-20-16-24
Email: rigal@crdl.fr
www.rigal.fr

■ **DOMAINE DU PRINCE**
GAEC de Pauliac
Cournou, 46140 Saint-Vincent-Rive-d'Olt
Tel: 05-65-20-14-09 Fax:05-65-30-78-94
Email: domaine-du-prince@libertysurf.fr

■ **CHÂTEAU LES RIGALETS**
Jean-Luc Bouloumié
Les Cambous, 46220 Prayssac
Tel: 05-65-30-61-69 Fax: 04-65-30-60-46

■ **CHÂTEAU DE LA ROSE ROUGE**
Sylvain Busser
Lasserre 46220 Prayssac
Tel: 05-65-22-46-64 Fax: 05-65-30-67-46
Mobile: 06-25-54-34-27
Email: s.busser@chateau-la-rose-rouge.com

■ **CHÂTEAU SAINT-DIDIER PARNAC**
Franck and Jacques Rigal
46140 Parnac
Tel: 05-65-30-70-10 Fax: 05-65-20-16-24
Email: rigal@crdl.fr
www.rigal.fr

■ **DOMAINE DES SALLES**
Sylvie and Philippe Lasbouygues
Les Salles, 46090 Villesèque
Tel: 05-65-36-94-32

■ **DOMAINE DES SAVARINES**
Rosie Kindersley and Eric Trouillé
46090 Trespoux-Rassiels
Tel: 05-65-22-33-67 Fax: 05-65-53-11-85
www.domainedessavarines.com
A fully organic vineyard belonging to the owners of Sheepgrove butchers in the UK. Look for rapid improvement in quality.

■ **DOMAINE DU THÉRON**
Vic Pauwels
Route du Chemin de Théron, 46220 Prayssac
Tel: 05-65-30-64-51 Fax: 05-65-30-69-20
Email: domaine.theron@libertysurf.fr

COTEAUX DU QUERCY

AREA OF VDQS: selected parcels within the communes of
TARN-ET-GARONNE: Bruniquel, Caussade, Labarthe, Lapenche, Lavaurette, Mirabel, Molières, Montaigu-de-Quercy, Montalzat, Montpezat-de-Quercy, Mont-Fermier Puygaillard-de-Quercy, Puylaroque, Réalville, Saint-Georges, Sauveterre, Vaissac and Vazerac.
LOT: Belfort-du-Quercy, Belmontet, Castelnau-Montratier, Cézac, Flaugnac, Labastide-Marnhac, Lascabanes, Le Montat, Montcuq, Montdoumerc, Montlauzun, Saint-Daunès, Saint-Pantaléon, Saint-Paul-de-Loubressac and Valprionde.

Red and rosé wines only.
GRAPE VARIETIES: cabernet franc (required to be at least 40% but not more than 60% of a vineyard), merlot, cot, gamay and tannat, none of which may exceed 20%.
ALCOHOL LEVELS: between 10.5% (minimum) and 13.5% (maximum).
MAXIMUM PERMITTED YIELD: 60 hl/ha.
PLANTING DENSITY: min. 4000 plants/ha. Max. 2.5 metres between rows, plants not less than 1 metre apart.
PRUNING: *méthode* Guyot simple (double Guyot permitted for cabernet franc) or *cordon bilateral*.

Straddling the A20 from east to west and the boundary between Lot and Tarn-et-Garonne from north to south, and occupying an area roughly equivalent to what used to be called Bas-Quercy, are the vineyards called Coteaux du Quercy, promoted to VDQS status in 1999 and awaiting full AOC recognition when the slow-coaches in Paris see fit. Local growers cannot help feeling that the *gros légumes* of Cahors are not exactly helping another appellation on its doorstep to find its feet.

THE *TERROIR*

The soil here is very chalky, but there are lush valleys too and wooded enclaves, home to the truffle and the *cèpe*. Barren in the north where the *causse* dictates that little but the vine will grow, the landscape changes as you travel southwards until you reach the fruit orchards of the Garonne Valley and the melon plantations of Mirabel.

The *terroir* dictates the choice of grape varieties, the most important of which is the *cabernet franc,* which must compose between 40% and 60% of a grower's red wine vineyard if he is to be allowed his *agrément*. The supplementary varieties are *auxerrois* (not surprisingly), *merlot, gamay* and *tannat*. Other kinds of grapes can only be allowed into *vins de pays*. All the wine within the appellation is either red or rosé; there is no recognition for white wines hereabouts.

The *cabernet franc* gives the Coteaux wines a character of their own, which enables the drinker at once to distinguish them from their neighbours in Gaillac or Cahors. The growers are determined to maintain this typicity, conscious that their wines are less tannic than cahors, but more gutsy and rustic than most red gaillac. Subtlety is not their hallmark, rather an open, no-nonsense fruitiness which asks for glasses to be refilled.

PRODUCERS OF COTEAUX DE QUERCY

CAVE LES VIGNERONS DU QUERCY
82270 Montpezat-de-Quercy
Tel: 05-63-02-03-50 Fax: 05-63-02-00-60

About half the production is in the hands of this *coopérative,* whose premises are unmissable on the east side of the old N20. Here they make a whole range of wines, including a nice sweet *muscat* which of course is sold as a *vin de pays.* Their main red is called **Bessey de Boissy** (**B) and is an excellent example of coteaux du quercy, better by far to my mind than the single-domaine wine which they sell called **Domaine de Peyre-Farinière** (B), which is pretentiously over-done.

The *coopérative* at Cahors also has members in the Coteaux, but its coteaux wines tend to play second fiddle to their own appellation. As so often, it is the band of independent producers who produce the most interesting wine, and this area sports two dozen or so of them. The following are the most consistent:

DOMAINE D'ARIÈS
Pierre Belon et fils
82240 Puylaroque
Tel: 05-63-64-92-52 Fax: 05-63-31-27-49
www.domainedaries.com

Pierre is president of the local *syndicat* of growers. His 2001 **rosé** (*A) won him a well-deserved gold medal in Paris, and his reds are no less attractive. The **Tradition** (*A) may be passed over, but not by me, in favour of his oaked **Cuvée des Marquis des Vignes** (*A). Unlike many growers, the Belons welcome visitors on Sundays and public holidays.

DOMAINE DE CAUQUELLE
Messrs. Palmié and Sirejol
46170 Flaugnac
Tel: 05-65-21-95-29 Fax: 05-65-21-83-30

The owners can often be found offering their wines at country fairs and markets. Attractive **good-value reds** (*A).

DOMAINE DE LAFAGE
Bernard Bouyssou
82270 Monpezat-de-Quercy
Tel: 05-63-02-06-91 Fax: 05-63-02-04-55
www.domainedelafage.free.fr

M. Bouyssou is not merely organic but bio-dynamic to boot. His rosé he describes as 'like spreading redcurrant jelly on toast of a summer morning'. It certainly has lovely red fruits. He also makes a pure *gamay* for summer drinking, but it is his **Rouge Tradition** (*A) which commands attention for its deep colour, its soft tannins and its hint of truffles. It will keep, too.

DOMAINE DE LA GARDE

Jean-Jacques Bousquet

Le Mazut, 46090 Labastide-Marnhac

Tel and fax: 05-65-21-06-59

www.domainedelagarde.com

Bousquet makes very good cahors, but it is his coteaux du quercy wines that also win the attention from the *Guide Hachette* juries, as well as prizes in the South-West wine shows. His unoaked **Rouge Tradition** (**A) is among the best of its peers, while the barrel version will no doubt get equal ratings from oak fanciers. The property is just on the edge of the *causse* and so the wines are closer to cahors in style than many.

DOMAINE DE MAZUC

Erick Carles

82240 Puylaroque

Tel and fax: 05-63-64-90-91

www.domainedelamazuc.com

The Carles family have been making wines here for four generations, during which time they have won widespread recognition for quality. Erick describes them as 'rich in colour, chewy in texture, with powerful aromas of red fruits, especially blackcurrants.' The **Rouge Tradition** (*A) is very good value.

DOMAINE DE MERCHIEN

David and Sarah Meakin

46230 Belfort-de-Quercy

Tel and fax: 05-63-64-97-21

Mobile: 06-16-07-75-39

Email: wine@merchien.net

www.merchien.net

Anglo-Saxons are not the only people to believe that David and Sarah are making the best wines from the Coteaux. Hachette thought so too about their 2001, giving it their coveted *coup de coeur*. Despite these successes, local jealousies have sometimes prevented the Meakins from gaining recognition from their peers and often from getting the *agrément* for their wines. The Meakins arrived in the 1990's along with their Newfoundland dog (hence the name of the property) and no experience of wine-making. After some initial help from friends in Cahors, they learnt fast and can be proud of what they have achieved. They will be pleased to welcome you most Sunday mornings to their stand at the Saint-Antonin street market, where you will be able to taste their range of wines, including a charming **rosé** (**A), a red **Tradition** (**A and B), another red from their **Vieilles Vignes** (**B) and a curious *vin de pays* which they call **JAS** (**B) because it is a blend of *jurançon noir*, *abouriou* and *syrah*, a wine that is as successful as it is untypical. The Meakins get full marks for enterprise, too: they have recently launched a dark beer called Bière de Belfort.

OTHER GOOD PRODUCERS OF COTEAUX DU QUERCY

CHÂTEAU DES ARDAILLOUX
SCEA Château des Ardailloux
See below under *Vins de pays* du Lot.

LE CARTELOU
Lino Cella
46090 Labastid- Marnhac
Tel: 05-65-35-26-01 Mobile: 06-86-11-24-18

DOMAINE DE GANAPES
Jean-Marc Séguy
Ambeyracq, 82240 Réalville
Tel and fax: 05-63-31-04-81

DOMAINE DE GUILLAU
Jean-Claude Lartigue
82270 Montalzat
Tel: 05-63-93-17-24 Fax: 05-63-93-38-06
Email: j.c.lartigue@worldonline.fr

DOMAINE DE PECH-BELY
Messrs. Richard and Jooris
Pech-Bely 82150 Montaigu-de-Quercy
Tel: 05-63-94-47-28 Fax: 05-63-95-31-79

LA TREILLE DE LAGARDE
Mme Laur
46800 Montcuq
Tel: 05-65-31-90-82 Fax: 05-65-31-89-54
(Not to be confused with Domaine de La Garde;
see above)

CHÂTEAU VENT D'AUTAN
Anne Godin
46800 Saint-Matré
Tel: 05-65-31-96-75 Fax: 05-65-31-91-78

VINS DE PAYS DU LOT

It has already been noted that several cahors producers also produce *vins de pays*, often because there is no such thing as white cahors (yet); see for example Clos Coutale, Château du Cèdre, Château Latuc, Clos de Gamot, Clos Triguedina etc. There are also producers who do not make any AOC cahors wines at all, but whose production consists entirely of *vins de pays*. The grapes favoured are, for the white wines, *viognier*, *chardonnay* (a grape otherwise seldom seen in the South-West), *chenin blanc* and *sauvignon*; for the reds, *malbec* (which is often used to make a kind of *vin nouveau*, not a style really suited to the grape), the two *cabernets*, *auxerrois*, *gamay*, *merlot* and *ségalin*. Sixty or so producers make *vins de pays* du Lot, the total production of which has increased by 50% since 1998. There are about 225 hectares devoted to these wines, two-thirds for red, a quarter for rosé and the rest for white.

PRODUCERS OF VINS DE PAYS DU LOT

DOMAINE BELMONT
Christian Belmont
46250 Goujounac (outside the AOC area)
Tel: 05-65-36-68-51 Mobile: 06-08-36-71-72
Fax: 05-65-36-60-59
www.domaine-belmont.com

Christian Belmont makes a red wine from equal quantities of *syrah* and *cabernet franc*: it is complex and fruity, and shows the characteristic spices of the *syrah*, well blended with the prunes and dried fruits of the *cabernet*. The wine is given 18 months in all-new barrels, and the result rather resembles a pure *auxerrois* wine of the new school.

Belmont also makes a pure **chardonnay** (**D), a grape making a rare appearance in the region. These wines, good though they are, do not come cheap. The vines are planted to a density of over 8000 plants per hectare, the soil is entirely worked by hand and the grapes are picked the same way.

DOMAINE DES ARDAILLOUX
SCEA Château Ardailloux
46700 Soturac
Tel: 05-53-71-30-45
Email: ardailloux@aol.com

Here you will find another pure **chardonnay** (**B), grown on nearly five hectares of soil, highly individual in style, powerful and with a flowery nose, big on the palate and with a splendid finish. Though not in the mainstream of the Coteaux du Quercy growers, this property also produces a fine example of that wine, based of course on *cabernet franc*.

DOMAINE DE SULLY
La Famille Bohy
46100 Capdenac-le-Haut
Tel and fax: 05-65-40-02-00
Email: info@vin-domaine-sully.com
www.vin-domaine-sully-com

This is a newly established vineyard in an area which was once prolific. The property currently extends to about only one single hectare, but the wine (all **red**;**C), made uniquely from a blend of *malbec, merlot* and *mansois,* has found favour with many of the best local restaurants. There is good fruit, with vanilla deriving from the very careful light oaking, carrying through to good plummy *merlot* style with nice acidity and reaching no more than 12 degrees of alcohol by volume.

THE WINES OF GAILLAC

GAILLAC

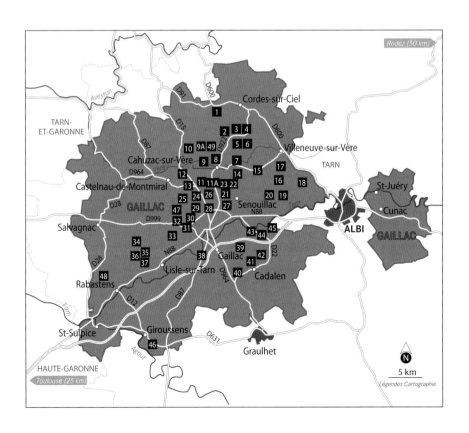

Rodez (50 km)

Aveyron

TARN-
ET-GARONNE

Cordes-sur-Ciel

D1

D600

D600

D15

D87

D964

1

2 **3** **4**

5 **6**

10 **9A** **49**

9 **8**

7

Villeneuve-sur-Vère

TARN

Cahuzac-sur-Vère

D922

17

15

Castelnau-de-Montmiral

12

13

11 **11A** **23** **22**

14

16

18

St-Juéry

D28

25

24 **26**

21

20 **19**

Tarn

Cunac

GAILLAC

47

29 **28**

27

Senouillac

N88

GAILLAC

D999

32 **30**

31

ALBI

Salvagnac

33

43 **44**

45

D28

34

39

42

D22

N88

36 **35**

37

38

41

Gaillac

40

Cadalen

48

Lisle-sur-Tarn

D964

Rabastens

D87

Tarn

D12

St-Sulpice

Giroussens

46

D631

Agout

Graulhet

HAUTE-GARONNE

N

Toulouse (25 km)

5 km

Légendes Cartographie

AREA OF AOC: selected parcels covering 4200 hectares.

CANTON OF ALBI: Arthès, Carlus, Castelnau-de-Lévis, Fréjairolles, Milhavet, Rouffiac, Sainte-Croix and Villeneuve-sur-Vère.

CANTON OF CADALEN: Aussac, Cadalen, Fénols, Florentin, Labessière-Candeil, Lasgraisses and Técou.

CANTON OF CASTELNAU-DE-MONTMIRAL: Alos, Andillac, Cahuzac-sur-Vère, Campagnac, Castelnau, Larroque, Montels, Puycelci, Saint-Beauzile, Sainte-Cécile du Cayrou, le Verdier and Vieux.

CANTON OF CORDES: Amarens, Bournazel, Les Cabannes, Campes, Cordes, Donnazac, Frausseilles, Livers-Cazelles, Loubers, Mouzieys-Panins, Noailles, Souel, Tonnac and Vindrac-Alayrac.

CANTON OF GAILLAC: Bernac, Brens, Broze, Castanet, Cestayrols, Fayssac, Gaillac, Labastide-de-Lévis, Lagrave, Montans, Rivières and Senouillac.

CANTON OF GRAULHET: Busque.

CANTON OF LAVAUR: **Giroussens and Saint-Sulpice.**

CANTON DE LISLE-SUR-TARN: **Lisle-sur-Tarn, Parisot and Peyrole.**

CANTON OF RABASTENS: **Rabastens, Coufouleux and Loupiac.**

Communes of Combéfa, Virac, Salvagnac, Saint-Grégoire, Itzac, and six communes near Cunac.

Communes listed in bold enjoy the superior appellation 'Gaillac premières Côtes' for white wines.

White wines from mauzac, len de l'el, muscadelle, ondenc, sauvignon and sémillon. Len de l'el and/or sauvignon must represent 15% of a grower's planting.

Red and rosé wines from principal varieties which must make up 60% of a grower's planting: duras, fer (aka braucol), gamay, syrah. Duras, braucol and syrah, must alone or in any combination total at least 30%.

OTHER PERMITTED VARIETIES: **cabernet sauvignon, cabernet franc and merlot.**

MAXIMUM YIELD: **60 hl/ha (45 in Premières Côtes and all doux) for whites; 45 for reds and rosés.**

Gaillac Mousseux made according to the Champagne method. Méthode Gaillacoise limited to one single fermentation, without addition of extra sugar or yeasts.

ANNUAL PRODUCTION: **195,000 hectolitres.**

THE OLDEST VINEYARD

Gaillac was once part of Narbonnensis, a large Roman province which extended from what is now Montauban in the west, through present-day Languedoc and up the Rhône Valley almost as far as Lyon. This was Rome's logical extension to its colony Provence, giving the necessary link to its conquests in Spain.

In the small town of Montans, to the south of Gaillac town, the results of archaeological digs are on show proving that in the first century A.D. at the latest the vineyards of Gaillac were already thriving, though they had been planted much earlier, probably in the second century B.C. Since these early times Gaillac has had its ups and downs. The barbarian invasions which followed the collapse of the Roman Empire would have brought about the destruction of the vineyard but for the devotion of the Church. The monks of the Abbey Saint-Michel at Gaillac laid the basis for a flourishing trade throughout the Middle Ages. As owners of much of the local terrain, they developed a kind of leasing contract under which land was made available to anyone prepared to clear it and plant vines. The tenant paid a tax based on the revenue of the land, a concept reflected later in the much-hated *dime* tax.

The development of a vineyard, which entails a cycle of 50 or more years, requires peace and stability, commodities which were in short supply. The constant battles between local feudal lords, the devastating struggles of the Albigensian crusade, and the wars between France and England had a disastrous and cumulative effect on the countryside. The English presence did, however, have one advantage: the development of an export connection, which made Gaillac a favourite wine at the English court, thus beginning a trade which lasted until the defeat of England at the end of the Hundred Years' War in 1453.

Prosperity returned slowly during the 16th century; the English connection was restored when François I met Henry VIII at the Field of the Cloth of Gold and gave him 50 barrels of Gaillac wine. Henry became a regular customer.

Proliferation of fraud and adulteration were direct consequences of the growing reputation of Gaillac. The growers needed to protect the name and quality of their wine, so, with the backing of the feudal lords, they developed a primitive system of *appellation contrôlée*. The device of a cockerel, today Gaillac's logo still, was used to brand containers as a guarantee of origin. The importation of wines from outside the area was forbidden, to prevent those of Gaillac from being stretched with others. Pigeon droppings were declared the only permitted form of fertilizer, a rule which persisted until the 19th century and explains the presence today of so many *pigeonniers* in the Gaillac countryside. To promote solidarity as well as trade, the growers founded one of the oldest French wine-fraternities, the forerunner of today's *Ordre de la Dive Bouteille*, whose ceremonial dress consists of a red cloak edged in black, a Rabelaisian red hat and a long red and black chain from which hangs the Divine Bottle in bronze.

A PRE-PHYLLOXERA SNAPSHOT

A survey of Gaillac immediately before the phylloxera epidemic would disclose some surprises. The total production of wine of all kinds in the area was over five times what it is today, notwithstanding that Gaillac is still, after the Bergeracois, the biggest producing area of the South-West. Secondly, less than one-quarter of 1% of the production was of white wine, whereas today it is about 35%, having reached a peak of nearly double that at one time in the middle of the 20th century. The switch to the production of white wine was largely a response to the competition of red wines from the Midi after the phylloxera. Gaillac growers wisely sought to establish their own niche in the market.

The range of wines at the close of the 19th century was probably as great as it is today. Gaillac seems always to have been able to provide bigger variety of choice than any other region in the South-West, perhaps in the whole of France. Their sparkling wines, *brut*, *demi-sec* and sweet, can claim equal ancestry with those of Limoux, certainly pre-dating Champagne by a century or more. The *méthode gaillacoise* differed from that of champagne in that the wine underwent only one fermentation, interrupted by the cold temperature of winter during which the wine was bottled. The fermentation began again quite spontaneously when the weather warmed up in the spring, and the resulting gas produced the bubbles without further human encouragement. There were thus neither added yeasts nor sugar, ingredients in the making of champagne which are known to cause allergies in some people. The Gaillac method has no additives whatsoever.

There was also a wine called *moustillant*, usually deriving in those days from the *muscadelle* grape, on account of its early ripening. This curiosity was a partly finished white wine, sold while still fermenting, and dispatched in large quantities by the newly arrived railway to the bars of Paris, where it had a considerable vogue for some years until the outbreak of the Second World War. This style is rarely commercialized today, but it is still made for local consumption round autumn fires with the season's new chestnuts. Wines like this can still be found in other parts of the South-West such as Jurançon, where they are sometimes called *vin bourru*.

Very little dry wine was made in those days, typically only when the weather was not good enough to ripen the grapes fully, other than to make a kind of *vin jaune* by leaving it to oxidize in barrel. The taste until the 1950's was generally for more or less sweet wines, and in these Gaillac excelled. Until about that time the quality as well as the quantity of red wine was nowhere near that of the white, usually being made from grape varieties which nowadays would be regarded as inferior, such as *jurançon noir* and *portugais bleu*. White wines achieved AOC status in 1938, whereas the reds had to wait until 1970.

GAILLAC'S MODERN RANGE

Gaillac has in modern times added to its range of wines, without dropping its traditional specialities. Alongside the sparkling wines by *méthode gaillacoise*, many growers make their *mousseux* by the champagne method, which here is by law required to be called somewhat confusingly and inaptly *méthode traditionnelle*. Here too the range can be dry, off-dry or sweet. *Traditionnelle* wines can be more easily controlled in their vinification, and are less likely to explode in bottle. Nevertheless, the old *méthode gaillacoise*, usually rather sweeter, is having something of a revival, appealing as it does to the taste of younger drinkers, who may well view it as a halfway house between Coca-Cola and Krug. It is usually considerably lower in alcohol than wine made by the champagne method.

Another modern development is the so-called *vin perlé*, a dry wine which has a slight prickle on the tongue. This is produced by allowing the wine to undergo a second fermentation during the course of which it is bottled. There is not, or should not be, any question of adding gas artificially. This wine has its fans, particularly holiday-makers in summer, but is frowned on by wine snobs.

Although the bulk of the production is of dry white and red wines, the great strength of Gaillac is in its sweet whites. Their style is less heavy and sugary than, say, monbazillac or sauternes, harking back to days when dry white wine was a rarity and the standard drink in village bars was a *demi-sec* style.

The dry and sweet white wines of Gaillac, as well as the reds, may be found aged traditionally in tanks or in old wood, or, increasingly, in new or nearly new barrels.

Gaillac is also proud of its *vin nouveau*, a Beaujolais lookalike made from the *gamay* grape and which often snatches prizes for this style of wine from under the noses of the Beaujolais makers. Developed in the early 1960's, these are wines to be drunk almost as soon as they are made, and are thus rarely seen during the summer holiday season. They will surely appeal to lovers of the *gamay* grape; for the rest of us the best that can be said for *gaillac nouveau* is that it is much better than the local *vins de pays nouveaux*, made often from grape varieties afraid to speak their name, and which are quite frankly awful.

GAILLAC'S ECCENTRIC GRAPE-VARIETIES

WHITE GRAPES

The grapes which are permitted for white gaillac AOC are *mauzac*, *len de l'el*, *muscadelle*, *sémillon*, *ondenc* and *sauvignon*.

Sauvignon. The all-conquering *sauvignon* grape is a recent importation to Gaillac when viewed against the long history of the others. Its chief worth locally is to give bite and a touch of its savage attack to the juice of other grapes, which sometimes lack acidity, particularly in hot years. However, *sauvignon* needs to be used with discretion if it is not to destroy the typicity of white gaillac, and there is a tendency among the great and the good in Gaillac—who, as in every appellation, carry a lot of weight—to standardize the gaillac style by over-using *sauvignon*. Financial help is also available to plant *sauvignon* at the expense of the truly indigenous grapes. The rules of the appellation require that 15% of the area in each grower's vineyard allocated for white grapes should consist of *sauvignon* and/or a rare variety called *len de l'el*.

Len de l'el. This grape derives its name from the fact that the bunches of grapes are on long stalks and are thus 'far from the eye' ('eye' meaning the bud in winespeak) which gave them birth. It is apparently grown nowhere else in France and has a long history in Gaillac. After the phylloxera it gave ground to *mauzac* because it is lower-yielding, but it has had a recent renaissance. The area planted with it has multiplied five-fold in the last 50 years. Because it ripens early, growers have the option of picking the grape dry for its acidity, or leaving it on the vine to give more sugar. It can thus be found in the driest and the sweetest wines of Gaillac. Its current popularity is due to the fact that its acidity does not fall as far or as fast as that of its companion-grape, *mauzac*. Many growers have thus discovered its excellence as a base for *vins liquoreux*.

Ondenc. This is another Gaillac speciality, nowadays to be found nowhere else. It used to be quite common in the area, but, because its buds burst early, it is particularly vulnerable to spring frosts, which are fairly frequent in Gaillac, especially on the lower ground of the Tarn Valley. After the phylloxera it was hardly replanted at all, and today the area planted with it does not reach double figures in hectares. It is, however, highly thought of by those growers who have it; they value the importance of preserving the presence of authentic indigenous grape-varieties. The deceptively pale juice can make some of the most luscious of Gaillac's sweet wines. Perhaps *ondenc* is due for a renaissance, like *len de l'el*'s.

Mauzac. Of the white grapes grown in Gaillac, *mauzac* accounts for about 60% of the total. After the phylloxera, and until the revival of *len de l'el*, it had a virtual monopoly. When picked young, *mauzac* has good acidity and is therefore ideal for making *vins mousseux*, a characteristic which it shares with the vineyards of Limoux, the only other area where *mauzac* is today planted in any quantity. As it ripens, the acidity drops away sharply, enabling growers to make sweet wines of extraordinary richness, even though sometimes prone to oxidization. *Mauzac* is certainly a native of the region, its name being possibly a corruption of the name of the town Moissac. It may be recognized by the curiously powdery aspect of the underside of its leaves, which develops as the growing cycle reaches its climax. Its flavour almost always recalls to a greater or lesser extent that of apples and sometimes pears. There are, according to one authority, six varieties of *mauzac* apart from the one commonly called *mauzac blanc*; among them there are *mauzac rose* (with tinted grapes) and *mauzac vert*. The variety called *mauzac noir* may or may not be a relation.

Muscadelle. This variety should not be confused with *muscat*, despite the shared perfumed quality from which it no doubt derives its name. It is valued for its above-average alcoholic potential and the richness which it can add to the sweet wines of the area. Introduced in Gaillac during the 1950's by the director of one of the local *coopératives*, its presence is today diminishing. This is largely because of the difficulty of controlling its yield, which its fans say is a fault of the *porte-greffes* commonly used rather than the variety itself.

Sémillon. Though a permitted variety, it is scarcely to be found in Gaillac, being just about as rare as *ondenc*.

BLACK GRAPES

There are four principal varieties permitted for AOC purposes: *braucol, duras, syrah* and *gamay*.

Braucol. We have already met this grape under its Marcillac alias of *mansois*. As in Marcillac, *braucol* is valued for its same aromatic qualities, its good colour, its currant fruit and its freedom from disease. It likes pebbly and poor soils. It has more weight than **duras**, which nevertheless has a spicyness and elegance not often to be found in the South-West. It also has good deep colour and a bouquet which strengthens with cellaring. *Duras* is not to be found anywhere other than Gaillac, except for pockets in the Côtes de Millau higher up the Tarn Valley. Each of the above two varieties must represent at least 10% of a grower's red AOC planting.

Syrah. A relatively recent import into Gaillac, *syrah* was introduced in the period leading up to the grant of AOC status for reds in 1970. The authorities (typically) considered that an AOC wine could not rely solely on local grapes. *Syrah* adds backbone and structure to red gaillacs, as well as a certain southern twang; a touch of toast, gaminess and chocolate sometimes as well. *Syrah* is not obligatory for Gaillac growers, but they must have at least 30% of their red AOC planting in any two of *braucol*, *duras* and *syrah*, or 60%, if to this list you add **gamay**, which is used exclusively for the making of *gaillac nouveau* (see above).

As supplementary varieties, growers who comply with the above rules may also have *merlot*, *cabernet franc* and *cabernet sauvignon*, but, as a general rule only the larger producers and the *coopératives* take advantage of them. These grapes do, however, enter into *vins de pays* and *vins de table*, as does **prunelard**, a close relative of the *auxerrois* but more akin to the *cot* of Touraine and a grape for the moment confined to the attention of a few specialist growers, some of whom make a pure varietal from it. It is not a permitted variety in the AOC, so can only be sold as a *vin de pays* or *vin de table*. In the old days, it accounted for a third of the red grapes planted in Gaillac and was much liked by the Bordeaux blenders. It can suggest fresh plums, liquorice, spices and sometimes, when mature, a touch of leather. The quality is infinitely better than that of **jurançon noir**, still valued for its fruitiness though not for its finesse (it has a long history in the South-West), and **portugais bleu**, another fruity grape giving supple but short-lived wines.

THE *TERROIRS*

The surface area presently under vine is about 10,000 hectares. As you approach from Toulouse, the vines begin on your left just beyond the pretty town of Rabastens. Here on the Côtes de Lisle, are some of the largest properties: Clément-Termes, Saurs, Lastours, for example.

On the other bank of the Tarn, gentle terraces, created by successive alluvial deposits from upstream, are composed mainly of *graves,* a pebbly soil mixed with clay, the whole on a chalky subsoil. Here the *syrah* grape is particularly successful for red wines and *len de l'el* for whites.

Further on to your left are steeper hillsides reaching deeper and deeper into the hinterland as far as the river Vère. This area includes the so-called Premières Côtes, where some of the best-quality wines are made on soil mainly of sandstone.

To the north of the river Vère is the chalky Plateau Cordais, reaching almost to the gates of that medieval hilltop city. Technically the appellation area extends further northwards and westwards, but in modern times nowhere beyond Cordes has been replanted to AOC requirements.

There is also a small pocket of vineyards to the east of Albi, called Cunac, technically within the AOC area of Gaillac, but its wines are all made and sold by one of the *coopératives* under the Cunac name as a brand.

THE CLIMATE

The Gaillac climate is more Mediterranean than that of any other vineyard of the South-West, but even so, the Atlantic influence is still strong. Spring frosts are a danger, particularly in the valleys of rivers and streams. A feature of the weather is the strong wind from the south-east called *vent d'autan*. It is hot and dry, its moisture having been exhausted during its passage over the Black Mountain. The *vent d'autan* plays an important part during the ripening season, keeping the bunches of grapes dry and thus less liable to disease. By the same token, it can also prevent the development of *Botrytis cinerea,* 'noble rot', the process of fungoid decomposition of the grapes by moisture in the atmosphere which makes the fortune of sweet wine makers in the Sauternes and Monbazillac. Here the sweetness in the juice is much more likely to develop by the grapes being allowed to shrivel in the sun on their own without the development of rot, a process called *passerillage*. Botrytis does, however, occur and is of course welcome when it does.

NÉGOCIANTS AND *COOPÉRATIVES*

In the immediate post-phylloxera period, most Gaillac wine was sold to *négociants* (dealers), 15 of whom were in the main square of the town alone as recently as the 1950's. Single-vineyard wines were unknown, let alone bottling at origin—developments of the 1950's and '60's. As long ago as 1903, in an effort to counteract fraud and over-production in the Midi, then about to result in the financial collapse of the wine industry, the first Gaillac *coopérative* was formed with about 100 members. Just before the Second World War there were 500 members, although in 1926 a breakaway organization had been formed. These two bodies accounted between them for about 40,000 hectolitres of wine a year.

The problem for Gaillac and its growers was that these bodies had no wine-making facilities, they were purely marketing organizations, whereas elsewhere in France *coopératives* had assumed the role of wine-maker. So there came into being in 1949 the *Cave,* which is nowadays called the **Coopérative de Labastide-de-Lévis**, after the village in which it is established. In the ensuing years it absorbed the Cunac growers in a separate annexe, a second small group devoted to the making of *vins mousseux*, and later the *Coopérative du Pays Cordais*, which specialised in the making of white AOC. Today this combined *cave* has about 300 members producing about 100,000 hectolitres of wine a year. This is about the same level of production as that of the **Cave de Rabastens**, founded in 1953 by growers whose vines were at the western end of the appellation. This *cave* originally followed a policy of bottling in *bonbonnes* (demi-johns), large glass containers usually encased within wicker. These were aimed at the Toulouse market. However, the cost of producing in this way eventually obliged the Rabastens *cave* to adopt the conventional style of bottling, and to seek a wider market. Today they are often noted for their good *vins mousseux* and, more recently, a pure *len de l'el* called **Astrolabe** (**B). A third *coopérative*, the **Cave de Técou**, was founded at about the same time as the Rabastens *cave*, and specialised initially in red wines produced by the growers on the south bank of the Tarn. Smaller than its two rivals, Técou has established the highest level of quality of the three, particularly with its range of wines aged in oak barrels, which are popular with local restaurateurs.

Meanwhile, of the two original *coopératives*, the first was dissolved, and the second, the *Union Vinicole*, became the *Cave de Gaillac*, gradually taking over the function of the old *négociants* and losing its cooperative character. Today it is in private hands, the main wholesale outlet for producers of Gaillac wines in bulk.

Today 50% of all Gaillac is still sold in the region, another 15% going to Paris, 10% to the north of France, 7% to other regions, and 20% is exported, largely to Belgium and Germany.

THE RISE OF THE INDEPENDENT *VIGNERON*

The second half of the 20th century saw fundamental change within Gaillac. After the war, the average size of a smallholding was between 6 and 15 hectares, barely providing a living for its owner, and only a part of this was given over to vines. Anyone who had more than 25 hectares was regarded as a rich proprietor. Tiny holdings of 2 or 3 hectares still persisted, usually in the hands of artisans who retained a handful of vines. During the early 1960's growers realized that they either had to get bigger or give up, but even so the size of a domaine rarely rose other than slowly. Production of white AOC Gaillac fell dramatically, partly because the AOC rules limited strictly the amount which could be produced, whereas no such restriction operated in respect to *vins de table*. By the same token, the production of red wine increased, largely because the old post-phylloxera hybrids had died out, making it possible to replant with modern varieties. The consequence of the grant of AOC for red wines in 1970 was an immediate increase in quality reds. White wine production at the AOC level remained static.

During this period, the impact of the Common Agricultural Policy encouraged growers of inferior vines to pull them up. This caused a sharp fall in the area under vine and the number of growers. On the other hand, the area of AOC production increased, aided by the restructuring of the vineyard in favour of high-quality grape varieties. Nevertheless, most of the vines are still in the hands of growers for whom the grape is only one crop among many. Only about one-tenth of Gaillac producers devote more than three-quarters of their land to the vine. Quality production outside the *coopératives* has concentrated itself in the hands of 100 or so *vignerons* who bottle and commercialize their own product. In the 1960's there were fewer than 10. Thus today there is an increasing number of good artisan growers.

VINS DE PAYS DES CÔTES DU TARN

The area of the *vins de pays* is slightly bigger than that of the AOC, and it includes the whole AOC area. It covers an extra 41 communes to the east, south and west of it. The southern area is particularly important because it includes the vineyards of Lavaur and the Agout, which themselves have a long history. The growth of the *vins de pays* is a logical consequence of the restructuring of the AOC. The adoption of good-quality grapes to replace the old hybrids, but particularly the banishment of the *portugais bleu* and *jurançon noir* varieties from the AOC, has produced a natural increase in both quantity and quality of the *vins de pays*. The whites are made principally from *mauzac* and *muscadelle*, the popular rosé from *jurançon noir*, and the reds largely from that grape and *portugais bleu*, although increasingly one finds the AOC varieties making their contribution as well.

Vins de pays are available from all three *coopératives,* in bottle or *en vrac*; many of the independent growers sell them too, and they can be extremely good value. But taste before buying.

VIGNERONS DU COEUR DE GAILLAC

One of the paradoxes in Gaillac is the consistent refusal by the tasting committees to grant the *agrément* (the right to call the wine by its AOC) to the most influential of its growers. The problem is not limited to Gaillac but here displays its most complete absurdity. It arises through the development during the last quarter of the last century of a tendency to favour only those wines which correspond to the least typical of the area, those which are found on the shelves of the supermarkets and village shops. Such wines tend to come from the larger and more influential producers, who have been responsible among other things for distorting the character of true Gaillac by over-reliance on 'foreign' grape varieties such as *sauvignon*, the two *cabernets* and *merlot*. How can one explain the rejection of Plageoles's beautiful *mauzac* wines as 'untypical, tasting of apples', when that very flavour is the signature of the grape variety? One of the consequences of this blinkered attitude is that the best independent growers, impatient with the restrictions placed on them by the wine authorities, which sometimes in their view inhibit them from making Gaillac wine true to the *terroir*, have formed an association under this name. The president is Robert Plageoles, and the vice-president Patrice Lescarret, but the list of members also includes mainstream Gaillac celebrities such as the Alberts of Domaine Labarthe. The object is not to hierarchize the producers of Gaillac with a *Charte de Qualité* as in Cahors, but to aim towards the production of wines of character, which are seen as being the only way to bring back to wine lovers an appreciation of good wine. They see the way forward as working with the traditional grape varieties, as naturally as possible in the vineyard, having as little recourse as possible in the *chais* to artificial processes such as inverse osmosis, artificial enrichment of the must, acidification, artificial yeasts and enzymes. The members of this group of producers are shown by the letters **CDG** in the following pages.

TODAY'S GROWERS

The diversity of styles produced today by Gaillac growers makes it difficult to suggest any pecking order in terms of quality. Some of the most talented make only some of the styles, and usually they are specialists in those styles. For other wines of comparable quality you may need to look elsewhere. On the other hand there are some who, while making a full range of wines, do not necessarily make the best of any one kind. These are usually the larger and sometimes oldest-established producers, and they can be counted on to be thoroughly reliable throughout the range. They are perhaps a good place to start a journey round Gaillac.

PRODUCERS OF GAILLAC

■ MAS PIGNOU
Jacques and Bernard Auques
Laborie, route de Castelnau-de-Montmiral
81600 Gaillac
Tel: 05-63-33-18-52 Fax: 05-63-33-11-58
Email: maspignou@free.fr

Auques Père says he doesn't mind being called pear-shaped as long as you praise his wines. Good they are, too; they can be relied on to give pleasure without fail. The stars are grouped under the name Cuvée Mélanie, after his great-grandmother who was left in charge of the vineyards when her husband went off to the Great War. When he returned, Mélanie refused to hand back the reins. Gradually she switched production from the *vin bourru*, so beloved of Parisians, to conventional table wines.

The red **Mélanie** (**B) is from 40% *braucol* and 30% each of *cabernet franc* and *merlot*, and is given a full three weeks' maceration, rather longer than the **basic red** of the property (*A), which is made mainly from the local grapes and has real gaillac character, even if it is less ambitious than the Mélanie. **Mélanie** also appears as a dry white, (**A), usually half *len de l'el* and half *sauvignon*. Auques, who is gradually handing the vineyard over to his son Bernard, completes his range of AOC whites with a stylish **perlé** (*A) and a honeyed beauty called **Hauts de Laborie Doux** (**A), from 100% *mauzac*. There are also good *vins de pays en vrac,* the red largely from *duras*; for the rosé, Auques adds a little *syrah* and *jurançon noir*.

Bernard Auques, who has largely taken over from his father, has revived the old *moustillant* style, which he markets as **Vin Bourru** (**A); it rates a mere 3.5 degrees of alcohol, is only medium sweet and is quaffable in huge quantities at any time of day or night.

■ CDG DOMAINE DE LABARTHE
Jean-Paul Albert
81500 Castanet
Tel: 05-63-56-80-14 Fax: 05-63-56-84-81
Email: labarthe@vinlabarthe.com
www.vinlabarthe.com

Gaillac has come a long way since Jean-Paul's grandfather planted his first *gamay* grapes, destined to go into one of the earliest *gaillacs nouveaux*. This is one of the pioneering estates in the appellation, with a wine-making history going back many generations. Jean-Paul still makes the delicious **blanc moelleux** (**B) in a style which seems to be getting squeezed out between *blancs secs* on the one hand and the fashionable ultra-sweet style on the other.

Some of the *mauzac* vines here are used to make the **blanc perlé** (**A), one of the best of its kind. In a good year, some of the grapes are left to over-ripen on the vine to give the wine a little richness. Jean-Paul's first **blanc sec** (*A) is *sauvignon*-based, as if to distinguish it clearly from the other whites, and it has on oaked cousin called **Héritage** (*B), skilfully raised but tending rather to veer away from gaillac in character. There is also a **Gaillac Blanc Premières Côtes** (**A), a delicious dry wine all from *mauzac*. The range of whites is completed by a choice of dry and off-dry sparklers made by the *méthode traditionnelle* (**B).

As well as a charming **rosé** (**A) which features a good dose of *syrah*, there are two reds: The premium wine is called **Cuvée Guillaume** (**B), a dark keeper mostly from *braucol* but with some *merlot* too. Despite an *élevage* in wood, the oak manages not to smother the basic fruit too much. There are good peppery spices too as a rule. At the other end of the scale, the *vins de pays* are consistently good value here, so don't forget to bring your *bidon*. If you do, there is always *le baginbox*.

▦ CDG DOMAINE D'ESCAUSSES
Rosaline and Jean-Marc Balaran
La Salamandrié, 81150 Sainte-Croix
Tel: 05-63-56-80-52 Fax: 05-63-56-87-62
Email: jean-marc.balaran@wanadoo.fr
www.domainedescausses.com

The Balaran family are another of the sure values in Gaillac. They have 20 hectares of vines within the appellation, 14 for red grapes and six for white. The property is just off the main road from Albi to Cordes, about midway between the two.

Jean-Marc found himself plunged into the deep end when his father was killed in a motor accident. Since then he has been nodding in the direction of a more modern style for his gaillacs. Not for his quaffable **rosé** (*A) or the equally thirst-quenching **perlé** (*A), but in his reds and whites. His white **Vigne de l'Oubli** (***B) will most likely contain half *sauvignon* (given a preliminary cold fermentation) and a quarter each *mauzac* and *muscadelle*, the whole barrel-fermented in French oak, one-third of it new. The top red is called **La Croix Petite** (**B) and will probably come from 30% *braucol*, 45% *syrah,* 15% *merlot* and 10% *cabernet sauvignon*. The *syrah* is usually given a preliminary pre-maceration and *microbullage* in vat. The best *cuvées* are aged in oak, but only some of the barrels are new. The older barrels are reserved for another red called variously

La Vigne Blanche or **La Vigne Mythique** (*A). These are the most typically gaillac of the reds, which are no worse for being spared oak barrels that would surely have smothered their freshness.

There are two sweet wines: **La Vigne Galante** (*A), a typically old-fashioned *moëlleux,* contrasts with the more modern styled **Vendanges Dorées** (***B).

To complete his range, Jean-Marc will propose a delicious dry **mousseux** (**B) by the old *gaillacois* method. If you happen to be in Gaillac in November from the third Thursday in the month onwards, drop in for his *vin nouveau*. At other times in the year, and by appointment, you can sample a range of five cheeses and the wines of the property for a modest 4 euros.

▦ CHÂTEAU VIGNE-LOURAC
Alain Gayrel (Les Domaines Philippe Gayrel)
Ravailhe, Senouillac 81600 Gaillac
Tel: 05-63-33-91-16 Fax 05-63-33-95-76
Also at the Cave de Gaillac,
103 Avenue Foch, 81600 Gaillac
Tel: 05-63-81-21-05 Fax: 05-63-81-21-09
Email: ccso@wanadoo.fr

Gayrel is a busy man. What with the *Cave de Gaillac* (one of the biggest *négociants* in the region), which he took over in 1997, and his 70-hectare domaine, he has his work cut out to keep up with himself. But although seemingly without a spare moment, he can relax to host a tasting that is spiced with reminiscences about mutual experiences and acquaintances.

He makes rather more white wines than reds, for frankly commercial reasons, but they sell easily and well, though apparently not in France. The UK is his best market. The wines are seldom to be seen in restaurants or shops in the region of production, although they are available throughout the Campanile chain of hotels.

At Ravailhe are all but six hectares of the vineyard, the remainder to be found at Meritz, six kilometres away on the Cordes plateau where the chalky soil produces lighter, more aromatic wines. The whites range from a pure **sauvignon** (*A), at its best within months of production and rather faded one year after the vintage. When fresh, it is spicy and the ultra-gooseberry flavour amounts almost to caricature, perhaps because of the skin contact. The 100% *mauzac* **Vieilles Vignes** (the vines being 20 to 70 years old) (**A), with 5 months on the lees, is altogether more serious and ages well; the *mauzac* character is not immediately apparent, the bouquet being floral, fruity with a touch of lemon and very fresh; the wine is bone dry, developing notes of honey, hazelnuts, butter and even aniseed, long on the palate but without heaviness, and with good acidity. '

The **perlé** (*A) is from 60% *mauzac*, 20% *len de l'el*, and 10% each *muscadelle* and *sauvignon*. The prickle is achieved by stocking the wine with its CO_2 in vats at sub-zero temperatures, and compressed 44 mm corks are used to ensure preservation of the mini-bubbles. Not authentic, but effective.

The **vin doux** is 60% *len de l'el* and 20% each *mauzac* and *muscadelle*. Gayrel is willing to make up a *vin de pays* blend to suit bulk buyers. The one which he makes for the mainstream market is agreeable but nothing special.

The red **Rubis de Vigné-Lourac** (**A) is delightful, made from *duras*, *braucol* and *syrah* and given 18 days on the skins. Light and easy drinking, with pepper, spices and a good suggestion of cassis, it apparently does not attract UK buyers like the red **Vieilles Vignes** (*A), admittedly more powerful and ambitious, but rather lacking in charm. This is not a fault to be found in his seductive summer *vin de pays* from 70% *duras* and 30% *cabernet*, exuberant and more-ish, for picnics and barbecues.

Gayrel is frank about his commercialism but manages at the same time to keep one foot in his *terroir*. Many would give their right arm for his marketing skills.

■ CDG **DOMAINE ROTIER**
Alain Rotier and Francis Marre
Petit Nareye, 81600 Cadalen
Tel: 05-63-41-75-14 Fax: 05-63-41-54-56
Email: rotier.marre@domaine-rotier.com
www.domaine-rotier.com

Alain Rotier may not be the longest-established of Gaillac winemakers, although his father was a *coopérateur* in the old days. His domaine, formerly called Le Petit Naraye (a name which he says the French found difficult to either pronounce or remember), has long been recognized for its mixture of loyalty to the traditional grapes of the region and a certain readiness to explore new techniques to maximize the quality of the wines. He is proud that he was one of the first to rediscover the excellence of *len de l'el*, raising it from its long eclipse since the phylloxera era to one of the strengths of Gaillac. Similarly, he has played a part in the revival of *duras*, one of the oldest of the local gapes, now much valued for its colour, alcoholic potential, soft but substantial body and peppery spices.

Alain and his brother-in-law have 35 hectares, a sizeable holding by Gaillac standards, all on the second terrace of the left bank of the Tarn. The soil is *graves*, with plenty of big round pebbles, called *galets*, such as you find in river beds. Alain has neighbours who are determined to use insecticides, which he does not approve of, instead trying as hard as he can to follow biological principles. As he replants his vineyard little by little, he does so to greater density and trains the vines closer to the ground than his father did. He also follows Luc de Conti in Bergerac in planting oats between the rows of his vines to improve the soil.

The *chais* is a succession of large barnlike chambers, reached through doors, each of which leads to the next area, as in Bluebeard's Castle. The *salle de dégustation* leads direct into a barrel-store, which in turn leads to the vinification *chais*. That leads in its turn to the *élevage en barriques*, beyond which is the store-room and labelling area.

In the *chais* Alain is a devotee of the technique of *microbullage*, the introduction into the maturing wine of tiny elements of oxygen. The effect of this when applied at the end of the fermentation process, while the wine is still on its skins, is to soften the tannins and stabilize the colour of the juice. After the malolactic fermentation is over, *microbullage* can increase the complexity of the flavours and continue the process of softening the tannins. Constant racking of the wine, another way of introducing oxygen into the wine, is avoided, thereby minimizing the disturbance of the wine on its lees.

The top wines of the property are called, appropriately, **Renaissance** (***B), and they come in red as well as dry and sweet white versions. All share the benefits of hand-harvesting (particularly the white grapes), low yields and *élevage* in wood (but never more than 15% is ever new oak). Additionally the whites are barrel-fermented. The **sweet white** (***C), a 100% *len de l'el*, has achieved exceptional renown and is one of the best of the appellation.

Not at all to be spurned is the more modest range called **Les Gravels** (**A), wines which can be drunk young but which will nevertheless keep well. There is also a range called **Les Initiales** (*), exceptionally fruity and destined for easy and copious consumption, sometimes containing grapes which have been bought in from nearby growers.

GAILLAC'S ECCENTRIC TRIO

(All distinguished by having some of their wines regularly refused the *agrément*.)

■■ CDG **LES VINS DE ROBERT ET BERNARD PLAGEOLES**
Domaine des Très Cantous
81140 Cahuzac-sur-Vère and
Domaine Roucou-Cantemerle
81140 Castelnau-de-Montmiral
Tel: 05-63-33-90-40 Fax: 05-63-33-95-64
Email: bernard.plageoles@wanadoo.fr

Robert, who has now handed over to his son Bernard, was always a traditionalist and an inventor. He insisted on using only the historic Gaillac varieties for wines which he bottled and commercialized himself. He has one of only two plantations of *ondenc* in the region, from which Bernard—whose wines are at least as good as his father's—makes a range of three whites: a traditionally vinified **dry white** (**B) for drinking young while its aromas of quince and mock orange are still fresh; a **dessert wine** from overripe grapes fermented and matured in the barrel (**B); and his great speciality, **Le Vent de l'Autan** (***D), for which only Robert's own words are adequate: 'Five years of research to rediscover five centuries of oblivion. A sweetmeat at once full and honest, hugely original. A wine of which one could say that it was comparable to no other. It is the wine of the wind and the soul.' It is hard to add to that except to say that this wine is recognized as one of the great sweet wines of France. Plageoles claims it will keep for between 20 and 100 years.

Robert, though more or less retired, is busying himself writing a learned book on the local grape varieties, which may prove as controversial as some of his wines. In the *mauzac* range—all of Plageoles's are varietals from single grape varieties—he grows four of the six different subspecies (or five of the seven if you include the '*noir*'). From the *vert*, he makes an apple- and lime-scented **dry white** (***B) of great character; from the *roux,* a pale yellow **sweet wine** (***B), ideal as an aperitif or with

from an obscure grape of the same name which he has rescued from his father's museum.

There are four red varietals: a **duras** (**B) with a unique flavour of crushed blackberries seasoned with pepper; a **syrah** (**B) with good body and structure and a long finish that ages well, developing fine tannins, red fruit flavours and a hint of spice; and finally two typically Plageoles specials, a 100% **prunelart** (***B), with flavours of plum and liquorice set off by spice and, with age, a touch of leather; and the **mauzac noir** (**B), today a rare variety, but in the old days widely cultivated alongside the *prunelart*, *duras* and *négrette*. The *prunelart,* though one of the oldest of the local varieties, has been excluded from the list of AOC grapes for some reason unexplained. It is probably the same grape as the *cot à queue rouge*, and thus not the same as the *auxerrois* of Cahors.

It is an irony that Robert Plageoles, the most famous and widely admired grower in Gaillac, should also have been the *enfant terrible* of the Establishment—until, that is, one day along came his disciple.

CDG DOMAINE DE CAUSSE MARINES

Patrice Lescarret
81140 Vieux
Tel: 05-63-33-98-30 Fax: 05-63-33-96-23
Mobile: 06-07-11-80-83
Email: causse-marines@infonie.fr
www.causse-marines.com

Patrice, a devotee of sweet wines, who chose Gaillac because he could not afford a vineyard anywhere else, has created so many waves that he has probably made more enemies than friends in the Gaillac oligarchy. This is rash in any appellation firmly controlled by the great but not necessarily good. Nevertheless, Patrice is accorded enormous respect and admiration by everyone else for the quality of the wines he makes. He is also much praised by the media, whom he affects to despise when it suits his polemic. 'The majority of competitive tastings are only masquerades, where the level of expertise of the tasters is feeble to the point of

foie gras, and an extraordinary **Vin de Voile** (***D), so called because it is allowed to oxidize as it ages under a kind of skin, or 'veil,' which forms on the surface, as in a *vin paillé* or a sherry. From *mauzac gris* and *rose* there comes another Plageoles speciality, a gaillac *mousseux ancestrale* which he calls **Mauzac Nature** (***B), a wine of great finesse, off-dry usually and intended to be drunk during the first year; do not be put off if a sediment sinks to the bottom of the bottle.

Before leaving the Plageoles whites, mention must be made of the pure **muscadelle** (***B), vinified and aged in oak, a wine which is Bernard's own creation; and a varietal wine called **Verdanel** (**B),

(**A). Both are excellent examples of their *cépages*, whatever INAO or ONIVINS might say. He does not seem to have had the same trouble with his other dry white wine, called **Les Greilles** (***A), a blend of *len de l'el*, *mauzac*, *muscadelle* and *ondenc*. Here the *muscadelle* is gradually giving way to *ondenc*, as Patrice's recent planting of the latter ('the largest recent plantation of *ondenc*, 80 ares, in the world') comes on stream. Nor should one pass over his quaffing red, called **Peyrouzelles** (**A), made from the younger vines on the property, *braucol*, *syrah* and *duras*, with a touch of older *jurançon*, *prunelard* and *alicante*.

But it is the range of sweet wines on which Patrice bestows his passion. The most conventional of these is called **Grain de Folie Douce** (**B), being a blend of *muscadelle* and *len de l'el* (both botrytized, with any luck) and *mauzac* (overripened without botrytis); the grapes are harvested at a potential of 17 degrees alcohol, vinified traditionally, and the wine is aged in old barrels for two years. It is bottled when Patrice thinks it is ready. Much of the sugar is not fermented, leaving the alcohol level at a gentle 12 or 13 degrees volume.

But now come the three wines from *ondenc*, which he says attracts botrytis well—and if botrytis does not materialize, *ondenc* shrivels well in the sun, drying out like currants. Every year he is able to make a wine called **Délires d'Automne** (***B), which has 250 grams per litre of residual sugar; but only in exceptional years can he go on from there to produce **Folie Pure** (***D), with 420, and **Graal** (***D), with 550. The fermentation of these wines lasts more than a year, or 'a blurp a day' as Patrice says, the pure natural yeasts being slow to act. There is 'no filtration, no added sugar nor acids, no inverse osmosis, no cryoextraction, just grape juice'.

As if this were not enough *ondenc*, Patrice is also planning a dry wine from his young vines. He also makes an *eau-de-vie* from it called Eau Dingue, and to round off Patrice's eclectic range, there is a *vin de voile* from *mauzac* called **Mysterre** (***C), as well as a semi-sweet fizzy by the *méthode ancestrale* called **Présambulle** (***B), both clearly

being laughable. Having served on these juries I know what I'm talking about.' His annual newsletters make for racy reading.

Furious at not being allowed by law to put the name *mauzac* on his label, he promptly baptised his wine from that grape **Zacmau** (***B) anagrammatically, and described it as a *vin de table* when the tasting committee refused to allow him his AOC. They said it was typical of neither the grape nor the appellation, their idea of typicity being that which they had invented for themselves and with which they have flooded the *grandes surfaces*. By the same token, his pure *duras* wine he calls **Rasdu** owing something to Plageoles's influence. Whether or not Patrice's natural impatience will keep him to the steady path of wine-making we shall see. His energy was once channelled into a wine-bar, since sold, in downtown Gaillac, as well as a wine-making relationship with Bernard Angles in Marcillac (see p. 36), which entitles him to bottle and market some marcillac of his own.

Patrice has a new partner to help him with his 15 hectares of vines. His former no. 2 has come back too after a bad motor accident. So a period of bad luck has perhaps come to an end, but Patrice is still concerned that his vineyard is too much for him, even though he has his eyes on further interests in Marcillac to add to his burdens. If Patrice decides to shrink his vineyard (but 'which of my vines must I tear up?' he asks in despair), he would not be the first perfectionist to go down that route. He promises, however, to keep his *ondenc* at all cost.

■ CDG DOMAINE DE LA RAMAYE

Michel Issaly
Sainte-Cécile d'Avès, 81600 Gaillac
Tel: 05-63-57-06-64 Fax: 05-63-57-35-34
Email: contact@michelissaly.com
www.michelissaly.com

This small vineyard, tucked away in a fold of the hills to the northwest of Gaillac town, is scarcely more than four hectares in size, all on chalk and clay. It has been in Michel's mother's family for six generations at least. He and his father, Maurice, started to make red wine on a serious scale only when appellation status came in 1970. Today it represents nearly three-quarters of their production of about 20,000 bottles. Simple calculation shows that the yields here are very low, and the policy is the highest possible quality at the expense of quantity, even if this means higher-than-average prices.

Michel, who manages a rare balance between passion and thoughtfulness, puts his skills as a trained oenologist at the service of tradition. 'The genius of wine is in the plant,' he says. So, in high respect of the environment, the vines are planted in the midst of hedgerows and trees; the soil is worked by digging deep, forcing the roots of the vines to penetrate the soil as far down as possible; the weeds and grasses are cut by hand and left as a top dressing to protect the plants from the heat of the summer sun. The low yields are achieved by fierce pruning in winter, a total ban on artificial supplements and the cruellest sacrifice of surplus grape-bunches in summer. Harvesting is by hand, and the must is not manipulated by the addition of any foreign substances other than the minimum of sulphur, or by any purely scientific 'improvements'. The wines are aged on their lees in cement tanks.

There is no *élevage en barriques neuves*. Close to the *chais*, Michel has an extensive orchard of fruit trees, of whose produce he is something of a connoisseur, his love of good food deriving clearly from his mother, who is a famous local cook. He also has what he calls a *vignothèque*, a row or two of each of the grape varieties he grows, where he experiments with different methods of pruning and training of the vines. One of his plans is to grow some vines *en foule*, that is to say not in rows, but randomly, like they used to in the old days, to see whether the plants respond better to a little less regimentation.

Michel's range of whites starts with a *sec* called **Les Cavaillés Bas** (***B), from equal quantities of late-picked *mauzac* and *len de l'el*. He recommends serving this wine at cellar temperature and not colder. A sweeter wine from the same percentages of grapes but from different parcels is called **Le Sous-Bois de Rayssac** (***C), for which the last picking of *mauzac* may take place as late as Christmas-time. This is a wine for foie gras, blue cheese and fruit-based desserts. In very great years Michel also makes an ultra-sweet 100% *mauzac* wine which he calls **Quintessence Grains par Grains** (***D), Gaillac's version of a *Trockenbeerenauslese*. For sheer luxury and complexity, these sweet wines are hard to beat. Michel believes that the secret with sweet wines is to maximize the minerality and to leave the sugar to look after itself. He is experimenting with growing the fruit on vertical stakes, rather than trained along wire, allowing the vegetation to climb as high as possible before toppling over downwards towards the ground. By forcing the sap of the plant to the top of its growth, he believes that the lower shoots of the vine on which the bunches of grapes grow are forced to seek deep into the soil for nourishment and thus produce fruit whose juice is what he calls *aërienne*.

Before turning to Michel's red wines, mention must be made of his **Vin de l'Oubli** (***D), in a style like Plageoles's which used to be commonplace in Gaillac in the old days. After natural clarifying, the wine is drawn off into old barrels more than 15 years old and left there for seven years without replenishment. The cellar temperature will be the same as outside. From the second year on, the veil will start to form, and the wine will start oxidizing and assuming a madeira-like character. About a third of the quantity is lost through evaporation during this time. The wine is fined but not filtered before bottling. Michel says this wine will keep for more than 50 years in a good cellar. His love for this wine is such that he labels it by hand, meticulously affixing stamps from a bowl of bubbling yellow wax. For the fearless he makes an *eau-de-vie* called **La Blanche de Mauzac**, a wine-based brandy from 100% *mauzac*.

The first of Michel's reds, **Le Pech de la Tillette** (**B), is, for him, less traditional than his other wines, being a blend of 70% *merlot* and 30% *syrah*. The *cuvaisons* are rather short too, and the bunches of grapes are destalked, which is unusual at this domaine. This is perhaps Michel's idea of a *vin de soif*, but it will keep a good few years in bottle and is by no means a lightweight. *Duras* and *braucol* in equal quantities are at the base of **La Combe d'Avès** (***C), which is given 30 days in enclosed tanks after the fermentation is over. It is then aged for nearly three years in barrels which are at least five years old. Finally, there is a relative novelty from 50% *prunelard* and 50% *braucol* called **Le Grand Tertre** (***D), which, because of the *prunelard* content, has to be labelled as a *vin de pays*. The price of this wine reflects the tiny yield from the *prunelard* vines, at the rate of a mere 18 hectolitres per hectare. *Prunelard* also enters into a more modest red called **La Cuvée Y** (**B), where it is balanced by equal quantities of *duras* and *braucol*.

Michel, with his relatively small production, has been clever to find a niche in the restaurants of Paris, where a faithful band of *sommeliers* are only too happy to take up a large proportion of his supply. By concentrating on an appreciative sector of the market, he is able to make his small vineyard viable.

THE CORDES PLATEAU

▓ CHÂTEAU D'ARLUS

Lucien Schmitt

Les Homps, 81140 Montels

Tel and fax: 05-63-33-15-06

Email: info@chateau-d-arlus.com

www.chateau-d-arlus.com

Schmitt is a German businessman and leaves this excellent vineyard largely in the hands of his resident wine-making team. The property is the result of the merger of two former holdings, once in the separate hands of two *coopérateurs* who sold to Schmitt in 1999. Since the former owners had no wine-making facilities, the winery here is brand new and no expense has been spared in equipping it with the latest state-of-the-art equipment.

Schmitt found that he had purchased some very old vines indeed, some of them more than 100 years old, but he has also planted some *syrah* and *cabernet sauvignon* for his red wines, and some *sauvignon* and *muscadelle* for his whites, all trained in the modern manner on wire rather than grown *en gobelet*.

It is something of a tribute to the early wine-making team here that, as early as their second year, they were already winning medals, initially for their speciality wines, **Château d'Arlus Mauzac** (**A) and **gaillac doux** (*B), another *mauzac* wine. There is also a blended **blanc sec** (*A), which contains *muscadelle* and *len de l'el* in addition to *mauzac*. A **perlé** (*A) completes the range of whites, and there is only one **gaillac rouge** (*), which comes in oaked (B) and unoaked form (A).

The *vrac* wines here are excellent. Sheer value for money makes this one of the most attractive prospects in Gaillac.

▓ DOMAINE DES CAILLOUTIS

Patricia Baisse and Bernard Fabre

81140 Andillac

Tel and fax: 05-63-33-97-63

Having spent some time in Burgundy, this young couple took over this seven-hectare domaine on the chalky Plateau Cordais in 1998, since when they have made a name for themselves. They have been working organically since 2001 and conversion is now therefore fully complete. The wines to go for here are the reds; the **gaillac rouge** (**A) aims not so much for concentration or deep colour as a good spicy, herby character with good bite. The **Cuvée Prestige** (**B) is *syrah*-based, though sometimes Bernard adds a little *braucol*; the wine is partly raised in oak. It is bigger, rounder and has deeper fruit than the unoaked version, and the wood is not too prominent. The *vin de pays* based on *jurançon* and *gamay* is not in the same class as the other two reds.

▓ DOMAINE DE LA CHANADE

Christian Hollevoet

81170 Souel, par Cordes

Tel and fax: 05-63-56-31-10

Email: hollevoet.christian@wanadoo.fr

The *chais* is in an old stable, but with fully state-of-the-art stainless steel tanks, thermoregulated for the whites; and there is new concrete for the reds. The family were Flemish, grandfather leaving Belgium for the south of France during the First World War. He was a *vigneron,* but his son was not. The family lived not far away from La Chanade, which Christian bought in 1997. In the local patois, *chanade* means 'midsummer day', recalling the days when the locals used to light beacons on the nearby hilltops in the region to celebrate the occasion.

Christian's **blanc sec** (**A), from equal quantities of *mauzac* and *len de l'el*, is surprisingly full, almost rich, perhaps because it is matured on its lees. His **blanc doux** (**B) is from *len de l'el* and is aged in barrels made from local oak from the forest of Grésigne by the local *tonnelier* Alibert, who was an uncle of Christian. The wine is made in the Burgundian style with regular *bâtonnage* of the lees.

As a prelude to his reds, Christian will propose his rosé called **Les Riols** (***A), one of the best of the region. He will ring the changes with the grapes he puts into his reds, but where he uses oak, he will put the lees into the barrels with the wine. For example, a virtually pure **braucol** (**A) given treatment *en barrique* was delicious, although in danger of taking on too much wood, and a 2001 **syrah** (**A) had plenty of ripe cassis, finer than some Mediterranean *syrah*, with good acidity and silky tannins. He also sells a **duras** (*A) sometimes as a *mono-cépage*.

A **blend 2/3 duras to 1/3 syrah** (**B) was very promising. It had a touch of *prunelard,* which Hollevoet is very proud to have kept. Another blend from roughly equal **braucol, cabernet,** and **syrah** was dominated by the red fruits from the **braucol** (**A). A wine for lovers of the latter grape.

Damien Miralles, a *maître de chais,* is in residence next door; his mobile number is 06-22-78-88-71 and he will help you if Christian is absent among his vines.

■ **DOMAINE PEYRES-ROSES**
Astrid and Olivier Bonnefont
81140 Cahuzac-sur-Vère
Tel: 05-63-33-23-34 Fax: 05-63-40-53-01
Mobile: 06-09-22-52-73
Email: olivier.bonnafont@wanadoo.fr
www.domaine-peyresroses.com

The Bonnefonts are a very serious-minded and totally bio couple who work the vineyard with a horse and believe, like Luc de Conti in Bergerac, in maintaining in the vineyard a complete ecological range of plants and insects. Needless to say, no chemicals are allowed near the grapes or the vines, nor any artificial fertilizers of any kind, and grasses are given a free range between the rows of vines. The care really does show in the quality of the wines, which include a very minerally **blanc sec** (*A) from *mauzac, len de l'el* and *muscadelle*, and a **Jeunes Vignes** *vin de table* (**A). The latter is something of a misnomer because the vines are from eight to 14 years old, but Olivier wishes to distinguish it from his red **Vieilles Vignes** (**B), purple and rather classy. And above all there is a superbly fine and elegant **blanc doux** (***B), not rating higher than 5/10 on a sweetness scale, but having beautiful balance and just the right touch of acidity.

OTHER GOOD WINEMAKERS
ON THE PLATEAU

▌CHÂTEAU ADELAIDE

Christine Cornet

Cinq-Peyres, 81140 Cahuzac-sur-Vère

Tel and fax: 05-63-33-92-76

Email: chadelaide@aol.com

www.chateauadelaide.com

Noted for their whites: a rich dry blend of *mauzac* and *len de l'el*, and a range of *doux*, good enough for Ducasse's restaurant in Paris (**B).

▌MAS D'AUREL

Brigitte and Jacques Ribot-Molinier

81170 Donnazac

Tel: 05-63-56-06-39 Fax: 05-63-56-09-21

A thoroughly reliable range of wines, of which the **Cuvée Alexandra red and white** (*B) are especially good. Good *vrac* wines too.

▌DOMAINE DE BERTRAND

Eric Cunnac

81170 Donnazac

Tel: 05-63-56-09-30 Fax: 05-63-56-06-52

Good middle-of-the-range stuff; note an aperitif called Hypocras, from spiced wine.

▌CHÂTEAU BOURGUET

Jean and Jérôme Borderies

81170 Vindrac-Alayrac

Tel and fax: 05-63-56-15-23

Email: jean.borderies@libertysurf.fr

www.chateaubourguet.neuf.fr

Note especially a rather jurançon-like *doux.*

▌CHÂTEAU MONTELS

Bruno Montels

Burgal, 81170 Souel, par Cordes

Tel: 05-63-56-01-28 Fax: 05-63-56-14-46

Admirers of oaked wines will not be disappointed by the top red here.

▌VIGNOBLE LE PAYSSEL

Eric and Arielle Brun

Frausseilles, 81170 Cordes-sur-Ciel

Tel: 05-63-56-00-47 Fax: 05-63-56-09-16

Email: lepayssel@free.fr

Another oaked red features here, but the *classique* is less forbidding and the dry white very agreeable.

▌DOMAINE PEYRES-COMBE

Victor Brureau

La Combe, 81140 Andillac

Tel and fax: 05-63-33-94-67

Email: peyres-combe@wanadoo.fr

Here is an organic producer who makes a nicely balanced dry white and a range of reds in which *cabernet* and *merlot* are used to tone down the local *duras* and *braucol*. Also a very good **méthode gaillacoise** (**B).

▌DOMAINE SALVY

Michèle and Anne Marc

Arzac, 81140 Cahuzac-sur-Vère

Tel: 05-63-33-97-64 Fax: 05-63-33-97-29

Email: salvy@wanadoo.fr

www.domainesalvy.free.fr

Perhaps a run of tricky vintages did not help, but the wines from earlier years, though quite outstanding, were hardly noticed commercially. There has been a revival, though. The 2004 red Tradition is particularly nice.

COTEAUX DE GAILLAC
PRODUCERS

◾ DOMAINE BARREAU
Jean-Claude Barreau
Boissel, 81600 Gaillac
Tel: 05-63-57-57-51 Fax: 05-63-57-66-37
Mobile: 06-80-65-24-54

Just out of Gaillac, on the road north to Cordes and just as you start to climb the hillside, you will find Jean-Claude's domaine right on the road. He is one of the most consistent gaillac producers, much respected by his fellow growers.

From his wide range of wines, his **Mousseux Méthode Ancestrale** (**A) is one of the best of the sweet wines made in this style, while his oaked still *doux,* called **Caprice d'Automne** (**B), wins prizes regularly. Of his two dry whites, one is made for drinking *en primeur* (*A) and contains up to 70% *sauvignon*, while the other, **Blanc Sec Fût** (**B), which will age quite well, has only a touch of that grape, being mainly from *mauzac* and *len de l'el*.

◾ DOMAINE (MAS) DE BICARY
Roger and Claude Rouquié
81600 Broze
Tel and fax: 05-63-57-07-93

The 20 hectares of this estate are divided just about equally between white and red wine production. Of the whites, the **perlé** (**A) is good, if you like the *perlé* style, but the **vin doux** (***A) is outstanding, with luscious overtones of honey and almonds. It is not exaggeratedly sweet, being rather more in the old *moëlleux* style; a lovely wine

as an aperitif or with foie gras, because it is not too heavy. Note also the **Rouge Tradition** (**A), vinified ultra-traditionally without destalking and with long *cuvaisons* of up to four weeks, a wine which keeps remarkably well and improves in the bottle. Madame Rouquié will probably be your host in the tasting room, and she is very attentive and informative.

◾ DOMAINE DE LARROQUE
Patrick and Valérie Nouvel
81150 Cestayrols
Tel: 05-63-56-87-63 Fax: 05-63-56-87-40
Email: domaindelarroque@wannado.fr
www.domainedelarroque.fr

Patrick is Jean-Paul Albert's nephew, and his domaine is just across the valley from Labarthe, although you have to go all round the world to get from one to the other. He must have studied his uncle's wine-making well, because Patrick's reds are among the best of the whole appellation. His basic **Tradition** (**A) is good enough, but the **Privilège d'Antan** (***B) is outstanding, rather better perhaps than the top-of-the-range wine raised in oak. There are no concessions to modern technology here, but the wines are clean as a whistle and attractively presented. Patrick often has stands at local wine and food shows.

■ CHÂTEAU DE MAYRAGUES
Alan and Laurence Geddes
81140 Castelnau-de-Montmiral
Tel: 05-63-33-94-08 Fax: 05-63-33-98-10
Email: geddes@chateau-de-mayragues.com
www.chateau-de-mayragues.com

These growers are well known to Anglo-Saxon residents in the region almost as much for the delightful concerts they organize in their beautiful home as for their elegant wines. This is a real château, dating back to the Middle Ages, complete with *tour de ronde* and fortifications, lovingly restored under the expert eye of Laurence, a one-time curator of the Carnavalet Museum in Paris. Alan was a high-powered chartered accountant in an international firm with Bordeaux clients to audit, but he gradually took a shine more to the wine than the figures. He and Laurence decided to buy their own home in the South-West and to make wine themselves.

Their first and almost immediate success was with their **doux** (***B), with which they have won prizes and kept up a consistently high standard. Made wholly from *len de l'el*, it shows the aptitude of the grape to the sweeter style of wine. Over the years their reds have improved to the same standard; their **Mages** (**B), with a good dose of *cabernet sauvignon,* reflects Alan's former Bordeaux connection. Visitors should be sure to make an appointment.

■ CDG CHÂTEAU DE PALVIÉ
Jérôme Bézios
Avenue des Potiers, 81600 Montans
Tel: 05-63-57-19-71 Fax: 05-63-57-48-56
Email: croixdesmarchands@wanadoo.fr
www.croix-des-marchands.com

Jérôme represents the younger generation at La Croix des Marchands, a big property on the south bank of the river where the family are large and successful players in Gaillac. The so-called Château de Palvié is not really a château at all, but the name given to a vineyard which Jérôme has acquired on the other side of the river, not far from Robert Plageoles.

For the Palvié wines Jérôme has taken on mostly *syrah* and some *braucol*, with which he is making what many consider to be the finest red wine in Gaillac. Incontestably ***B. Some may say that it is not typically gaillac, and it is true that the wine manages to reflect something of the Rhône Valley as well as an elegance reminiscent of Bordeaux; but the quality is unmistakeable as well as irresistible. Jérôme makes it in oaked (C) and unoaked versions, and which you prefer is a matter of taste. To taste and buy, go to Les Croix des Marchands at Montans on the south bank. There are no tasting facilities at the Palvié vineyard itself.

■ DOMAINE DE SALMES
Jean-Paul Pezet
81150 Bernac
Tel: 05-63-55-42-53 Fax: 05-63-53-10-26

Rather remotely situated at the eastern end of the *coteaux*, this domaine has a long and distinguished history. The wine-making is traditional, based on the local grapes and a great deal of skill born of experience. One of Pezet's grandfathers was called Ligoury, and he has bequeathed his name to a delicious *braucol*-based **red wine** (**A), which Pezet makes only in good years. He gives it a very gentle oaking, which is hardly perceptible but no doubt adds to the character and complexity of the wine. Blackcurrants and peppers are featured, as they are in another red, a **blend** of *braucol* and *duras* (**A), deep and dense in appearance, with a flowery and fruity nose. It ages well. Pezet has also just brought on stream a *prunelard* varietal, available from 2009 onwards. The grape seems to be fashionable all of a sudden.

Among the whites, his *doux* are outstanding; first a pure **mauzac** (*A), which combines an immediate fruitiness with a little acidity, and then a rather richer blend of *muscadelle* and *len de l'el* called **Douceur d'Automne** (***B), which manages also to achieve a certain finesse and elegance. The **perlé**

(**A), a blend of *len de l'el*, *mauzac* and *sauvignon* in equal quantities, is one of the best examples of this style of wine. Low-brow it may be, but it sells well.

▪ DOMAINE DE LA TRONQUE

Claude Leduc

81140 Castelnau-de-Montmiral

Tel: 05-63-33-18-87 Fax: 05-63-33-22-18

Email: leduc.claude@wanadoo.fr

www.domainedelatronque.com

Claude must have the strictest organic principles of anyone I know. Even during a year when disease threatened to kill the whole of his red wine crop—and it did—Claude refused to have recourse to unacceptable chemical sprays. You cannot help admiring such steadfastness, but it must have made a huge hole in his finances, not only for that year but until he could replace the dead vines with others mature enough to yield grapes for quality wine-making.

Claude was one of the first to pioneer the revival of the *méthode gaillacoise,* and his **Perle d'Antan** (***B) is still one of the best versions. Most people reserve this wine for the end of a meal to accompany desserts, but it is unbeatable as an aperitif, or indeed as a refresher at any time of the day.

▪ CHÂTEAU LECUSSE

Mogens Olesen

Broze, 81600 Gaillac

Tel: 05-63-33-90-09

Fax: 05-63-33-94-36

Email: post@chateaulecusse.com

www.chateaulecusse.com

This talented Dane also has a plantation of truffle oaks and supplies roses to the Queen of Denmark. The wine is pretty good too. It shows his pursuit of optimum quality. Note especially his medal-winning 100% *braucol* **red** (**A), and a beautifully balanced **doux** (**B). He is something of a *muscadelle* specialist, which unusually contributes as much as 35% towards his perlé. This property is on the rise.

OTHER GOOD WINEMAKERS ON THE COTEAUX DE GAILLAC

▪ MAS DE DOAT

Henri Plageoles

81600 Senouillac

Tel: 05-63-41-78-78 Fax: 05-63-81-51-29

and

▪ CHÂTEAU RAYNAL

Nelly and Patrick Raynal

81140 Senouillac

Tel: 05-63-41-70-02 Fax: 05-63-81-51-29

Two properties twinned for marketing purposes, where they make real, honest country red gaillac without frills. At Raynal there is also a lovely little museum of wine and other artefacts.

▪ DOMAINE FERRET

Bernard and Nathalie Ferret

Mauriac, 81600 Senouillac

Tel and fax: 05-63-41-51-94

The *caveau* is just near the Château de Mauriac. Note particularly a very clean pure dry *sauvignon* and some well-matured older reds.

▪ CHÂTEAU DES HOURTETS

Edouard and Anne Kabakian

Laborie, 81600 Gaillac

Tel: 05-63-33-19-15 Fax: 05-63-33-20-49

Their *mauzac* and *len de l'el* have a wonderful exposure towards the sun, and make a dry white wine which is their excellent speciality. Traditional grapes only here.

■ DOMAINE DE MATENS

Martine Lecomte

81600 Gaillac

Tel: 05-63-57-43-96 Fax: 05-63-57-43-82

www.matens.free.fr/vin

A biological vineyard whose reds age beautifully, sometimes acquiring a Rhonish character. Note
a pure *duras* and another AOC red called **Combe aux
Acacias** (**B).

■ CHÂTEAU MIRAMOND

Pascal Trouche

Mas de Graves, 81600 Gaillac

Tel: 05-63-57-14-86 Fax: 05-63-57-63-44

Email: pascal.trouche@wanadoo.fr

Best for his prize-winning sweet whites,
although the whole range is enjoyable.

■ CDG DOMAINE DU MOULIN

Nicolas and Jean Paul Hirissou

Chemin de Bastié, 81600 Gaillac

Tel: 05-63-57-20-52 Fax: 05-63-57-66-67

Email: domainedumoulin@libertysurf.fr

www.hirissou.com

The *cave*, set in the hillside to the north of
Gaillac town, is unmissable. The family have vineyards on both sides of the river and make a good
commercial range of wines of all styles.

■ CDG DOMAINE DES TERRISSES

La Famille Cazottes

81600 Gaillac

Tel: 05-63-57-16-80 Fax: 05-63-41-05-87

Email: domaine.des.terrisses@wanadoo.fr

www.domainedesterrisses.com

Long-established over seven generations, this
domaine specializes in wines which are aromatic,
typical of the appellation, and show real class
(**A/B). Note especially the *méthode gaillacoise*
range.

■ CHÂTEAU DE SALETTES

Roger le Net

81140 Cahuzac-sur-Vère

Tel: 05-63-33-60-60 Fax: 05-63-33-60-61

Email: salettes@chateaudesalettes.com

www.chateaudesalettes.com

A swanky hotel and restaurant with a vineyard
attached, where the owners of Domaine Lacroux
make a range of rather modern style wines of which
the *doux* is the most interesting.

■ CHÂTEAU MOUSSENS

Alain Monestié

Moussens, 81150 Cestayrols

Tel: 05-63-56-86-60 Fax: 05-63-56-86-65

www.chateaumoussens.com

The dry white and the *primeur* wines are the
ones to note here, but the traditional red is pretty
good too.

■ DOMAINE DE CANTOPERLIC

Ursula and Sune Sloge

Cantoperlic, 81600 Gaillac

Tel: 05-63-57-25-56 Fax: 05-63-57-58-91

Email: cantoperlic@telia.com

www.cantoperlic.com

The domaine's name means 'song of the par-
tridge', and today the best wine, a fresh peppery
and spicy red, is called Covée Rouge (*covée* meaning
'covey'). Formerly owned by English couple Alex and
Claire Taylor, it became well loved by anglophiles in
the neighbourhood for its Cuvée Claire, a bone-dry
mousseux by the *méthode traditionelle*.

GROWERS ON THE COTEAUX DE LISLE

The road west from Gaillac to Montauban serves as a dividing line between the two banks of the *coteaux*. Those round Lisle-sur-Tarn, which overlook the river as far as Rabastens, are particularly suited to the *muscadelle* grape.

◼ DOMAINE DE BORIE-VIEILLE

Pascale Roc-Fonvieille
Saint Salvy, 81310 Lisle-sur-Tarn
Tel: 05-63-40-47-46 Fax: 05-63-40-31-93
Mobile: 06-81-48-97-61
Email: borie-vieille.pascale@wanadoo.fr

The family bought this estate of 60 hectares, of which 25 are under vine, as long ago as 1910. The vines are on a mix of poor sand and gravel, facing south down the river. This *terroir* suits Pascale's dry *muscadelle*, **Domaine de la Belle** (***A), to perfection. This is their best wine, even if it has to be marketed as a *vin de pays*. Pascale also makes a **chardonnay** (*A)—good, but not in the same league as the *muscadelle*, which is a regular prize-winner. A rosé, two reds and a *doux* complete the range.

◼ DOMAINE DE LONG-PECH

Christian Bastide
La Peyrière, 81310 Lisle-sur-Tarn
Tel: 05-63-33-37-22 Fax: 05-63-40-42-06
Email: dom.longpech@wanadoo.fr
www.domaine-de-long-pech.com

This property takes some finding, lost as it is in the hills behind Lisle. Perseverance pays, however, because the **Doux** (**B) is particularly fine, outstanding among a range of consistent quality.

◼ DOMAINE DE SARRABELLE

Laurent and Fabien Caussé
Les Fortis, 81310 Lisle-sur-Tarn
Tel: 05-63-40-47-78 Fax: 05-63-81-49-36
Mobile: 06-63-08-19-18
Email: fabien@sarrabelle.com
www.sarrabelle.com

Wine has been made here for seven generations, but only the present one has taken it seriously. From 37 hectares the Caussés make a large range of wines of consistently good quality, one or two of them quite original. The domaine includes a ruined Cathar chapel and a spring said to have been a lovers' rendezvous in distant history. The legend is perpetuated in the very sweet **Esprit de la Source** (**D), which seems loaded with currants and sultanas, sweet spices such as cinnamon and cloves too. There is just enough acidity to keep the wine floating.

At the other end of the scale, the Caussés make a range of varietals which they put into hideous bottles for the transatlantic market. More conventionally packaged here are a delicious **chardonnay vin de pays** (*A) and a **sauvignon** (*A) which manages a delicate balance between gooseberries and *gras*. Even better than these is a pure **mauzac** (**B), a blend of the white and pink varieties, which has rich fruit and a long finish. A traditional **rouge** (**A) has an unusual leathery nose in some years. It is well made, so that even in the hot year of 2003 there was no evidence of grilling of the grapes, partly because there is a lot of sand in the soil which forces the vines down deep into the earth to find moisture. Varietal reds include a delightful **Saint-André** (**B), a pure *braucol*, deeper in flavour but less redcurranty than many; and a gently oaked **syrah** (**A), reminiscent of Bezios's Palvié. If the Esprit de la Source is too sweet for you, try the delicious **Doux** (**A), everything a *moëlleux* should be. Some *muscadelle* gives wonderful perfume to blend with the acidity of the *mauzac*.

OTHER GOOD GROWERS ROUND LISLE

▇ DOMAINE DE MAZOU

Jean-Marc Boyals

81310 Lisle-sur-Tarn

Tel: 05-63-33-37-80/ 05-63-40-47-47

Fax: 05-63-40-46-93

Email: domainedemazou@wanadoo.fr

www.mazou.com

This long-established domaine has a good following in local restaurants. The reds are always reliable and they accompany the local cuisine well. Good *vrac* wines here too.

▇ CHÂTEAU DE SAURS

Marie-Paule Burrus

81310 Lisle-sur-Tarn

Tel and fax: 05-63-57-09-79

Email: info@chateau-de-saurs.com

www.chateau-de-saurs.com

The old cellars at this beautiful property are worth a visit on their own account, but the wines are of good quality too, especially the reds. Note the **Cuvée Elévier** (**B), which is quite southern in style.

▇ L'ENCLOS DES BRAVES

Chantal and Nicolas le Brun

D 18, route de Saurs, Vertus

81800 Rabastens

Mobile: 06-08-30-27-81

Email: lebrun.Nicolas@cegetel.net

Nicolas is a trained oenologue with wide-ranging experience, and it shows in the wines, which often owe more to the *chais* than the vineyard. Nevertheless, his wines are well made. Try his **L'Enclos Braucol** (**B) with its cassis and green pepper flavours, raised in three-year-old barrels.

GROWERS ON THE SOUTH (LEFT) BANK OF THE TARN

▇ DOMAINE DE GINESTE

Armelle and Frédéric Delmotte

Sigolène and Emmanuel Mourgeais

Gineste, 81600 Técou

Tel: 05-63-33-03-18 Fax: 05-63-81-52-65

Email: domainedegineste@wanadoo.fr

www.domainedegineste.com

Mourgeais (who comes from Beaujolais, having trained in Bordeaux) and Delmotte are brothers-in-law. They have 23 hectares of clay and chalky terraces, covered with *graves*, on the left bank of the Tarn, including four hectares which have just come into production. They took over the property in 2000.

Mourgeais has since reduced the range of wines drastically from 14 to six, sacrificing along the way the delicious *méthode gaillacoise,* which he finds hard to sell, despite an apparent fashion for the style. As the vines fall, to be replanted, he will aim for much greater density, up to 6000 to the hectare, and will concentrate on the traditional grapes: *braucol* and *duras* for the reds and *mauzac* and *len de l'el* for the whites. He tends towards organic production but has not signed up formally.

The dry white **Domaine de Gineste** (**B) is made from hand-picked grapes given a *macération pelliculaire* and raised in oak barrels from Bordeaux which have already been used once. The blend of *sauvignon*, *mauzac* and *len de l'el* is carefully assembled so that no one *cépage* dominates. The sweet **Cuvée Blonde** (**B) is 100% *len de l'el* and yields only 15 hl/ha. Residual sugar ranges from 110 to 125 g/l. The result is *moëlleux* rather than *liquoreux*. There is, however, a real *liquoreux* **La Coulée d'Or** (***D), from 100% *chardonnay* and thus 'demoted' to *vin de pays* status; the grapes are left on perforated trays (*claies*) until the middle of December before being pressed and vinified. The yield is a mere 8 hl/ha. Only 2000 50-centilitre bottles or so are made each year.

The reds, though good, are not on quite the same level. **Cuvée Pourpre** (*B), from *duras* and *syrah,* shows the spices and loads of red fruit one would expect from such a blend. The must gets three or four weeks *cuvaison,* and the wine is neither filtered nor fined. The bigger red, **Grande Cuvée** (*B), is atypically from *cabernet sauvignon*, *merlot* and *braucol*, and, after the grapes have been destalked, spends 25 to 30 days in vats at 32 degrees for maximum extraction, then 15 months in barrels after the malolactic fermentation is finished. Again there is no filtration or fining. This wine has plenty of coffee and cocoa on the nose, as well as red and black fruits. Mourgeais says this New World style will keep 10 years.

◾ LE HAUT DES VERGNADES

Jean-Philippe Blanc
Route de Cadalen, 81600 Gaillac
Tel: 05-63-33-02-02 / 05-63-33-01-70
Fax: 05-63-81-54-76

There is nothing New World about the wines here. It would be difficult to imagine a more resolutely typical gaillac range, full, sturdy, a touch rustic but very satisfying. The family has been growing grapes here since 1860 from their 33 hectares of vines. The wines are always enjoyable.

The one red, called **Cuvée Empeyre** (**A), wins medals for its smooth texture but also for the flavourful punch it packs. It is pure *braucol* and a fine expression of that grape when grown on gravelly soil. The good whites get *A: the dry from **len de l'el** with 'a few *sauvignon* tears'; the sweet, wholly from late-picked **len de l'el**; a charming *syrah*-based rosé; and two sparklers, one dry, the other *demi-sec*, again both from *len de l'el*.

This is a no-frills domaine, and a wonderful value for the money.

◾ DOMAINE DE PIALENTOU

Jean and Kai Gervais
81600 Brens
Tel: 05-63-57-17-99 Fax: 05-63-57-20-51
Email: domaine.pialentou@wanadoo.fr
www.domainedepialentou.com

Jean was formerly a very senior executive with Seagrams before he moved from Spain to buy this well-known estate from Jean-Pierre Ailloud in 1998. There are 13 hectares, all in one uninterrupted parcel on west-facing ground 150 feet above the river Tarn, just 'a bridge away from Gaillac town', as Jean says. The soil is a mix of typically gravelly alluvial deposits with pebbles and clay.

The domaine has built on its previously high reputation to the point where it is producing some of the most interesting left-bank wines. There are two ranges: Nuances de Cocagne and the more ambitious usually oak-aged Les Gentilles Pierres. Of the two whites, the **Nuances Blanc Sec** (**A) is half *mauzac*, half *sauvignon,* and has the characteristic stamp of apples and grapefruit; to my mind it is a better blend than the **Gentilles Pierres Blanc Sec** (*A), where the *sauvignon* content is raised to two-thirds. In the Nuances range, a *syrah*-based **rosé** (*A) is surprisingly strong and deep-coloured.

The **Nuances Rouge** (**A) is a delightfully fresh and light summer red from a blend of the three basic Gaillac grapes, spicy and refreshing, while the **Gentilles Pierres** version (*A), where the *cabernet* and *merlot* are majority grapes, is less typical but attractive all the same. There are oaked and unoaked versions.

Although red wines dominate the production here, there is a lovely sweet **mauzac** (**B), for which the grapes are hand-picked at the end of October and fermented and aged in new barrels. Only a few hundred bottles are made each year.

To round off the range, Pierrentou is the name given to a light and fruity red *vin de pays*.

■ **DOMAINE D'EN SEGUR**

Pierre Fabre

81500 Lavaur

Tel: 05-63-58-09-45 Fax: 05-63-58-65-03

Email: ensegur@wanadoo.fr

www.ensegur.com

This domaine is way outside the Gaillac AOC area, and almost on the limit of the Côtes du Tarn boundary, being just a few kilometres down the river Agout from Lavaur.

Pierre Fabre is a local industrialist who bought this property in 1989 with the idea of replanting it entirely with a mix of international grape varieties (*merlot*, *sauvignon*, *gamay*, the two *cabernets* etc.) and also the local *braucol* and *duras,* as well as *syrah,* which falls into both categories. Though he is denied the right to produce AOC wines, the attention devoted to the vines in the vineyard and the care which goes into the state-of-the-art vinifica-tion often exceed those bestowed by more illustrious producers.

Particularly to be admired are a dry **sauvignon** (**A) aged for six months on its lees; a lively *chardonnay* called **Cuvée Madeleine** (**A), which is given some oak-ageing; **Le Rouge** (**A), a fruity blend of the local grapes (including *gamay*); and an interesting off-dry white called **Sauvignon d'Or** (**B), light, fresh and fruity, admirable as an aperitif.

Off the beaten track, this property is well worth the trouble of seeking out.

OTHER GOOD LEFT BANK
AOC GROWERS

◼ DOMAINE DES ARDURELS
Sébastien Cabal
81150 Lagrave
Tel and fax: 05-63-41-74-79
Email: cabalseb@aol.com

The red **Cuvée Alby** (*A) adds *duras* to *braucol* and *syrah* to make a light peppery red, while the **Muscadelle Doux** (*B) is a worthy rival to Borie-Vieille's.

◼ LA CROIX DES MARCHANDS
La Famille Bézios
81600 Montans
Tel: 05-63-57-19-71
Email: croixdesmarchands@wanadoo.fr
www.croix-des-marchands-81.com/

◼ TERROIR DE LAGRAVE
Arnaud, Blatché, Bounes, Calmet and Lagasse
81150 Lagrave
Tel: 05-63-81-52-20 Fax: 05-63-56-09-16

A partnership of growers, producing a range of wines from their combined production. The red **Sigolène** (**A), light but stylish, and the unoaked **doux** (*B) stand out.

◼ CHÂTEAU TOUNY-LES-ROSES
Marc Lavite
81150 Lagrave
Tel: 05-63-57-90-90 Fax: 05-63-57-90-91
Email: chateau@tounylesroses.fr
www.tounylesroses.fr

A very pretty venue for receptions and weddings, where they also make very good wines. The **Cuvée du Poète** (**B) is raised in barrels; there is also a white from *muscadelle* and a rosé to complete the range.

WHERE TO TASTE A GOOD RANGE
OF GAILLAC WINES

LA MAISON DES VINS
Abbaye Saint-Michel
81600 Gaillac
Tel: 05-63-49-48-98 Fax: 05-63-57-70-61
Email: civg@vins-gaillac.com
www.vins-gaillac.com
Open from 7 a.m. to 7 p.m.

AU CHAI ROLLAND
Adjoining restaurant La Table du Sommelier
34 place Thiers, 81600 Gaillac
Tel: 05-63-57-01-37 Fax: 05-63-57-48-08
Email: rolland.et.fils@wanadoo.fr
Open Monday through Friday.

CAVE CONFIDENCES DU TERROIR
1 place Sainte-Cécile, 81000 Albi
Tel and fax: 05-63-54-05-78
Open from 7 a.m. to 7 p.m., except Sunday afternoon.

FRONTON AND THE WINES OF THE TOULOUSAIN

FRONTON

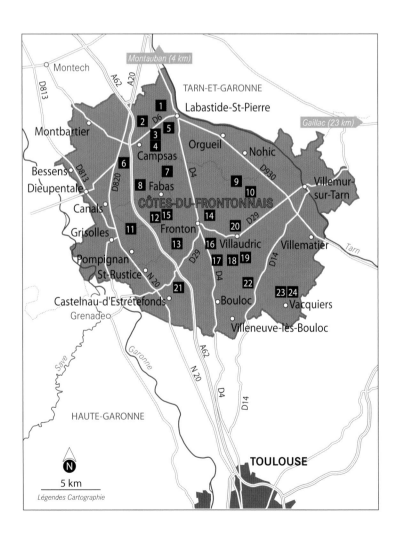

Montech

D813

A62 A20

Montauban (4 km)

TARN-ET-GARONNE

1
2 D6
3
5

Labastide-St-Pierre

Gaillac (23 km)

Montbartier

4

Orgueil

Nohic

Campsas

D4

D930

6

Bessens

D813

D820

7

Villemur-
sur-Tarn

Dieupentale

8 Fabas

9

10

Canals

CÔTES-DU-FRONTONNAIS

12 **15**

14

Grisolles

11

Fronton

20 D29

Tarn

13

16 Villaudric

Villematier

Pompignan

17 **18** **19**

D14

St-Rustice

N 20

D29

22

21

D4

23 **24**

Castelnau-d'Estrétefonds

Bouloc

Vacquiers

Grenade

Save

Garonne

A62

Villeneuve-lès-Bouloc

N 20

D4

D14

HAUTE-GARONNE

N

5 km

Légendes Cartographie

TOULOUSE

AREA OF AOC: selected parcels covering 2000 hectares in the communes of Bessens, Bouloc, Campsas, Canals, Castelnau-d'Estrefonds, Dieupentale, Fabas, Fronton, Grisolles, Labastide-Saint-Pierre, Montbartier, Nohic, Orgueil, Pompignan, Saint-Rustice, Vacquiers, Villaudric, Villematier, Villemur-sur-Tarn and Villeneuve-lès-Bouloc.

Red and rosé wines only.

PRINCIPAL GRAPE VARIETY: négrette (which must represent between 50% and 70% of a grower's vineyard).

COMPLEMENTARY GRAPE VARIETIES: gamay, mérille, cinsault and mauzac. Together or singly: max. 15%, reducing to 10% by 2012 and to 5% by 2019. Mauzac to be phased out altogether by 2012.

Côt, fer servadou and syrah, each subject to a maximum of 25%.

Cabernet franc and cabernet sauvignon, singly or together subject to a maximum of 25%.

All wines must be a blend of three varieties, of which négrette must be one.

Above percentages relate to the mix of grapes in a grower's vineyard, not to any assemblage in bottle.

PRUNING: en gobelet, guyot simple or double, cordon royat.

MAXIMUM NUMBER OF EYES: 10, whatever growth type.

MAXIMUM YIELD: 50 hl/ha.

ANNUAL PRODUCTION: 100,000 hectolitres.

PLANTING DENSITY: 4000 plants per hectare, with transitional relief to 2012.

THE KNIGHTS OF SAINT JOHN OF JERUSALEM

The river Tarn, which downstream from Gaillac seemed to be heading straight for Toulouse, makes an abrupt right turn and flows in the direction of Montauban. On the left bank, there rise three successive terraces, eroded by the river and top-dressed by the alluvial deposits which it washed down on its way from the Cévennes. Here are the vineyards of Fronton and Villaudric, today united under the common banner of AOC Fronton. The terraces are not always easily discernible, the impression often being that of a rather flat plateau, somewhat dull and feature-less in comparison with other vineyards in the South-West. There is nothing dull about the wines, however.

Like Gaillac, Fronton can claim a history going back to Roman times. The nearby city of Montauban had been the western outpost of the Romans in the days before they went on to conquer the rest of Gaul under Julius Caesar. The remains of elaborate villas, once occupied by Roman officials or by Gauls who had adopted the Roman way of life, attest to the infusion of civilization into a once barbarous region, and with it the cultivation of the vine. One such villa, unearthed in 1834 near the village of Saint-Rustice, had particularly fine mosaics, now housed in the Museum of Toulouse.

The fall of Rome was followed by a long period of chaos. Despite the rise of the Christian church, the local people existed in a cultural vacuum, which successive invasions of Visigoths and Saracens did nothing but perpetuate. The grandees made a point of boasting that they could neither read nor write. In a mood of desperate fatalism, many people believed that the world would come to an end after the first millennium, but when the year 1000 passed without disaster, faith and a greater spirit of optimism revived and large estates found their way by donation or legacy into the hands of the Church, often by way of thanks to God for having averted, or at least delayed, Armageddon. At about the same time, the Knights of Saint John came to the area of Fronton and started raising funds to support their charitable activi-ties, the giving of food, shelter and protection to pilgrims on their way to and from the Holy Land. In this way they became the owners of churches, abbeys and appurtenant estates, including the vineyards. As the years went by, the knights became lords of the whole region. They are not to be confused, as they often are, with the Knights Templar, an order of military rather than ministering monks.

THE *NÉGRETTE* GRAPE

Legend has it that the knights brought with them from their base in Cyprus a grape called *mavro* ('black' in Greek), which is said over the years to have acquired the name *négrette* on account of its very dark skin and juice. This pretty story certainly fits both the idea of the Order's exclusive ownership of the vineyards, and also the fact that today the grape is known practically nowhere outside the area of Fronton. It also makes good copy for the Fronton PR machine and those who write publicity material for today's wine-makers. However, experts now prefer the view that *négrette* is a member of the *côt* family, which includes the *auxerrois* of Cahors and the *tannat* of Madiran, and that all these varieties originated in the Quercy region of South-West France, having been brought there from Spain during the Middle Ages. Robert Plageoles believes that *négrette* first flourished in Gaillac, who 'lent' it to Fronton. It is still an authorized but unused grape in Gaillac.

Whatever the historical truth, *négrette* has been the mainstay of Fronton wines for many hundreds of years, and today the growers understand well that they need the grape to distinguish their wines from others in the South-West. The fruit is perfectly spherical. Despite its dark colour, it makes a wine which is subtle, aromatic, often suggesting violets and wildflowers, round, fruity and generous, sometimes with notes of spice and liquorice. But the grape has its problems too: it sometimes lacks acidity, and its wine does not age well; it has a thin skin and is liable to mildew and rot in a rainy year. For these reasons, growers now usually blend it with other grapes which counteract or at least cover up these deficiencies: the more austere *cabernets*, the hefty *côt* and structure-giving *syrah*. The proportions in which these other grapes are grown depend very largely on the style of each grower and the kind of wine which he wants to make. However, under the rules of the appellation, neither of the *cabernets*, nor the *syrah* nor *gamay,* should constitute more than 25% of any AOC *assemblage*, while *côt* is limited to 10%. *Négrette* must form between 50% and 70% of the *encépagement* in a grower's vineyard.

Bunches of *négrette* are small and rather oval in shape, and the grapes pack themselves tightly together. They, too, are small. The fruit ripens fairly early compared with other varieties, and the harvest normally takes place about the middle of September. The character of the wine is generally lighter than that of some other wines of the South-West, and thus fronton has established a particular niche in the local bars and restaurants, where the wine is sometimes called 'the Beaujolais of Toulouse'.

For the rosés, which represent 20% of the total fronton output, the *gamay* is often introduced for its fruit and summery freshness. White fronton does not exist as such, although a few growers make white wines as *vins de pays*, using grapes from neighbouring regions, *mauzac* for example.

THE FRONTON VINEYARD

The vines extend over 2400 hectares, covering an area roughly the shape of a rugby ball, lying between the river Tarn to the north-east and the Canal du Midi to the south-west; from the village of Labastide-Saint-Pierre close to Montauban in the north to Bouloc near Toulouse in the south; and from Villematier in the east to Montbartier in the west.

There used to be a fierce rivalry between the growers in Villaudric and those in Fronton, both towns at the heart of the modern vineyard. Until 1975, there were indeed two separate areas of VDQS, then combined to make Côtes du Frontonnais, nowadays more simply Fronton AOC. The merger was not to the taste of everyone. The former Villaudric *Coopérative*, since closed, defected to Gaillac as a haven for disaffected growers, whose grapes then went to the Rabastens *cave*. To satisfy the pride of the two camps, each is allowed to add the name Fronton or Villaudric as appropriate to the AOC on the label, and Villaudric growers sometimes still present their wines in Burgundy-shaped bottles to distinguish them from the Bordeaux-type bottles used by the *Frontonnais*. Some say that the wines of Villaudric have more finesse and body than those of Fronton itself, which according to others are said to be fruitier and more alcoholic. One would only upset both sides by suggesting that the distinctions are marginal, deriving perhaps from the individual *terroir* of each grower and his mix of grape varieties.

THE FRONTON *TERROIR*

A subsoil of iron and quartz is common to the whole area and gives the wine through the roots of the vine its fullness and bouquet as well sometimes as an agreeable suggestion of bitter almonds on the palate. *Boulbènes* is a word without equivalent in English, being local to Toulouse in origin. It signifies a mixture of soft soil, sometimes sandy, with small pebbles and crushed quartz. This type of terrain is also common to all Fronton. But there are local differences. In the south, there is a band of red soil called *rouget*, mixed with the *boulbènes* and small pebbles. Towards the east the stones are larger, reminiscent of the large pebbles to be found in the southern Rhône. As you go further north the soil becomes more sandy and less stoney, but the stones of whatever size are still everywhere. It is hardly surprising that little but the vine grows successfully in the area.

LA CAVE COOPÉRATIVE DE FRONTON

Following the grant of VDQS status to Villaudric in 1945 and just ahead of a similar grant for Fronton two years later, the *cave* at Fronton was founded in 1946. One hundred seventy growers joined, and the first vintage produced 11,200 hectolitres. Since then production has quadrupled, and the *cave* has plenty of space for even more expansion. Today it produces roughly half the output of the appellation. It also produces large quantities of *vins de pays*, often from grape varieties which are no longer permitted in the AOC wines, such as *prunelard*, *mérille* and sometimes *fer servadou*. The *cave* was very largely responsible for putting Fronton on the map because, even as late as 1983, there were a mere dozen independent growers bottling and marketing their own wines. Today there are more than 50.

PRODUCERS OF FRONTON

▉ LA CAVE COOPÉRATIVE DE FRONTON

Avenue des Vignerons

31620 Fronton

Tel: 05-62-79-97-79

Email: export@vins-fronton.com

www.vins-fronton.com

The *Cave* has increased its standards to match the competition from the independents. Its full range of red and rosé wines sold under the AOC (*A) are remarkably good value and give a general overview of what to expect from the Fronton style. For instance, a wine called **Cour des Consuls** (**A) has an attractive bouquet of cherry jam, a bit cahors-like, while the taste is spicy with sweet ripe fruit and plenty of sunshine. The *Cave* makes wines from seven or so single domaines, some of which are given the full treatment in oak barrels. Of its *vins de pays*, the most interesting is a pure **négrette** (*A), which gives a visitor the chance to assess the character of that grape when not blended with others.

RECOMMENDED INDEPENDENT GROWERS

▉ CHÂTEAU BAUDARE

Claude and David Vigouroux

82370 Labastide-Saint-Pierre

Tel: 05-63-30-51-33 Fax: 05-63-64-07-24

Email: david@chateaubaudare.com

vigouroux@aol.com

www.chateaubaudare.com

Claude, David's father, inherited just one hectare from his own father, who, like his ancestors, had been making rather indifferent wine for some years. Claude dug up the five hectares of rather feeble fruit trees on the estate and started building the present vineyard, which today extends to 25 hectares. The family is now monocultural except that they have a small plantation of sunflowers by a stream where the soil is too damp for vines. Claude's son David has largely taken over the vineyard. He, like so many of the younger generation, is a trained oenologist and a dab hand at marketing. He has been especially successful in exporting to the Far East.

The vineyard is in one unit, which explains the homogeneity of the wines. The vines themselves enjoy rather more clay than is true of some other Fronton estates. It gives a certain richness and ageing potential to the wine.

The **sauvignon vin de pays** (*A) makes a good kir and is attractive on its own, without being remarkable. The **rosé** (***A), one of the best in an appellation which is strong on pink wines, is another matter, a multi-medal winner, quite full and

in some years suggesting wild strawberries on the palate. There are no fewer than four reds: first, the **Tradition** (**A), notable for its perfume of violets; the wine from **Vieilles Vignes** (***A) is spicier and blackcurranty, an ideal partner for a good entrecôte steak; the **Cuvée Prestige** (***A) is aged in old *foudres*, with no taste of wood but natural notes of vanilla and a gorgeous limpid appearance. The **Secret des Anges** (B) is a secret perhaps best kept in heaven; for all but the most intrepid oak-fanciers, it is over the top and not in any way characteristic of the appellation.

Finally, there is a real *foie gras* wine from the **sémillon** (**A) grape: a *moëlleux* of the old-fashioned kind, sadly out of fashion, light, very fruity and even with a hint of the petrol on the nose so sought after in Alsace. This domaine, always near the top of the Fronton ladder, continues to improve.

▓ CHÂTEAU BELLEVUE LA FORÊT
Philip Grant
Avenue de Grisolles, 31620 Fronton
Tel: 05-34-27-91-91 Fax: 05-61-82-39-70
Email: contact@chateaubellevuelaforet.com
www.chateaubellevuelaforet.com

Not only the largest vineyard in Fronton but the second largest in the South-West, this estate is by far the biggest producer of Fronton after the *coopérative*. It is not surprising, therefore, that the wines are so well known. The domaine was created and developed during the 1970's by Patrick Germain. He started with 25 hectares, which he bought just about the time AOC was granted, abandoning his earlier ideas of making wine in Algeria and Morocco. There was not even a house, let alone a cellar, to go with his Fronton purchase. While the vines were growing to maturity, Patrick, with the aid of the famous pioneer-oenologist the late Emile Peynaud, built his magnificent *chais,* and in 1990 he added some underground storage space for his oak barrels. At the same time, his daughter Diane joined him in partnership, and today she is respon-

sible for just about everything following the recent sale of the property to Irishman Peter Grant.

The vineyard extends to 112 hectares, of which 60 are given over to the *négrette* grape, 17 to *cabernet franc*, 12 to *cabernet sauvignon*, 16 to *syrah* and 7 to *gamay*. This extensive estate represents about 5% of all the fronton production. There are no white grapes. The vines are all trained on wire and pruned using the method known as *guyot simple*, which consists of allowing only one main leader with a maximum of eight or so eyes. Vinification is traditional save that the must is treated to *microbullage* at the end of each fermentation.

Diane is particularly keen on her rosés, which represent a quarter of Patrick's production. She makes two. One, from pure *négrette,* is called **Allégresse** (*B) and is flowery and very distinctive, but the traditional version, called simply **Le Rosé** (**A), which has 37% *syrah* and 13% *gamay*, is more vinous and rather bigger.

Of the reds, the **Rouge Classique** (**A), made from a cocktail of the authorized grapes, is good middle-of-the-road fronton. The **Cuvée d'Or** (*A) can be darker and fruitier, though sometimes lighter in body. Perhaps the most interesting wine is the pure *négrette* called **Ce Vin** (**A), which Patrick originally created for the now retired Gascon chef André Daguin to accompany the latter's fine cooking at his hotel-restaurant in Auch. The grapes come from two different *terroirs*, the first very stoney, producing grapes which require a relatively high vinification temperature, the other more sandy and vinified at a lower temperature to bring out the fruit, suppleness and finesse of the wine. This can have quite a kick on the finish and is not lacking in acidity and tannins, sometimes absent from pure *négrette* wines. Germain also makes two oaked wines, the better known of which is called **Optimum** (*B), much admired by the guides and press, but which one would be hard put to identify as fronton in a blind tasting.

▌CHÂTEAU BOUJAC

Michelle and Philippe Selle
Chemin de Boujac, 82370 Campsas
Tel: 05-63-30-17-79 Fax: 05-63-30-19-12
Email: selle.philippe@wanadoo.fr
http://perso.wanadoo.fr/chateau-boujac

Philippe is the nephew of the owners of the perhaps better-known Château Bouissel. One hopes that he will not be embarrassed, nor his uncle and aunt offended, by my view that the nephew is making the better wines. Philippe brings to his vines and his *terroir* an unusual passion and a sense of being part of a perpetual evolution. 'A respect for the past is reflected in the task of the present and projects forward into the future', he says. *Vignerons* are sometimes given to this kind of flowery philosophizing, and his wines make the point better than Philippe does.

The **Tradition** (*A) is half *négrette* and has a good fruity attack and good volume on the palate. There is a fairly gently oaked wine called **Éole** (*B), in which the wood is very discreet, but the best of the three reds is the **Cuvée Alexanne** (**A/B), which is given a longer maceration than the Tradition and is altogether richer and more substantial.

▌CHÂTEAU CAHUZAC

Claude Ferran
Les Peyronnets, 82170 Fabas
Tel: 05-63-64-10-18 Fax: 05-63-67-36-97
Email: chateau.cahuzac@wanadoo.fr

Claude claims that his is the oldest wine-making family in Fronton, going back to 1776. In the intervening time they have built a vineyard from a nucleus of just a few rows of vines into a substantial holding of 43 hectares, a long way off Bellevue-la-Forêt, but still big by local standards. The family took advantage of the calamitous frosts of 1956 to improve the *encépagement* of the property, preparing the way for the high standards of viticulture and wine-making for which Cahuzac is now well known.

Claude had intended to make his career in forestry, but when Fronton received its award of AOC status, his father persuaded him to stick with the family vineyard, which suddenly seemed to hold out much more promise than had been the case in earlier years. To age and bottle their wines, Claude built an extra *chais*, which at the time seemed ambitiously large but today is needed to mature and store the ever-increasing proportion of wine bottled at the property.

Cahuzac was one of the first Fronton properties to attract international attention and continues to be one of the top estates. The *entrée de gamme* red, **Rouge Tradition** (**A), is as good an example of its genre as it is good value, with floral elegance and beautiful balance. The next red, **Authentique** (***A), can do with some cellaring, but it has a beautiful dark ruby colour, a generous bouquet of ripe fruit including prunes, as well as touches of tobacco and pepper. Long in the mouth, the wine develops with age suggestions of autumn leaves and fruits preserved in *eau-de-vie*. This is certainly among the top handful of all Fronton wines. I wish I could say the same about the **Fleuron de Guillaume**, much praised by those who only award prizes and medals to wines raised in new barrels, but . . . By now I need hardly say more.

Mention should also be made of a novelty **rosé** (**A), raised in wood but so that you would not really notice. It is full of body and summer fruits.

▌DOMAINE DE CALLORY

Guy Pérez
82370 Labastide-Saint-Pierre
Tel: 05-63-30-50-30 Fax: 05-63-30-16-17
Email: callory-perez@wanadoo.fr

The property belongs to Mme Pérez, née Montels, who works in the local pharmacy and whose father was mayor of the commune. The latter returned the family domaine to viticulture, his own father having temporarily given it up. Like Ferran, Montels *père* substantially replanted the family vineyard after the 1956 frosts. Today there are 27 hectares on the typical *boulbènes* of the region. Guy looks after them and the wine-making, while Madame deals with the business side of the domaine.

Tradition rules here, with longer-than-usual macerations. Because of the fairly flat landscape, picking by machine is almost universal, and Pérez prefers to avoid having to hire pickers. They are difficult to find and none too reliable. Madame recalls that when the first Gulf War broke out, and just at the moment when the annual pruning had to be done, two Moroccans left to fight, and she and Guy were left to do it all on their own.

Guy also finds that the modern machines are so selective and gentle that he does not need to destalk his grapes, so his wines have an extra element of authenticity. Forty percent or so of his output is a **vin de pays** (*A), a delicious blend of *cabernet sauvignon*, *syrah* and *merlot*, fresh, aromatic, supple and well balanced. He used to make only one red, but today he makes three appellation wines: first is **Saveurs** (*A), with a nostalgically rustic nose, plenty of flowers and fruit and good grip on the palate; then a **Fronton Rouge Tradition** (***A), so traditional as to defy the professional oak-fanciers not to like it. It is aged in enormous old *foudres*, one of which contains 402 hectolitres (as opposed to a mere 2.25 in a modern oak barrel); the wine is matured for 18 months before being bottled, but the wood is so old that it carries no oak flavours. Not that Guy fails to give a nod to slightly newer wood; his third red, **Cuvée Spéciale** (**B), is aged in casks which have already been used three or four times, and whose effect is therefore very gentle; it enhances the character of the wine rather than masking it. Guy produces wines which are full of body but which manage also to preserve the freshness of the *négrette* grape.

■ **CHÂTEAU CAZE**

Martine Rougevin-Bazille

45 Rue de la Négrette, 31620 Villaudric

Tel: 05-61-82-92-70 Fax: 05-61-82-09-95

Email: chateau.caze@libertysurf.fr

www.chateaucaze.com

It would be hard to think of a more appropriate name and address for a Fronton grower, hard too to find one who so consistently provides such delightful wines. 'Delightful' is the singularly appropriate word to describe the more elegant and subtle style sometimes attributed to the Villaudric reputation.

This domaine is not only in the centre of Villaudric village, but the front door opens directly off the street, giving immediately into the *chais*. Opposite you two huge barn doors open onto a courtyard at the back, where the grapes are brought at vintage time. On your right is the wine-making area, a huge building in the shape of a V, as if in tribute to the name of the village itself. This cellar is in the shape of the prow of a galleon, although the rows of old *foudres* which line its sides have never contained rum. Today they form an important part of the fascinating little museum of ancient artefacts with which Martine decorates her unique *chais*.

Martine's father was an officer in the French

Air Force, and left to his employees the business of wine-making. Martine herself decided she wanted to take a closer interest, though none of her four sisters showed any inclination to join her. She left home to study oenology in Montpellier and later Toulouse. Martine is, however, no slave to fashion: she makes wine in a traditional way.

The characteristic of the wines of this property is their ability to demonstrate to the utmost the character of the *négrette* grape. There is no concession here to the fashion for overextraction, just the determination to express the natural fruit of the principal grape variety. After the **rosé** (**A), surprisingly fresh and full of fruit, there are two reds, usually from 50% or more *négrette* with the balance made up from the two *cabernets* and *syrah*. The **Tradition** (***A) is exceptionally charming and elegant, one of the best interpretations of the fronton style. It is a lively thoroughbred wine, with lots of flowers, liquorice and gentle spices. Lip service is paid to barrel ageing in Martine's wine, which she makes from older vines and from grapes coming from her best parcels. The barrels are hand-me-downs from a friend in Pomerol, usually two or more years old. The wood adds just a touch of complexity and concentration, but you would not otherwise know that casks had been used. This is how to handle barrels. The wines age well, probably because of the *cabernet* stiffening, which provides tannins that the *négrette* on its own can lack.

■ CHÂTEAU CLAMENS

Jean-Michel and Béatrice Bègue
720 Chemin du Tapas
Quartier Caillol, 31620 Fronton
Tel: 05-61-82-45-32 Fax: 05-62-79-21-73
Mobile: 06-27-39-03-91 / 06-16-17-81-55
Email: chateauclamens@orange.fr
www.chateau-clamens.fr

These growers manage themselves to bottle and sell the whole of the production from their 22 hectares of grapes, which they grow on the upper two terraces of the Tarn. The two *cabernets* and *syrah* complement their statutory plantation of *négrette*. Their equipment is of the most modern, with thermoregulated stainless steel tanks to keep both reds and rosés at the right temperature during vinification. The wines here are noted for their fruit when young and their reflection of liquorice when mature.

They recommend their **Cuvée Julie Rosé** (*A), a blend of *syrah* for its colour and body and *négrette* for its fruit, a dry pink to go with grilled fish or charcuterie, or quite simply as an aperitif. The basic **Cuvée Sélection Rouge** (**A) has buckets of flowers and spice, while the **Cuvée Julie Rouge** (*A) is an unusual blend of 70% *syrah* and the rest *négrette*, all from old low-yielding vines and with a strong red and black fruit character. The *syrah* certainly asserts itself.

The Bègues are one of the handful of growers to make a pure *négrette* wine, which they call **Expression** (**A), showing plenty of blackcurrants and blackberries as well as the typical violets. The two oaked wines, **Cuvée Fût de Chêne** (B) and **Cuvée Caractère** (B), have only 10% and 20% *négrette* respectively and will no doubt please oak fanciers, who like their fronton to taste of anything but the local grape.

■ CHÂTEAU LA COLOMBIÈRE

Diane and Philippe Cauvin
31620 Villaudric
Tel: 05-61-82-44-05 Fax: 05-61-82-57-56
Email: vigneron@chateaulacolombiere.com
www.chateaulacolombiere.com

Madame Cauvin and her husband took over this property in 1999 from her father, M. le Baron de Driesen. He had been a fierce Villaudric partisan, even though he arrived in the region from Provence in 1983, after Fronton and Villaudric had merged. He came in search of some inexpensive vines, close to a town with good transport links, and anyway he already knew Toulouse well. La Colombière, an attractive house whose name no doubt derives from the prominent dovecote on the grounds, was once the home of the intendant of the Abbey of Dorade, formerly one of the *préceptories* (learning centres) of the Knights of Saint John. Alas, the abbey is now no more. There are 25 hectares with soil typical of the clay mixed with round quartz pebbles to be found in Villaudric. The owners think that Villaudric produces better-structured wines than Fronton itself, which is why M. le Baron saw no point in trying to produce a pure *négrette* wine. His daughter is more devoted to the local grape, from which she makes **Vinum** (**A), a round, fruity and well-balanced wine, smooth, aromatic and peppery, very *négrette*.

In his early days, the baron used to make at least some of his wine by *macération carbonique*, because the skins of the *négrette* are thin and the grape lends itself well to vinification whole. However, this process requires the grapes to be picked by hand so that they reach the tanks virgin and undamaged, which would be impossible if the bunches were picked by machine. The difficulty in finding people to harvest by hand has led the family to adopt machine picking, and so they no longer go in for *macération carbonique*.

Mme Cauvin does make her rosé in a way which is unorthodox, at least for Fronton. It is made by pressing the grapes, half *négrette* and half *gamay*, without leaving them on the skins at all. The wine is then vinified as for a white wine, a kind of *blanc de noirs*. She calls it her **vin gris** (**A), so pale is its colour. It took the authorities a long time to give it its *agrément* for this reason. Its great virtue is its long finish rather than its bouquet.

Just as original as her rosé is the way she names her red wines. Most growers give their wines more and more impressive names as you go up the ladder of excellence, or at least price. Not so this family. Her *entrée de gamme* is called **Réserve** (*A) and tends to be lightweight but easy and pleasant enough all the same, pretending to be nothing more. The 100% *négrette* **Coste Rouge** (**A) is a complex and rather hefty wine. The **Baron de D** (*A), from small-yielding old vines, a blend of half *négrette* and the rest a mix of the *cabernets*, has

much better body, attack and ripe jammy fruit as well as spice and pepper, while the modestly named **Tradition** (**B) is what the baron used to call *'le fleuron du château'*, and it is indeed the top wine here, with good fruit and elegance as well as real Fronton style and fine balance. It is from 80% *négrette* which is only partially destalked. The wine is aged for two years on its lees. Its spicy character suits strongly flavoured foods such as tagines and the gentler curries.

■ **CHÂTEAU CRANSAC**
SCEA Domaine de Cransac
Allée de Cransac, 31620 Fronton
Tel: 05-62-79-34-30 Fax: 05-62-79-34-37
www.chateaucransac.com

This is a real and very grand château, a survivor of fire and riots in its time and now bought by a supermarket king and lavishly equipped for making wine from its 35 hectares of vines. The owners, through a team of young enthusiasts headed by Jean Cristophe Briet, practice best vineyard principles, what the French call a *culture raisonnée*, as laid down in a charter called Terra Vitis. The wines are vinified in an unusual way in tanks called Ganimede, an Australian invention. The *cuves* look perfectly ordinary from the outside, but inside there is a funnel which traps the gas coming off the wine as it ferments. The weight of the must above the funnel provides gas pressure; this can be used to irrigate the *chapeau*, the crust which forms on the top of the wine and which needs to be kept moist. This is normally achieved by pumping the wine back over the *chapeau*, but the Ganimede system avoids the need for this, thereby avoiding disturbance to the must. It is a fairly simple and elegant solution to the problem of cap irrigation.

Whether Ganimede contributes to the character of the wines is hard to say, but the **Rouge Tradition** (**A) is certainly very aromatic and fruity, peppery too. It contains typically 50% *négrette*, the remainder being made with *syrah, cabernet franc* and just a touch of *malbec*. The oaked **Cuvée Renais-**

sance (**B) was a Gold Medal winner in Paris and is lighter than most of its kind. It sports no less than 50% *cabernet franc* and a mere 20% *négrette*. The wood is so well handled as to be hardly noticeable.

The domaine also produces an agreeably fresh **Cuvée Tradition Rosé** (*A) from equal proportions of *négrette* and *cabernet franc*, with just a touch of *côt* and *syrah*. It is also remarkable for a delicious pure **Blanc Renaissance** (**A), 100% *sauvignon* fermented and aged in the barrel. It is surprisingly light and aromatic but has *gras* too to make it a good all-purpose white.

■ CHÂTEAU FERRAN

Nicolas and Catherine Gélis

31620 Fronton

Also at

CHÂTEAU MONTAURIOL

31340 Villematier

Tel: 05-61-35-30-58 Fax: 05-61-35-30-59

Email: contact@chateau-montauriol.com

www.chateau-montauriol.com

Nicolas took over this property from his uncle in 1995. Basically a handsome building going back to the Empire, it had become a little sad, though the wines had enjoyed a good reputation following the uncle's withdrawal from the *coopérative* in 1985. Under Nicolas and his wife, Catherine, the vineyard has continued to flourish, growing to its present size of 24 hectares, and they have kept some of the old *cépages* which survived the replanting in 1970 when the AOC was granted to Fronton: some *mérille* and *côt*, still used in the red wines of the property, and some *mauzac* and *cinsault*, now outlawed in the appellation wines. Daniel's uncle once said that, in the old days, it was common to add some early-picked *mauzac* to the *négrette* to give the wines a little touch of acidity, which the *négrette* tends to lack.

Nicolas's **Rouge Tradition** (**A) has a certain rusticity which needs time to soften it, but is well made and regularly wins prizes. One gets the impression that little has changed since Uncle's day,

when the vinification was traditional and simple, the wine was not given long macerations, temperature control was nonexistent, and the wine was aged in concrete vats. This is by no means a criticism because the modernization of a *chais* is sometimes a perfect example of the law of diminishing returns. Ferran makes an interesting contrast with Château Montauriol, which the Gélis family purchased soon after taking over Ferran. There everything is state of the art and the wines are aged in new oak, something which Daniel's uncle would never have countenanced. 'La négrette n'est pas son truc', he used to say, and he was no doubt right.

■ CHÂTEAU JOLIET

François and Marie-Claire Daubert

Route de Grisolles, 31620 Fronton

Tel: 05-61-82-46-02 Fax: 05-61-82-34-56

Email: chateau.joliet@wanadoo.fr

www.chateau-joliet.com

The Dauberts came to Fronton from the West Indies in 1978 to buy this 20-hectare domaine. They started to bottle and market their own wines six years later. The soil of the vineyard has plenty of sand, and there is a deal of iron in it too. At first François found it difficult to do much with his *négrette*, and a so-called expert advised him to dig it up and plant something else. Thank goodness he didn't because perseverance has paid off to the point where François thinks it the most wonderful grape in the world, to the extent of making one of his *cuvées*, **Fantaisie** (***A), almost entirely from it. The label bears a pretty picture of a bunch of *négrette* grapes with the name of the *cépage* underneath. When I asked him whether this transgressed the French law which forbids the naming of the grape on the label of an AOC wine (at least in Fronton), he replied that the name was used as part of the picture and not part of the label. Was he trained as a lawyer, one wonders? In any event, this is certainly his most original as well as perhaps his best wine, very aromatic, lightly vinified and good for drinking in its youth; a cherry-red colour, with the characteristic violets on the nose, red fruits and other flowers too.

The more conventional red, called **Mélodie** (**A), has the other permitted grapes of the appellation as well as *négrette*. Deeper in colour than Fantaisie, it suggests the darker soft fruits and sweet peppers, perhaps deriving from the *syrah*. For his red aged in oak, **Symphonie** (**B), François reserves the grapes from his best parcels of ground and gives the wine 10 months in casks. The resulting wine is deep ruby, with a bouquet of jammy fruits and some vanilla from the wood; the finish shows good balance and soft tannins and the oak is not too prominent.

The Dauberts also make two sweet *vins de pays* from *mauzac* vines which were already planted when they bought the property. **Sérénade** (**A), without the benefit of oak, and **Madrigal** (**B), with, are both delightful in their different styles, surprising and full of character. Sérénade accents the apples-and-pears quality of the grape, quince too with some honey. It should be drunk young, while Madrigal derives complexity from its toasty vanilla and spices and will keep.

The **rosé** (*A) is agreeable without being particularly special.

▌CHÂTEAU LAUROU

Guy Salmona
2250 Route de Nohic, 31620 Fronton
Tel: 05-61-82-40-88 Fax: 05-61-82-73-11
Email: chateau.laurou@wanadoo.fr

This large 45-hectare domaine produces a wine regularly medalled and much appreciated by consumers. One of the characteristics of the wine-making is the long maceration, which Gay Salmona thinks is needed to extract the aromas and colour of the wine. He also uses *microbullage* to stabilize the wines and soften the tannins.

The wines are typically fronton, with a bouquet of red fruits and flowers, spices and liquorice on the palate. There are three reds. The **Tradi-tion** (**A) and its oak-raised complement (**A/B) are fine in their respective styles. The wine styled **Haute Expression** (**B) will delight those who like oak more than I do. Note also a good **rosé** (**A).

▌CHÂTEAU PLAISANCE

Marc Pénévayre
31340 Vacquiers
Tel: 05-61-84-97-41 Fax: 05-61-84-11-26
Email: chateau-plaisance@wanadoo.fr
www.chateau-plaisance.fr

Marc left home to study wine-making formally and then went to the Loire Valley where he ran a wine research centre. One day his father, who was already making and bottling his own wine under the name Domaine Louis Pénévayre, rang him to say that a neighbour at Vacquiers was going to dig up his vines unless the Pénévayres would agree to rent them from him. That call brought Marc dashing home. Since then the family domaine, now expanded to 24 hectares, has never looked back. Some would nominate him as top of the class in Fronton.

The home and *chais*, like those of Château Caze, open directly on to the main street of the village. The vines are dotted round the neighbourhood in various small parcels. Marc prefers not to destalk his grapes, but on the other hand adopts short rather than long vinifications, with one exception noted below. Generally speaking he allows the *gamay* only six days, the *négrette* eight or nine, and a little longer for the *cabernets* and *syrah*.

His *entrée de gamme* is what the French call a *vin des copains*, a wine to drink with chums (usually all male), probably in large quantities to foment debate on rugby football. It is called **Grain de Folie** (**A) and is not in any way serious; it is very fresh, perfumed and loaded with fruit, ideal for barbecues or picnics. This is the kind of wine which is scorned by highbrow wine critics, but lapped up by everybody else. His **Rouge Tradition** (***A) is another matter, much more substantial, but elegant all the same, beautifully balanced and with a good long finish. Marc finds that some customers, of which he has more than 1000 private ones, like this wine aged longer in the tank than others. Marc does not therefore necessarily bottle it all at the same time.

When Marc became a father, he named his first oaked red after his son, **Thibaut** (***B). This wine, generously oaked, is hugely admired, even by the author, who happily gives it three stars. If it has the usual problems associated with the use of oak, they are nothing compared with those affecting Marc's latest creation, **Tot Co Que Cal** (C) (meaning in French *Tout ce qu'il faut*), which may be the kind of *vin de dégustation* admired by professionals, but is not really a fronton at all, let alone a wine for accompanying a meal. Sorry, Marc, but your Rouge Tradition is so much more enjoyable.

■ DOMAINE DES PRADELLES

François Prat
44 Chemin de la Bourdette, 31340 Vacquiers
Tel and fax: 05-61-84-97-36
Email: fprat@domaine-pradelles.com
www.domaine-des-pradelles.com

This vineyard has been in the same family since 1869, and is reached by taking the road to La Magdelaine north-east out of Vacquiers village. There are 16 unbroken hectares of vines, of which *négrette* represents half, the two *cabernets* 30%, *syrah* 10% and *gamay* and *cinsault* each 5%, the last-named being reserved for *vins de table*.

M. Prat's oaked red wine was disappointing, not because of the wood, but because it was dusty, at least in the one vintage recently tasted. The **Rouge Tradition** (**A) was, however, excellent, with abundant flowers, fruit and spices on the nose. The entry on the palate was at once smooth as velvet but with a good attack all the same, plenty of black fruits and good long finish.

The domaine also produces dry and sweet whites *en vrac,* a *muscat*, two grades of red and a rosé.

■ CHÂTEAU LE ROC

La Famille Ribes
31620 Fronton
Tel: 05-61-82-93-90 Fax: 05-61-82-72-38
Email: leroc@cegetel.net
www.leroc-fronton.com

Frédéric and his brother Jean-Luc, whose second passion is the blues, took over the 13 hectares of this domaine when their father retired in 1988, and they have now doubled it in size. They had already tried their hand at wine-making before persuading their father to quit the *coopérative* and allow them to prove to him their worth as wine-makers. Frédéric's wife, Cathy, is described by them as 'the heartbeat of the home, lending a sensitive touch to the wine and a feminine voice to the estate'. Pierre Salama is the fourth member of this team, a sort of *vigneron* without portfolio, able to turn his hand

to whatever aspect of the work is needed on the domaine. Frédéric finds time to devote himself to local affairs, such as the presidency of the local *syndicat* of growers and acting as a leading light in the campaign to save Fronton from being turned into an international airport, an absurd proposal which seems now to have bitten the dust.

The Ribes now have a harvesting machine, but care is taken to sort the grapes carefully by hand before emptying them without any destalking or pumping into small concrete tanks. This is done with only the lightest of preliminary crushing. Frédéric gives the *négrette* 17 days, the *syrah* and *cabernets* 21. These are longish periods for this appellation. After a year's ageing, the *négrette* is dense, ripe and deep with plenty of body and matter. After a second year, what Frédéric calls 'the exuberance of the *négrette*' becomes rounded.

It can be imagined that the house style here is rather different from most others. The Ribes believe that they can keep the typical character of the *négrette* while at the same time making a firmer-structured wine for keeping. After *assemblage* their wines are quite complex.

Since their father retired, grapes are the sole crop, though Frédéric likes to keep a few sheep to indulge his passion for a good roast leg of lamb. There are a few chickens and cows too. Nowadays the *encépagement* is standard except that the domaine does not bother with *gamay*, a grape which does not fit with the house style. To help the cashflow, and to compensate for the fact that he ages his wine longer before bottling and sale than most other Fronton growers, Frédéric makes a **rosé** (**A) from 15–20% of his crop. It is pale in colour because he leaves the juice on the skins for a mere four hours. This is a wine which he agrees needs to be drunk within the year.

There are two styles of red wine. What most growers would call their 'Tradition', the **Cuvée Classique** (***A) is a wine which, after only two years, tastes more like a wine twice its age. From 70% *négrette*, it is obviously intended for drinking young. The more serious **Cuvée Réservée** (***B)

is for once a wine which really justifies its nine months' ageing in oak barrels, of which only 10% are new each year so that there is no floorboard effect. There is less *négrette* here, only 50%, and correspondingly more *cabernet* and *syrah*. The wine-making is copybook; with daily *remontage,* the *chapeau* is at the same time broken up and submerged in the fermenting must. The wine is powerful and concentrated, in many ways less typical of the appellation than most, but undeniably top class. **Don Quichotte** (***B) is aged in old *foudres* rather than oak *barriques*. It has a floral bouquet, developing notes of liquorice. The same flowers explode in the glass, releasing spices and a fine structure without astringency. Concentrated but fruity, this is a wine that can be enjoyed young or old, particularly with spicy food or plain grilled meat.

In 1994 the Ribes bought Château Flotis, once a leading domaine in Fronton, but which had suffered an eclipse due to the former owner's apparent preference for thoroughbred Arab horses over his wine-making. The rebirth is heralded by a fair **Tradition** (*A) and a rather better **Elles** (**B), with just a touch of barrel-ageing.

OTHER GOOD GROWERS

▌CHÂTEAU DE BELAYGUES

Karine Bonjour and Guillaume Veyrac

Belaygues, 82370 Labastide-Saint-Pierre

Tel: 05-63-30-00-86

Good **Rouge Tradition** (*A).

▌CHÂTEAU BOUISSEL

Pierre and Anne-Marie Selle

82370 Campsas

Tel: 05-63-30-10-49 Fax: 05-63-64-01-22

Email: annemarie@chateaubouissel.com

www.bouissel.com

▌CHÂTEAU COUTINEL

Gérard Arbeau

82370 Labastide-Saint-Pierre

Tel: 05-63-64-01-80 Fax: 05-63-30-11-42

Email: vignobles@arbeau.com

www.arbeau.com

An important house whose commercially styled wines are frequently to be found in supermarkets. They also have a substantial business as *négociants*.

▌CLOS MIGNON

Olivier Muzart

Villeneuve-les-Bouloc, 31620 Fronton

Tel: 05-61-82-10-89 Fax: 05-61-82-19-14

Email: omuzart@aol.com

www.closmignon.com

▌CHÂTEAU LA PALME

Madame Éthuin

31340 Villemur-sur-Tarn

Tel: 05-61-09-02-82 Fax: 05-61-09-27-01

A large estate making wines in a rather lighter style than many. There are also 16 hectares of haricot beans, and the château is very beautiful.

▌DOMAINE DE ST-GUILHEM

Philippe Laduguie

31620 Castelnau-d'Estrefonds

Tel: 05-61-82-12-09 Fax: 05-61-82-65-59

Email: philippe.laduguie@orange.fr

www.domainesaintguilhem.com

Wines largely in a modern style.

▌DOMAINE VIGUERIE DE BEULAYGUE

Jeanine Faure

Beulaygue, Chemin de Bonneval

82370 Labastide-Saint-Pierre

Tel and fax: 05-63-30-54-72

▌DOMAINE URBAIN BLANCAL

Urbain Blancal

31620 Villaudric

Tel: 05-61-82-44-09

The doyen of fronton growers. Visit as much for the *ambiance* of the old *chais* as for the wine. Sadly, M. Blancal seems to have frightened off his family from following in his footsteps.

VINS DE PAYS DU COMTÉ TOLOSAN

This catch-all title, including some fine jewels as well as paste, is used to hold together all the wines in the South-West which cannot present themselves under any other title: wines made in the Frontonnais which either come from unauthorized grape varieties or are white or where the yield from the vines exceeds the permitted limits; wines from other vineyards in the Tarn-et-Garonne and the Haute-Garonne which have no more localized name of their own; and wines from further west in AOC areas where wines are made which don't conform to the rules current in their areas of production. Outside the recognized appellations, most of these wines are made by local *coopératives,* but one of them has a raison d'être all its own because it is the centre of a small area of VDQS wines.

LAVILLEDIEU-DU-TEMPLE

VINS DE LAVILLEDIEU

AREA OF VDQS: selected parcels covering 65 hectares in the communes of Albefeuille, Barry-d'Islemade, Bressols Castelsarrasin, Escatalens Lacourt-Saint-Pierre, Labastide-du-Temple Lagarde, Lavilledieu, Les Barthes, Meauzac, Montbeton, Montech and Saint-Porquie.
Red and rosé wines.
PERMITTED GRAPE VARIETIES:
REDS: Main varieties which must constitute between them 80% of the grower's red wine vines: négrette (must constitute 35%), mauzac, bordelais, morterille, chalosse.
OTHER VARIETIES: syrah, cabernet franc, tannat and milgranet (max. 25% each), gamay (10% max.). Blend of at least four varieties required, which must include négrette.
MINIMUM ALCOHOL CONTENT: 10.5%.
MAXIMUM YIELD: 60 hl/ha.
ANNUAL PRODUCTION: 2100 hectolitres.
PLANTING DENSITY: 4000 to 4500 plants per hectare.

This VDQS has had its ups and downs. Until very recently a magnificent *cave coopérative* drew together producers of this VDQS and also of Coteaux de Quercy and Coteaux et Terrasses de Montauban. Sadly, the *cave* closed during the winter of 2008 and its members scattered, some simply giving up commercial production, others joining the *Cave Coopérative* of Donzac in the Côte de Brulhois. Two independent growers continued to produce under the appellation Lavilledieu. The 2008 was their first vintage, so it is impossible to assess the quality of their wines, but for curious amateurs here are the domains to follow:

DOMAINE DE GAZANIA
Patrice Colombie
Caufour, 82290 Labastide-du-Temple
Tel: 05-63-31-63-25 Fax: 05-63-21-51-02

DOMAINE DU ROUCH
Franck Mezan
Les Clottes, 82290 Lavilledieu-du-Temple
Tel and fax: 05-63-31-68-61

COTEAUX ET TERRASSES DE MONTAUBAN

PRODUCER

DOMAINE DE MONTELS

Philippe and Thierry Romain

82350 Albas

Tel: 05-63-31-02-82

Email: info@domaine-de-montels.com

www.domaine-de-montels.com

Aline Romain, who has now handed over her domaine to her two sons, Philippe and Thierry, was responsible almost single-handed for the creation of this recently established *vin de pays*. After a varied agricultural career in North Africa and later in Alsace, Aline discovered the South-West in 1973 with her husband and their small babies, and they bought this estate to carry on farming. Tragically, her husband died almost immediately thereafter.

Aline decided she wasn't going to farm; she was going to make wine. She went to study at Montauban, Toulouse and Bordeaux and went about digging up the old hybrid grapes on the farm and replanting with modern ones. Today the domaine includes *gamay*, *syrah*, *cabernet franc*, *tannat*, *merlot* and *jurançon noir*. Nor was she satisfied with making only a *vin de table,* the property being in no known wine-growing area. Her application to be included in Fronton was turned down because she was too far from there, nor would the Coteaux du Quercy have her because of differences in *terroir*. It was all too much for the bureaucrats to accommodate just one grower, and a woman at that.

So Aline created her own appellation. With other locals she gave birth to the *Vin de Pays des Coteaux et Terrasses de Montauban*. Most send their grapes to the Lavilledieu *coopérative*, but there are some independents. Aline was for a long time the head of the *Groupement des Producteurs*.

Today her son Philippe looks after the 25 hectares of vines, while Thierry deals with the marketing and business side; he is often to be seen manning a stall at local markets. They make an excellent pure **cabernet franc** (**A), as well as a blend which includes the other red grapes mentioned above and an oaked version of it too. A nice **dry white** (*A) from *jurançon à jus blanc* makes a good change, and there is an agreeable **rosé** (*A). They are a courageous, hard-working and quality-minded family who deserve the notice which they have been getting from the French media and guides. Recommended without hesitation.

OTHER PRODUCERS OF COTEAUX ET TERRASSES DE MONTAUBAN

DOMAINE DU CAYROU

Maurice Brunet

Léojac, 82000 Montauban

Tel: 05-63-64-57-12

DOMAINE DE PUYSEGUÈRE

Michel Serles

Saint Martial, 82000 Montauban

Tel: 05-63-03-11-57

WINES OF SAINT-SARDOS

PRODUCERS

LA CAVE COOPÉRATIVE DE SAINT-SARDOS
Le Bourg, 82600 Saint-Sardos
Tel: 05-63-02-52-44 fax: 05-63-02-62-19
www.cave-saint-sardos.com

Saint-Sardos is a tiny village in the sparsely populated area on the left bank of the Garonne called the Lomagne. As well as being a centre of garlic production it is home to a *cave coopérative* with just over 100 members which makes wines, elevated to VDQS status in 2005, in all three colours. As at La Ville-Dieu, the *Cave* was constructed in a time of huge optimism, but subsequently many members were tempted away by grants and by improvements in irrigation techniques to produce cereals, fruit and vegetables rather than grapes. Production almost fizzled out altogether, but today the vineyard has been reborn.

The reds and rosés are based on *syrah* (recommended minimum 40%), *tannat* (20%), *cabernet franc* and *merlot*, the latter usually less than 10%. The eclectic mix of grapes results from the advice of the wine authorities, who were asked to recommend what kind of *encépagement* would have the best chance of the vineyard securing promotion to VDQS status. Their application for this took 10 years to process, a not unusual period of gestation with the French authorities.

The soil here is in part chalky clay, what the French call *argilo-calcaire*, and partly on the same type of *boulbènes* as at Fronton. And everywhere there are loose stones.

As at Fronton and Gaillac, the members of the *coopérative* have very small holdings of vines, rather less than two hectares each on average. They prefer to spread the climatic risks by growing other crops as well. But the quality standards on which their management insists ensure that most of the wine is sold locally, either at the *Cave* itself or in regional shops. Plantation must exceed 4000 plants to the hectare, the wines are fermented under strict temperature control and the *assemblages* are made with the best technical advice. They include an attractive dry white called **Domaine de Marquestus** (*A), from *sauvignon*, *muscadelle* and *chardonnay*; a nice fruity unambitious red currently called **Prestige de Naudin** (*A); a rather more ambitious **Grand Selve** (*A), which would go down a bomb in wine bars; and their top wine, **Domaine de Cadis** (**A), from low yields and hand-picked grapes.

DOMAINE DE LA TUCAYNE
Jean-Claude Delpech
82600 Bouillac
Tel and fax: 05-63-27-70-43

The success of Saint-Sardos was in large part due to the efforts of one dedicated grower called Jean-Claude Delpech. For many years he sent his grapes to the *coopérative*, but since 1998 he and now his son have been making their own wine at their 27-hectare estate, where you can find some attractive wines: a rosé called **Cuvée Tourroumbail** (**A), *saigné* from *syrah* and *cabernet franc*, a **dry white** (*A) blend of *sauvignon* and *chardonnay* and a **moëlleux** (A) from *sémillon* and *sauvignon*. The reds are rather more interesting. **Cuvée Antonin** (**A), half *syrah*, the rest *cabernet franc* and smaller quantities of *tannat* and *merlot,* is floral and supple. A rather bigger wine, named after the **Domaine** (**A), is from *syrah* and *tannat*. These wines are well worth looking out for, and in the unlikely event that you find yourself in this remote part of the Garonne basin, a visit would be interesting.

DOMAINE DE RIBONNET AND THE WINES OF ARIÈGE

After the phylloxera, *Toulousains* looked north to Fronton rather than southwards for their wine. The vineyards south and east of the city became just part of the pattern of local polyculture. *Coopératives* such as those to be found today at Escalquens, Longages and Bérat were the modest best of which the city could boast.

Further towards Spain, Ariège was for many years the only French *département* in the Midi unable to boast a wine above the status of plonk. Phylloxera came late to Ariège. Not until the early years of the 20th century was its effect fully felt, by which time other vineyards in the South-West had already started to re-establish themselves, Gaillac and Fronton in particular gaining a hold on the local market, which became difficult to break into. Wine production in the area never took off again. The towns of Pamiers and Varilhes were once well known for their wine, but by 1990 only two farmers were known to have more than one hectare of vines.

DOMAINE DE RIBONNET

Christian Gerber

31870 Beaumont-sur-Lèze

Tel: 05-61-08-71-02 Fax: 05-61-08-08-06

Email: vinribonnet31@aol.com

www.vin-ribbonet.com

Today this sad situation is changing fast, thanks in large measure to the vision and the resources of Christian Gerber, a rich Swiss businessman whose father bought this imposing domaine in 1975, but died soon after, leaving the estate in the hands of his son Christian, then a young man and inexperienced in agriculture let alone wine-making. The domaine, strictly speaking in the Haute-Garonne but close all the same to the Ariège borders, had had an interesting history. It dates back to the 15th century, when châteaux were built on the tops of hills so that invaders could more easily be spotted while there was still time to organize defence. This one is at the centre of a large estate which includes 32 hectares of vines. It had belonged at the beginning of the 20th century to Clément Ader, a pioneer-aviator of whom the people of Toulouse are proud. Ader replanted the vineyards with modest grapes, from which he made large quantities of not very remarkable wine. He sold it all *en négoce*, bottling none of it himself.

When Christian Gerber arrived on the scene he gradually replanted the vineyard with superior *cépages*. Being in an area with no modern viticultural reputation, he was bound by fewer rules than most in the selection of grape varieties. He followed the varietal path, making wines from single unblended varieties while experimenting to find which suited his *terroir* best. A visitor might well find himself offered a blend of *chasselas* and *sylvaner*, with a wonderful banana nose; a rich, fruity, exotic and very full pure *sauvignon*; a *pinot grigio* or an *aligoté*; various cuves of *pinot noir*; an oak-fermented *marsanne* or a pure *sémillon*; *viognier* as well as *chenin blanc* and the more conventional *cabernets* and *merlot*. Whatever Christian may propose will be excellent (**A/B).

Christian may well invite you to taste in his office, with picture windows overlooking the valley as far as the Pyrenees. Here he will tell you about his latest co-venture with four other growers: nothing less than the re-establishment of the Ariége as a wine-producing area.

LES VIGNERONS ARIÉGEOIS

Christian Gerber inspired a compatriot, Christian Zeller, and his wife to buy a property just to the south of Ribonnet, over the border into Ariège, called **Domaine de Lastronques**. Another part of the jigsaw was a local *Association pour Adultes et Jeunes Handicapés,* one of many charitable institutions providing an organized working life for handicapped people. The centre had six hectares which it was prepared to plant with vines, and it had a good site on which to build a *chais*. The fourth interested party was Philippe Babin, also willing to plant vines to the south. The four of them formed a group, each retaining their land and vines, initially pooling the cost of running the vineyards and marketing their wines together through a separate company. With one eye to future official recognition, the grape varieties chosen were the two *cabernets*, *merlot*, *syrah* and *tannat*. The initial costs were met partly by local enthusiasts and friends, thus repeating the funding process which Christian Gerber had already tried so successfully at Ribonnet 20 years previously. Dividends were to be in wine, and the subscription lists closed almost as soon as they were opened.

Nowadays there is enough wine, after the investors have been satisfied, to market commercially, either under the names of the individual properties or under the group brand *Les Vignerons Ariégeois*. The wines are getting better all the time (*A). Recently, a dry white has been added to the range, a blend of *chardonnay, sémillon* and *sauvignon*.

THE GROWERS

DOMAINE DE SABARTHES
L'Association pour Adultes et Jeunes Handicapés
Marc Vigneau
Le Sabarthes, 09120 Montégut Plantaurel
Tel: 05-61-05-39-39

Note red and white wines called **La Gulhatié**, the latter selected for *Guide Hachette* in 2009.

DOMAINE DE LASTRONQUES
Christian Zeller
09120 Lézat-sur-Lèze
Tel: 05-61-69-12-13 Fax: 05-61-69-18-44

LE DOMAINE DES COTEAUX D'ENGRAVIÈS
Philippe Babin
09120 Vira
Tel: 05-61-68-68-68
www.coteauxdansengravies.com

Biological growers, with two excellent reds, one *merlot*-based (*A), the other mostly *syrah* (**A).

New member of group:

DOMAINE DU MOULIN DE BEAUREGARD
09130 Le Fossat

THE WINES OF THE
DORDOGNE VALLEY

BERGERAC

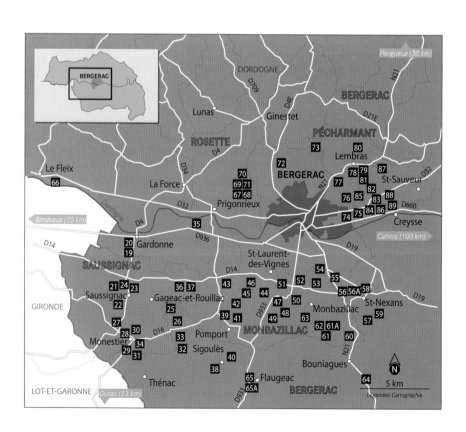

BERGERAC, BERGERAC SEC AND CÔTES DE BERGERAC

AREA OF AOC: selected parcels in the following communes in the *arondissement* of Bergerac: Baneuilo, Bergerac, Boisse, Bonneville and Saint-Avit-de Fumadières, Bouniagues, Campsegret, Carsac-de-Gurson, Colombier, Conne-de-Libarde, Cours-de-Pile, Creysse, Cunèges, Eymet, Faurilles, Flaugeac, Le Fleix, Fonroque, La Force, Fougueyrolles, Fraisse, Gageac-et-Rouillac, Gardonne, Ginestet, Issigeac, Lalinde, Lamonzie-Saint-Martin, Lamothe-Montravel, Lanquais, Les Lèches, Lembras, Lunas, Maurens, Mescoules, Minzac, Monbazillac, Monestier, Monfaucon, Mommadalès, Monmarvès, Monsaguel, Montazeau, Montcaret, Montpeyroux, Mouleydier, Moulin-Neuf, Nastringues, Naussannes, Nojals-et-Clotte, Plaisance, Pomport, Port Sainte-Foy-et-Ponchapt, Prigonrieux, Queyssac, Rampieux, Razac d'Eymet, Razac-de-Saussignac, Ribagnac, Rouffignac-de-Sigoulès, Sadillac, Saint-Agne, Saint-Antoine-de-Breuilh, Saint-Aubin-de-Cadalech, Saint-Aubin-de-Lanquais, Saint-Capraise-d'Eymet, Saint-Cernin-de-Labarde, Sainte-Eulalie-d'Eymet,

Saint-Germin-et-Mons, Saint-Géry, Sainte-Innocence, Saint Julien-d'Eymet, Saint-Laurent-des-Vignes, Saint-Leon-d'Issigeac, Saint-Martin-de-Gurçon, Saint-Méard-de-Gurçon, Saint-Michel-de-Montaigne, Saint-Nexans, Saint-Perdoux, Saint-Pierre-d'Eyraud, Saint-Rémy, Saint-Sauveur, Saint-Seurin-de-Prats, Saint-Vivien, Saussignac, Serres-et-Montguyard, Sigoulès, Singleyrac, Thénac, Vélines, Verdon, Villefranche-de-Lonchat.

Red and rosé wines, white dry and sweet.
GRAPE VARIETIES:
REDS: cabernet sauvignon, cabernet franc, merlot and malbec. Also allowed but not much seen, mérille and périgord.
WHITES: sémillon, sauvignon, muscadelle, chenin blanc. Ondenc and ugni blanc also allowed, but the latter is subject to a maximum of 25%, balanced by an equal quantity of sauvignon.
MINIMUM PLANTING DENSITY: 3000 plants per hectare with transitional relief for nonconforming vineyards.
Plants must be at least 90 cm apart in their rows.
MAXIMUM YIELDS:
RED: côtes de Bergerac and white Bergerac moëlleux: 50 hl/ha.
RED AND ROSÉ BERGERAC: 55 hl/ha.
DRY WHITE: 60 hl/ha.
MINIMUM ALCOHOL CONTENT: Côtes de Bergerac reds must reach at least 11%; 10.5% for Bergerac tout court.
White moëlleux must have at least 11.5%; the dry whites 10%.

It is very nearly true to say that 'Dordogne' in wine terms means Bergerac. In the rest of the valley and the *département*, wine making had, until very recently, virtually disappeared except for the small amount made by the farmers of the region for their own consumption. Occasionally one comes across small producers of modest table wines, sometimes grouped into little *cooopératives*, but what has happened to the one-time famous vineyards of Brantôme or the wines of Périgueux itself?

FORMER GLORY

At one time, before the havoc caused by the phylloxera plague, Périgord boasted an honourable list of wines. South of Sarlat, the hillsides of Gaumiers, Florimont and Daglan produced wines whose bouquet is said to have rivalled that of the finest cahors. The vines of Domme, Coste Calve, Saint-Cyprien, Bézenac and Saint-Vincent shared with truffle-oaks dry and chalky slopes which yielded wines of real quality. There was fierce local pride for the wines of Bourdeille, Chancelade, Saint-Pantalys, Brantôme and Montpon, which were loaded into old casks and ferried down the river, like the old wines of the Corrèze way upstream.

The journey downstream was slow, punctuated by stops to pay tolls demanded at Bergerac, where those with rights over the river, in imitation of the Bordeaux merchants, either demanded money or, if their own wines had not yet been sent down the river for sale, blocked completely the passage of those grown to the east. Libourne was the next to extort money, so as to defend the wines of Saint-Emilion, and at Lormont, the monks sold the boatmen a branch of bay, which, on presentation at Bordeaux, gave the right to unload the wines on the Quai des Chartrons. So risky were the problems to be overcome, it was touch and go whether the barrels from inland Périgord might be returned to sender for one reason or another.

The destruction of the Dordogne vineyards by the phylloxera was total. In the space of a few years, the 600 square kilometres of vines upstream from Lalinde disappeared for over 100 years. In other areas of the South-West, one finds occasionally small pockets of vines which survived, but none whatever in the Dordogne. As at Cahors, poverty was such that growers could not afford to buy and replant the new American rootstocks. Lack of alternative crops in the hillier parts of the *haut-pays* caused mass emigration; the loss of life in two world wars and the depression of the 1930's accentuated the decline.

But downstream from Lalinde, entering the Bergerac region, there is suddenly a sharp contrast. The countryside is richer and the farms have always been more prosperous. Other crops can thrive, and the landholdings are larger. There are other factors as well, buried in ancient history, which favoured the rebirth of the Bergerac wine trade.

FRENCH AND ENGLISH—AND THE DUTCH

In 1225, Bergerac gave its allegiance to the English Crown. In return, Henry III gave it a substantial degree of autonomy. Recognizing the problem of governing his vast French territories, the king realized that a special relationship with Bergerac might open up trading in the whole county of Guienne. Bergerac obtained important rights: as well as the privilege of taxing the wines made upstream as they passed through the town, Bergerac was also exclusively exempted from the Grand Privilège exercised by the Bordeaux dealers. Even after the return of Bergerac to the French Crown, its special position was preserved.

During the Hundred Years' War, Périgord loyalties were split: in the north in favour of the French Crown, in the south in favour of the English. During the wars of religion, the north was Catholic, the Bergeracois Protestant. It was therefore natural for the Bergerac growers to develop trading links with Protestant Holland, where they had already begun to establish markets. The ties were to be reinforced after the disastrous revocation of the Edict of Nantes by Louis XIV, when many Bergeracois emigrated to Holland. These expatriates were well placed to favour and strengthen trade with the town of their birth.

It was the Dutch connection, too, which saved Bergerac from the consequences of the loss of its privileges during the Revolution, because, in its golden age of trade with Holland, the bonds had grown so strong that Bergerac did not feel the loss of revenue from the tolls it had previously extracted from its neighbours upstream. It had also started to develop the concept of single-domaine wines, after the Bordeaux pattern. There emerged a hierarchy of quality with the brands of the vineyard owners stamped on the bottom of their casks, and sometimes too the name of the exact area from which the wine had originated. These wines were referred to as *marques hollandaises*, a term still current to identify estates enjoying a long history. For many bergerac producers, Holland remains their most valuable export market. Just as the British remained loyal to claret for hundreds of years, so the Dutch have remained faithful to bergerac, despite changing fashions in wine—the switch from white to red and from sweet to dry.

PRE-PLAGUE PRODUCTION

Before the phylloxera, Bergerac made a certain amount of red wine, mostly on the right (north) bank of the river, but by far the greater proportion was white, made from vines on both banks. Those from the left (south) bank were regarded as superior and were almost without exception sweet. The Dutch called them the 'madeiras of the Périgord'. The red wines from the right bank were used entirely for blending, and were exported as such, often losing their bergerac name at the hands of the dealers. Because these wines fetched much less money than the left-bank dessert wines, the right bank was not immediately planted after the phylloxera. The continuing Dutch connection gave every inducement to replant the quality vineyards of the left bank.

I was told by an aristocratic old-timer, the owner of a large left-bank estate, that before the phylloxera there were twice as many vines in the Bergeracois as there are today, but the yield was much lower; in 1837 it was as little as nine hectolitres to the hectare. The vines were planted at random and not in rows. The vineyards were on the hillsides; there were none in the plain, where the farms were all rented out by the landowners for other crops. Following the slow death from the phylloxera, the right bank was allowed to revert to woodland, while the left initially developed polyculture as a way of survival. In those days oxen were used in the vineyards. Larger and stronger beasts were needed to work the higher sloping ground where the best vines grew, so the vines had to be well spaced; lower down, the gradients were less steep and vines were planted closer together, so smaller oxen could be used. Paradoxically, the better land was less densely planted than the more ordinary land, the opposite of modern viticultural practice. The growers developed a kind of double yoke for their beasts which enabled the latter to work in pairs on either side of the vine rows. The height of the yoke, normally close to 1.1 metre, dictated the height of the stakes supporting the plants, and thus the height of the growth of the vines. With the coming of tractors after the Second World War, the distance between vine rows became wider, nobody foreseeing the modern kind of mini-tractor which can work in relatively small corridors between the vines.

It was about this time, too, that a dry style of white bergerac began to emerge to meet the changing taste in wine. Some say that this was a natural concomitant of the change of diet, a more sedentary population needing less sugar. A drier and lighter style of wine would also suit better a leaner and less fatty diet. Certainly the postwar years showed a sharp swing away from sweet wine styles. Today Bergerac manages to keep a balance between the production of sweet monbazillac and saussignac, for example, and the dry whites from Montravel and elsewhere in the Bergerac region.

The 13 appellations within Bergerac cover 12,220 hectares, and the total AOC production is some 650,000 hectolitres. This is over four times that of Gaillac, the next largest wine-producing area of the South-West. Of the 1240 growers, just over half sell their grapes to the *coopératives,* of which there are eight, and many others sell their wine *en négoce*. Red wine comprises nearly 60% of the total volume, white just under 40%, and rosé a tiny 2% but rapidly growing to meet a revived demand for this style.

BORDEAUX SATELLITE?

Bergerac has enjoyed the benefits as well as some disadvantages of its proximity to Bordeaux. The fast transport links it enjoys through Bordeaux international airport and the TGV network underline the impression in some quarters that Bergerac is a Bordeaux satellite. Many growers, however, seek to assert its independence and to emphasize differences in *terroir*. It is nevertheless an inescapable fact that the Bergerac vineyards are a natural eastward extension of Bordeaux. The wines of Montravel on the right bank rub shoulders with those of the Côtes de Castillon, which themselves adjoin Saint-Emilion without a break. The structure of the soil is also a continuation of that which underlies the red wines of those two areas, so it is not surprising that the red wines grown on the right bank have a natural kinship with those of their more famous Bordeaux neighbours. It is not until you reach Pécharmant, at the very eastern end of the Bergeracois, that a particular kind of pebbly-sandy soil with a touch of iron below gives an unmistakeably different *goût du terroir* to the red wine. On the left bank, the Bordeaux district of Entre-Deux-Mers adjoins Saussignac in the Bergeracois, and Saussignac adjoins Monbazillac in turn.

The kinship with Bordeaux is further highlighted by the use of the same grape varieties in both areas. The red wines are thus made from *merlot* (about a half of the total vineyard is now planted with this grape, which was once only a minority *cépage*), *cabernet sauvignon* and *cabernet franc* in roughly equal quantities. *Malbec* appears from time to time, particularly in the east of the appellation. *Fer servadou* and *mérille* (once called locally 'Périgord') have disappeared. The white wines, both dry and sweet, are still largely made from *sémillon,* which accounts for nearly three-quarters of the white vines. *Sauvignon* is the other main *cépage,* and *muscadelle* is liked by some growers for its aromatic character.

The only physical distinction between Bordeaux and Bergerac is political; the vineyards of the former are in the *département* of Gironde, while the Bergerac vineyards are almost all in the *département* of Dordogne. If it were not for this artificial boundary, might the two areas have merged? Could not the inner appellations of

Bergerac, such as Monbazillac and Pécharmant, survive alongside the inner appellations of Bordeaux, such as Sauternes and Saint-Emilion? But the Bordelais might argue that they have enough problems selling their own wine without taking on the burden of an expanded vineyard.

CONFUSION

The creation of areas of *appellation contrôlée* for the Bergerac vineyard began in 1936. Over the years, the rules have become exceedingly complex and most confusing for the consumer. It is easier perhaps to consider the red wines separately from the white.

There are two basic appellations for the reds, which cover the entire Bergerac region: Bergerac and Côtes de Bergerac. The difference is not in the altitude or geographical position of the vineyards, but in the de facto decision by Côtes growers to designate a superior *cuvée,* often raised in barrel. Technically, the Côtes wines are required to have a slightly higher minimum alcoholic content, but this is academic because in practice all Bergerac wines exceed the bare minimum.

Then there are two inner appellations for red wines: Montravel and Pécharmant, names which can be given only to wines made within those strictly delimited areas.

For white bergerac, there are three appellations covering the whole region: Bergerac sec, Côtes de Bergerac (which also has a higher minimum alcoholic strength of 11 degrees and may contain slightly more sugar), and finally Côtes de Bergerac moëlleux, where the respective figures for alcohol and sugar are higher still.

There are three inner areas whose names may be given only to sweet wines: Monbazillac, Saussignac and Rosette. A fourth area, Montravel, may, according to which particular part of the appellation the vines are located, give its name to three different styles of white: *sec*, *moëlleux* and something bordering on *liquoreux*, but not strictly speaking entitled to call itself such. Wines from any of these areas, even if they qualify under the rules for their own inner appellation, may also call themselves under the generic bergerac names if they so wish, and they frequently do. Perhaps the situation will seem less complicated as we visit each of the subregions later. But outside of these inner appellations, there are reds and whites produced simply as bergerac or côtes de bergerac which rank among some of the best of the district, and so we look at these first.

PRODUCERS OF
RED AND WHITE BERGERAC

CHÂTEAU DE LA COLLINE

Charles Martin

24240 Thénac

Tel: 05-53-61-87-87 Fax: 05-53-61-71-09

Email: charlesm@la-colline.com

www.la-colline.com

You do not find many Welsh winemakers. Charles, though Welsh, spent most of his youth in Brighton, where his father had a wine business. He also travelled the world extensively, learning from the Australians, Californians and South Africans before doing a seven-year stint at the Ryman-owned Château La Jaubertie in Bergerac. When the going got rough there (warfare between Ryman *père* and *fils*), he decided to set up on his own and in 1994 bought this beautifully situated domaine at the very southern tip of the Bergerac appellation, south even of Saussignac, from which the growers in Thénac were for some obscure political reasons excluded. At 196 metres above sea level, it is one of the highest vineyards in the Bergeracois. Today it covers 19 hectares.

Charles bought the domaine from an Englishman who was more interested in quantity than quality. Restructuring the vineyard, he has raised the average density of plantation to a more fashionable 5000 hectolitres per hectare, his *sauvignon* for example being planted in rows two metres apart, but the plants only 50 centimetres away from each other.

His aim is for as much freshness in the wine as possible, so his widespread use of barrels is careful and well mastered. Thus his 100% *sémillon* called **Calista** (**B) is handled simply and with a minimum of intervention during its fermentation and ageing in wood; and the red **Carminé** (**B), nearly all *merlot* with just a touch of *cabernet sauvignon* to comply with the rules, enables Charles to achieve a classic structure and concentration from his best red grapes. The côtes de bergerac **moëlleux** (**B) is a really seductive *liquoreux,* which would have been called a saussignac if the vineyard were just a few kilometres further north.

The vines are in two contrasting areas: the Côté Sud gives grapes from which Charles seeks a maximum of fruit, while the Côté Ouest enables him to make wines with bigger structure and complexity. The contrast is well demonstrated in his basic whites, where the **Colline Blanc Sec** (**A) is floral and fresh, a very good-value commercial aperitif style of wine, while the **blanc sec** from the Côté Ouest (**B) is a food wine with a deeper flavour.

Similarly with the reds, **La Colline Rouge Sud** (*A) is a good upmarket wine bar sort of wine, while the **Ouest** (**B) has much more guts and ideally needs some good red meat to go with it.

This is a property making attractive middle-of-the road wines to the modern taste: plenty of fruit, good weight and balance but without frightening tannins. His success in export markets, particularly in Holland and Belgium, comes as no surprise.

CHÂTEAU GRINOU

Catherine and Guy Cuisset
Route de Grinou, 24240 Monestier
Tel: 05-53-58-46-63 Fax: 05-53-61-05-66
email: chateaugrinou@aol.com

Guy's grandfather bought this vineyard in 1929 and perhaps it should be listed under Saussignac, because grandson Guy makes as fine an example as you could wish. His **saussignac** (**D) is fashionably aged in new barrels, but seemingly more traditional in style than many of the new school. But Guy has 36 hectares, of which two-thirds are planted with white grapes and one-third with red, so there is a full range of Bergerac wines as well as the star of the domaine.

There are two **blancs secs** (*A and B, respectively), the one raised *en cuve* with quite rich fruit, the other *en barrique,* which Guy suggests is fat enough to go with a *magret de canard*. Of the reds,

the **Cuvée Tradition** (*A) is a very easy tannin-free quaffer, made from young vines of *merlot* and the two *cabernets*, an excellent summer wine for barbecues and open-air eating. The **Réserve** (**B) is all *merlot* and is given six months' barrel-ageing, though you would hardly know it. The **Grand Vin** (B) is altogether too much, and I suspect Guy thinks so too, but the world expects *vignerons* to do this sort of thing and so he is happy to oblige. It is again all *merlot* and Guy thinks it would keep for up to 15 years.

CHÂTEAU TOUR DES GENDRES

Famille de Conti, Les Gendres
24240 Ribagnac
Tel: 05-53-57-12-43 Fax: 05-53-58-89-49
Email: familledeconti@wanadoo.fr
www.chateautourdesgendres.com

This property, formerly the wine farm attached to the Château de Bridoire when it extended to over 200 hectares, today covers 45 hectares and is located a few kilometres to the south of Monbazillac. Luc de Conti is the wine-maker, his cousin Francis looks after the vines, and his cousin Jean oversees the rest of the family farm. The ladies deal with reception and the paperwork.

Luc bought the property in 1981 originally as an extension of the family farm. Following his father's retirement, Luc has suddenly become the locomotive in the renaissance of bergerac, occupying the same sort of position as Alain Brumont in Madiran and Henri Ramonteu in Jurançon. The family dedicated a special red wine to Luc's father, named after Marcel Pagnol, **La Gloire de Mon Père** (**B). It is rich in fruit and firm-structured, made from wines on the highest ground of the vineyard, almost on a plateau, half *merlot* and half *cabernet sauvignon*. Here there is a lot of chalk in the soil. The grapes (like all the wines of this property) are hand-harvested and given a long fermentation of up to 30 days. The wine is transferred to barrels, half new and half once used, for its second malolactic fermentation. After 22 months the wine is bottled without fining or filtering.

Moulin des Dames (***B) is the name given to a pair of wines, one red and one white. These are usually the top wines of the property. Typically the red would be a blend of half *cabernet sauvignon* and a quarter each *merlot* and *malbec*, given a long 40 days to ferment and macerate. The characteristics of this wine are huge length, a New World fruitiness and a capacity to age. Decanting is essential. The white is half *sauvignon*, the balance *sémillon* touched off with a little *muscadelle*. Forty-eight hours' skin-contact would be normal before vinification in barrels, some new some old, with regular *bâtonnage* over a 12-month period. The wine is neither filtered nor subjected to any detartrating process. Deep gold in colour, it has a peachy, quincey, mineral character and needs keeping.

In great years like 2000 and 2005, red and white super-*cuvées* are made under the name **Anthologia** (***C) from vines grown on biodynamic principles. Both red and white versions are barrel-fermented, the casks of red being turned by rolling them for the gentlest possible extraction. There is no *pigeage*. Do not miss either the white **Cuvée des Conti** (***C), a *sémillon*-based wine with 20% *muscadelle*, aromatic and complex with some sweetness from overripening of the fruit. Luc de Conti recommends decanting before enjoying the wine with fish or meat in a creamy sauce.

At a more modest level, and very attractively priced (all A), is a basic range (*) of rosé, red and sweetish white **Côtes de Bergerac**, and a **dry white** matured on its lees with a hint of *muscadelle* to give it richness.

Luc has now completed the conversion of much of the vineyard to organic production, nurturing the total environment of the vines so as to encourage desirable insect and plant life. He makes all his own fertilisers and has outlawed weedkillers. Weeds are everywhere allowed to grow between the vine rows, so as to oblige the vine roots to plunge deeper and deeper into the subsoil to find strength and nourishment. Some of the spaces between rows are planted with oats, the vivid green of those plants contrasting with the dull greeny brown of the

gaps weeded by hand. Luc believes that the application of his principles enhances the *terroir* character of his wines. Certainly the plants which benefit from this treatment have a livelier colour and a fresher, more healthy look than plants which are sprayed in the normal way and allowed to grow in soil which has been partly sterilized by weedkillers. The soil smells of fresh earth too, rather than dust.

He is also a convert to micro-oxygenation, which he uses for nearly all his reds and whites so as to soften the tannins and encourage maturity and sweetness in the fruit. The technique also avoids frequent racking of the wines, thus disturbing them less and allowing them to mature naturally and quietly.

The wines of Tour des Gendres are unquestionably among the finest of the South-West.

■ VIGNOBLE LES VERDOTS

David Fourtout, Les Verdots
24560 Conne-de-Labarde
Tel: 05-53-58-34-31 Fax: 05-53-57-82-00
Email: fourtout@terre-net.fr
www.verdots.com

As a boy, David Fourtout detested working in the vines of his family, who had been *vignerons* in Bergerac for four generations, though their main business was milling. As an adolescent he preferred Coca-Cola and cheap whisky to wine. But one day a family friend working at Château Mouton-Rothschild invited him for a stay in the Médoc. After visits to all the leading properties there, David quickly reassessed his opinion of wine; for him, the road back from Bordeaux was the road to Damascus. Quick to learn by observation, he preferred to go round the world and see what other countries were doing, rather than undertake formal training in France. His analytical eye noted good and bad practices everywhere.

He started in 1991 with 15 used barrels given to him by Mouton-Rothschild, and these saw him on the way to creating what is today one of the most extraordinary operations in Bergerac. He has over the years extended the vineyard to 34 hectares, planted roughly two-thirds with red grapes, one-third with white, the latter including six hectares of vines in the Monbazillac appellation. He has built a post-modernist *chais*, incorporating an underground storage facility through the middle of which runs the river Conne. There is a large reception area at ground-floor level, and two flanking towers which contain *chambres d'hôtes*. The *chais de vinification* is notable among other things for the ranks of *cuves tronçonneuses*, which differ from the normal Burgundy variety in being custom-built in stainless steel rather than wood. They combine all the advantages of computerized temperature control with an improved system of mechanized *pigeage*. With their cut-off-cone shape they also cause the crust to rise more slowly, keeping it in more permanent contact with the must.

But, as David Fourtout says, the only purpose of technique is to serve the grapes. With these he makes, like Christian Roche (see p. 166), three ranges of wine, not to mention the red, white and rosé which he sells in bag-in-box format. **Le Clos des Verdots**, a group all made and raised in tanks, includes a remarkable **blanc sec** (***A) very largely from *sémillon*, as well as a thirst-quenching **rosé** (**A), a highly rated **rouge** (**A) and a **moëlleux** (**A). The value for the money here is astonishing.

The second range is called simply **Château Les Tours des Verdots** and here the **blanc sec** (***B) is again outstanding. The wines are aged in wood, none of which is new. The **Côtes de Bergerac rouge** (***B) contains one-third old-vine *merlot*, and the **moëlleux** (***C) won a silver medal at the International Wine Challenge in 2004.

Prices start to steepen with the top range, called **Les Verdots selon David Fourtout,** or sometimes simply **Vin,** a conceit redeemed only by the wines' quality. The **blanc sec** (***C) is three-quarters *sauvignon*, of which one-third is *sauvignon gris*. The **rouge** (***C) is a huge wine, and the 2003 version, called **Cuvée Paul,** seems, because of the hot character of the vintage, more like a montpeyroux than a bergerac. There are two sweet whites, a côtes de bergerac **moëlleux** (***D) and the **Monbazillac** (***D+), priced at the very top of the appellation and worth every euro. It will have spent 30 months in the barrel, but no wood shows except in the complexity of the wine. The wine is mentioned here because it is a minority production from a property otherwise outside the Monbazillac area.

In exceptional years, David also makes a 100% *muscadelle* from very old vines, also called simply **Vin** (***C), which has a vividly perfumed bouquet and an astonishing flowery depth.

DOMME

Mention must be made of the attempts to replant small areas of vines upstream in the neighbourhood of Domme. Before the phylloxera there were 2700 hectares of vines, roughly a quarter of the size of present-day Bergerac. In 1993 les Amis du Vin de Pays de Domme was formed to revive the vineyard. By 2000 15 hectares had been planted with 60% *merlot* and 40% *cabernet franc*. In 1997 a *coopérative* was formed by the Vignerons des Coteaux du Céou and a fine *chai* was built in 1999 at Moncalou.

LES VIGNERONS DES COTEAUX DU CÉOU
Moncalou, 24200 Florimont-Gaumier
Tel: 05-53-28-14-47 Fax: 05-53-28-32-48
Email: vignerons-du-ceou@wanadoo.fr

The *cave* has emerged as an important *locomotive* in this project, controlling five hectares. The Domme **Tradition** 2004 (B*) has good colour and plenty of body with encouraging minerality. It is sturdy and mouth-filling.

OTHER GOOD GROWERS
OF RED AND WHITE BERGERAC

▓ DOMAINE CONSTANT
Jean-Louis Constant
24680 Lamonzie-Saint-Martin
Tel: 05-53-24-07-08 Fax: 05-53-24-28-43

▓ CHÂTEAU LES FONTENELLES
Famille Bourdil
GAEC Les Fontenelles
24500 Saint Julien d'Eymet
Tel: 05-53-58-82-01 Fax: 05-53-61-32-07
Email: chateau.fontenelles@free.fr

▓ CHÂTEAU DE LA JAUBERTIE
S. A. Ryman
24560 Colombier
Tel: 05-53-58-32-11

After some ups and downs, this estate is back in top form with its exemplary dry white bergerac.

▓ CHÂTEAU MEYRAND LACOMBE
M. Lorenzon
24240 Cunèges
Tel: 05-53-58-46-32 Fax: 05-53-58-29-61

▓ CHÂTEAU DE MARNIÈRES
Christophe Geneste
Les Brandines, 24520 Saint-Nexans
Tel: 05-53-58-31-65 Fax: 05-53-73-20-34

A property which has come into prominence in recent years. Good all-rounders.

▓ CHÂTEAU MONTDOYEN
Jean-Paul Hembise
24240 Monbazillac
Tel: 05-53-58-85-85 Fax: 05-53-61-67-78
Email: chateaumontdoyen@wanadoo.fr
www.chateau-montdoyen.com

Of note is the **Cuvée La Part des Anges** (**D).

▓ CHÂTEAU MONESTIER LA TOUR
Philip de Haseth-Möller
24240 Monestier
Tel: 05-53-24-18-43
www.chateaumonestierlatour.com

▓ CHÂTEAU DE PANISSEAU
M. Becker
24240 Thénac
Tel: 05-53-58-40-03 Fax: 05-53-58-94-46

▓ CHÂTEAU LE PARADIS
Madame Tonneau
Les Mayets, 24560 Saint-Perdoux
Tel: 05-53-61-92-00

▓ CHÂTEAU LA RAYRE
Vincent Vesselle
24560 Colombier
Tel: 05-53-58-32-17 Fax: 05-53-24-55-58
Email: vincent.vesselle@wannadoo.fr
www.chateau-la-rayre.fr

Also good monbazillac.

▌ CHÂTEAU LE RAZ
Gil Barde
24610 Saint-Méard-de-Gurçon
Tel: 05-53-82-48-41 Fax: 05-53-80-07-47
www.le-raz.com

▓ CHÂTEAU LA ROBERTIE
Jean-Philippe and Brigitte Soulier
24240 Rouffignac-de-Sigoulès
Tel: 05-53-61-35-44 Fax: 05-53-58-53-07
Email: chateau.larobertie@wanadoo.fr

▓ CHÂTEAU TOUR DE GRANGEMONT
Christian Lavergne
24560 Saint-Aubin-de-Lanquais
Tel: 05-53-24-31-50 Fax: 05-53-24-56-77

MONBAZILLAC

AREA OF AOC: selected parcels in communes of Colombier, Monbazillac, Pomport, Rouffignac-de-Sigoulès and Saint-Laurent-des-Vignes.

TOTAL POTENTIAL AREA OF VINEYARD: 3600 hectares.
In spring before the vintage, growers must supply a list of parcels which will be producing as Monbazillac AOC.
SWEET WHITE WINES ONLY: there are complex restrictions on the amount of other white wines which may be made by a Monbazillac maker.
PERMITTED GRAPE VARIETIES: sémillon, muscadelle, sauvignon.
MAXIMUM YIELD: 30 hl/ha. Hand-picking only in two or more *tries,* which are compulsory.
PLANTING DENSITY: 3300 plants per hectare with transitional relief to year 2020.
MINIMUM ALCOHOL CONTENT: 13% by volume.

This is no doubt the most famous wine of the Dordogne *département*, as well as the oldest of its vineyards. Today it covers 2500 hectares and produces 50,000 hectolitres of wine, more than 10% of the total production of the Bergerac region. The figures vary very much from year to year. Monbazillac is always sweet; there is no such thing as dry monbazillac. Dry wines produced here must be sold as bergerac *sec*. However, as some growers move towards an ultra-*liquoreux* style, others may try and secure a secondary appellation for the more traditional *vins moëlleux*. Like Sauternes, monbazillac is based on the *sémillon* grape, some growers adding a little *muscadelle* and/or *sauvignon*.

The road to the vineyard leads south out of Bergerac town. As you leave the valley, the ground starts to rise in shelves. The rich, fertile soil of the plain gives way gradually to layers of sandstone and then clayish chalk. The hill of Monbazillac itself appears like a striped green curtain in front of you, and beyond it the landscape changes to one of gently rolling hills. It is on the north-facing slopes of the Monbazillac hill that many of the best wines are made. This exposure brings the danger of frosts in spring, but it also accounts for the unique character of the wine. The climate is temperate, so that in autumn the lie of the land causes the formation of morning mists which are slow to clear, because the sun does not reach the vines until it is high in the sky. Only after midday does the warm October sunshine draw the moisture first southward up the slope of the land and then into the atmosphere, dispelling the mist, which has in the meantime produced a microscopic fungoid growth. This is *Botrytis cinerea*, the noble rot which shrivels the skins of the grapes and causes the juice inside to concentrate. The reduced volume of liquid is correspondingly more loaded with sugar. This is the same phenomenon as occurs in the wines of Sauternes, but rarely in other parts of the South-West, even where the

making of sweet wines is a speciality. To extract the maximum natural sweetness from the grapes, the pickers go over the plants several times instead of picking all the grapes at one visit. The idea is that every grape should be gathered at maximum ripeness. In the South-West this is called *tries successives*. It explains why in Monbazillac the grapes must not be picked by machine: if they are, today's grower loses the right to use the name Monbazillac.

Before the Revolution, when honey was the usual source of sugar, the cultivation of bees was forbidden in Bergerac, in order to prevent excessive sweetening of the wines. But the Dutch insisted on a regular supply of monbazillac, year in and year out and irrespective of whether the autumn season had been propitious to the development of botrytis. Sugaring of the wine came to be abused, some growers even adding *eau-de-vie* to beef up the wine in a poor year. Especially after the Second World War, the standard of monbazillac fell sharply. In 1939 it fetched the same price as a good Sauternes, but during the fifties and sixties the price fell to about a quarter of that of its rivals. It still had its devotees, but was consumed rather as a cheap aperitif than as a dessert wine. Bernard Ginestet, a distinguished French expert on the wines of Bergerac, has likened the wine at this period to an ageing actress—still much talked about but no longer able to hold the front of the stage. The image of the wine had slipped, but the potential for quality was always there. Today there has been a marked revival in the demand for monbazillac, mirroring the situation in Jurançon, where a new generation of producers has concentrated on making wines which accentuate the *typicité* of the *terroir*.

OUTSTANDING PRODUCERS OF MONBAZILLAC

■ **CAVE COOPÉRATIVE DE MONBAZILLAC**

Route de Monbazillac

24240 Monbazillac

Tel: 05-53-63-65-00 Fax: 05-53-63-65-09

Email: monbazillac@chateau-monbazillac.com

www.chateau-monbazillac.com

This *cave*, operating out of an unmistakably ugly complex of buildings on the road south from Bergerac to Eymet, was one of the pioneers in the revival of monbazillac, and even today it claims nearly half of the total production. There is a large and impressive retail shop where, as well as the local wines, you can buy single-malt whiskies, foie gras and other gastro-goodies. Although it is possible also to buy wine here *en vrac*, the accent is on the top-of-the-range wines, including some which it makes for other domaines. The *Cave* has been particularly successful since the 1990's, when, after a period of wrangling and dispute, a new team was appointed to run it and the policy of quality rather than bulk production was firmly adopted.

The most important social function of this *Cave* is its ownership of the **Château de Monbazillac** (**C), a superb building overlooking the valley of the Dordogne, with a history going back to the Middle Ages. The wine from the château is also by far the finest for which the *Cave* is responsible, and it sells at prices comparable to those fetched by some of the best independent growers. The château receives over 40,000 visitors a year to its 16th-century interior, which houses some of the most highly polished furniture you are likely ever to see, as well as priceless manuscripts of Erasmus and other Protestant writers, the property having once been a stronghold of the most fanatical religious dissenters of the area. Also much worth seeing is the wine museum. A mid-morning tour of the château, followed by a tasting (not free) and picnic in the woods adjoining is a very pleasant way of spending a hot summer day.

Of the other monbazillacs which the *Cave* makes, **Château Septy** (*B) is an old established estate which was one of the original 32 *marques hollandaises*, and today it has been exploited as a joint venture between the *Cave* and outside interests. It is said that the situation of this property is so good that the harvest is often finished before the grapes at Château Monbazillac are fit to pick. Other properties for which the *Cave* makes wine are **Château Touron** (another *marque hollandaise*) and **Château la Sabatière**, but perhaps their best single-domaine wine is not monbazillac at all but red bergerac that comes from **Château Pion** (*B), notable for its high percentage of *merlot* vines. The wine is powerful, with a deep and complex bouquet; the fruit is very ripe, and gentle oak-ageing gives just the right added complexity without adding extraneous flavours. Although, like many bergeracs, it can be drunk young, it would undoubtedly age well.

■ DOMAINE DE L'ANCIENNE CURE
Christian Roche
24560 Colombier
Tel: 05-53-58-27-90 Fax: 05-53-24-83-95
Email: ancienne-cure@wanadoo.fr
www.domaine-anciennecure.fr

This handsome domaine, named after the presbytery of the tiny hamlet of Colombier, is the hub of the village, dominating from its hillside perch the Route Nationale 21 south out of Bergerac and the surrounding countryside. A few years back, Christian Roche converted an old family barn on the main road into a tasting and reception area, though the wine is still made on the top of the hill. The family, like so many others in the district, were *polyculteurs*, growing and rearing a bit of everything; the vines were something of a side line, although Christian points out that the family have been growing them for three generations.

Today, however, Christian devotes all his time to the vines. Apart from being a brilliant wine-maker, he has developed promotional skills to the point where he can hardly begin to count the medals and citations he has earned in just a few years. They are well deserved too, because his is undoubtedly one of the flagship properties of Monbazillac.

Like all true *vignerons*, he begins with the *terroir*, and Christian maintains that the renaissance of monbazillac is due to the realization that quality comes not from planting vines anywhere and hoping for the best (as most farmers did in the old days), but from a basic understanding of how different *terroirs* should be interpreted. Over his 42 hectares he has a wide variety of soil, chalk, *boulbènes, argilo-calcaire* and *argilo-limoneux,* giving a great deal of flexibility when the eventual grading of the grapes according to quality and finally their *assemblage* come to be made.

Christian makes three ranges of wine, 'Les Classiques', 'Cuvée Abbaye' and 'L'Extase', and each range includes dry white and red bergerac, as well as the monbazillacs for which he is famous. In the **Classique** range, the **blanc sec** (***A) is exceptional in terms of quality and value for the money; from 60% *sauvignon* and 40% *sémillon,* the wine is aged on its lees without sulphuring. Though fully dry on the palate, it has aromas of peaches and apricots and a surprising fullness. The **bergerac rouge** (**A) is as good an example of its kind as you are likely to come across, as is the **monbazillac** (**B), made in the traditional way from the first *trie* of grapes, not too heavy or oversweet, though redolent of honey and acacia flowers and with plenty of barley-sugar on the palate. Neither the **bergerac moëlleux** (**A), a beautiful wine to accompany foie gras, nor the pretty **rosé** (*A) appears in the upper ranges. As a group of *entrée de gamme* wines, these are hard to beat.

The **Cuvée Abbaye** wines are all vinified and aged in wood, about 20% of which is new each year. The **blanc sec** (**B) is made from very ripe fruit, picked before the onslaught of botrytis. The wine has less bite than its Classique counterpart, but correspondingly more elegance and class. The **bergerac rouge** (**B) will usually come from 60% or so *merlot*, the rest mainly from *cabernet franc* with just a touch of *cabernet sauvignon*. The wine has the benefit of *microbullage* to soften the tannins and give balance, but it still needs time to show its best. The **monbazillac** (***C), from the second and third *tries*, is in a rather different league, fermented in new barrels for 24 months, but without any wood flavours showing through in the wine, which is extraordinarily rich and decadent.

In the **Extase** range, the **monbazillac** (***D) is made only in exceptional years (recently 2001, 2003 and 2005) and is nothing short of fabulous with its overtones of preserved fruits, vanilla, toast and toffee. Again there is no apparent influence of oak, unlike in the **bergerac rouge** (*C), where the wood tends to get in the way of the fruit, at any rate until the wine is more than six or seven years old.

Mention should also be made of the **pécharmant** (**B), which comes in oaked and unoaked versions. An unusually high proportion of *cabernet sauvignon* gives the wine complexity, and the *cuvée* raised in wood is well handled. The wine is bought from Pécharmant growers and sold by Roche *en négoce*.

■ CHÂTEAU LA BORDERIE
AND CHÂTEAU TREUIL-DE-NAILHAC
Armand Vidal
224240 Monbazillac
Tel: 05-53-57-25-63 Fax: 05-53-63-00-94
Email: chateau.la.borderie@wanadoo.fr
www.pays-de-bergerac.com/vins/chateau-borderie

Family ties link these two old-established Monbazillac estates. Madame Vidal's family has for many generations owned Treuil-de-Nailhac, which was one of the first properties to market its wine in bottles rather than casks. The château is on top of the Monbazillac hill just off the road to Eymet.

Although Armand has been making wine at La Borderie for 40 years, he is a relative newcomer, being *languedocien* by origin; he has brought to Monbazillac all the passion and temperament one associates with the deep south. Today the wines of both properties are made at La Borderie.

As always in Monbazillac, it is the sweet wines which are the attraction. The monbazillacs from the two estates have subtle but different characters of their own; the **Treuil-de-Nailhac** (**B) is much

more muscaty because of the high proportion of *muscadelle* in the blend, while the **Borderie** (*B) has more citrus and tropical fruits in its build. Vidal's skill in the use of oak is reflected in the relative delicacy of these wines. His pure **muscadelle** (*B) is well worth looking out for too.

■ CHÂTEAU BÉLINGARD
Laurent and Sylvie Bosredon
24240 Pomport
Tel: 05-53-58-28-03 Fax: 05-53-58-38-39
Email: contact@belingard.com
www.chateaubelingard.com

Not all the best vineyards look down northwards to the Dordogne Valley. Just over the top of the ridge and out of sight of the river is this large domaine of 60 hectares. There are another 25 hectares in the direction of Monestier, outside the Monbazillac appellation. The Bosredon family and their ancestors the Clauzels have owned this estate for many hundreds of years. They themselves go back to the 10th century. Blanche, the beloved grandmother of the present Count Laurent, died not long ago, just before her 103rd birthday, having relished daily to the date of her death old vintages of Bélingard, such as 1959 and 1948. Laurent acknowledges that she is still the presiding genius of the vineyard, and he names some of his top *cuvées* after her.

Bélingard looks west down the valley towards the Côtes de Castillon, where General Talbot met his death on the battlefield at the close of the Hundred Years' War. In the immediate foreground there used to be a château from which the local barons launched the first attack of that war on the city of Bergerac. Bélingard is the only place in France from where you can see the start and finish of that marathon struggle. It took 100 years for soldiers to make a net advance of 30 miles.

The prospect from the terrace of Bélingard is exceptionally pleasing, the folds of the hills producing an endlessly fascinating pattern of cultivation, the various parcels divided by alleyways of grass.

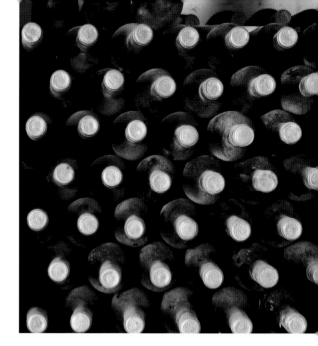

The effect is of an abstract monochrome in green. You can sit, as no doubt Blanche did, for hours on end enjoying the interplay of the sunlight on the different angles and shades in the vine rows.

Bélingard means in Celtic 'the stone of Belin', the sun god of the Celts. On a hilltop nearby is the small tumulus called Moncuq, which means 'the hill of twilight'. The Druids were once very important here. Their priests were not averse to a kind of wine which they made from honey and the juice of the wild vine. Their flock were lyingly told that it was made from mistletoe and thus non-alcoholic. The Bosredons have unearthed a druidical sacrificial chair in an amazing state of preservation. It is thought to have been used in human sacrifices to Belin, so perhaps Bélingard is the oldest vineyard in France?

Within a strictly limited yield of not more than 20 hectolitres to the hectare and sometimes as little as 10, it is the policy at Bélingard to make as much monbazillac (rather than other bergeracs) as the conditions of the vintage will allow. The total production of monbazillac is thus relatively small for such a large estate, about 350 hectolitres on average. The *encépagement* is 80% *sémillon* and 10% each *sauvignon* and *muscadelle*. Usually there are two or three *cuvées* made in ascending order of richness; the first, bearing just the **Château Bélingard** name (**B), is lighter and fruitier in style than the others, some of the grapes being picked before the onslaught of botrytis. The fermentation is stopped when the wine has reached 13 degrees of alcohol, and the wine is matured in tanks before being transferred to old barrels. **Monbazillac Cuvée Blanche de Bosredon** (***C) is altogether richer and more sumptuous, from wholly botrytized grapes and raised in barrels.

There are dry whites too at Bélingard. A straight dry **bergerac blanc** (*A) in both oaked and unoaked form is not quite in the same class as the 100% *sauvignon* **L'Ivresse** (**B), which is fermented and aged in wood. It is made from very late picked grapes, but before botrytis has attacked the fruit. It is barrel-fermented and aged in wood for 18 months; bone dry chemically, it has an extraordinary sucrosity and richness, and Laurent says he himself prefers to drink it after rather than before the reds. There are four of these: the basic **bergerac rouge** (**A), a straight *merlot/cabernet* blend raised in tanks; **Cuvée Alliance** (*A), which gives more than a nod of acknowledgment to the influence of New World wine-makers, the wines being supple and not shy about their oak-ageing in American barrels; the red **Cuvée Blanche de Bosredon** (**B), a worthy partner for the monbazillac of the same name; and the top red wine of the estate, called **Ortus** (*C), to which I meanly give one star because for my taste it is over-oaked. Laurent de Bosredon describes it as a marriage between power and femininity, and lovers of new wood will doubtless agree and upgrade it accordingly. I wonder if Blanche would have liked it.

▪ CHÂTEAU LE FAGÉ

François Gérardin
24240 Pomport
Tel: 05-53-58-32-55 Fax: 05-53-24-57-19
Email: info@chateau-le-fage.com
www.chateau-le-fage.com

This property, like Bélingard, has been in the same family for many generations, and the wine is often to be found in the UK. François Gérardin must be proud of what is one of the most beautifully situated of all the Bergerac estates. Crowned by a long low Chartreuse-type building completed by a classical pediment, the vines start at the top of the Monbazillac ridge, where the *sauvignon* and *muscadelle* are planted. The high ground enables them to give finesse and suavity to the wines. Planted in vertical rows in the direction of the slopes, *de haut en bas* as the French say, the *sémillon* takes over on the lower ground, where grape variety and *terroir* combine to give maximum sugar and structure. A feature of the property is the excellent natural drainage: even in the wettest weather the water runs away quickly. The *cave* where the wine is made has been built at the bottom of the slope, so that the grapes can all be taken downhill instead of up the steep gradients to the château.

Before the Revolution, the vineyard, like many others, was planted mainly with red grapes. In modern times it was François Gérardin's grandfather, Albert Géraud, who built the reputation of the wine, largely by promoting it himself at country fairs. In those days it was one of the more expensive *crus*. He became mayor of his commune and a much respected member of the community, but never recovered from the death of his son who had been a prisoner for five years during the Second World War. When he retired, he handed over the vineyard to his son-in-law, Maurice Gérardin, François's father, and François in turn took it over in 1983. François is an articulate and highly persuasive advocate for the wines of smaller growers, he himself having been president of the Association of Independent Vignerons for three years (1999 to 2002).

Modern techniques can nowadays make it possible to produce acceptable wine even in poor years, but in Monbazillac, where everything depends on the botrytis, you are almost totally at the mercy of the weather. He describes the challenge as rather like going to the casino. If you win, you win a lot; if you lose, you end up with a lot of bergerac *sec*. So François makes the entire range of red, white and pink wines, and while he modestly concedes that his may not always be the best

in any particular style, overall his total production earns high marks.

His basic **monbazillac** (**B) is lighter and less honeyed in style than many, because he uses a good proportion of unbotrytized fruit. It has good acidity, some elegance and is not cloying, making it a better partner for food than many heavier wines. There are only small quantities of *sauvignon* and *muscadelle* in this wine; they and the *sémillon* are all vinified together in enamelled concrete, which is François's preferred material, though he now recognizes the practical advantages of stainless steel. The **Grande Réserve** (**C) is an oaked version of the same wine, raised in barrels which have already seen one wine. Although the wood is not prominent, the result is totally different, and equally delicious.

From fruit which is all unbotrytized, François makes a **côtes de bergerac moëlleux** (**A), from equal quantities of *sémillon* and *muscadelle*. It is given between 12 and 18 months ageing in tank. For his **bergerac blanc sec** (**A) he uses only *sauvignon*, which he gives skin contact before a slow fermentation at 16 degrees celsius. He ages it for four months in cement tanks. There is a barrel-aged version too, called **Cuvée Maurice** (**B), named after his father, the wine being deliciously fruity and with an extraordinarily long finish. The **rosé** (**A) is not drawn off the red wine, but made by leaving the grapes, all *cabernet franc*, to macerate on their own for 72 hours before pressing them.

There are two **côtes de bergerac rouge** (**A and **B) respectively, the one aged in tanks, the other in barrels, both made very largely (80%) from *merlot*, with just 20% *cabernet sauvignon*. Both have round, almost sweet, smooth fruit. François was once reluctant to use barrels, but he finds that he has moved with the times and is proud to offer a complete range, which he is not ashamed to finish off with some excellent bag-in-box examples. He is an advocate of this form of presentation, enabling both private and restaurant clients to draw off wine as and when needed rather than having to consume an entire bottle within a relatively short time span. Nor would he like to be labelled 'old-fashioned', a term which is almost an insult in some sectors of the wine trade. He has, for example, appointed the fashionable Jean-Marc Dournel as his *oenologue*. François sees the future of monbazillac as being in the exploitation of fruit: honey and flowers are no longer enough on their own; for him it is the fruit which must shine through and give the wines the acidity and freshness they need to avoid being heavy and cloying. For those who like to get away from overweight, international styles, François's wines come as a merciful contrast.

■ GRANDE MAISON
Thierry Desprès
24240 Monbazillac
Tel: 05-53-58-26-17 Fax: 05-53-24-97-36
Email: thierry.despres@free.fr
www.grande-maison.fr

This ancient property, acquired by Desprès in 1990, was once an outpost of a much bigger château destroyed during the Wars of Religion. The old stone house is of that period and is today the heart of one of the most interesting of all Monbazillac vineyards. The four hectares which Desprès bought were in a shocking state, but in the meantime, by means of purchase and exchange, he has 20 under plantation, three-quarters of which have been replanted to a modern density and on well-considered *porte-greffes*. The soil has a deal of clay and limestone and a strong element of flint, which Desprès says gives a certain acidity to the *terroir*. The steep slopes all face south. Three-quarters of the vineyard is planted with white grapes, of which *sémillon* accounts for half, *muscadelle* just over a third, and the rest is *sauvignon*.

Desprès was always a bio person, and so from the moment he started to make wine he adopted full bio principles for which he enjoys Ecovert certification. Thus, to avoid the debasement of the *terroir*, there are no weedkillers, chemical fertilizers or synthetic pesticides. Added to this are certain aspects of biodynamic principles, including adherence to the cycles of the moon and the spraying of juices from wild plants such as nettles and bracken. Then there is the question of removing the long shoots from the interior of the vine plants, the usual *vendanges en vert*, a cleaning-up by hand after the passage of mechanical weeders, and a removal of surplus leaves from both faces of the plant in August.

The grapes are all picked by hand, with up to five *tries* for the grapes destined for the dry wine, as well as for the botrytized grapes. Sometimes Desprès uses techniques of supra-extraction, the freezing of the grapes followed by pressing at low temperature. Sulphur dioxide, permitted in bio circles, is added at once to prevent oxidization. Fermentation without additional yeasts starts in tank, then continues in barrel for all the sweet wines and most of the dry ones too. The dry wines are aged for nearly a year, and the sweet for nearly two.

As may be imagined, such counsel of perfection produces wines of absolutely top quality. Nothing that Desprès makes is less than ***, even his basic **blanc sec** (B), raised unusually for him in tank like his basic red, **Cuvée d'Antoinette** (B), virtually all *merlot*. The more prestigious **sec** (C) is correspondingly more complex, as is the second **rouge** (C). There are no fewer than four **monbazillacs,** the first (C) delicious for its emphasis on fruit, and superior to many other growers' top *cuvées*; a pure *sweet sauvignon* (C), which is an astonishing tour de force; a more traditional *sémillon/muscadelle* blend (D); and the richest wine of all, called **Cuvée des Monstres** (D+), pure nectar of which only the gods are worthy.

Needless to say, the walls of Desprès's *caveau de dégustation* would be covered with his medals and diplomas were there space for them all.

■ CHÂTEAU HAUT-BERNASSE

Jules and Marie Villette

24240 Monbazillac

Tel: 05-53-58-36-22 Fax: 05-53-61-26-40

Email: contact@haut-bernasse.com

www.haut-bernasse.com

In 1977 this property was acquired by a Paris businessman named Jacques Blais, who not only loved wine but played the cello well too. In those days there were only nine hectares of vines, and Blais soon showed himself to be a pioneer in the renaissance of the Monbazillac vineyard, introducing many of the techniques which are today commonplace. In 2002 the property was sold to its present owners. Monsieur Villette is a businessman from Nice, and he has been wise to retain the services of Xavier Giannorsi, who trained under Blais; he has also appointed a new *maître de chais*, Sébastien Dieuaide, who is also in charge of the sales side.

In 30 years there have been so many changes in Monbazillac that the regime created by Blais seems in the eyes of the youngbloods now in charge to need bringing up to date. To start with, they have 24 hectares of vines to look after, of which 18 are devoted to monbazillac, all one single plantation of vines grouped round the *chais*. Planted to a high density of 5000 plants to the hectare, they give grapes which are picked very late indeed, sometimes into December. Yields are low, averaging about 15 hectolitres to the hectare. Once the grapes are in the *chais,* they are pressed in old vertical presses dating back 100 or so years.

There are two monbazillacs. **Les Coteaux de Bernasse** (**B), from 85% s*émillon*, 10% *muscadelle* and 5% *sauvignon*, is fermented and aged in tank and is of the style of an old-fashioned monbazillac, not too honeyed, more of a *moëlleux* type. On the other hand, the **Château Haut-Bernasse** (**D) is fermented in wood, half the barrels being new and half one season old, and the wine is aged for up to 20 months before being bottled. It is then stored another year before being marketed. The colour of the wine is a deep gold, with a honeyed, nutty and intense bouquet. Rich and fat in the mouth, the finish has a good acidity to keep the palate fresh.

■ LES HAUTS DE CAILLEVEL

Sybille Chevalier and Marc Ducroz

24240 Pomport

Tel and fax: 05-53-73-92-72

Email: caillevel@wanadoo.fr

Sybille's parents were farmers in Normandy. She went to work in Paris, where she met her husband. After a while they wanted to make a new start, something creative with new values. They pondered this for four years and ultimately nudged each other towards making wine. Ultimately they responded to advertisements: 'The devil took us to the top of this hill, showed us the view from the *terrasse,* and we fell.' The property is at the very southernmost edge of the Monbazillac appellation, facing full south.

Husband and wife had in the meantime done some training at technical college, but apart from this they are self-taught. They are either remarkably lucky at having found lovely *terroir* with some 100-year-old vines, or they are potential geniuses—or perhaps both, because the wines are top-class. For their dry **Fleur de Roche** (***A), they waited till late September to pick in the heat-wave 2003 vintage, and, following much-needed rain at just the right moment, were rewarded with good acidity in the grapes. The wine is both fat and fresh, raised in tank only and quite exceptional.

They have experimented with an oaked white which lives up to its name of **L'Atypique** (*B), an interesting and unusual blend of *muscadelle*, a little *ugni blanc* and the rest *sémillon*. They are very keen on *muscadelle*, even though it is a difficult plant to grow, being liable to disease. Sybille is not the first grower to complain about the quality of the single modern clone of this variety.

Their **rosé** (**A) is almost a *clairet*, all from *cabernet sauvignon*, half *saigné* and half pressed direct. Very concentrated and not for babies—or grandmothers.

The reds here are as good as the whites, which is not always the case in Monbazillac. The basic **bergerac rouge** (**A) is typically 40% *merlot*, the two *cabernets* making up the balance in equal shares: a good *assemblage* with a nice sweet fruity flavour, good acidity and soft tannins. The superior **Terres Chaudes** (**B) is from equal quantities of the three grapes and high class indeed. There is a choice of dessert wines. The **unoaked monbazillac** (***B) is refreshingly elegant and not overblown. The **oaked** version (**B) was good too but more in the general run. There is also a version from pure *muscadelle* called **Muscad'Elle** (***D), which is highly perfumed but not cloying. This is an unpretentious but first-class domaine with talented and enthusiastic owners who are sure to get even better.

▪ **LES VIGNOBLES DE POULVÈRE ET BARSES**
Francis and Bernard Borderie
24240 Monbazillac
Tél: 05-53-58-30-25 Fax: 05-53-58-35-87
Email: francis.borderie@poulvere.com
www.poulvere.com

These growers are surprising in at least one respect: They do not vinify the different grape varieties separately, at any rate in years when all the grapes are healthy.

The vineyard combines Château Poulvère, the Domaine des Barses and the Domaine Haute Brie et du Caillou. Despite the family name, they have nothing to do with the Domaine Borderie down the road, which is rather confusing. The Borderies have been here since 1923, and Bernard, Francis and Yolande represent the third generation, nowadays assisted by Frédéric, Bernard's son. With 91 hectares of vines, the estate is one of the biggest in the Bergerac region. The scale of operations remains human nevertheless, while enabling the Borderies to offer their customers the whole range of Bergerac wines.

The vineyards were almost entirely destroyed by the catastrophic frosts of 1956, and there are still some parcels of vines which show the sufferings of that winter. The Borderies have to be careful to perpetuate the vineyard; a few hectares are replaced each year to ensure the rejuvenation of the domaine and to keep the yield up to scratch. The grapes from the oldest vines give the best juice, but no plant is immortal. The average age of the vines is 30 years.

For their traditional **monbazillac** (**B), the Borderies do not necessarily want to extract the last gram of sugar, so they allow botrytis to develop on only 80% of the grapes. It is made from 30% *muscadelle*, the rest mainly *sémillon* with just a little *sauvignon*. The juice is drawn off the skins and pips at low temperature and fermented for at least a fortnight in steel or concrete. The wine is then aged in tanks for at least a year before bottling.

There is also a **barrel-aged monbazillac** (**B), fermented nevertheless in tanks and not wood. The barrels are replaced on a four-year cycle, and there is no evidence of undesired flavours in the wine, which is spicy and exotic.

▪ **CHÂTEAU THEULET**
Alard Père et Fils
24240 Monbazillac
Tel: 05-53-57-30-43 Fax: 05-53-58-88-28
Email: antoine.alard@wanadoo.fr

Pierre Alard thinks he is the sixth generation of his family to make wine at Theulet. His two sons will be the seventh. One of his forebears founded a *maison de commerce* in Holland to promote the trade in Bergerac wines after the revocation of the Edict of Nantes. Féret, whose commentary on the wines of Bergerac, first published in 1903, is still much sought after and respected, rated the wines of Theulet particularly highly, even though, after the phylloxera, the vineyard had been replanted mostly with red-wine grapes. Pierre explains that with the sugar shortage in the First World War, there was a sudden demand for sweet monbazillac wines, so a lot of replanting was carried out, this time with the traditional white varieties.

According to Antoine Alard, about one-third of the total production at Theulet is of monbazillac, for which the typical *encépagement* is 80% *sémillon,* 12% *muscadelle* and 8% *sauvignon.* They like to make as much of the wine as they can as monbazillac, because it fetches the better price and is in any case the *vin du terroir.* But they will always make some dry white wine, and in some years considerable quantities if conditions are not right for the sweet. The dominance of *sémillon* in the *encépagement* gives the dry wines an unusual richness, what the French call *gras,* which distinguishes them from many wines based more on *sauvignon.*

It is still the monbazillac which is the basis of Theulet's reputation, and Alard's are some of the best. Nowadays all three versions are aged in French oak barrels. The basic **monbazillac** (**B) has unusual freshness, a viscous texture supporting exotic fruits, with the wood lurking somewhere in the background. A mature bottle of the **Cuvée Prestige** (***C) may show a fine balance between exotic and citrus fruits, while the top **Cuvée Antoine Alard** (***D) is as ambitious as any in the appellation. It is raised in 100% new oak, which gives huge complexity without any taste of floorboards. Antoine Alard is not afraid to play the monbazillac card, and his is very rich and sweet, redeemed by a lovely twist of acidity right in the middle of the palate.

The dry whites come in two ranges, and the bergerac reds in three: Cuvée Tradition, Cuvée Prestige and Cuvée Antoine. For the whites, the basic **blanc sec** (*A) has a preliminary maceration of its largely *sauvignon* grapes, while the **Cuvée Antoine** (**B) may lose some of its zip from its *élevage* in wood, but gains finesse and class. The red wines show huge fruit and rich tannins and clearly need time, even the **Tradition** (*A); both **oaked versions** show more wood on the nose than on the palate (**B and **C respectively) and are real keepers.

Note: In 2004 the family acquired the Pécharmant property La Métairie, which in earlier years enjoyed a high reputation for its wines. Antoine has made this venture his own, and it is one to watch. He has recently further extended his interests in Pécharmant by acquiring the Château de Biran.

CHÂTEAU TIRECUL-LA-GRAVIÈRE
Bruno and Claudie Bilancini
24240 Monbazillac
Tel: 05-53-57-44-75 Fax: 05-53-61-36-49
Email: infos@vinibilancini.com
www.vinibilancini.com

There are only eight hectares in production at this smallish estate, put together by the Bilancinis while Bruno was working as an *oenologue* at the *cave coopérative* at Monbazillac. The strategy was to go straight to the top, and they have certainly got there. First, the *terroir* is extraordinary: two slopes, each draining perfectly and naturally into a central stream, chalky on the higher ground with increasing amounts of clay down the hill and, on the north side, some sandy clay. The vines face north and east, their mini-valley forming a perfect trap for the autumn mists, which generate the much-prized noble rot. Bruno says that there has been only one year for him when there was no botrytis, while for many other growers it is a hit or miss affair whether they get the benefit.

Production is almost entirely of monbazillac, although small quantities of a *vin de pays du Périgord* are made from a few *sauvignon* grapes, tempered by some of Bruno's *muscadelle.* For Bruno the fact that nearly half his vineyard is planted with *muscadelle* has been a large factor in his success. He appreciates that for many others, *muscadelle* is bad news: there is only one clone currently available and it is a bad one at that, although work is being done on producing a new one. The grape is liable to disease, it produces a lot of greenery and therefore needs extra work in the vineyard, and the usual *porte-greffes* encourage high yields which need strict control. Furthermore, *muscadelle* is not attacked in a regular fashion by botrytis; often only some of the grapes in a bunch will be affected. Bruno, however, is lucky; his *muscadelle* was already there when he rented and then bought the vines, and as he needs to replace them he does so by *sélection massale* without recourse to the poor modern clone. Since his vineyard is so small, he bows with good grace to the extra work which *muscadelle* demands, while he feels able to control the diseases by using only the acceptable bordeaux mixture and copper sulphate. His high botrytis record is also an advantage, which he improves on by making sure that as many individual grapes as possible have separate and unimpeded access to the autumn air.

Such fanatical attention to each and every plant, almost every bunch of grapes, results in tiny yields, sometimes as little as eight hectolitres to the hectare, but never more than 12. But the aim is not to produce the richest and sweetest, but the best balanced of wines, and here again the *muscadelle* plays a vital part in adding its mineral and fruit flavours to the *gras* of the *sémillon*. The grapes are pressed briefly for five or six hours and then left to settle for two days or so. The juice is then drawn off by gravity direct into barrels, which vary in age between one and five previous seasons. Here the wine is fermented and aged for 18 months or more.

The Bilancinis—it is important to stress that Claudie is as important to the success of the operation as Bruno—make usually just two *cuvées*. The first, called modestly **Monbazillac Château Tirecul-la-Gravière** (***D), is already ahead of most if not all of the field in this appellation. The **Cuvée Madame** (***D+) is, however, in a class of its own, having achieved equality in status on the international market with the best sweet white wines of the world. Sadly, such quality does not come cheap, the pain heightened by the bottles holding only 50 centilitres (unless reckless extravagance suggests a magnum of 150 centilitres).

■ CHÂTEAU LES CLOS DES VERDOTS
David Fourtout
See above under Bergerac winemakers.

OTHER GOOD MONBAZILLAC PRODUCERS

■ CHÂTEAU BAROUILLET
Gérard Alexis
24240 Pomport
Tel: 05-53-58-42-20

■ CHÂTEAU BELLEVUE
Gérard Lajonie
24240 Monbazillac
Tel: 05-53-57-17-96

■ CLOS BELLEVUE
Michel Royard-Blanchard
24240 Flaujac
Tel: 05-53-58-40-23

■ DOMAINE DU BOIS DE POURQUIÉ
Marlène and Alain Mayet
24560 Conne-de-Labarde
Tel: 05-53-58-25-58

■ DOMAINE DE COMBET
Daniel Duperret
24240 Monbazillac
Tel: 05-53-58-34-21

■ CHÂTEAU FONTPUDIÈRE
Christiane Alary
24240 Pomport
Tel: 05-53-57-47-27

■ DOMAINE GRANGE NEUVE
La Famille Castaing
24240 Pomport
Tel: 05-53-58-42-23

Note their good côtes de bergerac blanc
moëlleux.

■ DOMAINE DU HAUT-MONTLONG
Alain Sergenton
24240 Pomport
Tel: 05-53-58-81-60

■ CHÂTEAU LADESVIGNES
Michel Monbouché
24240 Pomport
Tel: 05-53-58-30-67
www.ladesvignes.com

■ CHÂTEAU DE MALFOURAT
Christian and Patrick Chabrol
24240 Monbazillac
Tel: 05-53-58-33-10

■ DOMAINE DE PÉCOULA
Marc and René Labaye
24240 Pomport
Tel: 05-53-58-41-89

■ CHÂTEAU DE PLANQUES
Jacques de Meslon
24560 Colombier
Tel: 05-53-58-30-18

■ CHÂTEAU LA RAYRE
Vincent Vesselle
24560 Colombier
Tel: 05-53-58-32-17
www.chateau-la-rayre.fr

■ CHÂTEAU DE SANXET
Bertrand de Passemar
24240 Pomport
Tel: 05-53-58-37-46
www.sanxet.com

SAUSSIGNAC

AREA OF AOC: selected parcels in the communes of Gageac-et-Rouillac, Monestier, Razac-de-Saussignac and Saussignac.

TOTAL POTENTIAL AREA OF PRODUCTION: c. 900 hectares
Qualifying parcels have to be identified and approved in advance of each vintage.
Sweet white wines only.
PERMITTED GRAPE VARIETIES: sémillon, sauvignon and muscadelle.
PLANTING DENSITY: 5000 plants per hectare in rows not more than two metres apart and with the vines not more than 90 centimetres from each other in their rows. Transitional relief to the year 2020.
Vines must be trained on wire; height of foliage must be at least three-fifths of the distance between the rows.
Hand-harvesting in successive *tries* obligatory. Freezing of grapes (*cryosélection*) forbidden.
MAXIMUM YIELD: 25 hl/ha. There are similar restrictions on the production of other whites, as in Monbazillac.

The vineyards of Saussignac link those of Monbazillac to the east with those of Entre-Deux-Mers to the west, creating an unbroken line between left-bank Bergerac and Bordeaux. As at Monbazillac, the vines start on the north side of the ridge rising from the Dordogne Valley and spread over the top into the rolling countryside behind.

Saussignac is one of the most recent (1982) of the Bergerac inner appellations, and it was originally intended to distinguish the range of medium-sweet wines produced there from the more generic côtes de bergerac *moëlleux*. However, the use of the Saussignac name did not take off as quickly as had been expected, producers fearing to leap into the unknown with an unfamiliar name when the Bergerac label seemed so safe. Many therefore produced their 'saussignac' under the Côtes de Bergerac name. The style was in all respects similar and the wines scarcely distinguishable.

After a few years, however, a small group of producers decided to make an altogether sweeter style of saussignac, a counterpart to the revived *liquoreux* of Monbazillac. To do this they had to apply each year to the INAO for permission to apply the Saussignac name to wines which were too sweet to qualify strictly under what were then the Saussignac rules. These placed an upper limit on the amount of residual sugar the wine was supposed to contain. Gradually the popularity of the new style began to overtake the demand for the older less honeyed wines, so that today all saussignac is required to meet the higher sugar requirements inherent in a *liquoreux* wine, at least in botrytis years. As might be expected, the character of saussignac has approximated much more closely that of monbazillac, to the point where it takes experience to tell blind the best of one from the best of the other. Very broadly the monbazillacs, or most of them, are closer to Sauternes in style, more honeyed and sweet, while the saussignacs have a touch more vivacity, almost certainly, it is said, due to a higher chalk content in the soil.

There are many excellent dry white, red and rosé wines made by Saussignac growers, but, as in Monbazillac, these have to be marketed as bergerac or côtes de bergerac as appropriate.

OUTSTANDING SAUSSIGNAC PRODUCERS

◼ **CHÂTEAU COURT LES MÛTS**
Pierre-Jean and Bernadette Sadoux
24240 Saussignac
Tel: 05-53-27-92-17 Fax: 05-53-23-77-21
Email: court-les-muts@wanadoo.fr

The Sadoux family have the largest independent domaine in Saussignac; it covers 83 hectares, the result of a sustained policy of expansion undertaken largely with the object of making a *sauvignon*-based dry white wine. The production of saussignac is relatively small, but its quality is excellent. Pierre-Jean Sadoux can take a deal of the credit for the creation of the Saussignac appellation, and it was fitting that he became the first president of its *syndicat* of growers. His father, who came back from Algeria in 1960, bought this domaine, which consisted at the time of only 14 hectares of vines, although in its time it had enjoyed a fine reputation. At the beginning of the 20th century it was still planted with 40 hectares of ungrafted vines, having miraculously survived the phylloxera up to that time.

Today Sadoux makes both the old-style saussignac, which he must now sell as **côtes de bergerac moëlleux** (**B), and the new ultra-sweet **AOC** (**B), which he had been making under derogation from the authorities during the period when growers were not allowed to produce a wine with so much residual sugar. The former is deliciously lightened by its citrus flavours, while the latter is not at all overblown and with a few years in bottle acquires a homogeneity and balance between acidity and sugar which is very satisfying. The wines of this property are to be found in some retail outlets under the name **Château de Bramefant**.

◼ **CHÂTEAU DES EYSSARDS**
Pascal Cuisset
24240 Monestier
Tel: 05-53-24-36-36 Fax: 04-53-58-63-74
Email: eyssards@aquinet.tm.fr

The Cuissets are a family of important players in this appellation, Pascal having the largest of the domaines. His father bought it in 1984, when the vineyard was very run down and a lot of replanting was needed, even though at the time it consisted of a mere six hectares, mainly in *sémillon*. Pascal says he has learnt everything he knows either from his father or from experience: 'Il y a un grand décalage entre l'école et la réalité' (there is a large gap between what you learn at school and real life), he says. He is no follower of fashion, despising those who betray the *typicité* of their region nearly as much as the large brands and the globalizers. 'Le vin n'est pas le popcorn.' At the same time, he appreciates commercial reality, and his policy is to marry fidelity to his *terroir* with an acceptance that he needs to produce wine which people will buy. Forty hectares take a bit of marketing. His success is evidenced by his notable export record: nearly 40% of his production is sold to the United Kingdom.

His prices are extremely keen; his saussignac **Cuvée Flavie** (**B) is something of a bargain, and is unusual in that he puts in some *chenin blanc*, a permitted but little-seen grape in Bergerac. He makes it somewhat in the older style, being wary of the plasma-screen versions which have taken front stage in recent years, but he manages successfully to highlight the fruit in the wine, and he gives it seven or eight months in used barrels.

His bergerac wines are in the same mould: a delicious **blanc sec Prestige** (**B) is largely *sauvignon* but with 20% *sémillon* to give a peachy flavour. The wine is fresh and exciting, heightened by a gentle ageing in barrel. His **basic white** (**A) is hardly less good.

Pascal planted a little *chardonnay* to make some wine for his own amusement, and it was so successful with his friends that he now markets it under the name **Adagio** (**B) as a *vin de pays*, the grape not being permitted in the appellation. He gives the same name to his **Adagio Rouge** (**B), a mostly *merlot* wine of which he makes about 15,000 bottles a year and which sells well with a fancy label to local restaurants.

The basic **bergerac rouge** (*A) is half *merlot*, half *cabernet franc*, and in 2003 he clearly had problems with the heat and drought. Normally it is a typically good middle-of-the-road wine of its style. A gently oaked **côtes de bergerac** (*B) is another locally popular restaurant wine.

a very chalky clay, and a full range of bergerac wines is made to suit the whole range of English taste. Most of the production is destined for the pubs (particularly the gastro-pubs) and restaurants which are the brewery's clients in the United Kingdom. Welsh makes full use of the recently won right to put the names of the grape varieties on the label, while using the Fayolle name as a kind of brand.

If all this sounds very un-French, the wines represent Bergerac styles well and are a splendid value for the money, even if they don't reach the top flight. Nor do they pretend to. The classic range of **dry white, rosé** and **red** (all *A) are a fine introduction for Anglo-Saxons to Bergerac styles: the first from a *sauvignon-sémillon* blend, the second from a blend of the two *cabernets* and the red mostly from *merlot*. Lightly oaked wines include a **dry sémillon** (*A) and **Cuvée Marcassin** (**B), a blend of *merlot* and *cabernet franc*. *Marcassin* is French for the young of the wild boar, which is the logo of Welsh's brewery, so it is not surprising that he names his top oaked red (too oaked?) **Sang du Sanglier** (*B). The range is completed by a sparkler made by *méthode champenoise* over in Bordeaux and his flagship **saussignac** (**C), not at all cloying and a wine which will give folks in Hampshire something to think about over their *crème brulée*.

▨ CHÂTEAU DE FAYOLLE

David Welsh

24240 Saussignac

Tel: 05-53-74-32-02

Email: chateau.de.fayolle@wanadoo.fr

www.chateaufayolle.com

Welsh claims he is the only English brewer (Ringwood Brewery, Hants.) to be sole proprietor of a French vineyard, and that is certainly true of the Bergeracois. Soon after his purchase, Welsh set about restoring and refurbishing this very pretty estate, and today it is under the management of Laura Southgate. There are *gîtes,* reception and even wedding facilities.

There are 17 hectares of vines, mostly on

▨ CHÂTEAU LESTEVÉNIE

Jolaine and Dominique Audoux

Le Gadon, 24240 Gageac-et-Rouillac

Tel: 05-53-74-24-48 Fax: 05-53-74-24-49

Mobile: 06-11-30-83-76

Email: d.audoux@wanadoo.fr

A short mention must be made to highlight the tiny volume of really fine **saussignac** (***D) produced by this newly arrived business couple turned *vignerons*. The backwoods of the Dordogne are a far cry from Birmingham and even Grenoble, where Dominique obviously did well in his previous commercial incarnation. There is a good range of other bergerac wines (all *A), especially a good dry white. The Audoux are charming hosts and extremely promising in their newfound career. *À suivre*, as they say.

■ **CHÂTEAU LA MAURIGNE**
Patrick and Chantal Gérardin
24240 Razac-de-Saussignac
Tel and fax: 05-53-27-25-45
Email: contact@chateaulamaurigne.com
www.chateaulamaurigne.com.

This old stone-built farm, dating back to the 17th century, its *pigeonnier* still intact, was built on the site of a Gallo-Roman villa, the foundations of which are still visible. The previous owner, a poly-cultural farmer, made his own wine, which was not the greatest, and sold it off *en négoce*. Some of the vines are more than 70 years old, and in places the grape varieties are all mixed up together, which makes harvesting them rather a problem.

The vines are mostly white varieties, roughly 80% *sémillon* and 20% *muscadelle*. There is a small amount of ancient *sauvignon*, an old-fashioned kind which has tiny grapes producing a very aromatic juice. Patrick aims to propagate from these himself by *sélection massale*. He has no time for the modern *sauvignon* clones. The black grapes are mostly *cabernet sauvignon* (72%), with 25% *merlot* and 3% *malbec*. Patrick reserves the *malbec* for his top red *cuvée,* believing it to give notes of dark fruits and roundness.

Of the 17 hectares, only six are planted with vines, which are all picked by hand, now obligatory in the case of the sweet saussignac. The soil is shallow for the most part, a mere 20 centimetres in depth, which means that the vines have to find their way below the top surface and plunge far for nourishment. This enables the well-established older plants to shrug off the effects of drought in hot, dry years. Weeds are allowed to grow in between the vine rows where the plants are sufficiently vigorous.

Nearly all the wines are aged in wood, the whites fermented in it too. The *élevage* is so well handled that the wood is not noticeable and in fact adds considerably to the complexity of the wines, particularly the whites. The barrels are renewed when the cash-flow permits, on average a fifth of them each year. The *chais* is very simple. Patrick has retained the old cowstalls, while recognizing that the inexorable call for more and more space may mean they have to go one day. There is no formal tasting room as yet. In summer visitors are invited to sample the wines under the trees in the garden, otherwise in the Gérardins' home.

The reds are well enough made, usually needing time. The **basic red** (*A) is not aged in wood, but the **oaked version** comes in two grades (*A), both of which have extra complexity and seem sweeter in fruit. The 2001 wines (**A) were particularly successful and will last a long time, with a lovely attack and soft tannins.

The whites are in a different league, all of them very fine, even the basic **bergerac sec** (***A), which, though aged in expensive wood, is a bargain. Given 18 months in older barrels, it remains completely fresh and rather subtle.

The sweet **saussignac** comes in two quite different versions, both marketed in 50 centilitre bottles. The **basic** wine (**B) from 2001 won a gold medal in Paris in 2003 with its attractive load of honey and currants. The *haut-de-gamme* version called **Florilège** (***D) is aged for four years in barrels and is in the ultra-sweet style, light in alcohol (11.5 degrees would be normal) but with heaps of residual sugar.

Patrick sells almost entirely to private customers, which is not so difficult if you only have about six hectares of vines.

■ **CHÂTEAU LES MIAUDOUX**
Nathalie and Gérard Cuisset
24240 Saussignac
Tel: 05-53-27-92-31 Fax: 05-53-27-96-60
Mobile: 06-10-69-83-77
Email: gerard.cuisset@wanadoo.fr

Gérard is the youngest and perhaps the most original of the Cuisset family, who play such a large

SAUSSIGNAC
181

role in Saussignac. Together with Richard Doughty and later joined by Patricia Atkinson (see below), Gérard was one of the pioneers of the new saussignac *liquoreux* and was astonished by the success of his 1990, his first effort in this style, for which he had to ask permission from the authorities to exceed the permitted sugar levels. Gérard made the mistake of not asking enough money for the wine and it quickly sold out. Unhappily, there were three bad years in a row after that, in which he managed to produce only tiny quantities, but, undeterred, he has persevered and has been blessed in recent years by a run of good vintages. To tide him over when the weather lets him down, he has a good sideline in prunes, which he makes from his eight hectares of plums. Gérard has recently completed his conversion to organic production, partly out of conviction and partly egged on by Richard Doughty.

Gérard does not limit himself to the risky business of botrytized sweet wine. He makes a fresh and lively **blanc sec** (**A) aged conventionally in tanks, but his oaked version, called **Inspiration** (***B), from a blend of *sauvignon*, *sémillon* and *muscadelle* is even better, indeed one of the best of this style made in the region, because the fruit is not drowned by technical virtuosity. There are two reds to match the whites, both raised in barrels, but you will find only the gentlest hints of wood on the **bergerac fût** (**B), a wine of good concentration and a harmonious marriage between fruit and oak. The more complex red **Inspiration** (**C) gives a generous nod in the direction of Bordeaux; it is made from Gérard's best parcels of *merlot* (80%) and *cabernet franc* (20%), and its tannins will ensure a long life.

Then there are the sweet wines; first, a **côtes de bergerac moëlleux** (**A) which must be what saussignac was like before the new rules came into being, a delicious foie gras wine, only three parts sweet and much lighter in texture and flavour than the **saussignac** (***C), which is undoubtedly in the top rank of Bergerac sweet wines, a wine which has suppleness and a fine length to support its range of preserved and exotic fruits.

■ **CHÂTEAU RICHARD**
Richard Doughty
La Croix-Blanche, 24240 Monestier
Tel: 05-53-58-49-13-13 Fax: 05-53-58-49-30
Email: info@chateaurichard.com
www.chateaurichard.com

Richard has many claims to fame: the first anglophone to make wine in Saussignac; the first there to adopt entirely bio principles; the only one so far to preach the virtues of really old barrels; and one of the pioneers of the new saussignac *liquoreux* style—not to mention the fact that he makes some of the best wines in the region.

Trained as a geologist, Richard exercised his profession all over the world before deciding that he needed a career change. He went to study wine at La Tour Blanche in the Sauternes, then the only training ground for those wishing to specialize in the making of sweet wines. His teacher persuaded him to become a producer, but he could not afford a vineyard in Bordeaux so opted for the Bergeracois, where he bought his present domaine in 1988.

He has expanded his vineyard from the original five hectares, today having 13 and another four, which he rents. He makes two **white bergeracs**: the first being a sharp and lively unoaked wine (**A), only part *sauvignon* with a generous admixture of *sémillon* and *muscadelle*. The second, from the same grapes, is quite different. It is aged in wood. The barrels, eight years old and more, come from the **Allier** (***A), which gives the wine its name. It is full-bodied, round, a little toasty and nutty and ages well; a quite distinctive and individual *blanc sec*.

From the two *cabernets* which go into his red wines, Richard draws off the juices to make an attractive thirst-quenching **rosé** (**A). His basic **bergerac rouge** (**A) is given nearly a year's ageing in tank and is nicely rounded and smooth, while the **côtes de bergerac** version (***A) is treated to his very old barrels. Richard maintains that, even after eight years, a barrel still has a lot to give a wine in terms of complexity and smoothness. In some years he makes a wine which he calls **Cuvée Osée** (A), a high-risk affair as its name implies, because he eschews the use of sulphur altogether. Sometimes it works, and sometimes it is a disaster.

It is the sweet saussignac style which is Richard's true passion; with Gérard Cuisset and Patricia Atkinson he pioneered the switch in style in Saussignac from just another kind of bergerac *moëlleux* to an authentically different kind of *liquoreux*. He no longer needs a *dérogation* from the authorities to make this kind of wine because it has become the mainstream saussignac style. Richard's versions are still some among the best; his *entrée de gamme*, sometimes called **Novembre** or **Charmes** (***B), is extremely fine and elegant, lighter than some others and not aiming to be a Sauternes lookalike. Although in some years it can be made from as many as eight different pickings, Richard also puts some unbotryticized juice into the blend, giving the finished wine freshness and a nice point of acidity.

Coup de Coeur (***C) may also be an *assemblage* of many *tries*, sweeter in style, with a fine balance between the honey and acidity. Its hallmark flavours are preserved fruits, apricots, quince, sometimes pineapple too.

Richard believes that his combination of biological principles with a total absence of additives (no extra sugar, for example, even when this was permitted under the rules, which it no longer is), and the use of *sauvignon* and *muscadelle* as well as *sémillon* in the blend, make for wines which are both fruity and lively, avoiding the heaviness of some other *vins liquoreux*. **Cuvée Noble** (***D), his top-of-the-range wine, is a fine example, luscious but at the same time what the French call *nerveux*.

Richard, who will lecture his visitors on what others may believe to be old-fashioned wine ideas, can be a revolutionary experimenter too, living in a different world from the mass producers, a firm believer that opening a bottle of wine is a journey of discovery, not simply a repetition of what you opened last week. He stands at quite the opposite pole from what supermarket buyers are trained to look for.

■ **CHÂTEAU LE TAP**
Olivier Roches
24240 Saussignac
Tel: 05-53-27-53-41 Fax: 05-53-22-07-55
Email: chateauletap@orange.fr
www.pays-de-bergerac.com/vins/vinsolites

Olivier left the bosom of his Pécharmant-famous family to buy 12 hectares of vines here in 2001. The property is in the lee of the Château de Saussignac, which is not a wine domaine but a combined museum and antique shop.

There's not much to see at Le Tap except the lovely view across the valley down to the Dordogne in the distance (*tap* in the local language means 'hole'). The buildings are in the course of modernization, and in fine weather tasting takes place on the terrace behind the modest house.

Olivier has increased the plantation density, although the vines were in good shape when he bought them. Since then he has planted some *sauvignon gris* just below his *terrasse*.

Meanwhile, his bergerac *sec,* **Cuvée Grand Chêne** (**B), raised in barrel with frequent *bâtonnage*, is mostly *sémillon*, a delicate and elegant wine. A cask sample was very fruity, rich almost, quite viscous. A red from the barrel had had a maceration of 30 days, was made *en cuve* and then aged in cask.

There are two reds, one plain **bergerac** (**B) with good fruit, firm structure and excellent balance, and raised in tank, the other, the **côtes de bergerac rouge** (*B), aged in barrels, one-third of which are new. The wine is not fined and needs plenty of time on account of the firm tannins.

Olivier's **saussignac** (**B) is very elegant and fine. Although quite rich, it is not excessive in either weight or sugar, and has excellent balance. As might be expected, it is the star wine of the property. Olivier is a relative newcomer to this appellation, if not to the region, but he has already made his mark in Saussignac, and his future looks bright.

The wines are marketed through the family property, Haut-Pécharmant (see page 192).

CLOS D'YVIGNE
Patricia Atkinson
Le Bourg, 24240 Gageac-et-Rouillac
Tel: 05-53-22-94-40 Fax: 05-53-23-47-67
Email: patricia.atkinson@wanadoo.fr
www.cdywine.com

Everyone in Bergerac adores Patricia for her courage and her talent, for the way in which, by sheer hard application, she has become one of the region's top wine-makers, acquiring en route a passion for wine which has gradually replaced the necessity to earn a bare living from a wholly new way of life. The story of how she and her former husband came to Gageac, of his illness and their eventual separation, and of her gritty passage to success in a male-dominated profession, is movingly told in her memoir, *The Ripening Sun* (Century Books, London 2003). Suffice it to say that a group of discerning growers, notably Richard Doughty and then Bruno and Claudie Bilancini (see pages 173–74), took up her vinous education to the point where she has almost become a regional mascot, the toast of all the *gros fromages* of Monbazillac and Saussignac.

Patricia started with a mere four hectares ('more like two and a half', she says cryptically), but has gradually expanded the vineyard to its present 21. Although much of the drama and excitement of her life as a wine-maker surrounds her sweet **saussignac** (***D), she makes relatively little of it, a mere four to 10 barrels depending on the vintage. The wine is quite simply the envy of most other growers, and worthy to take its place among the top sweet wines of Bergerac. With its nice suggestion of citrus as well as sweet fruit, it bears the hallmark of all Patricia's wines: elegance and finesse and a total absence of vulgar excess. In good years, she goes over the vines as many as five times to pick only those grapes which have reached the right stage of noble rot.

The rest of her range is in the same mould too, the wines named after characters in French novels. There is an unoaked *blanc sec*, **Princesse de Clèves** (**B), a *sauvignon-sémillon* blend named for the heroine of the first French romance. This wine opens like a flower in the mouth. Then there is her own favourite, **Cuvée Nicholas** (***B); this one has some *muscadelle,* and the blend is vinified and given eight or nine months in barrel. Her two côtes de bergerac rouge obviously come from the same family, but, as in families, you look for the differences as much as the resemblances. **Rouge et Noir** (**B), made from 75% *merlot* and 25% *cabernet sauvignon,* has perhaps more substance, reflecting its Stendhalian inspiration, but also a little more austerity than the charming **Le Petit Prince** (**B), where the *merlot* climbs with Saint-Exupéry's biplane to a dizzy 90% of the *assemblage,* joined by a mere 10% *cabernet franc*. Both these reds show a masterly use of oak; you will not be conscious of it at all, provided you have cellared the wines for a few years.

OTHER GOOD SAUSSIGNAC PRODUCERS

▓ **CHÂTEAU LE CHABRIER**
Pierre and Eliéna Carle
24240 Razac-de-Saussignac
Tel: 05-53-27-92-73 Fax: 05-53-23-39-03

Note also the dry whites, which are kept unusually in tank or barrel for two years or more.

▓ **CHÂTEAU TOURMENTINE**
Armelle and Jean-Marie Huré
24240 Monestier
Tel: 05-53-24-18-43

ROSETTE

AREA OF AOC: selected parcels in communes of Bergerac, Lembras, Creysse, Maurens, Prigonrieux and Ginestet.

AREA CURRENTLY PRODUCING: 18 hectares. Volume produced: 483 hectolitres.

GRAPE VARIETIES: sémillon, sauvignon and muscadelle.

Grapes as picked must contain 204 grams of sugar per litre. The wine must contain between 8 and 54 grams of residual sugar per litre after fermentation, and may be between 12 and 15 degrees in alcohol by volume.

MAXIMUM YIELD: 40 hl/ha.

Rosette is the Cinderella of white bergerac, which is not to cast monbazillac and saussignac in the role of ugly sisters. Rosette is tiny, slightly sweet, and for drinking young, sometimes with rather more power than you might guess. It has nothing to do with *vins rosés*, as its name might suggest, and this perhaps explains why it has made little headway in the marketplace. It is named after a small village hidden in the hills behind Bergerac, in an amphitheatre of vineyards which protect the town from the north winds and which once formed the heart of the Bergerac vineyard. Nowadays the wines of this little district tend to be marketed as bergerac, but rosette has a distinct character of its own. There are only 10 or so growers who declare their wine as rosette, and although 125 hectares qualify for the appellation, less than a fifth of this area produces wines officially declared under it.

The growers do not necessarily wait for the arrival of botrytis, though the noble rot is a bonus; often the grapes are picked as soon as the required sugar levels are reached. The style of wine has an air of innocence, *moëlleux* rather than sweet, very refreshing and perfect in moderation as an aperitif. It is more than a curiosity: its character of wildflowers and freshly cut summer hay does not often recur in Bergerac wines, and its makers deserve the plaudits of wine lovers for their efforts in promoting this charming inner appellation.

Colette Bourgès, one of the growers, cannot understand why more producers do not take advantage of the distinctive name; it had gone entirely out of use until 1981, when her neighbours at Puypezat revived the style and persuaded Colette to join in. Colette believes that rosette was the precursor historically of monbazillac. According to her, the French Crown imposed taxes in the Middle Ages on the monasteries of the north bank, forcing the monks to flee to the opposite side of the river, which was in English hands, and there they started to make monbazillac as we know it.

Rosette is made essentially from *sémillon*. *Sauvignon* is not forbidden by law, but its use is regarded as a heresy by the custodians of the rosette Grail. Sometimes *muscadelle* is added to the assemblage, and nowadays some growers give the wine a light *élevage* in old barrels.

GOOD PRODUCERS
OF ROSETTE

■ * DOMAINE DE LA CARDINOLLE
Nicolas Eckert
24130 Prigonrieux
Tel: 05-51-63-28-77

■ CHÂTEAU COMBRILLAC
François Eckert
24130 Prigonrieux
Tel: 05-53-24-69-83

René Girou
also at CHÂTEAU COMBRILLAC
24130 Prigonrieux
Tel: 05-53-58-02-06

■ ** CHÂTEAU ROMAIN
Colette Bourgès
vinified at Clos Les Côtes, Les Costes
24100 Bergerac (see also under Pécharmant)
Tel: 05-53-57-59-89

■ ** DOMAINE DE COUTANCIE
Nicole Maury
Coutancie, 24130 Prigonrieux
Tel: 05-53-58-01-85
Email: coutancie@wanadoo.fr

■ DOMAINE DU GRAND-JAURE
See Pécharmant.

■ CHÂTEAU MONTPLAISIR
Marie-Françoise Blanc
Peymilou, 24130 Prigonrieux
Tel: 05-53-58-91-86

■ ** CHÂTEAU PUYPEZAT-ROSETTE
Les Frères Bernad
24100 Bergerac
Tel: 05-53-57-27-69

■ CHÂTEAU DE SPINGUELÈBRE
Philippe Prévot
24130 Prigonrieux
Tel: 05-53-58-85-29

PÉCHARMANT

AREA OF AOC: communes of Bergerac, Creysse, Lembras and Saint-Sauveur. 392 hectares currently under production.

YIELD: 18,000 hectolitres. Red wines only.

GRAPE VARIETIES: cabernet sauvignon, cabernet franc, merlot and côt (malbec).

PLANTING DENSITY: 5000 plants per hectare with transitional relief to 2020 for existing plants.

MAXIMUM YIELD: 45 hl/ha.

PRUNING: *méthode* Guyot single or double.

Wines must be aged at least until the first September in the year following the vintage before commercialization.

Nowadays the region of Pécharmant produces almost exclusively red wines. But this has not always been the case. According to Xavier de Saint-Exupéry of Château de Tiregand, his grandfather, famous among other achievements for having built the railway from Paris to Orléans, devoted a large part of the family vineyard to the making of rosette. As recently as 1956, the estate was given over exclusively to the production of white wine from vines grafted from Château d'Yquem, whose then owners, the Lur Saluces family, were relations.

The appellation Pécharmant was created in 1946, although the name had long been in use to describe a superior-quality bergerac. The white wines of the area cannot use the name and are entitled only to call themselves bergerac or côtes de bergerac. The district of Pécharmant lies within four communes on the right bank of the Dordogne, and its wines owe their particular quality to the iron in the subsoil lying under a layer of sand and pebbly clay. Locally this characteristic terrain is called *tran*. The whole vineyard of Pécharmant extends to a mere 400 hectares or so, of which over a third is in the ownership of but three growers. The name is thought to mean *pech* (hilltop) *charmant,* but that is probably no more than guesswork. *Armant* could well have been someone's name.

The wines are, under the Pécharmant rules, supposed to be a blend of at least three of the authorized grape varieties, but it seems that this requirement is not always enforced. They tend to be bigger structured, sturdier and capable of longer ageing than the other red wines of Bergerac, and the growers were among the first in the region to adopt the use of new wooden barrels for maturing their wines. The grape varieties are the same as in the rest of Bergerac: the two *cabernets*, *merlot* and *malbec*. A decision has recently been made to increase the minimum of plantation density from 4000 plants per hectare to 5000 by the year 2020.

Pécharmant is rich in colour, the bouquet tending to be restrained in early years but filling out as the wine ages. Full-bodied, the wines have chewy tannins, a sure sign of long life. They start to soften at three years old, reaching their peak seven years after the vintage. Those raised in wood need correspondingly longer. They call for hearty meat dishes and hard cheeses.

OUTSTANDING PÉCHARMANT PRODUCERS

■ DOMAINE DES BERTRANOUX
Daniel Hecquet
See Châteaux Puy-Servain-Calabre and Puy-
Servain-Terrement under Montravel.

■ CHÂTEAU CHAMPAREL
Françoise Bouché
Pécharmant, 24100 Bergerac
Tel: 05-53-57-34-76

This lovely property is somewhat isolated, towards the end of a country lane which leads almost out of Pécharmant altogether. Madame Bouché bought Champarel in 1970 with just over six hectares of vines. A wine lover with no experience of wine-making, she is self-taught. Wisely, she started by sending her grapes to the local *coopérative*, but after four years she decided there was only one way forward: to make her own wine. Modestly she says that any improvements are the fruit of her own experience, 'for which I have paid'.

Madame Bouché has never wanted to extend her vineyard, even if she had ever been offered the chance. She has enough to occupy her without losing the total control which she insists on having over her operations. Her husband, a Bergerac dentist, exchanges his drill at weekends for a pair of *sécateurs* and helps when he can, and they have a vineyard manager who looks after the vines, while they concentrate on the vinification and *élevage* of their wines.

The Bouchés are builders as well as wine-makers; not content with making a beautiful home

out of the former farm buildings, they have constructed an underground cellar beneath the vineyard, as at Château Ausone perhaps, but Madame points out that at Ausone the cellar is natural, whereas hers cost a great deal of money.

The vineyard is half *merlot*, half *cabernet sauvignon*. The wine-making itself is conventional, Madame Bouché having stayed with the techniques she developed when she started. The wines are aged for up to two years in barrels, renewed on a three-year cycle. There are two **cuvées** (both **B), the **Prestige** coming from selected vines and sometimes given rather longer in the wood. In neither case is the wood in any way obtrusive; it just confers additional elegance and finesse to the wines.

Since Madame Bouché has but 6.5 hectares of vines, her son Paul has flown the nest and established himself down the road with five hectares of his own (Château Neyrac), where he has got off to a good start.

■ LES CHEMINS D'ORIENT
Régis Lansade and Robert Saleon-Terras
19 Chemin du Château d'Eau, 24100 Creysse
Tel: 06-75-86-47-54 Fax: 05-53-22-08-38
Email: Regis.Lansade@wanadoo.fr
www.les-chemins-d-orient.com

This micro-estate of five hectares split between two locations, one in the hamlet of Pécharmant itself, the other on higher ground at La Germanie, is relatively new on the scene. Their first vintage was the 2000, a year in which wine-makers of merit, like these, had no problem in establishing a reputation. Today they could well be described as Pécharmant's cult-*vignerons,* not because they are changing the style of the appellation, but because they are reminding everyone of exactly what the true pécharmant style should be. After 15 years, working together with Médecins Sans Frontières, both decided on a change of career; each separately trained in oenology, Lansade subsequently becoming a consultant to the Bergerac Wine Committee, Saleon-Terras qualifying in medicine. Lansade started with a tiny holding of just over one hectare, and Saleon-Terras joined him shortly afterwards with some more. Thus was born Les Chemins d'Orient.

If you have any doubts about the influence of the famous *tran*, these growers are sure to convince you. It gives their wines a minerality which illustrates the *terroir* perfectly. The vines are planted at a high density of 6000 plants to the hectare and cultivated without weedkiller; the soil is worked by hand, the base of the vines being covered over for the winter and laid bare again in the spring. Their main pécharmant *cuvée* is given a different name each year—Ariane for example in 2000, Oxiane in 2001, Nouria in 2002. The 2003 **Cuvée Syrus** (***C), from the famous heat-wave year, had spices, rich fruit, fine balance between acidity and tannins, and concentration of flavour rather than maximum extraction of matter, even if the character of the vintage resulted in a wine reaching 14 degrees of alcohol by volume in the bottle. The quality is perhaps due in part to the masterful handling of barrels, one-third of which are new each year, but which, while adding complexity and style to the wine, give no hint of oak flavours.

There is a second wine called **Caravanserail** (**B), designed for drinking young on its fresh ripe fruit.

The balance here between tradition and modernity is an object lesson to Bergerac growers generally, and producers of pécharmant in particular.

■ **CHÂTEAU DE CORBIAC**
Bruno de Corbiac
Pécharmant, 24100 Bergerac
Tel: 05-53-57-20-75 Fax: 05-53-57-89-98
Email: corbiac@corbiac.com
www.corbiac.com

Bruno de Corbiac, working in tandem with his wife, Thérèse, who looks after the administration and marketing, and their son, Antoine, who is gradually assuming the reins from his father, trained as an agricultural engineer before returning in 1970 to this property, which had been in the family for many years. Since then, Bruno has done much to modernize the plant and buildings, while Antoine currently aims to achieve the required target of 5000 vines to the hectare in due time.

Corbiac is on some of the highest ground in Pécharmant and today covers 17 hectares, planted to 60% with *merlot* at the top of the hill, while the *cabernets* account for 35% in the pebbly soil of the hillside. The small quantity, 5%, of *malbec* is grown in sandy soil with plenty of iron below. Fertiliser comes exclusively from sheep, which the Corbiacs also raise in the meadows of the property. The vines are pruned and trained in arched form, giving a yield of 45–50 hectolitres of wine to the hectare. The vinification is traditional in a modern *chai*s with modern temperature control and frequent *remontages*. The wine is aged over two winters before being bottled.

There is just the one red, bottled simply under the name of the property, **Château de Corbiac** (**B). A favourite with the *Guide Hachette,* it is elegant and round on the nose, sometimes quite powerful, with ripe fruit and some spice. The palate is smooth with silky tannins.

▦ DOMAINE DES COSTES

Nicole and Jean-Marc Dournel

Les Costes, 24100 Bergerac

Tel: 05-53-57-64-49

The 12.5-hectare vineyard looks out over a small industrial estate, and the Dournels are neighbours of Colette Bourgès at Les Côtes, which is confusing, particularly as the wine-making styles at the two properties are poles apart.

The property was bought by Nicole in 1992, and since then she and her oenologist husband, Jean-Marc, an increasingly powerful and fashionable voice in Bergerac, have inspired each other to produce some of the most avant-garde wines of the region. Jean-Marc refers to the vineyard as 'the Haut-Brion of Bergerac' because it is, like Haut-Brion in Bordeaux, surrounded by the town.

At Les Costes, there is an obvious strategy to produce a New World style of pécharmant, apart from a **Tradition** made by Nicole's parents. Jean-Marc has said, 'There used to be lots of tannins in the wines but not much fruit. Now we are learning to adapt to the maturity of the fruit.' Even so, these deeply coloured wines show a good deal of oak on the nose, with roasted coffee aromas, tobacco and liquorice; on the palate, there is some sweetness, the wood fairly well integrated, more tobacco in the style of cigar boxes, and fruits preserved in alcohol. Some tasters have compared the palate with Pomerol, wondering whether this is due to the iron in the soil.

Les Costes (C) without doubt reflects a style of bergerac which seeks to attract the professional tasters while also striving to differentiate itself from the wines of Bordeaux. If the wine conjures up images of Robert Parker– or Michel Rolland–style blockbusters, there will be plenty of takers on that account alone. Readers can award stars here in line with their personal tastes.

▦ CLOS LES CÔTES

Colette Bourgès

Les Costes, 24100 Bergerac

Tel: 05-53-57-59-89 Fax: 05-53-24-20-24

Email: clos.les.cotes@wanadoo.fr

Just a few metres separate the estates of two wholly different wine-makers. Colette has two hectares of land outside the town where she grows grapes from which she makes rosette, and she has about six hectares in Bergerac itself for her pécharmant, as well as another four from which she makes straight bergerac (pink and red). The vineyard was replanted by her grandfather after the phylloxera, and Colette eventually took the estate over from her father in 1985. She realized that she needed some formal training, so she took a course at the agricultural *lycée* in Monbazillac.

Her vines in Bergerac are up the hill from the *chais*, and command a fine view of the whole town. She has a little *malbec* in addition to the two *cabernets* and *merlot*. The slopes of the hill are sufficiently steep to need terracing, and Colette weeds the rows only every other year to allow the soil to firm up after being disturbed. This helps to prevent erosion so that mini-tractors may pass easily and safely between the vine rows. Machine-harvesting would be possible, but Colette prefers to pick by hand. The vines face due south over the valley to Monbazillac and this exposure means that the grapes can ripen fully without the removal of surplus foliage in July and August. She does not destalk her bunches of grapes and vinifies each variety separately for three weeks. It is surprising that her wine is as round and gentle on the palate as it is, the tannins entirely resolved. She does not believe in new wood, although in 2002, to please her son, she bought three barrels just to try. Her **Clos les Côtes** (**B) is invariably rich in blackcurrant and prune flavours with good length, and is one of the best of the traditional style of pécharmants.

1995. Her first vintage from her new vineyard was 2003.

Jocelyne has created waves in Bergerac, building on her already established fame. Her wine is often to be found in restaurants, its distinctive labels stressing its feminine source. But when it comes to power and guts she can easily hold her own with her male colleagues.

She makes two wines, no whites or rosé. **Château d'Elle** (**C) in 2003 came from 40% *merlot*, 35% *cabernet sauvignon* and 25% *cabernet franc*. The fruit was gorgeously ripe in that hot year, the wine reaching 13.5 degrees in alcohol. Extraction was fairly gentle, a long slow fermentation of 28 days at about 28 degrees celsius, followed by an *élevage* of seven months in once-used barrels. The wine was a little gamey even in its early years. **Une Femme Un Vin** (**D) from the same year had as much as 40% *cabernet franc* and the same amount of *cabernet sauvignon*, with only 20% *merlot*, and was a rather bigger proposition; prunes and *griottes* backed with vanilla from the wood, which was rather more prominent than in the Château d'Elle.

Both wines are fermented in steel, and she uses no *vin de presse*, just the free-run juices. The only filtering is through a *crépine*, a kind of coarse perforated cloth, 'to keep the flies out'; nor are the wines fined. They will keep well, although the tannins are already well absorbed. Cask samples of a 2004 *cabernet franc* suggested that that year will be finer and more elegant, with perhaps not so much sheer power, but all the better for that.

■ **DOMAINE DU HAUT-PÉCHARMANT**
Michel Roches (also Clos Peyrelevade)
24100 Bergerac
Tel: 05-53-57-29-50 Fax: 05-53-24-28-05
Email: dhp2@tiscali.com
www.haut-pecharmant.com

This 33-hectare vineyard is at the top of the hill which dominates the village of Pécharmant. Sand, gravelly stones, and grey and red clay overlay the famous *tran* with its iron backbone. The vine-

■ CHÂTEAU D'ELLE
Jocelyne Pécou
La Briasse, 24100 Pécharmant
Tel and fax: 05-53-61-66-62
Mobile: 06-32-81-04-79
Email: contact@chateaudelle.com
www.chateaudelle.com

Jocelyne plays the lady-*vigneron* card in no mean manner from her 2.5-hectare micro-domaine in the suburbs of Bergerac. She built herself a formidable reputation as a wine-maker when managing her family's property Les Bertranoux in the 1990's. To be her own mistress she bought this little vineyard in 1991, planting new *cabernet sauvignon* (45% of the total) the following year and *merlot* (35%) in

yard, facing due south and enjoying the best of the hot sunshine, consists of 40% *cabernet sauvignon*, 30% *merlot*, 20% *cabernet franc* and 10% *malbec*. The wines, notable for their dark colour and their firm structure, while subtle on the nose and round and supple on the palate, nevertheless benefit from long ageing more than most other pécharmants; a 15-year-old 1990 tasted in 2005 was still lovely and full of life. It is possible to drink the wines young, but they must in that case be decanted well in advance.

Michel Roches has been joined at the domaine by his son Didier, who trained for some while with the Buzet *Coopérative*, where he could not but fail to acquire additional expertise to that which could be learned at home. He was at that time responsible for three of the best Buzet estates, Gueyze, Padère and Bouchet.

Didier says that at the time the cork is pulled the wines from Haut-Pécharmant are closed, but two hours later they reveal aromas of raspberry and typical *cabernet* tannins. The same bottle three days later will show oaky vanilla, softened tannins and a burst of fruit. He is sure that the fine-grained tannins will melt away with the passage of time to allow the wine to expand.

As well as the basic **pécharmant** (***B), there is another *cuvée* made from the best parcel of vines and named **Veuve Roches** (***B), after Michel's mother, who was largely responsible for achieving the high quality for which the estate is today famous. *Cabernet franc* is the main grape, and the wine may be aged in oak for up to 18 months, depending on the nature and development of the tannins in the wine. This *cuvée* is powerful and intense and may take up to 10 years to reach its peak.

Clos Peyrelevade is a property immediately opposite Haut-Pécharmant. It was formerly the property of Michel's father, who sold it to pay for Haut-Pécharmant itself. When the chance came to buy it back, Michel Roches did not hesitate. The soil here is sandy clay. The 10 hectares of old vines are mostly *merlot*, from which Roches makes a

pécharmant (**B) both firm and fruity, which can be enjoyed much younger than the wines of Haut-Pécharmant itself.

We met Michel's other son, Olivier, in Saussignac. The family have now formed a company to market and distribute all the family wines. Château Le Tap can be tasted here as well as at Saussignac.

LA MÉTAIRIE
Pierre and Antoine Alard
24100 Bergerac
See Château Theulet under Monbazillac, page 172.

CHÂTEAU LA RENAUDIE
Line, Yves and Olivier Allamagny
24100 Lembras
Tel: 05-53-27-05-75 Fax: 05-53-73-37-10
Email: contact@chateaurenaudie.com
www.chateaurenaudie.com

This is a much improved and rapidly developing property in the north-west corner of the appellation. It is notable for the relatively high (15%) proportion of *malbec* in the vineyard. The wines are very lightly and rather cleverly raised in wood. There are two *cuvées,* the **Tradition** (**B) and the **Vieilles Vignes** (**C).

TERRE VIEILLE
Gérôme and Dolorès Morand-Monteil (also Domaine de Grateloup)
24520 Saint-Saveur
Tel: 05-53-57-35-07 Fax: 05-53-61-91-77
Mobile: 06-20-04-52-50
Email: gerome-morand-monteil@wanadoo.fr
www.terrevieille.com

Le Domaine de Grateloup was the birthplace of an illustrious philosopher, Maine de Biran (1766-1824). He was clearly an adroit politician, starting out as a *député* for the Dordogne *département* after the Revolution and then holding high office under the Empire and the Restoration. The historian Alexis

Monteil says that de Biran liked to potter in his vineyard between sessions of meditation in his library. The wines must have been good because they are mentioned favourably in the 1903 edition of Feret.

The soil in these vineyards is made up of iron-rich clay and silex, which give the wines their minerally character. The present owners maintain the same care as their distinguished predecessor in harvesting by hand and rejecting less than perfect fruit. The ageing in oak lends character and elegance to the wines in time, the wines gaining a deep ruby colour, good harmonious fruit on the nose and the roundness and suppleness on the palate which you would expect to find in the best growths of the region.

The 27 hectares of vines provide three different red pécharmants. The *entrée-de-gamme* **Chevalier Saint-Sauveur** (**B), from more or less equal quantities of younger vines of *merlot* and the two *cabernets*, though vinified for only two weeks in stainless steel, has nevertheless a deep colour and a surprising strength of dark fruit, cherries particularly both in the bouquet and on the palate. Tannins are ripe and the final impression is of sweetness. The wine will age, although it can be drunk with pleasure in its youth. The **Cros de la Sal** (**B) has more *merlot* and less *cabernet franc*, but is aged for a year in barrels. The oak is noticeable but is well blended in with the fruit. Like the first wine, this one is agreeable when young and can be enjoyed on its fruit, but it will develop too in the bottle. The top wine is usually the **Château Terre Vieille** (***C), with a high 70% or more *merlot* content. It is aged for 18 months in barrels, but only a quarter of the casks are new. The presentation is in old-fashioned heavy bottles with long corks, and the wine is clearly aimed at serious private buyers, top wine shops and grocery stores and famous restaurants. The colour is dark but the appearance brilliant, the nose showing cassis and blackberries and suggestions of vanilla and toasting from the wood, more so than on the palate, where complex and concentrated aromas are released. The wine is a real keeper.

In truly fine years there is a micro-*cuvée* called **L'Ambroisie** (D) from 85% *merlot*. Even in 2000 only that number of bottles were made. The wine bears all the hallmarks of the ubiquitous consultant-oenologue Jean-Marc Dournel: lots of extraction and hefty oak, which will take many years to come round.

▮ CHÂTEAU DE TILLERAIE

Bruno and Dominique Fauconnier
Pécharmant, 24100 Bergerac
Tel and fax: 05-53-57-86-42
Email: contact@vignobles-fauconnier.fr
www.vignobles-fauconnier.fr

The château itself has 3.5 hectares of fine grounds round it, overlooking the town of Bergerac. It is more of a manor house really, going back to the late 18th century. The alley of lime trees (*tilleuls*) leading up to it gives it its name. For 200 years and more it has been well known for the quality of its wines.

Bruno and Dominique Fauconnier acquired the property in 1992 and have been winning medals over and over again. High standards reign here, the grapes being picked by hand in several *tries* to ensure maximum ripeness of the fruit.

The **pécharmant wines** (**B) are aged in barrels for 12 months, but oaky flavours are avoided. Characteristics are curranty fruit on the bouquet, often with animal notes as well. The wines are supple on the palate and usually boast a good finish. They are in a rather lighter style than some pécharmants, but none the worse for that, maturing relatively young. It is a policy of the house to make wines which can be drunk on their fruit but which will age too. There are also other wines sold as **bergerac rouge** and **rosé** (both *A), which are less serious but more approachable when young.

The Fauconniers are also proprietors of another 18th-century property called **Château de Malbernat** over to the east in the commune of Creysse, whose wines (all pécharmant) are destined exclusively for the hotel and restaurant trade, while for the wholesale business the same wines are sold as **Domaine de Leymonie**.

■ **CHÂTEAU DE TIREGAND**

Les Héritiers de Madame F. Saint-Exupéry

24100 Creysse

Tel: 05-53-23-21-08

Email: chateautiregand@club-internet.fr

www.chateau-de-tiregand.com

Bergerac seems to have attracted newcomers from all walks of life and all countries to try their hand at wine-making, which must make the Saint-Exupérys smile: they represent one of the oldest families in France, have a long tradition in the region and own what must be the most beautiful of all the wine-châteaux in Pécharmant. They may wonder whether the new competition is a good or bad thing for them. Perhaps it is both: nothing is harder than to lead from the front, which is where Tiregand has been for half a century.

There was an 'old château' here once, of which little remains except the present *chais* and the bread oven, buildings which are some distance from the present family home but which are well worth a visit on their own account. They stand in the middle of a park adorned with centenarian trees. At one end of the *chais* a window opens onto what used to be a passage giving access to the 'old' château, and it is here that visitors can taste the wines.

After the calamitous frosts of 1956, the family faced a fundamental strategic decision: either to send their grapes from then on to the *coopérative* at Bergerac, or to spend the considerable sums which would be needed to rebuild the vineyard. Only four hectares of vines had survived (today there are 43). Xavier de Saint-Exupéry had already decided to study agricultural engineering and oenology, so the family chose to replant, but this time it would be entirely, or nearly so, with red-wine grapes.

There are in fact 1.8 hectares devoted to white grapes, 80% *sauvignon* and 20% *sémillon*, from which the family make as delicious a **dry white**

bergerac (**A) as you might hope to find. They do commercialize it, but it is mostly used as an *entrée de gamme* at tastings and formal receptions. This is a light, flowery and easy wine, not intended to be 'serious', but a wine to encourage the palate to go on to further adventures. The grapes are macerated for 12 hours under carbonic gas before fermentation proper, which lasts for 10 days at a cool temperature of 16 degrees. The wine is then matured on its lees for six to eight weeks before bottling.

With younger *merlot* grapes, mostly from the terraces on the higher ground praised by Feret a hundred years ago as being some of the best *terroir* in Bergerac, Tiregand makes a wine for drinking young on its fruit, called **Clos de la Montalbanie** (**A).

The mainstream red **Château de Tiregand** (***B) is typically 60% *merlot*, 20% *cabernet sauvignon*, 15% *cabernet franc* and 5% *malbec*. The grapes are destalked and given longish *cuvaisons* of up to four weeks, perhaps rather less for the *merlot*. Stainless steel is the preferred material for the vinification because the tanks can be used for ageing the wine as well as making it. There is some gentle oaking, 10% only of the casks being new. The wine is for keeping, up to 10 years, though in hot years like 2003, when there was less acidity than usual, the wine may come on rather quicker. This wine is quintessential Tiregand, fragrant on the nose and firm-bodied on the palate, with a long and powerful finish.

In 2000, a particularly good year in Bergerac, the family embarked on a new project with the assistance of the ever-present Dournel, a fully committed barrel-aged red called **Grand Millésime** (***C). The third star is given in the expectation that the wood will one day open to the tastebuds the undeniably fantastic wine, which it covers when the wine is young. There is a complexity which is extraordinary, and it is not surprising that the wine won a gold medal in Paris in 2005. It is symptomatic of the policy at Tiregand to stay ahead of the field in Pécharmant, a policy which is reflected in the determination to convert the vineyard over a period up to 2020 to the required density of 5000 plants per hectare. This will entail partial digging up of some vines, and elsewhere planting between the existing rows, an enormous financial commitment in such a large estate.

OTHER GOOD PÉCHARMANT PRODUCERS

■ CAVE COOPÉRATIVE BERGERAC LE FLEIX

24130 Le Fleix
Tel: 05-53-24-64-32 Fax: 05-53-25-64-46
Email: service.commercial@cave-bergerac-le-
fleix.com
www.cave-bergerac-le-fleix.com.

Price B. The pécharmant is made at the Cave in
Bergerac, 72 boulevard de l'Entrepôt, and the wines
include several single properties such as *Domaine
Brisseau Belloc, *Château Métairie-Haute and
*Domaine Vieux Sapin.

■ CHÂTEAU LES FARCIES DU PECH

Vignobles Dubard
24100 Bergerac
Tel: 05-53-82-48-31
(same ownership as Château Laulerie at
Montravel; see page 205)

■ DOMAINE DES GALINOUX

Francis Romain
24100 Bergerac
Tel: 05-53-57-97-88

■ DOMAINE DU GRAND JAURE

Georges Baudry
24100 Lembras
Tel: 05-53-57-35-65

■ CHARTREUSE DE PEYRELEVADE

Gilbert Dusseau
24100 Bergerac
Tel: 05-53-57-44-27

■ DOMAINE DE TOUTIFAUT

André Coll
24100 Creysse
Tel: 05-53-63-40-73

MONTRAVEL

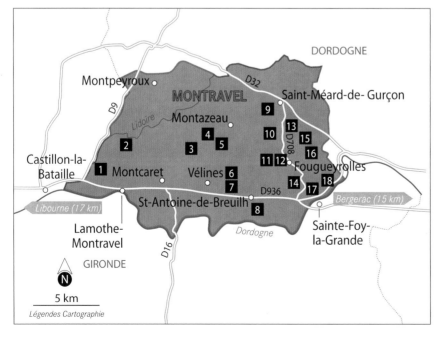

DORDOGNE

Montpeyroux

MONTRAVEL

D32

Saint-Méard-de- Gurçon

D9

Lidoire

Montazeau

9

13

10

15

Castillon-la-
Bataille

2

4

5

3

D708

16

11 **12**

Fougueyrolles

1 Montcaret

Vélines

6

14

18

7

D936

17

Libourne (17 km)

Bergerac (15 km)

St-Antoine-de-Breuilh

8

Lamothe-
Montravel

Dordogne

Sainte-Foy-
la-Grande

GIRONDE

N

5 km

Légendes Cartographie

AREA OF AOCS: communes in bold are in the area of Côtes de Montravel; those in italics are in the inner area of Haut-Montravel.

SELECTED PARCELS IN THE COMMUNES OF: **Bonneville**, *Fougueyrolles*, Lamothe-Montravel, Montcaret, Montpeyroux, Montazeau, *Nastringues*, Ponchapt, *Port Sainte-Foy, Saint-Antoine-de-Breuilh*, Saint-Michel-de-Montaigne, Saint-Seurin-de-Prats, Saint-Vivien, *Vélines* and part of Saint-Méard-de-Gurçon.

APPELLATION	SURFACE AREA	VOLUME PRODUCED
Montravel blanc sec	289 ha	12,686 hl
Montravel rouge	53	2,000
Haut-Montravel	50	1,636
Côtes de Montravel	51	1,837

Red and white wines (dry and sweet).

GRAPE VARIETIES:

REDS: merlot (at least 50%), cabernet sauvignon, cabernet franc and côt (malbec).

WHITES: sémillon (min. 25%), sauvignon and muscadelle.

MINIMUM PLANTING DENSITY: 5000 plants/hectare; max. no. of buds: 50,000 per hectare.

Extent of foliage must be a minimum of 6000 square metres per hectare.

PRUNING: *méthode* Guyot single or double, Cordon Royat and *taille à cot.*

MAXIMUM YIELDS: dry whites 58 hl/ha; others 50 hl/ha.

ALCOHOL CONTENT: dry whites min. 10%, reds 11% (max. 13.5 when chaptalization authorized), sweet whites between 12% min. and 15% max.

Red and white wines allowed AOC status from the 2001 vintage onwards.

Montravel covers 15 communes on the right bank of the Dordogne in the hills beside the main road which leads from Bergerac to Bordeaux. Its name is said to be derived from the Latin 'In Monte Revelationem'. It was also the name of a small fortified village in the Dordogne Valley which was destroyed in 1622 by Louis XIII.

In 1937, AOC status was granted to the white wines of the district: montravel sec, which can be made anywhere within the 15 communes; côtes de montravel, a slightly sweet wine made from grapes grown in some communes only; and thirdly haut-montravel, a much sweeter style made in yet other communes in the heart of and entirely surrounded by the Côtes de Montravel, Russian doll fashion. Growers in Montravel may also use the generic Bergerac appellations.

Until 2003, the red wines of the district were sold either as bergerac rouge or côtes de bergerac, although the local growers, supported by the evidence of many professional tasters, have always maintained that their wines are of a slightly different style from those made upstream in the rest of Bergerac. Red fruits are said to be more prominent in the younger wines, while mature vintages suggest resin to some; the tannins are said to be softer than usual in the region.

No grower in Montravel is obliged to use any of the montravel appellations for which he may qualify; he can always use, as many do, the basic bergerac and côtes de bergerac names. All of this makes for a situation which is very confusing for the consumer as well as the producer, particularly because, as we shall see, only some producers of red wines in Montravel may use the montravel name.

THE WHITE MONTRAVELS

The dry whites may be made in any of the 15 communes which make up the district. They are sometimes more *nerveux*, more minerally than other white bergeracs, especially in good years. The areas of Côtes de Montravel and Haut-Montravel are mutually exclusive, though some growers have vines in both.

Côtes de montravel, although officially called *moëlleux,* is less sweet than most wines of that style. On the other hand, haut-montravel is a truly sweet wine, after the manner of monbazillac or saussignac, but may still not call itself *liquoreux,* because the sugar levels necessary to obtain the right to that title are above those permitted in Haut-Montravel, unless growers obtain special permission by *dérogation* to exceed the sugar limits. This is unfortunate for makers of haut-montravel, who are thus put at a disadvantage when compared with growers in Monbazillac and Saussignac, and may help to explain the decline in production under this name. The situation is expected to change in the near future so as to ensure that côtes de montravel becomes a truly *moëlleux* style and haut-montravel a truly *liquoreux* wine after the fashion of monbazillac and saussignac. Application has been made to INAO to effect these changes in the rules.

The production of dry white montravel has been more or less stable in recent years, and currently runs at about 12,000 hectolitres a year. But this masks the growth in Montravel of the production of red wines, even though until recently these might only be sold as bergerac. The production of the sweeter styles fell dramatically during the second half of the last century; the côtes from 34,000 hectolitres after the Second World War to 3000 in 1991; and haut-montravel even more notably from 20,000 hectolitres at the earlier date to a mere 630 hectolitres in 1991. Since that time the production of the *moëlleux*-style côtes de montravel has fallen further, but that of haut-montravel has had a slight recovery (see table above).

RED MONTRAVEL

Twice as much red as white wine is produced in the Montravel district today, but not all of it may be sold as montravel rouge. The *terroir* for the red wines recalls slightly that of Pécharmant, with a good deal of flint in the ground and iron underlying the surface.

It took 56 years from the date when AOC status was awarded to the white montravels for the reds to achieve their own montravel appellation. Success was due largely to the determined and sustained efforts of a small band of enthusiasts. Thirteen growers qualified for the first vintage in 2001 under the strict rules which they themselves created, and the number of postulants is growing. Their intention is to create something very special, and this is reflected in the relatively high prices asked for the wines: there is nothing to be had at under 10 euros. Montravel rouge is the only appellation which requires the grower to submit samples by lot and mark the lot number on the cork of each bottle in the lot. It is claimed that in this way it can be established exactly how much wine the grower has produced under the appellation and the date when it was granted its *agrément.* This in turn is intended to help eliminate fraud.

The rules for red montravel are very stringent. A grower must declare in advance of the wine cycle for which of his parcels of vines he is going to claim appellation rights. It appears that scientific tests have established that growers had inadvertently hit upon the best parcels of their vineyard without analysing their virtue; some of the best *terroir* apparently has threads of greenish clay mixed with fossilized oysters, which some *vignerons* marked out by intuition rather than scientific process.

A group composed of representatives of the syndicate of growers and other experts visits the vineyard and checks that density of plantation of these parcels reaches the required minimum of 5000 plants per hectare, that the pruning, the size of the plants and their *bon état cultural* conform to the rules. *Merlot* is an obligatory 50% of the selected parcels. During the spring following the vintage a first independent tasting is held to determine whether the wine is likely to age well; if not, it must be declassified to bergerac status. Having passed this test, the wine must then be aged for a further minimum of 15 months, either in tank or barrel, and pass a second tasting test for quality at the end of this time before it is bottled with its lot number. It may then be called montravel rouge. This is claimed to be the only appellation in France which requires a tasting after bottling before the *agrément* is finally granted.

The first results (in 2001) were mixed. In an effort to differentiate their wines as far as possible from other red bergeracs and so justify the existence of the separate appellation, the growers tended to overripen their fruit (not difficult in 2001, which was a heat-wave year), over-extract in the maceration and over-oak in the *élevage*. Even the French press, who generally go along with these sorts of techniques, saw fit to criticize, and 2002 saw a modification of the earlier excesses, again partly perhaps because the vintage was rather different in character and lent itself more to modesty of product. Perhaps in due course, the montravel enthusiasts will settle down to make wine which is more on a par with pécharmant, and a proper counterweight to that excellent wine, rather than try to beat the New World at its own game, in the process denying the character of their own *terroir*. On the other hand, Jean Rebeyrolle at Château la Ressaudie told me that montravel rouge must establish itself as the producer's *haut-de-gamme* wine. The rules on density, for example, involving as they do some replanting for many growers, made it more expensive to produce; the wine had to justify the price, and this was the reason for the ultra-modern style of some of the wines. His view was that it was now the turn of the other montravel styles to bring themselves up to the quality-level of the reds.

OUTSTANDING MONTRAVEL PRODUCERS

▌**CHÂTEAU DU BLOY**

Bertrand Lepoitevin and Olivier Lambert

24230 Bonneville

Tel and fax: 05-53-22-47-87

Email: chateau.du.bloy@wanadoo.fr

A former barrister from Le Havre, Lepoitevin found Le Bloy in 2001 and bought it from the brothers Guillemer, who were already making good wine there. Bertrand had always been a passionate wine lover but had no experience at all of wine-making. He had decided on a career change, and his lawyer's logic pointed him in the direction of becoming a *vigneron.*

The French have a system whereby anyone wishing to dispose of agricultural property has to put it at the disposal of a local quango whose acronym is SAFER and whose function it is to rationalize landholdings. Lepoitevin considers himself lucky that this property of 20 hectares was not of a size to be sought after by neighbours, so SAFER was happy for him as an outsider to take it on. One curious aspect of the layout of this vineyard is that, although the vines are *dans un seul tenant* all round the buildings on the property, there is also in the middle of it all a golf course which belongs to someone else.

Lepoitevin clearly has an enormous talent, his wines being some of the most exciting of all montravels. He puts elegance and finesse at the head of his list of wine virtues, and his use of barrels is well mastered and never too indulgent.

There are two white montravels: **Blanc Sec Lilia** (**B), half *sauvignon*, the remainder equally *sémillon* and *muscadelle*, is raised in tanks for five months with regular *bâtonnage* and may in a good year clock up 13.5 degrees of alcohol by volume. It is fresh and lively, with good acidity and grip while avoiding any suggestion of cats' pee: a dry white very much to the English taste. The second white, **Montravel Blanc Sec Le Bloy** (***C), drops the *muscadelle,* which is replaced by more *sémillon.* The wine is vinified and aged in barrels after the grapes have been pressed whole. Again there is regular *bâtonnage* and the wine is only lightly filtered and fined. The barrels are renewed on a five-year cycle. The wine has rich flavours of grapefruit and peaches.

The bulk of the production at Le Bloy is of red wine, white grapes accounting for only a quarter of the vineyard. Before tasting the montravels, do not pass over the bergeracs; the best of them, called **Sirius** (**B), is a joy to look at, brilliant, limpid and ruby, with elegant fruit and good firm style. It is three parts *merlot*, one part *cabernet franc*, vinified in tanks with regular pumping over and *délestages.* Seventy percent is aged in barrel, 30% in tank for 18 months, and the wine is bottled without filtering or fining. Fantastic value for the money.

If there is but the one **Montravel Rouge Le Bloy** (***C), it is to many minds the best of the new appellation. Half *merlot* and half *cabernet franc* (a grape which Lepoitevin obviously loves), the macerations may vary between four and as much as seven weeks in length according to the vintage. Oaking is gentle, a mere six months in 2001 for example; in less good years only old barrels may be used. The *robe* is once again pure pleasure, dark but brilliant, almost shining. The fruit is powerful, the balance perfect and the finish long. This is a wine to put alongside the best that the Bergerac region can offer.

▌ CHÂTEAU JONC BLANC
Isabelle Carles and Franck Pascal
24230 Vélines
Tel and fax: 05-53-74-18-97
Email: jonc.blanc@free.fr

Franck quotes Hegel, 'Nothing is accomplished without passion', and passion is certainly not lacking here. He calls to mind Plageoles and Lescarret in Gaillac, but is less loquacious than either. Curiously enough, he nearly bought Durantou in Gaillac, next door to Plageoles, but the price was too high.

Franck is surprisingly charming for someone who is not too keen on casual visitors. Prior appointments are strongly advised. He is serious-minded and does not want to be distracted from the job, so he keeps Jonc Blanc off the official Route des Vins. Isabelle and Franck are gravely concerned that the French government, in an effort to make French wine more competitive with the wines of the New World, will dumb down the product by permitting the addition of water (as already practised in some parts of the US), the use of wood chips, antiseptic chemicals to kill yeast and bacteria at the point of bottling, the addition of dead yeasts to enrich the wines, and the subtraction from wine of water (to concentrate the must), sugar (to reduce the potential alcoholic strength) and alcohol itself by osmotic process. At Jonc Blanc, meanwhile, vineyard practice is copybook: no artificial yeasts, no filtering or fining, no acidification or chaptalization, not even any sulphuring; in fact, no artificial additions or subtractions whatever. Isabelle and Franck will carry on making what is naturally good, clinging to values which to them seem more and more fundamental.

Trained in general agriculture, Franck has travelled a great deal and has good English. I asked him how he chose Montravel. He said it was one of the few regions where high density was already established. He thought this was because Montravel was less of a polycultural region than most, more given over to the vines, so didn't need wide spaces between the vine rows to allow tractors (formerly oxen) to pass. The vines were in good shape when he took over in 2000. So was the *chais*. The previous owner was a conscientious grower, but did little bottling of his own wine before he retired at the age of 64. Franck started off, therefore, with no storage facility either for barrels or for packaged stock.

He has few private customers, selling mostly to merchants and restaurants. He exports a little, and won a tender to the Norwegian government, which runs the wine business in that country as a state monopoly. There is no white wine here, which is strange for a property in an area which has specialized in three styles of white. He does make a good **rosé** (**A), however, in which the *cabernet sauvignon* is pressed directly, while the *merlot* is *saigné*.

Although they won gold medals galore with their former red called Blanches Pierres, they entirely changed their range of wines from 2004 onwards and also their presentation. The new range, under the banner Paysans-Vignerons, will consist of a *vin de plaisir* which they call **Les Sens du Fruit** (B), a wine to be enjoyed on its fruit, with soft tannins. There will also be a *merlot*-based sulphur-free wine to be called **Coup de Foudre** (B), a play on words because it will be aged in an Alsatian *foudre* more than a hundred years old. Franck is not too keen on new wood, but he and Isabelle have several 400-litre barrels from the Allier, which they prefer to the more orthodox 225-litre casks. So their **montravel rouge** (**C), which one hopes they will continue making, can be guaranteed fresh and minerally. It may be too soon to assess the change of direction at this domaine, but the quality is so good and the wine-makers are so serious that one can predict two or more likely three stars for whatever they do.

■ **CHÂTEAU LAULERIE**

Vignobles Dubard

Le Gouyat, 24610 Saint-Méard-de-Gurçon

Tel: 05-53-82-48-31 Fax: 05-53-82-47-64

Email: vignobles-dubard@wanadoo.fr

www.vignobles-dubard.com

In days gone by, the Dubard family, pillars of Montravel, used to reserve the name Laulerie for their top oaked red, the other wines being made under the name Domaine de Gouyat. Today, however, they have adopted Laulerie more as an umbrella name for all their wines which they make in Montravel. The enterprise is run by a brother and sister, who are assisted by the fully trained son of another brother now retired. The hallmark of this property is consistency of quality, attained no doubt by the variety of *terroirs* which they are able to exploit from their 83 hectares, without at the same time losing the artisanal quality of the wines. Nearly half the vineyards are given over to white grapes, planted to a high density of 5000 plants to the hectare. The family follow modern practice in allowing the weeds to grow between the vine rows.

The **montravel sec** (**A), raised in tank, is beautifully fresh and fruity. The oaked version, called **Cuvée Comtesse de Ségur** (*B), will appeal to those who like a highly technicoloured dry wine in the New World manner, but some may find the style overdone. The adoption of the name Comtesse de Ségur derives from the vines now managed by the Dubards which adjoin the château, which used to belong to the countess, a well-known writer of children's story-books. The name is also given to the Dubards' **montravel rouge** (**C), which is made from 40-year-old vines grown on the best parcels. The wine is given four weeks' maceration, the juice being pumped over twice a day. The phenolic extraction is gentle and gradual. The wine is aged in casks for a year. When mature, the wine is powerful on the nose, with plenty of dark fruits and liquorice. Big on the palate, the wine maintains its fruit and spices develop with aeration. It certainly needs a long cellaring.

There is also a traditional **bergerac rouge** (**A), representing the bulk of the production of red wines at this property. Typically it will be largely *merlot*, but also with some of the other grapes, including *malbec*. The wine is raised partly in used barrels, and partly in old 50-litre *foudres.* The bouquet is fruity and spicy, and on the palate the fine tannins are complemented by more fruits and gentle toasting from the wood.

The range would not be complete without an attractive **rosé** (**A), a big, dark example, made from draining off about 20% of the juice from red-wine tanks, and a charming **côtes de montravel** (**B), admirable as a mid-morning appetiser or with *le five o'clock.*

The Dubard family also own a **pécharmant** (**B) property, Château les Farcies du Pech, where a largely *cabernet encépagement* (only 30% *merlot*) is aged in oak for one year. The nose is complex, with coffee, tobacco and cinnamon present, as well as other spices. It is a big wine in the typical pécharmant style.

■ **DOMAINE DE LIBARDE**

Didier and Pierre-Bernard Banizette

24230 Nastringues

Tel: 05-53-24-77-72

Email: banizette24@aol.com

www.banizette.isasite.net

Jean-Claude, the father of the present owners, was president of the local syndicate of Montravel producers for four years, and the property is perhaps best known for its **haut-montravel** (***B), which represents a third of all the wine they make and about half of all the wine made under that appellation. The family can trace wine-making back to 1903, so it is not surprising that they are expert in a style which was then so much more popular than it is today. The family's passion for it is, however, undimmed, just as they are proud of their efforts to promote its renaissance.

The degree of richness of the wine is dependent on the vintage; in a poor year like 1992 or 1993, for example, the wine barely attains 12 degrees, whereas in years such as 1989 or 2001 it achieves the same levels of sweetness as a monbazillac. The Banizettes believe in the keeping power of their wines, which close up about four years after the vintage and then start their development all over again.

Bernard, who is in charge of the *chais*, does not make only sweet wine. There are 40 hectares of vines altogether, producing roughly equal quantities of red and white, the latter including a particularly snappy **dry white** (**A) which reminds one of peaches and apricots, though crisp and refreshing. The **Rouge Tradition** (**A) is amazingly good value for the money, as is the recently introduced **barrel-aged version** (**A); Bernard makes this because clients ask for it, but he is careful to use only barrels which have already seen two wines. The Banizettes are lucky to have a friend at Château Filhol in the Sauternes who supplies them with hand-me-down barrels for the red wine, which they like to mature in cask for six months or so. Sometimes they make do without the wood, in which case they will only partially destalk the grapes and then lengthen the period of maceration. As a result their **bergerac rouge** (**A) has good structure and takes rather longer to come round than most other wines of its style. The wood does a good job, without imparting oaky flavours, and the hallmark of the wine is its dark, sweet fruit.

The wines here are staggeringly good value and rank among the best-kept secrets of the appellation.

■ CHÂTEAU DE LA MALLEVIEILLE
Philippe, Hélène and Thierry Biau
24130 Monfaucon
Tel: 05-53-24-64-66 Fax: 05-53-58-69-91
Email: chateaudelamallevieille@wanadoo.fr

Once a *relais de poste* beside the road going from Sainte-Foy into the northern Périgord, the property was many years ago converted to make a charming country house. Philippe, a fully trained *oenologue,* took the property over in 1983 from his father, who left Algeria during the troubles in the 1950's. In those days there were but six hectares of vines, but today there are about 18, and son Thierry acquired another seven at Fougueyrolles, just over the boundary into the Montravel appellation. Thierry, who joined his parents in working the domaine in 1997, is hoping that he will be lucky with his first attempt at meeting the stringent requirements of montravel rouge, the 2005 vintage.

Meanwhile, a delicious **montravel blanc sec** (***A), matured on its lees in tank after vinification at low temperature, awaits. Aged in rare barrels of acacia, about 30% of which are renewed each year, the wine is beautifully honeyed, though quite dry; the character is no doubt due to the *muscadelle*, which seems to enjoy the acacia wood and is a high 50% of the blend, sharing equal honours with *sauvignon*.

Most of the vines are outside the Montravel appellation, so are made as bergerac or côtes de bergerac. For example, the **bergerac blanc sec** (*A) is attractive but not in the same class as the montravel mentioned above. The **Rouge Tradition** (**A) is rather more interesting, its minerality giving a little bite and austerity to the fruit. **Mallevieille cuvée fût** (**B), which has rather more *merlot* so as to prevent hardness, has very delicate oak-ageing, and is a rather better value than the otherwise admirable **Imagine** (**C), which derives special character from the 20% *malbec* which goes into the blend. A good value **bergerac rosé** (*A) and **bergerac moëlleux** (**A) complete a range of very attractive and highly drinkable wines. A bergerac red is available also in *bag-in-box*—a format the usually conservative French have adopted much more readily than the UK market has.

■ CHÂTEAU MASBUREL
Julian Robbins
33220 Fougueyrolles
Tel: 05-53-24-77-73
Email: chateau-masburel@wanadoo.fr
www.chateau-masburel.com

This property, which includes an absolutely magnificent vineyard and home, was developed and nurtured by Englishwoman Olivia Donnan, though recently it was acquired by Julian Robbins. The remarkably tough and determined Olivia is married to the former European director of Mars Bars, who took early retirement. When they saw Masburel in 1997, that was it. It was very run down; the house was a mess, and all the outbuildings were in bad need of attention. But the property had a fine reputation historically for wine, though the previous owner only bottled about 20% of it himself, selling the rest off *en négoce*.

Today Masburel is a showplace. If the locals are jealous, they don't show it. They developed considerable respect for this English lady who took them all on single-handed, helped only by her *maître de chais,* who came from Château Sigalas-Rabaud in the Sauternais. There are 23 hectares under vine and a further 10 of woodland. The vines used to be grown *en hautain*, but it was decided to bring the vines nearer to the ground by truncating the main stem. One-third of the vineyard was replanted and the cellars furnished with state-of-the-art equipment.

She started to plant with absurdly high density (up to 13,000 plants per hectare, compared with the montravel rouge requirement of 5,000), which amused her neighbours intensely. She used a lot of new wood, bought on a three-year cycle. The property is up on a ridge, so gets little attention from botrytis. Therefore there are no sweet wines. Most of her production was exported to the UK.

During the transition to new ownership, who have declared an intention to continue in Olivia's footsteps, the Donnan wines from 2007 backwards will continue to be found on the market. There were two ranges of Bergerac wine. The first was called Lady Masburel, the other simply Château Masburel. The **Lady Masburel Blanc** (**B) was sometimes barrel-fermented and raised in wood (but neither in hot 2003). The yields were about 25–30 hl/ha. There were *agrumes* and exotic fruits on the nose and palate with some buttery richness. The 2001, for example, was rather delicate and there was little

evidence of the oak. Nor was there on the **Château Masburel Blanc** (***B), where the 2001 had more grip and bite and a more *sauvignon* character than the 2000.

The reds showed more evidence of the wood, sometimes perhaps too much, the **Lady Masburel Rouge** (**B) less so than the **Château** (**B). The red Lady was given her malolactic fermentation in barrels and then aged for 11 months in the same barrels. The wine is typically half *cabernet sauvignon*, 30% *merlot* and 20% *cabernet franc*. The red Château surprisingly had 75% *merlot* and only 25% *cabernet sauvignon*, macerated for eight weeks before being aged in entirely new wood. Both the reds will continue to keep and improve for many years and should be decanted well ahead of drinking. The 2000 (which Olivia agreed had a bit of rice pudding on the nose) was still pretty tannic after five years, but has suddenly started to come round and will go on improving for many years.

Olivia's first venture into montravel rouge was the 2003 vintage. The wine was called **Mon Ravel Bolero** (C), and the tune is written out on the label. This is a huge wine which will take many years to come round. The character of the vintage overlays the deep fruit, and the tannins will take some resolving.

The 2002 was not the greatest vintage in Bergerac, but the reds particularly seemed better than any of the preceding more illustrious years. The reason for this may be that for the first time the whole of the red *cuvée* Lady Masburel was given an experimental treatment by Thermo Flash Détente, a process whereby the temperature of the wine is raised for a mere fraction of a second to 70 degrees celsius. The effect seems to be to concentrate the flavours and soften the tannins as well as accentuating the phenolic contribution from the grapes. Purists frown, but in this case the results speak for themselves.

The wines here had been improving all the time, although severe hail in 2004 decided Olivia to sell off her reds *en négoce* rather than risk damage to the good name of Masburel.

Watch to see how Olivia's outstandingly hard work will be built on by the new owner.

▌CHÂTEAU MASMONTET

Thibaut Guillermier
24230 Vélines
Tel: 05-53-74-39-56 Fax: 05-53-74-39-60

Thibaut has 23 hectares which he took over following the retirement of his uncle and a family division of lands. Formerly there were 45 hectares, the rest being some ways away. The division was neat. The vines are not, however, *dans un seul tenant.* There are eight hectares round the house, and another 15 at Montcaret and Bonneville, nearby villages. The *chais* is primitive but functional, very cramped and somewhat casual. However, it is spotlessly clean.

Thibaut has trained in agriculture and vinification so brings new ideas to the family property. He makes bergerac in its two red styles, a montravel sec and both côtes de montravel and haut-montravel, having vines in both of the sweet appellations. The grapes for the sweet wines, especially the haut-montravel, are all hand-harvested, the rest gathered by machine.

For his reds he prefers long fermentations without too much reliance on new oak, with which he is sparing. He prefers *demi-muids* to the smaller sizes, and uses acacia barrels for his *liquoreux* to add floral rather than oak flavours.

I tasted his **montravel rouge** (**B) from the cask. The 2002 was much less aggressive than I thought it was going to be. Thibaut had been careful with the wood, and the wine had good fruit, nice acidity and length. This is perhaps the way montravel should go with its reds. Thibaut is as outgoing as he is well built and a cheerful and charming host: a wine-maker to follow.

▌CHÂTEAU MOULIN CARESSE

Sylvie and Jean-François Deffarge
24230 Saint-Antoine-de-Breuilh
Tel: 05-53-27-55-58 Fax: 05-53-27-07-39
Email: moulin.caresse@cegetel.net

Jean-François was until the spring of 2004 the president of the local *syndicat* of growers responsible for the creation of AOC montravel rouge. He is rightly proud of his achievement. He is also a thoughtful man, anxious to interpret the modern world in the light of the natural and to keep scientific man in his place.

His wines are among the best not only of Montravel but the whole of Bergerac, winning medals all over the place and a coveted *coup de coeur* from Gault Millau for his overall production.

The château, which has lovely views south over the Dordogne Valley, also houses *gîtes* and *chambres d'hôte* of a high standard.

There are three *blancs secs*, two raised in wood, one not. The **unoaked dry** (**A) is quite fat and has nice citrus-fruit. Half the grapes are given a *macération pelliculaire*, half are pressed straight away. The wine is cold-stabilized at the end of the vinification. The first oaked version is called **Magie d'Automne** (**B) and is more *sauvignon* weighted, with a bit of *muscadelle* too, barrel-fermented and raised in casks which are replaced on a four-year cycle. Obviously much richer than the unoaked wine, it is not overblown by any means. The *haut-de-gamme* white, called **Cent pour 100** (***B), has as much as 60% *muscadelle*, balanced by 30% *sémillon* and 10% *sauvignon*; it is a beautifully elegant wine with minimal sign of wood. Jean-François says of *muscadelle* that the problem is not the clone, but the overproductivity of the *porte-greffes* used by most people.

The traditional red bergerac, also called **Magie d'Automne** (**A), shows the benefit of a *culture raisonnée* (*vendanges vertes*, no chemicals etc.) and has nice balance. The **Prestige** (**B) has a little *malbec* too to give it structure in the wood. But it was the **montravel rouge** (**C) which I was curious to taste, coming as it did from the fountainhead of the *appellation*. The 2002 had a wealth of powerful fruit but needed a good two or three years for the wood to be integrated.

I asked Jean-François how the second tasting *after* the bottling worked. He said the committee consists of one local *vigneron,* two *sommeliers,* two dealers and two technical experts from Bordeaux or some other exterior region. It is organized by the Bergerac *Syndicat*. Each grower submits lots, numbered, and the number is printed on the cork. The *agrément* is given to the lot and not necessarily to all the lots submitted. Perhaps a committee of this type is going to favour wines which belong to the *vin de dégustation* school rather than the type most likely to be favoured by everyday consumers; and perhaps this explains the preponderance of overoaked wines from the first (2001) vintage. Were growers perhaps frightened that, unless they produced real blockbuster wines, they would not pass the test?

▦ CHÂTEAU PIQUE SÈGUE
Philippe and Marianne Mallard
33320 Ponchapt
Tel: 05-53-58-52-52 Fax: 05-53-63-44-97
Email: chateau-pique-segue@wanadoo.fr

As well as winning a prize for their French champion limousin bull, the Mallards, who have an important cattle herd on their 264-hectare domaine, have won countless prizes and medals for their montravel and bergerac wines. From their 85 hectares, which make them one of the biggest growers in Montravel, they make about 600,000 bottles a year. Seventy percent of the production is exported, largely to Belgium, Germany, the UK, Canada and Holland. The vines are situated on some of the highest ground in Montravel, notable for the absence of trees. There is little shade from the summer sun or the winds in winter, but this setting suits the cultivation of grapes very well.

The Mallards bought the property in 1990. Philippe, who is of English origin, is perhaps more orientated towards the cattle side of their business,

and Marianne to the wines. She is proud of the part they played in the establishment of montravel rouge. The wines raised in barrel are mainly produced under the name of an adjoining *lieu-dit,* **Château Dauzan La Vergne**, which is more of a brand than a distinct domaine. Under this banner the Mallards sell their multi-medalled **blanc sec** (**B), a blend of all three white-wine grapes, a particularly good partner for fish and white meat in sauces, or fresh ewes' milk or goats' cheeses. Their **côtes de bergerac rouge** (**B) is a fitting counterpart, with its aromas of red fruits supported by gentle oaking. It is under this marque that the property makes its **haut-montravel** (***C), one of the finest in this precarious appellation.

The Pique-Sègue label is used for the *entrée-de-gamme* wines, which by no means play second fiddle to the Dauzan La Vergne *cuvées*. The **montravel sec** (**A) is unusually fruity, with grapefruit, pineapple, lime and passion fruit overtones, a delicious aperitif particularly. The **bergerac rouge** (*A) suggests cherries as well as blackcurrants and raspberries and is *gouleyant*, which translates roughly as 'gluggable'. An attractive **rosé** (*A) fills successfully the market which has recently opened up for pink wines, and the **côtes de montravel moëlleux** (**B) makes an ideal foie gras wine, but is also good on its own as an aperitif, Montravel's answer to rosette.

The range is completed by the montravel rouge (**C), called **Terre de Pique-Sègue**, **Anima Vitis**. It is raised of course in barrels, the 2002 being more moderate in style than the flamboyant 2001.

▦ CHÂTEAUX PUY-SERVAIN-CALABRE and PUY-SERVAIN-TERREMENT
Daniel Hecquet
33320 Port Sainte-Foy-et-Ponchapt
Tel: 05-53-24-77-27 Fax: 05-53-58-37-43
Mobile: 06-85-42-02-20
Email: oenovit.puyservain@wanadoo.fr
www.puyservain.com

Much of the impetus behind the projection of Montravel, for its white as well as its red wines, has been from Daniel Hecquet, whose grandfather acquired a property in the Montravel area some years ago. Daniel, after a full training for his national Diploma in Oenology, during which he based his thesis on Château d'Yquem, moved to a good post at the Chamber of Agriculture for the Loire Valley. Returning to his native Montravel and armed with his technical qualifications, he became a consultant oenologist to a number of leading Bergerac producers as well as developing the vineyards and *chais* at his family home. As if that were not enough to keep a man busy, he also became the chief technical adviser to the *Comité Interprofessionnel des Vins de la Région de Bergerac,* a post which he held for eight years. After that he took over the presidency of the Montravel growers and for a while led the campaign for the creation of the red montravel AOC.

Today Daniel has dropped many of his outside commitments to devote himself more to his own vineyards, and also to bringing back to its former eminence the Pécharmant estate of Les Bertranoux, which had fallen on difficult times and which he could not resist taking on in what he calls a weak moment.

Puy-Servain, a name in old French meaning 'windy hilltop', is on some of the highest ground in Montravel, and hard by the tall water tower which can be seen from many miles around. Here Hecquet makes two ranges of wines. Under the name of **Calabre** the accent is on wines which are easy to drink and to market and which are not raised in wood; there is a striking **montravel blanc** (***A), a pure *sauvignon* (sometimes with just a hint of *sémillon*); the style is racy, minerally rather than grassy because a large part of the *encépagement* consists of *sauvignon gris,* rather than the more normal *sauvignon blanc*. In the glass the wine has enormous fruit and concentration and shows off perfectly Hecquet's skills in the cellar. In the Calabre range there are also an excellent quaffable **rouge** (**A) and a strawberry-like **rosé** (**A).

Two other dry whites bear the Puy-Servain name. The **Terrement** version (***A) is rather more

typical and original than the **Marjolaine** (***B), which nevertheless has an extraordinary length.

The wines called **Puy-Servain** are in an altogether different style. The basic **red bergerac** (***A) is 80% *merlot* and 10% each *cabernet sauvignon* and *franc*, all hand-picked and destalked. The macerations are long and the wine is aged in barrels for up to a year, one-fifth or one-sixth of the casks being renewed each year. The wood on the nose gives way to a powerful basket of fruits, while on the palate you may well find hints of woodland floor, even mushrooms. Balance and suppleness are other hallmarks, and in some years you may find touches of liquorice. If Daniel's technique as a wine-maker is well to the fore, there is no denying the richness and complexity which the superb *élevage* gives this wine.

There are two styles of bergerac raised in wood; the **Terrement** (**B) grapes are picked by machine, those for **Vieilles Vignes** (**B) by hand; the one is raised in barrels of which only 15% are new, the other for rather longer in casks of which 60% are new. Both wines have rather more of the two *cabernets*, and both have an animal character which itself calls out for good red meat or game to accompany them. They are complex and dense and improve with long keeping.

Hecquet is not content with making just one *cuvée* of montravel rouge. He always makes two and usually three. The most notable, called **Songe** (***C), is a huge almost port-like wine in every respect. It is almost black in colour, with big sweet fruit on the nose and a huge presence in the mouth; the finish goes on forever and the tannins are massive. This is one of the most demanding of bergerac wines, and will need long cellarage.

To wind up your visit to this most interesting and communicative of wine-makers, on no account miss out on the remakable **haut-montravel** (***D), the most persuasive defence-witness for this sadly dwindling appellation. Luscious but lively, the wine manages to be *liquoreux* without decadence.

OTHER NOTABLE MONTRAVEL PRODUCERS

█ CHÂTEAU LE BONDIEU
Didier Feytout
24230 Saint-Antoine-de-Breuilh
Tel: 05-53-58-30-83

█ CHÂTEAU LAROQUE
Jacques and Elisabeth de la Bardonnie
24230 Saint-Antoine-de-Breuil
Tel: 05-53-24-81-43 Fax: 05-53-24-13-08
Mobile: 06-86-55-40-00
e-mail: laroquevigneron@cegetel.net
Biodynamic producer for many years, with full
range of excellent bergeracs.

█ CHÂTEAU DE MONTAIGNE
Madame Mahler-Besse
24230 Saint-Michel-de-Montaigne
Tel: 05-53-58-60-54
www.chateaumontaigne.com
(Former home of the writer Montaigne, and
worth the visit on that account alone.) Specialist in
côtes de montravel.

█ CHÂTEAU LA RAYE
Itey de Peyronnin
24230 Vélines
Tel: 05-53-27-50-14

█ CHÂTEAU LE RAZ
Vignobles Barde
24610 Saint-Méard-de-Gurçon
Tel: 05-53-82-48-41
Email: vignobles-barde@le-raz.com
www.le-raz.com

█ CHÂTEAU LA RESSAUDIE
Evelyne and Jean Rebeyrolle
33220 Port Sainte-Foy-et-Ponchapt
Tel: 05-53-24-71-48
www.laressaudie.com
Full range of wines including montravel rouge.

█ CHÂTEAU ROQUE-PEYRE
GAEC Roque-Peyre (Domaines Vallette)
33220 Fougueyrolles
Tel: 05-53-24-77-98
Email: vignobles.vallette@wanadoo.fr
Full range in montravel rouge and *vins de pays*.

█ CHÂTEAU DES TEMPLIERS
GFA Ley
Bonnefare, 24230 Vélines
Tel: 05-53-58-68-15

THE WINES OF THE MIDDLE GARONNE

CÔTES DE DURAS

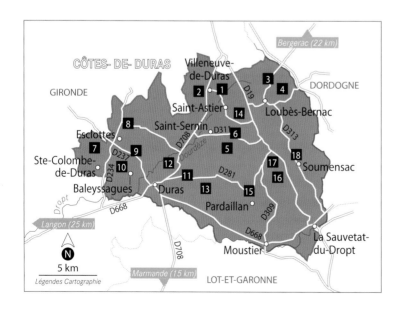

CÔTES- DE- DURAS   Villeneuve-
                    de-Duras
GIRONDE   [2] ○ [1]   [3]   DORDOGNE
                                              D19   [4]
                  Saint-Astier ○   [14]   Loubès-Bernac
             [8] Saint-Sernin
Esclottes ○   D708   ○ D311 [6]   D313
         [7] D237   [9]   [5]   [18]
Ste-Colombe- D234   [12]   [17]   ○ Soumensac
de-Duras ○   [10]   [11]   D281   [16]
Baleyssagues ○   ○ Duras   [13]   [15]
                  D668   Pardaillan ○
         Dropt   D309
Langon (25 km)   ○ La Sauvetat-
                        D708   D668   du-Dropt
              ▲   Moustier ○
              Ⓝ
         5 km   Marmande (15 km)   LOT-ET-GARONNE
      Légendes Cartographie

Bergerac (22 km)

AREA OF AOC: selected parcels in the communes of Duras, Auriac-sur-Dropt, Esclottes, Sainte-Colombe-de-Duras, Saint-Astier, Loubès-Bernac, Soumensac, Saint-Jean-de-Duras, La Sauvetat-du-Dropt, Moustier, Pardaillan, Saint-Sernin-de-Duras, Savignac-de-Duras, Villeneuve-de-Duras and Baleyssagues.

Red, white and rosé wines.

GRAPE VARIETIES:

REDS: cabernet sauvignon, cabernet franc, merlot and côt.

WHITES: sauvignon, sémillon, muscadelle, mauzac, rouchelein (pineau de la loire) and ondenc. The last two are not found in practice.

ALSO ALLOWED: ugni blanc (max. 25% and provided there is at least as much sauvignon in the vineyard).

MINIMUM ALCOHOL CONTENT: 10% by volume for reds, rosés and dry whites; 10.5% for white moëlleux.

RESIDUAL SUGAR: maximum 4% for reds, rosés and dry whites; minimum 4% for white moëlleux.

IF AUTHORIZATION FOR CHAPTALIZATION IS GIVEN: maximum alcohol by volume 13%; for moëlleux 15%.0

MAXIMUM YIELDS UNLESS OTHERWISE AUTHORIZED: 60 hl/ha for dry whites, 55 hl/ha for reds and rosés, 55 hl/ha for white moëlleux.

MINIMUM PLANTING DENSITY: 3300 plants per hectare.

To the south of Saussignac, and between the southern limits of the Bergeracois and Entre-Deux-Mers, are the vineyards of the Côtes de Duras. Duras is a small and pretty town with extensive views over the valley of the river Dropt (pronounced Dreau, to rhyme with château). Duras also has a historical and political importance far in excess of its size. Since the Middle Ages it has been the site of a fortified castle, which stood at the centre of most of the struggles which have characterized French political history in the South-West up to and including the Revolution.

The lords of Duras were ennobled to the status of duke by Louis XIV. They usually supported revolt and protest, but always managed to come out on top, even when they backed the losing side. In the Hundred Years' War they sided with the English Crown; in the religious wars of the Reformation they were Protestant for as long as it suited them; in the struggles of the Fronde they backed the rebels, and when the going got rough for them with their local subjects, they took refuge with their political protectors at Bordeaux and at the English Court. Yet they managed always to make their peace with the rulers of France, until, with the coming of the First Republic, they were swept away by the revolutionary tide, their château sacked and their influence smashed.

The ducal line died out in the 19th century, remembered by few and loved by none; they had been cruel overlords, exacting from their subjects every feudal due in the book. In particular the vineyards of the area were all held in tenancy from the duke, who arrogated to himself the right to make and process his own wines before anyone else was allowed to make theirs, ensuring him an unfair advantage in the markets downstream. Growers were also obliged to take a substantial part of their crop to the château by way of tribute. Under the *ancien régime* there was no yeoman tradition of wine-making in Duras, as there was in the Bergeracois. The Comté de Duras was ruled as a strict feudal serfdom.

IDENTITY CRISIS

It is not surprising that the local peasantry backed the extremists of the Revolution. The first Republican government sent a Monsieur Lakanal, a native of the Ariège, to expunge as far as possible all traces of the old nobility in Duras. Lakanal even required the residents to dismantle some of the fortifications and towers of the old château. He had plans, at first eagerly supported by the locals, to make the river navigable for wine traffic, but he refused to pay them for their demolition work on the château. This did not endear him to them, so they sent Lakanal back to Paris with a flea in his ear. To this day the decapitated towers of the ruined château bear witness to the uncompleted efforts of this maladroit politician.

The immediate local effect of the Revolution was that the ducal vineyards were put up for sale. The only people who had enough money to buy them, even at the knockdown prices ruling at the time, were the local artisans and small-time professionals who had feathered their nests very nicely in the wake of the chaos caused by the Revolution. So the vineyards came into the ownership of the *nouveaux riches* and those peasant-growers who had managed to keep a little gold hidden under their mattresses.

The feudal system had at least given the residents of Duras some cohesion. The Revolution destroyed it, and Duras has suffered a crisis of identity ever since. Politically and agriculturally it has nothing to bind it to the Bergeracois, and even less to Bordeaux. Its farming is geared to the production of sunflowers and maize and the making of prunes, emphasizing links with Agen rather than with the north or west. Yet the vineyards, which today cover nearly 2000 hectares, have a long and honourable history. Given the seal of approval by at least one pope—no matter that he was the uncle of the ruling lord of Duras at the time—they were admired by the English during the period of their occupation, and by François I, who called the wines 'nectar'. One achievement at least of the infamous dukes was to use their political influence abroad to spread the fame of the wines of Duras to the courts of 18th-century Europe.

THE PROBLEMS OF A BORDEAUX SATELLITE

Its historically long renown may be one reason why Duras was one of the first wine-growing areas to achieve AOC status (1937). But the problem of the AOC concept has always been that it is more concerned with local origin and unity than character or quality, and this is why it has taken so long for the growers in Duras to begin to make an impact on the marketplace. They have been both helped and hindered by using the same grape varieties as Bordeaux. They have sometimes been able to undercut their more famous cousins downstream, but they have found it difficult to establish a style which sets them apart. In the past, production was mostly of white wines, but today red wines have the upper hand, as in Bergerac, and in both cases this may be regrettable. The white wines are mostly dry and based on *sauvignon blanc,* which, unlike in Bergerac, has overtaken *sémillon* in the proportion 2:1. Thus there is already here in Duras something which sets their dry wines apart. The reds usually have more *merlot* than either or both of the two *cabernets*. *Malbec* is favoured by a few growers. The sweet whites, especially the less powerful kind, are making a comeback; this kind of wine, which used to be sold all over the region in cafés, is coming back to be the favoured aperitif, as well as being a style destined to make a better match with food than wines which are fully *liquoreux.*

MODERN PRODUCTION

There is little to distinguish the history of Duras after the outbreak of phylloxera from that of other regions, save to say that the re-creation of a viable trade in wine came later than in many other places. Partly for geographical reasons and partly through local rivalry, the foundation of the first *coopérative* was at Landerrouat, but not until the year 1930. It was not until the 1960's that the other part of the Duras camp founded their own *cave* just outside the town of Duras. For 40 years these two bodies competed for the same markets, a factor which no doubt held back the promotion of a unified concept of the wines of Duras. At long last the two *coopératives* merged, but not until the coming of the millennium. Today the two branches are known as Les Vignerons de Landerrouat-Duras.

PRODUCERS OF CÔTES DE DURAS

■ LES VIGNERONS DE LANDERROUAT-DURAS

SA Berticot
Route de Sainte-Foy-la-Grande
47120 Duras
Tel: 05-53-83-75-47 Fax: 05-53-83-82-40
Email: berticot@wanadoo.fr
www.berticot.com

Today the united *cave* is responsible for about half the planted area of the AOC. Particular care is taken over the work in the vineyards, with carefully controlled estimates of maturity of the grapes, selection of them parcel by parcel and a return to harvesting by hand.

As with many *coopératives*, the names and the styles of the wines are liable to change from year to year, but there will be inevitably two dry whites, both from pure *sauvignon*: an *entrée-de-gamme* **Cuvée Première** (A), straightforward and middle-of-the-road, and another, **Vieilles Vignes** (A*), which is aged on its lees. An oaked white called **Duc de Berticot** (*A) has a good deal of *sémillon* as well as a little *muscadelle* to add richness to the 40% *sauvignon*. It is fermented in barrels and then given eight months in wood.

The *merlot* grape is used to make a varietal wine, **Merlot Berticot** (A), by *macération carbonique,* and another varietal is the **Cabernet Sauvignon Berticot** (*A), which has rather more character. **Prélude** (A) is a *merlot/cabernet* blend for summer drinking, while the red **Vieilles Vignes** (*A) is 80% *merlot* and rather fuller, needing a little keeping. There is also a range of *barrique*-aged reds. **Sélection Berticot** (A*), the least oaky, is a frequent medal winner; **Duc de Berticot** (A) is more pretentious, boasting 12 months in cask; while in the best vintages there is a micro-*cuvée* called **Sans Nom** (*B), selected from only the best dozen or so barrels. The vinification here shows the influence of oenologist Michel Rolland, for many years consultant to the Berticot *Cave*.

Perhaps the best wines from this *cave* are the sweet ones: a straightforward old-fashioned **moëlleux** (*A) from late-picked *sémillon*; a barrel-fermented version called **moëlleux barrique** (*B) in which the *sémillon* is partnered by some *sauvignon*; and a *liquoreux* called **Premier Frimas** (**B) which is made only in exceptional years when the grapes are favoured by plenty of botrytis.

This *cave* is a dynamic one, and has done much to rescue the wines of Duras. The wines are all technically well made and very correct, enjoying considerable success in export markets. The problem, as with so many *coopératives*, is that there is still a tendency to resist limiting yields, in the mistaken belief that the income of members will suffer. The best independent growers in all regions have long ago proved this to be a fallacy. Furthermore, some thoughtful independent growers are exploiting their individual *terroirs* to produce wines which are not necessarily in the mainstream of Duras, but which are nevertheless wines of excellent quality.

NOTABLE INDEPENDENT PRODUCERS OF DURAS

▌**DOMAINE DES ALLEGRETS**

SCEA Blanchard

47120 Villeneuve-de-Duras

Tel and fax: 05-53-94-74-56

Mobile: 06-87-11-50-20

Email: contact@allegrets.com

www.allegrets.com

Julien Blanchard seems gradually to be taking over the running of this family domaine of 20 hectares. Wine-making here goes back five generations. There are no fancy departures from traditional grape varieties: just the *merlot* and the two *cabernets* for the reds, *sauvignon* for the dry white and *sémillon* for the *moëlleux*. Apart from a little rosé, equal amounts of red and white wine are made.

The dry white is available either with or without the benefit of oak barrels. The **unoaked vin blanc sec** (*A) has a nice fresh style to it and is very cleanly made, if perhaps without a great deal of individuality. The **sec en barriques** (**B) has much more depth and makes an interesting comparison with other wines of this style now available throughout the appellation.

The **Rouge Tradition** (**A) will have rich fruit and plenty of vivacity and is attractive in the way that red duras were not 20 years ago. There is also a version of **rouge en barriques** (**B), mostly from *merlot*, and the wood is very well handled. The wine nods in the direction of the modern style with its sweet fruit, but there is no concession to the Coca-Cola school of wine-making.

The sweet wines from this property are outstanding. The **moëlleux** (***B) is all that this old-fashioned style of half-sweet, half-dry wine should be: light, without serious pretension, and a much better accompaniment to food than many a more self-conscious heavyweight. The **liquoreux** (***B) is perhaps better still, showing good botrytis and a lovely touch of acidity on a very sweet base; a wine best drunk on its own as a *digestif*.

▌**DOMAINE CHATER**

Jackie and Iain Chater

Vignoble de la Lègue

47120 Saint-Sernin-de-Duras

Tel and fax: 05-53-64-67-14

Email: info@domainechater.com

www.domainechater.com/index.htm

It takes considerable talent and chutzpah to land in Duras from suburban London and walk off in your first year as an independent grower with gold medals from Paris and Bordeaux. Jackie is deservedly pleased with this initial success, perhaps rather less surprised, because she has an air of confidence which shines through her wines.

She and Iain bought this 9.5-hectare domaine in 2003 from a *coopérateur* whose contract with the Berticot *Coopérative* had but one year to run before it expired. This suited them well, because it was convenient to be able to send their grapes from their first vintage to the *coopérative* without any further obligation in future years. It gave them the breathing space also to build themselves a modern *chais de vinification*, where there was none before, and one to their own specification at that, without having to deal with any historical baggage.

Their very own first pink and white wines were a **rosé** (**A) *saigné* from *merlot* and *cabernet sauvignon* and an outstanding **sauvignon sec** (***B), raised in tanks. They also made a **barrel-fermented sauvignon** (**B) which was not ready for the competitions of 2005 but would have deserved to win yet another prize if it had been. Only 120 cases were made of this, but no doubt they will make more of this style as time goes by.

The reds are highly promising too; a **merlot/cabernet blend** (**B) has rich fruit, soft tannins and a long finish to commend it, while a pure **cabernet sauvignon** (**B), though not entirely typical of the grape variety, shows similar ripe fruit and good tannins which will ensure it long life.

These enthusiasts have made a very promising debut which catapults them straight towards the top in this appellation.

CHÂTEAU CONDOM PERCEVAL

J.-C. Lutaud
47120 Loubès-Bernac
Tel: 05-53-76-03-70 Fax: 05-53-76-03-79
Email: perceval@wanadoo.fr

Monsieur Lutaud claims his to be the smallest *chais* in Duras; he has just four hectares of vines in production, with a mere garage in which to make the wines, but these are special indeed. Although Madame comes from the region, they bought this attractive property in the heart of the village only in 1995. It once belonged to a minor nobleman who managed to survive the Revolution and even become a public servant of the new regime. The pretty village-house goes back to the 17th century. M. Lutaud bought without any vines attached, but he *grapillé* (scrambled together) four hectares dotted about the environs of the village, three of which are given to red wine grapes and one to white, the latter all *sémillon* and the source of the *liquoreux* for which he is best known.

He has been in the wine business most of his life, without any previous experience of wine-making, but the knowledge he had acquired in commerce, backed by a forceful philosophy of what wine should be about, seems to have been the only equipment he needed, apart from a few gleaming new steel *cuves* and a mix of old and new barrels from various makers.

Lutaud insists first on proper husbanding of the *terroir*: plantation to a density of at least 5000 plants to the hectare, sharp pruning of the vines, and severe disbudding in the spring, which he maintains avoids the necessity of *vendanges vertes* ('une mauvaise médecine', he calls them). At the same time, the fewer number of bunches on the plant at harvest time, the more likely it is that the grapes in each bunch will ripen evenly. Then the fruit must be at the right point of ripeness; picking too early produces sour juice and a lack of phenolic development, but picking too late produces too much sugar in a red wine and a lack of acidity in wines of both colours. Finally, the *vigneron* must be prepared to

take drastic decisions; if he makes a mistake in timing the harvest, then he may have to forgo his top *cuvées*, especially the botrytized white ones. Lutaud acknowledges that it is easier for him to adopt these draconian principles than it would be for a bigger grower whose entire livelihood depends on the wine crop; nevertheless, strict discipline is at the base of Lutaud's success in producing some of the best local wines.

He makes two reds. One he calls **Classique** (**B); half *merlot*, half *cabernet sauvignon*, after a long *cuvaison* of up to 40 days it is aged in barrels of which one-third are new each year. The other is **Cuvée Delph** (**B), named after his daughter Delphine; 90% *merlot*, it comes from his best *cuves* of *merlot* and *cabernet* and is aged in new barrels for 18 months.

The *sémillon*, with a minuscule yield of between nine and 12 hectolitres to the hectare, makes a **liquoreux** (***D) which is superb and in a class of its own. It is raised in barrels half of which are of oak and the other half acacia, the latter lending a floral extravagance to a wine which is never heavy or over-sweet, just perfectly balanced. If only all duras wines were this good.

DOMAINE DE DURAND

Michel and Marie Fonvielhe
47120 Saint-Jean-de-Duras
Tel: 05-53-89-02-23 Fax: 05-53-89-03-72
Email: info@domainededurand.com
www.domainededurand.com

Michel is probably the only wine-maker in South-West France who is also a hot-air balloonist—certainly the only fully biological one, in the sense that he is a fully paid up Agriculture Biologique licensee. It upsets him that many growers claim to be 'bio' but are not willing to sign up formally to the obligations entailed.

Michel, whose family has a wine-making tradition hereabouts which goes back to the 18th century, has equal quantities of red and white grapes in his 20-hectare vineyard, from which he makes a full range of wines. Like everyone else, he makes a **sauvignon sec** (*A) which does not wear its grape variety on its sleeve but has exceptional fruit. There is also sometimes a pure **muscadelle** (**B) which has all the flowery perfumes you might expect, with hints of apricots and exotic fruits. Another wine which is made only in good years is the **moëlleux** (**A/B), a traditional style which is not entirely sweet, having a good twist of citrus fruit towards the end, and is a long way from the *vendanges tardives* style which Michel has given up making.

A fresh and young-tasting **rosé** (**A) opens the way to the two red wines, a **Tradition** (*A) which is overshadowed by a **lightly oaked version** (**B) with good virile attack and tannins to see it through for a few years.

Since Michel became a fully biological producer in the 1990's, he feels that he has had to change his marketing techniques, and now covers mostly the Bio salons and shows, rather than concentrating on the fancy restaurants he cultivated when he first started. He is resigned to the unlikelihood of making a fortune from his wine-making; his enthusiasm for what he does and the way he does it is sufficient reward.

▌ **DOMAINE DU GRAND MAYNE**
Andrew and Edwina Gordon
47120 Villeneuve-de-Duras
Tel: 05-53-94-74-17 Fax: 05-53-94-77-02
Email: angordon@wanadoo.fr
www.domaine-du-grand-mayne.com

This property is well known to 5000 or so members of Wine Share, a rent-a-row scheme which Andrew pioneered when he left the wine trade in London in 1985 to take up a real challenge in this appellation, which at the time was hardly known. There were just 1200 *merlot* vines producing a mere 200 cases. Andrew started from scratch, restoring the *terroir*, then planting new vines and laying in the most modern plant. Today there are about 34 hectares of wines with every state-of-the-art refinement you can think of. His *régisseur*, Michel Coutin,

can manage with just two staff, such is the range of the technology in use. The vines are also all *dans un seul tenant*, which further saves on time and expense.

The south-facing slopes are on chalky clay, but most of the land also has a good deal of sand in the mix. Further clay is to be found in the substructure, and this seems to give the wines extra bite and freshness, as well as preventing stress in the vines during hot dry weather.

There are roughly twice as many red vines as there are white, and the latter are very nearly all *sauvignon*. *Merlot* outweighs the two *cabernets* put together in the red sector. Production of the *entrée-de-gamme* wines exceeds 200,000 bottles per annum, about 12 times as much as the prestige oak-aged wines. The latter are in turn being overtaken by the production of the ever more popular rosé.

The basic white **sauvignon** (*A) is a real winner, as is the oaked **Cuvée des Vendangeurs** (**B) from the same grape. The first may show white peaches, while the second has exotic fruits and almonds. The **rosé** (*A), made from drawing off 10% or so from some of the red wine tanks, reminds Andrew of strawberries and bubblegum, he says—a strange tasting note from a Master of Wine.

Until recently there were only two reds, the **Rouge Tradition** (*A) from 70% *merlot*—given just 8–10 days' fermentation, it is a lightish all-purpose red to suit all occasions—and the **oak-aged red** (**B), where the wood is more obvious on the nose than on the palate. This is a wine which has considerable strength built into its structure, and it keeps remarkably well, becoming in full maturity a Saint-Emilion style of wine of some character.

Andrew's latest experiment is with a barrel-fermented red entirely from *merlot* which he calls **Révolution** (***C). When he told me it was not only fermented in wood but also aged in it for two years, I was sure I wasn't going to like it, but quite surprisingly there was less evidence of new wood than on the earlier oaked red. A wine of fantastic richness, this will improve for many years to come.

With a small parcel of *sémillon* grapes, Andrew makes a delicious **moëlleux** (**C) which makes one want to reach for the Christmas cake.

▌**CHÂTEAU LAFON**
Pascal Gitton
47120 Loubès-Bernac
Tel: 05-53-94-77-14 / 02-48-54-09-59
Email: cavegitton@wanadoo.fr

Pascal, one of the principal players in the Sancerre market, might be expected to make an important contribution to the Duras appellation. A well-rounded (culturally and physically) and genial man-of-the-world could have much to teach the locals about marketing and promoting their wines. However, for Pascal this is a 'holiday vineyard' and he prefers to keep rather to himself. He comes to Duras to enjoy himself, not to get more headaches to add to those he has further north.

The need to root up some of his *sauvignon* grapes, which have suffered from the disease called eutypiose, has persuaded him to have a go with some less traditional grape varieties which are nevertheless permitted within the rules of the appellation: *mauzac*, *chenin blanc* and perhaps *ondenc*. Shades of Robert Plageoles in Gaillac? In any event, he has been pursuing for some while the idea of producing varietal wines which clearly announce their grape variety on the label. Legal sanction for this is now official, although there seems some doubt about whether the information should be contained on the front or back label of the bottles.

Thus Pascal produces charming examples of **merlot, malbec, sauvignon, sémillon** and so on (all **A or B), some of which demonstrate their ability to age gracefully. He makes the wines on the spot, but they are taken back to Sancerre to be bottled and stored. He has no trouble with the authorities about this (normally wines may be made and bottled only within the appellation concerned) because the wines are under the umbrella of his Sancerre company and may thus be processed in that district.

Pascal is of course not at Loubès-Bernac all the time, although he has a fanatical love for his 'second vineyard'; so an appointment should be made to visit this fascinating grower who brings to bear on the local scene the experience of a wine-maker whose savoir-faire covers the whole of the wine-making world.

▌**DOMAINE DE LAULAN**
Gilbert and Régis Geoffroy
Petit Sainte-Foy, 47120 Duras
Tel: 05-53-83-73-69 Fax: 05-53-83-81-54
Email: domaine.laulan@wanadoo.fr
www.domainelaulan.com

This is a benchmark property for the wines of Duras, especially *sauvignon*, a variety which Gilbert pioneered in the area, thereby earning himself the title 'brains of the appellation'.

Gilbert has proved that you do not have to be a native of South-West France to make good wine there. His family came from Burgundy. He trained as a farmer, because as a young man he wanted to go with his friends to study general agriculture at Montpellier rather than viticulture by himself nearer home. A combination of financial stringency and family deals found him in Duras, where he bought 10 hectares of vines in the early 1970's. He put in hand a total replanting of the vineyard, which at the time contained no red grapes, only the wherewithal to make sweet wines, which were not Gilbert's scene. Nowadays the family has 20 or so hectares, more or less equally divided between red and white grapes, mostly on a chalky clay above the valley of the river Dropt, but part also on higher ground where there is more chalk.

The only white grape the Geoffroys have is *sauvignon*, and from this they manage to make a fascinating variety of wines. Perhaps the most notable is the **sauvignon sec** (***A), with its heady nose of gooseberries and elderflower, a wine so perfect as a partner with shellfish as to suggest on the nose a *fumet de poissons*. It also marries well with fresh spring-time asparagus. There is an **oaked ver-**

sion of the same wine (★★★B) which is hardly less remarkable, only the personal preference of the drinker deciding which is the more attractive.

The red wines are good but, as so often in Duras, not quite as distinctive. The **Rouge Tradition** (★A), half *merlot* and half *cabernet*, is very dark and dense, perhaps a bit short on fruit, but with lots of acidity and soft tannins. In 2003, Gilbert made a **100% merlot** (★★A) from late-picked grapes in a one-off year. Perhaps this is a one-off wine too, raised in barrels which had already seen one wine. The fruit is very round and ripe, and the acidity was surprisingly good in a year which saw little of it. The **Duc de Laulan** (★B) is the oaked red of the house, conventional with a delicate use of wood to please the market but made so as not to upset the old customers.

Although Gilbert professed not to like the sweet wines of the area when he arrived, he makes an interesting **Vendanges Tardives** (★★C) entirely from *sauvignon*, in which a lovely sharpness balances the very rich fruit. He only makes this in certain years (1999, 2001 and 2005, for example), otherwise the wine turns out as a more conventional *moëlleux*.

■ **CHÂTEAU MOLHIÈRE**
(sometimes labelled LA MOULIÈRE)
Patrick and Francis Blancheton
47120 Duras
Francis: Tel: 05-53-83-82-83
   Mobile: 06-07-89-95-58
Patrick: Tel: 05-53-83-70-19
   Mobile: 06-86-57-49-51
Fax: 05-53-83-07-30
Email: patrick.blancheton@wanadoo.fr

Enjoying a strategic position astride the main road from the north into Duras, the tasting room on one side of the road and the family home on the other, and also within spitting distance of the Berticot *Cave,* the brothers Blancheton have made their wines some of the best known in the appellation.

The property is named after a certain M. Lamolhière, who arrived with a wave of immigrants at the end of the 16th century and rented the domaine from the dukes of Duras. His family became extinct when the last of the line was sent to the gallows in 1687 because of his Protestant fervour. The property thus reverted to the dukes of Duras, who re-let it to someone more reliable.

When Claude Blancheton, Patrick and Francis's father, arrived, like Lamolhière, from other parts in the 1950's, there were but six hectares of vines. Today there are 30, divided roughly in equal shares between red and white grapes. The red grapes are mainly *merlot* with some *cabernet sauvignon;* Patrick, who is responsible for the vines, does not seem to have much success with *cabernet franc*, which he reserves for his rosé. The red **Terroir des Ducs** (★★A) is thus a blend of the first two and often has a deep cherry nose and flavour, quite distinctive and one of the most interesting of its kind in the area. **Les Maréchaux** (★★A) is a slightly deeper version of the same, blended from selected *cuves*. **Cuvée Pierrot** (★★★C) is rather more ambitious, being from the best parcels of grapes and given two years in new barrels. A skilled wine-maker like Patrick does not allow the oak to impart unwanted flavours to the wine, which is an outstanding red duras.

Patrick also makes a **Terroir des Ducs rosé** (★★A), light in style but not in alcohol; it is largely from *merlot*, to which he adds his *cabernet franc* and a touch of *cabernet sauvignon* to make a wine in the provençal style rather than a wine to go with food.

The white wines are quite spectacular: a **blanc sec** (★★★A) from pure *sauvignon* aged in tank on its lees, which give some richness to balance the acidity nicely; and **Cuvée Pierrot** (★★★B), two-thirds *sauvignon* and one-third *sémillon* and raised in barrels for 16 to 20 months with regular *bâtonnage*, a tour-de-force in this style which is attempted by many but rarely as successfully as here. Patrick also has some old bottles of his **Grains Tardifs** (★★★D), an ultra-sweet style which he pioneered but has sadly discontinued. Others have since copied him, but he finds the wine difficult to market.

■ DOMAINE MOUTHES-LE-BIHAN

Jean-Mary and Catherine Le Bihan
47120 Saint-Jean-de-Duras
Tel: 05-53-83-06-98 Fax: 05-53-89-62-70
Email: domainemouthteslebihan@wanadoo.fr
www.siteschl.free.fr/mouthes

Jean-Mary and Catherine have 13 hectares of vines on this farm, where they also grow cereals and breed Arab horses. The long low farmhouse is just off a tiny road leading from Saint-Jean to Soumensac and so far there are no signposts. Visitors go straight into the living space, with a fine open fireplace at one end and pretty quarry tiles on the floor. The *chais* where the wines are aged in barrels is just across the courtyard. Jean-Mary would like in principle to raise all his wines in oak, but sometimes they do not turn out quite as expected, so he may keep some in tanks. He has no fixed policy about replacing used barrels; if he likes a particular cask he will keep it as long as it contributes to the finished wine, otherwise it is rejected.

Jean-Mary's first experiment in making his own wine was in 1999, his first serious efforts being in the following vintage. Best practices are the order of the day; he uses no chemicals whatever or artificial yeasts, and the wines are neither filtered nor fined. Jean-Mary will be anxious to show you first his work in progress from the barrel—perhaps a *merlot* from young vines growing on the typical chalky clay of the region, holding out promise for the years to come; a *cabernet sauvignon*, loaded with up-front fruit but not at the price of acidity or the soft tannins, both of which will contribute to a long life; or a delicious *cabernet franc*, perhaps still working a bit, but with good bite and fresh curranty flavours.

From the bottle you may start with the basic **vin blanc sec** (**B), a blend of *sémillon* and *sauvignon* of course, but with high (40%) *muscadelle*; an intriguing wine, sometimes with a hint of white

chocolate. The *sauvignon* is aged in barrels without racking, the other grapes in tanks on their lees. The top white is called **Pérette et les Noisetiers** (***C), Pérette being the name of one of the parcels. This is pure *sauvignon*, with a strong pineapple character and again white chocolate. The yields are less than 20 hl/ha, and the fermentation is started in tank. The must is then transferred to barrels of which one-third are new; here the alcoholic fermentation is finished, and the wines are allowed a malolactic fermentation too. They are then aged in wood for a further year. There is a **moëlleux** (**D) too, luscious rich and honeyed, but it really needs a bit more acidity to balance the luxurious character of the overripe and botrytized grapes.

The red wines are even more fascinating than the whites. **Vieillefont** (***B) is the principal *cuvée*, typically half *merlot*, 10% *cabernet franc*, 25% *cabernet sauvignon* and 15% *malbec*. After a gentle preliminary cold maceration, the grapes are vinified for four weeks without any additional enzymes or yeasts. Extraction is very gentle, no pumping over or emptying of the tanks, just gentle *pigeage*. The 2003 was somewhat atypical, being from the famous hot vintage and overloaded with rich fruit. The 2002 was more in the style of the house, better balanced and with less extraction, considerable elegance and finesse.

The top red is called **Les Apprentis** (***C) and is given up to six weeks' maceration and 19 months in the barrel. The bigger tannins therefore call for longer cellarage. But the wine is really fine, worthy to rank with any produced in South-West France.

Don't overlook a 'fun' *merlot* called **La Pie Colette** (**A), made for early drinking and fruity in the modern style. A bargain too.

■ **DOMAINE DU PETIT MALROMÉ**
Geneviève and Alain Lescaut
47120 Saint-Jean-de-Duras
Tel and fax: 05-53-89-01-44
Email: petitmalrome@wanadoo.fr
www.petitmalrome.com

Alain and Geneviève are near neighbours of Fonvielhe (see page 221), and like him, they are fully paid up biological growers, furthermore with biodynamic tendencies. Alain's great-grandfather was a farmer in the region from the 1920's onwards, but he had only a small parcel of vines, which were but one of his various crops. Alain and Geneviève did not themselves take seriously to wine production until 1997, at a time which coincided with the adoption of their biological convictions. Alain had worked for a while at one of the Bergerac *coopératives*, and later studied at the Institute of Oenology in Talence, Bordeaux.

Until recently they had only seven hectares of vines, all fully bio, and three more of walnut trees, but their son Nicolas has recently acquired five more hectares a little ways away which will soon be converted to bio over the usual three-year cycle. He has all the passion of the dedicated artisanal grower and plenty of charm to go with it.

Small the vineyard may be, but the wines are some of the best in Duras, all the grapes being hand-harvested. Their **sauvignon** (***A), raised in tanks, is a real value for the money, its *élevage sur lies* bringing out all the strength in the fruit. The **barrique version** (***B) is correspondingly richer, sometimes with a strawberry character. A fair enough **rosé** (*A) is *saigné* from the grapes which go into the two reds, and a **Tradition** (***A) is notable for a lovely balance between the fruit, the tannins and the attractive touch of acidity. The **barrique red** (**B) is entirely from *merlot,* and the handling of the wood is more than acceptable. As so often in Duras, the pleasant surprise is the **moëlleux** (***B), sometimes being in the old-fashioned lighter style but in the best vintages tending towards the *liquoreux* with its beautifully handled *élevage* in oak. This wine testifies to the excellence of these wine-makers. The wines here are also a wonderful value for the money.

OTHER GOOD DURAS GROWERS

▌DOMAINE AMBLARD
Guy Pauvert
47120 Saint-Sernin-de-Duras
Tel: 05-53-94-77-92
www.domaine.amblard@wanadoo.fr

▌DOMAINE DES COURS
Régis Lusoli
47120 Saint-Colombe-de-Duras
Tel: 05-53-83-74-35

▌CHÂTEAU LA GRAVE-BÉCHADE
Daniel Amar
47120 Baleyssagues
Tel: 05-53-83-70-06
Email: lagravebechade@wanadoo.fr
www.lagravebechade.fr

▌DOMAINE DES SAVIGNATTES
Maurice Dreux
47120 Esclottes
Tel: 05-53-83-72-84
Email: maurice.dreux@wanadoo.fr
www.les.savignattes.free.fr

▌DOMAINE DU VIEUX BOURG
Bernard Bireaud
47120 Pardaillan
Tel: 05-53-83-02-18
Email: contact@domaineduvieuxbourg.com
www.domaineduvieuxbourg.com/

AND TWO NEWCOMERS

▌DOMAINE GOURDON
Jonathan Coulthard
47120 Esclottes
Tel: 05-53-93-39-18
www.domaine-gourdon.com

▌CHÂTEAU HAUT-LAVIGNE
Nadia Lusseau and Michau Lavigne
47120 Saint-Astier-de-Duras
Tel: 05-53-20-01-94
Email: nadia.lusseau@tele2.fr
www.hautelavigne.free.fr

CÔTES DU MARMANDAIS

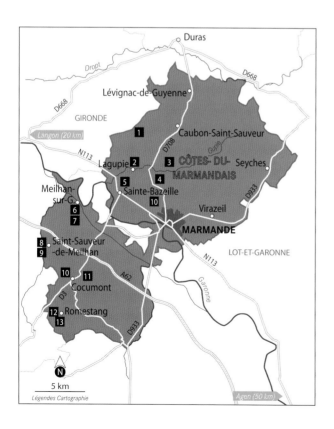

AREA OF AOC: selected parcels in communes of Beaupuy, Bouglon, Cambes, Castelnau-sur-Gupie, Caubon-Saint-Sauveur, Cocumont, Escassefort, Guérin, Lachapelle, Lagupie, Lévignac-de-Guyenne, Marcellus, Marmande, Mauvezin-sur-Gupie, Meilhan-sur-Garonne, Monteton, Montpouillan, Peyrière, Romestaing, Saint-Avit, Saint-Géraud, Saint-Martin-Petit, Saint-Sauveur-de-Meilhan, Sainte-Bazeille, Samazan, Seyches and Virazeil.

Red, rosé and white wines.

GRAPE VARIETIES:

REDS AND ROSÉS: cabernet sauvignon, cabernet franc and merlot (singly or together max. 75% of vineyard); abouriou, côt, fer, gamay and syrah (singly or together max. 50% of vineyard).

WHITES: sauvignon. Also permitted, up to max. 30% singly or together: muscadelle, ugni blanc and sémillon.

MINIMUM ALCOHOL CONTENT: 10% by volume.
MAXIMUM RESIDUAL SUGAR FOR WHITE WINES: 4%.
MAXIMUM YIELDS: 55 hl/ha for red and white wines, 66 hl/ha for whites.
MINIMUM PLANTING DENSITY: 4000 plants per hectare with transitional relief to 2020.

The district of Marmande, which straddles the river Garonne between Agen and Bordeaux, is gradually becoming as famous for its wine as for its tomatoes, even though this has taken many centuries to achieve. In the days when Bordeaux controlled access to the Bay of Biscay, the Marmandais beat off the demands of the merchants on the Quai de Chartrons by converting their wine into *eau-de-vie*. Equal resource was shown after the phylloxera epidemic, when the growers were quick to replant the vineyards on the immune American rootstocks.

Mostly the grape varieties were those used by the Bordelais, as was the case in Duras, but there was also a tradition in the region for a rare grape variety that is found only very occasionally elsewhere in France: the *abouriou*, a rustic plant giving juice of an amazingly deep colour and big, heavy tannins, a sort of super-*tannat,* in effect. Until the Revolution, the wines of Marmande were sold as bordeaux, being a virtual extension of the true Bordeaux vineyards, but the hapless Monsieur Lakanal, whom we met in Duras, decreed that only wines produced in the department of the Gironde were allowed to use the Bordeaux name. Marmande, like Buzet further upstream at a later date, had to reinvent itself, a process which took some time; it was not until the 1950's that the region was granted VDQS status and the *coopératives* at Cocumont and Beaupuy were founded. There followed a long period of restructuring of the vineyards so as to limit yield and increase planting density. Application was made to upgrade the wines to AOC status, a process which was successful as a result of the growers accepting the condition that, in order to differentiate their wines from those of Bordeaux downstream and those of Gascony to the south, one-quarter of the vines in every vineyard should consist of specific local grape varieties: *syrah*, *malbec*, *tannat* and/or the rare *abouriou*.

Abouriou is to be found more on the right bank of the river round Beaupuy, where the soil has more chalky clay, than on the left bank round Cocumont. At Cocumont the soil is sandier and more akin to that of Gascony, which adjoins to the south. Soil type may not, however, be the whole answer. The left-bank growers include many who have vines in the Bordeaux appellation as well as in Marmande, and they did not see why they should have to dig up a quarter of their bordeaux grapes in order to comply with the new AOC rules.

DIVISIONS IN THE APPELLATION

Growers on both sides of the Garonne are conscious of the deep division in the Marmandais which the river causes. The split is accentuated by the ban on planting grapes between the Canal du Midi and the Garonne, which are separated by a few kilometres of no-man's-land. The low-lying terrain between the two water-ways is almost certain to flood after heavy rains. The river was to a large extent also responsible for the emergence of two *coopératives* rather than a single one. It would not have been feasible to expect growers on one bank to deliver their wines to a winery on the other, if only because the one bridge at Marmande is a traffic-blocked bottleneck at all times. However, if the Marmandais had been able to make do with one *coopérative*, a unified effort might have obtained the right to *appellation contrôlée* a good deal earlier. It might indeed also have reduced the friction and fierce competition which developed between the two *caves* and which made their eventual merger so much harder to achieve.

PRODUCERS OF
CÔTES DU MARMANDAIS

■ LA CAVE DU MARMANDAIS

with premises at both 47250 Cocumont
and 47200 Beaupuy

Tel: 05-53-94-50-21 Fax: 05-53-94-52-84

Email: infos@origine-marmandais.fr

www.origine-marmandais.fr

In 2004 the two rival *coopératives* at Beaupuy and Cocumont merged. The vote of the growers was nearly unanimous, and at shop-floor level everything went smoothly, but, as with many mergers, it was at senior management level that arguments developed—who was to do what and who was to sit where. No doubt peace will be declared one day; meanwhile, the two separate establishments have been maintained, though each of the *caves* in principle stocks the wines of the other. The merger will need to generate more pull in the market than the two old *caves* ever did if the backlog of stocks is to be efficiently cleared.

Of the basic wines, the white come exclusively from *sauvignon* and are aged on their lees; the rosés combine *merlot*, *cabernets* and *abouriou*. Brands of these wines include **Grain de Bonheur**, **Grain de Plaisir**, **Esis**, **Osis** and **Mez Vinéa**.

Further up the scale, **La Vieille Eglise** represents Cocumont tradition and **La Cloître** that of Beaupuy. **Béroy** is Cocumont's next step up, **Confidentiel** Beaupuy's (incorporating a good dose of *abouriou*). Other brands in the pipeline include **Baron Copestaing**, **Perbos** and **Richard Premier** (an old Beaupuy brand-name).

Of various wines from single domaines, the *Cave* is proudest of **Château La Bastide** and **Château Bazin**, closely followed by **Château Sarrazière**, **Monplaisir**, **Marseau**, **Côte de France**, and **Soubiran**. All these wines are as unexceptionable as they are unexceptional (*A).

One of the wines which the people at the *Cave* don't talk about much is the **Château Mellet** (**A).

■ CHÂTEAU MELLET

Claudie and Christian Labeau

47180 Meilhan-sur-Garonne

Tel: 05-53-94-31-29 Fax: 05-53-94-36-40

Email: maison.labeau@wanadoo.fr

Although her wine is made at Cocumont, Madame sells the older vintages direct from her château at Meilhan, having bought them back from the *Cave*. As well as their vineyards, the Labeaus have an enormous pear plantation from which they make *eau-de-vie*. They also grow four hectares of kiwis.

The vineyard has 26 hectares on the same kind of terraces of *graves* as are found at Buzet, and their one red (which includes some *fer servadou* and *malbec*, but no *abouriou*) sells at the château at A-level price (for their 1998 vintage, for example). The quality is exceptional for the money, the wines being quaffable but with some class. Perhaps the *Cave* does not understand how much these wines improve with age, which is good news for the Labeaus.

INDEPENDENT PRODUCERS OF CÔTES DU MARMANDAIS

▌CHÂTEAU DE BEAULIEU

Robert and Agnes Schulte
47180 Saint-Sauveur-de-Meilhan
Tel: 05-53-94-30-40 Fax: 05-53-94-81-73
Email: contact@chateaudebeaulieu.net
www.chateaudebeaulieu.net

When the Schultes bought this now beautiful property in 1972, no vines went with it. Indeed, they would have had little time to devote themselves to wine-making, Robert being at that time a director of an international food firm and Agnes a PR specialist working for the Havas group. But they watched over the years, dreaming of the superb *terroir* which surrounded them. In 1991 the vineyard about them was put up for sale. The Schultes abandoned Paris and changed careers.

At the beginning there was no *chais de vinification*, so the grapes went to the *coopérative* at Cocumont, where the Schultes developed very good relations with the then director Henri Mourguet. When Mourguet retired and the *Cave* became less enthusiastic about competition from independent growers, they decided in 1995 to take full charge of their 30 hectares of vines, overlooking the left bank of the terraces of the Garonne and enjoying a superb *terroir*, part *graves* and part *argilo-calcaire*. The Schultes obtained the services of Marc Quertinier, for many years associated with Clos Triguedina at Cahors and Château de Frandat at Buzet, as oenologist. The repertoire of grape varieties is large: *merlot* (30%), *cabernet franc* (25%), *cabernet sauvignon* (20%), *syrah* (13% and growing), *malbec* (10%) and *abouriou* (2%). The Schultes do not like *abouriou* all that much; it is too rustic for their tastes.

There are no white or pink wines made at Beaulieu, just three reds. The *entrée de gamme* is called **Le Galapian** (**A), meaning in the local language 'urchin'. This is made from the young vines on the property. The grapes are given a short cold maceration before being vinified briefly at low temperature. The Schultes recommend a light chilling of the wine in summer, for it is meant to be enjoyed on its fruit and is ideal for drinking with grills and cheese, and for 'the *chasseur* to pack into his knapsack'. This wine may not be 'serious', but it is outstandingly attractive and more-ish. Brilliantly cherry red in colour, it has a bouquet that is fine and peppery. Tender on the palate, fresh and fruity, it finishes with a touch of mint.

The principal wine of the property is called simply **Château de Beaulieu** (***B) and it represents over two-thirds of the total production. The vines are all more than 25 years old and the grapes are harvested by hand. Vinification is traditional with frequent *remontages* and *pigeages*. *Cuvaisons* vary from three to four weeks according to grape variety and the character of the vintage. The wine is aged in oak barrels of which 20% are new each year. The colour is deep and the rich and complex bouquet is of red fruits with spices (the *syrah* content). On the palate the wine is soft, big, sometimes with touches of sloes.

The top wine is called **Clos de l'Oratoire** (**B) and is made from the oldest vines, with a low yield of about 20 hl/ha. It is named after a former chapel, a small place of worship located in one of the truncated towers of the property. The label bears a reproduction of a mural uncovered by the Schultes during their restoration of the property. The wine is from 15% *syrah*, 10% *malbec,* with the balance made up equally of *merlot* and the two *cabernets*. The wine is aged in barrels, three-quarters of which are new, and as may be imagined, the wood is evident on the nose though rather less in the mouth. The lack of a third star reflects personal taste rather than objective criticism, for this is a very good wine indeed. The colour is dense ruby, the nose spicy and toasted, the attack in the mouth powerful, and the flavour dense yet fresh, spicy with a touch of cocoa and backed by fine tannins.

One day a young man asked Robert Schulte if he could make his wines more sexy. So was born **Le Bel Insolent** (**A), a new wine meant for the young, easy to drink on its fruit, more-ish and simple. Sexy? Readers can judge for themselves.

■ **DOMAINE ÉLIAN DA ROS**
Élian da Ros, Laclotte
47250 Cocumont
Tel: 05-53-20-75-22 Fax: 05-53-94-79-29
Mobile: 06-83-25-37-27
Email: e_daros@club-internet.fr

It is easy to identify this cult-*vigneron,* although there are no signposts to his *chais*, the vines are not cut like an English lawn and the bottles lying around are Burgundy shaped. Still, it is useful to know that, as you arrive at Cocumont from Marmande, Élian's cellar is just less than a kilometre from the village, on the left. A square ugly building is rather less attractive than the wines made within, and there is absolutely no outward show of business.

Élian has 16 hectares of vines, which have been in the family for some while. They were *coopérateurs* until Élian decided to go out on his own and get training in an altogether different environment, from the famous grower Zind-Humbrecht in Alsace among others. He is heavily Burgundy-orientated in his technique, believing in small *cuves*, regular *pigeage* and so on.

He reproduces his vines by *sélection massale* rather than the officially authorized clones, using not very vigorous *porte-greffes*. Some of his *terroir* is *argilo-limoneux*, some *argilo-graveleux*, some *argilo-calcaire* on *molasses marnières* and *calcaires*, none of which is easy to translate. He has *malbec, abouriou* and *syrah* as well as the usual Bordeaux grape varieties; and for his whites he has some *sauvignon gris* as well as the ordinary *sauvignon* and *sémillon*. His principles are entirely biological, and he keeps his yields to a low 15–35 hl/ha according to the parcels of vines and the vintage. All the grapes are picked by hand and are first sorted at the vine.

The grapes are destalked, except in the case of some of his *abouriou*, and there is no question of using artificial yeasts. Élian insists on separate vinifications in open *cuves* by parcel and by *cépage*. *Pigeage* by foot and with hand stick punctuates long macerations. The malolactic fermentations happen in *barriques* or old *foudres*. The wines are all raised in wood for periods varying from 12 to 18 months. They are neither filtered nor fined. The wines are made and aged in his home-built *chais* and the underground barrel-store, which he also built himself and intends to extend.

The name of his basic wine changes according to caprice (**Le Vin Est une Fête**, or perhaps **Vignoble d'Élian**) and is always quaffable and stylish (**B). But it is the two top wines which have attracted all the attention. The **Chante-Coucou** (***B) may have violets on the palate (2002) or good mixed fruits (2001, which was more forward).

Go underground for tastings from the wood. A 2002 *merlot*, destined for the top **Clos Baquey** (***C), has proved sensational, like a big Loire, a style which Élian likes to emulate. A 2002 *cabernet franc* (a grape he loves) was very long, but had more acidity and tannins than the *merlot*, while a *cabernet sauvignon* was rather unorthodox and very un-Bordeaux-like.

Here you have a rare chance to taste pure *abouriou*; the 2002 was wonderfully floral but surprisingly tannic, puckering enough to gum up the face altogether, but faith in Élian's talent persuades you it will be lovely and an important element in a blend one day. A two-year-old version of the same wine was a bit dumb on the nose, not surprisingly, but the fruit was very ripe and there were the same frightening tannins. Recent results with this grape have, however, been much softer and less austere, attractive even for early drinking.

Finally back to ground level. From the bottle, a four-year-old Clos Baquey may be superficially quite soft, but will hide a tough backbone behind the fruit. Élian's wines are bound to keep well. A visit may finish with eccentric white wines, including a surprising neo-*moëlleux*, hard to classify and called **Coucou Blanc** (***B), a style of wine you might not expect from this grower. If you are really in luck, Élian will show off to you an amazing *liquoreux* which he makes from pure *sémillon*, but only in tiny quantities and not for sale commercially.

The philosophy here follows closely those of his friends in other appellations—Cosse-Maisonneuve in Cahors and Jean-Mary Le Bihan in Duras. So much so that there is an uncanny resemblance in the style of their wines, which are not necessarily typical of their respective appellations. This is not a criticism, for Élian, like his friends, is an exceptional wine-maker who makes his own rules. The results are more than top class.

■ **DOMAINE DES GEAIS**
Vignobles Boissonneau
Château de la Vieille Tour
33190 Saint-Michel-de-Lapujade
Tel: 05-56-61-72-14 Fax: 05-56-61-71-01
Email: vignobles@boissonneau.fr
www.boissonneau.fr

Monsieur Boissonneau anticipated the new AOC rules by planting his Marmandais vineyard to no less than 45% of the strictly local varieties, including *abouriou* and *syrah*. He has been much more enthusiastic in grasping the official policy than either of the *caves* were. The result is that his wines are no bordeaux lookalike; they have no need to be because he has much larger holdings in Bordeaux AOC than in Marmandais.

The family has been making wine here since 1839, and the vineyards go back a lot further than that. The local hamlet, called Lorette, has a diminutive church which was built for Eleanor of Aquitaine, and in the middle of his farm-buildings is an imposing *pigeonnier* which used to serve the entire local population, and which Boissonneau features on his labels to this day.

As with his bordeaux wine, vinification is highly sophisticated, even if the macerations are surprisingly short. Boissonneau vinifies some of his grape varieties together, for example the *merlot* and *abouriou,* which ripen at just about the same time, then the *syrah* and *fer servadou*, and finally the two *cabernets*. He uses no wood and leaves the wine in the tank until just before the next vintage, when he bottles it. His red **Domaine des Geais** (**A) is deliciously lively and fruity. He only makes the one *cuvée*, which is sometimes to be found in supermarkets under the name **Domaine de Saint Martin**.

▌DOMAINE BONNET ET LABORDE

Gilbert Bonnet and Eric Laborde

La Chalosse

47200 Lagupie

Tel: 06-14-74-78-90 Fax: 05-53-83-43-07

Email: bonnet.gc@libertysurf.fr

This is a partnership which started as friendship in school, and in 1998 was pursued with the idea of pooling wine-making resources in an area which at the time had little exposure in external markets. The combined area under vine, almost entirely replanted from scratch, is 30 hectares, on which are planted in addition to the usual *merlot* (30%) and *cabernet sauvignon* (30%), *malbec* (15%), *abouriou* (15%) and *fer servadou* (10%), so that at least 40% of the *encépagement* distinguishes the wines from downstream Bordeaux production. The vines are all on the north bank of the river, where the soil seems to suit the local *abouriou* grape so well.

Start with their lovely **rosé** (**A), so refreshingly fruity but dry, and move on to the red **Montpeyrac** (**A) made from the juice of younger vines, a good everyday quaffing wine, deceptively simple and light. The mainstream red is aged in a mixture of new and old barrels for two to three years, and the *élevage* is skilful and duly respectful of the basic character of the wine. **Clos de l'Adret** (*B) is the name given to their so-called top wine. The grapes are harvested by hand and grown on the best south-facing slopes, but the wine needs some keeping if the effect of the oak-ageing is not to intrude.

OTHER CÔTES DU MARMANDAIS
GROWERS
(not often found on the market)

▌CHÂTEAU BOIS-BEAULIEU

J.-P. Tarascon

Campot, 47180 Saint-Sauveur-de-Meilhan

Tel: 05-53-94-32-41 Fax: 05-53-64-65-11

Email: boisbeaulieu@aliceadsl.fr

▌CLOS CAVENAC

Mme Emmanuelle Piovesan

Cavenac Sud

47200 Castelnau sur Gupie

Tel: 05-53-83-81-20

Email: closcavenac@yahoo.fr

▌MONIQUE GAJAC

Route de la Réole

47180 Meilhan-sur-Garonne

Tel: 05-53-94-30-05

▌DOMAINE DE FONTALEM

Yvonne Renaud

33690 Grignols

Tel: 05-56-25-50-45

▌CHÂTEAU GRAND'CÔTE

Jean Philippe Tauzin

La Mole, 47200 Beaupuy

Tel: 05-53-20-90-19 Fax: 05-53-64-97-50

▌JEAN-PIERRE LAGAÜZÈRE

(a former president of the Syndicat of
Marmandais growers)

Clémenceau, 47180 Saint-Bazeille

Tel: 05-53-64-73-62

▌CHÂTEAU LASSOLLE

Stéphanie Roussel

47250 Romestaing

Tel and fax: 05-53-94-55-73

Email: chateaulassolle@wanadoo.fr

BUZET

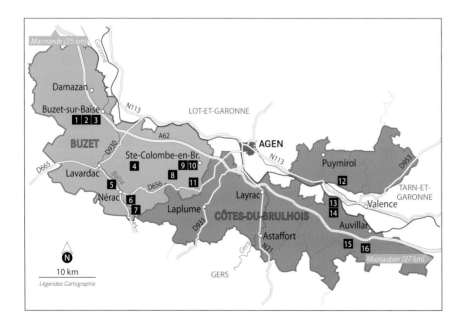

Marmande (25 km)

Garonne

Damazan

Buzet-sur-Baïse
1 2 3

N113

LOT-ET-GARONNE

BUZET

A62

D930

D665

Ste-Colombe-en-Br.
4

9 10

8

AGEN

N113

Puymirol

D953

12

Lavardac
5

Baïse

D656

11

TARN-ET-
GARONNE

Nérac
6
7

Laplume

Layrac

CÔTES-DU-BRULHOIS

13
14

Valence

Auvillar

D931

Astaffort

Gers

N21

15

16

Montauban (27 km)

N

10 km

GERS

Légendes Cartographie

AREA OF AOC: selected parcels in the communes of Ambrus, Anzex, Barbaste, Bruch, Buzet-sur-Baïse, Calignac, Caubeyres, Damazan, Espiens, Feugarolles, Lavardac, Leyritz-Moncassin, Moncault, Montagnac-sur-Auvignon, Montesquieu, Montgaillard, Nérac, Pompiey, Puch d'Agenais, Razimet, Sainte-Colombe-en-Brulhois, Saint-Léon, Saint-Pierre-de-Buzet, Sérignac-sur-Garonne, Vianne, Villefranche-du-Queyran and Xaintrailles.

Red, rosé and white wines.

GRAPE VARIETIES:

REDS AND ROSÉS: merlot, cabernet sauvignon, cabernet franc and côt.

WHITES: sémillon, sauvignon and muscadelle.

MINIMUM ALCOHOL CONTENT: 10% by volume for reds and rosés, 9.5% for whites.

Maximum alcohol content after enrichment (when permitted) 13% for reds and rosés, 12.5% for whites.
MAXIMUM PERMITTED YIELD**: 55 hl/ha.**
MINIMUM PLANTING DENSITY**: 4000 plants per hectare.**
PRUNING**: méthode Guyot (single or double).**

VENERABLE VINEYARD

The region which is today called the Côtes de Buzet lay in the inexorable path of the Romans as they progressed from their provincial capital, Narbonne, towards Bordeaux. It lies on the slopes of the left bank of the river Garonne between Agen and Marmande. Excavations a little further into the hinterland have unearthed ancient tools which could only have been used for pruning vines, proving that wine production at Buzet was in full swing as early as the second century BC.

As the importance of Bordeaux as a trading port grew, Buzet became an important source of wine to the dealers there, and the local growers expanded their production to meet the demand, well beyond the needs of their domestic consumption. Buzet was almost absorbed into the wine world of Bordeaux, its wines being sold as bordeaux.

The onslaught of the various 19th-century vine plagues occurred at a time when Buzet was enjoying its golden age. After the phylloxera, the growers decided to plant local rather than Bordeaux grapes; they grafted *malbec*, *bouchalès* and *mérille* onto immune American stock and the quality of the wine fell sharply. Then in 1911, after years of political lobbying and debate, the good and the great in Bordeaux managed to persuade the government of the day that only wines made in the *département* of the Gironde might be sold as bordeaux. Disinherited and without a name, the *vignerons* of Buzet suffered a long period in the commercial wilderness. Efforts at a renaissance were painful, and there were many false starts. Even the grant of VDQS status in 1953, following the agitation of a handful of enthusiasts, was not enough to kick-start Buzet as an appellation. This happened only two years later with the formation of the *cave coopérative*.

The first task was to restore the quality of the vineyard, which called especially for the planting of more *merlot*. Expert advice was sought on the identification of soil types and which grape varieties would best suit each one: porous, quartz soil for the *cabernet sauvignon*, lighter sandy and pebbly soil for the *cabernet franc*, and heavier clay soils for the *merlot*. The success of the *coopérative* even today rests largely on this pioneering analysis. Progress was sensationally rapid; at the beginning the members produced only 8% of their wine under appellation rules. By 1982 this percentage had risen to 75%, and the volume multiplied sevenfold.

PRODUCERS OF BUZET

◼ **LA CAVE COOPÉRATIVE**

des Vignerons de Buzet

BP 17, 47160 Buzet-sur-Baïse

Tel: 05-53-84-74-30 Fax: 05-53-84-74-24

Email: export@vignerons-buzet.fr

www.vignerons-buzet.fr

The *Cave* claims to be responsible for 'nearly 97%' of all wines produced under AOC Buzet. There are 281 growers and 22 individual châteaux and domaines, together covering 1872 hectares. Their dominant position means that they promote Buzet 'both as an AOC and as a brand name'. Perhaps this was the idea behind changing the name of the appellation from Côtes de Buzet to Buzet *tout court?* It seems hard on those who prefer to remain independent and at the same time enjoy the right to the Buzet name, but the *Cave* has always wanted to become a Buzet monopoly. Visitors will be told that there are only five independents, but in fact there are ten. The *Cave*'s slogan is 'One for All and All for One', and the aggressive stance is further instanced by the claim in their publicity literature that 'the style of the wines is closer to the elegance of Bordeaux wines than to the rustic character of some South-Western French wines'. Which are they referring to, one wonders?

The Buzet *Cave* is nevertheless highly successful and its achievements are impressive. Its equipment is state of the art; they can store 4500 barrels, many of which come from the local cooper, whose grandfather used to work for the *Cave* on its own premises. There are two satellite *caves*, one at

Espiens and the other at Château Padère, one of the *Cave*'s flagship domaines. Exports account for 15% of the production, which may not seem much but amounts nevertheless to 1.5 million bottles. The wines are mostly red (80%), but there is a significant amount of rosé (15%) and only a tiny amount (5%) of white.

The wines may best be described as sound rather than exciting. Quality can be expected to rise following the appointment as technical director of Pascal Lamothe, formerly the oenologist at Cos d'Estournel in Saint-Estèphe. Pascal is determined to modernize the style of the wines by relying increasingly on the prominence of ripe fruit, with perhaps less attention to acidity or phenolic maturity, though doubtless the flagship wines will continue to be made in a style which stays rather more with tradition. The new trend is noticeable already in the wines of the 2004 and 2005 vintages, which include a range of inexpensive reds under such names as **Cuvée 44**, a rather deeper **Rocher d'Hillac** and **Renaissance**, all *A and none of them aged in the barrel.

The single **white wine** of the *Cave* (A) is well enough made but has little character. The **rosé** (*A) is rather better, having enjoyed a preliminary maceration of six hours. It has good body and fruit and a dry finish, seemingly the requirements of today's pink wines. Of the basic reds, **Prince d'Albret**, **Roches d'Hillac** and the **Tradition** (only for restaurants and wine shops) are all satisfactory without raising much excitement (all A). **Domaine de la Prada** (*A), the first of the domaine wines, is a big leap forward, being the second wine of Château Padère. **Domaine de la Croix** (*A) (no. 3 on the map) is more in the modern style, half the wine having been given 14 months in barrels. Probably the best of the single domaines is the well-known **Château de Gueyze** (**B), an 80-hectare estate whose wines always need time. Others are **Châteaux Balesté** (*B), **Padère** (*B), **Bouchet** (*B) and English-owned **Mazelières** (**A), whose wines are expected to improve swiftly following new plantings on superior *terroir*. The best of the *Cave*'s own brands are the often-seen **Baron d'Ardeuil** (*B), named after a local aristocrat who earned favours from Napoleon for having lent his wife to the emperor; and the **Grande Réserve** (C), which is somewhat overpriced for what it is, a dense and tannic wine aiming for a New World–fancying public.

■ **CHÂTEAU DE FRANDAT**
Patrice Sterlin
47600 Nérac
Tel: 05-53-65-23-83 Fax: 05-53-97-05-77
Email: chateaudufrandat@orange.fr

This fine estate, whose soil seems particularly immune to the effects of drought, covers 60 hectares in all, of which 27 are planted with table-wine grapes and two with grapes for a small production of armagnac and floc de gascogne. The property is in both Buzet and Armagnac appellations, a reminder of how far south Buzet is in relation to Bordeaux and its satellites.

As a one-time student of agricultural engineering, Patrice likes to grow fruit and cereals as well as vines. The château itself can fairly call itself one, or just about. At first glance rather in the style of an 18th-century manor house, there are parts of the buildings which go back much further. The vineyard dates from the time of Napoleon. Patrice bought it from a member of the *coopérative* and had quite a hard time extracting himself from their clutches. Time, however, heals all, and peace has been declared between them.

He was lucky in his first vintage to have the benefit of the excellent conditions of 1990. Initially he made two reds, one oaked the other not, but today both his red wines are raised in barrel, the **Cuvée de Majorat** (**B) in French wood and the **Cuvée Privilège** (**B) (on the advice of his *oenologue,* Marc Quertinier) in American wood, which they both believe gives more suppleness without extra oak flavour. Both show well the typicity of buzet at its modern rather plummy best, full and rich and capable of long ageing in the cellar, indeed in good years needing it. These wines are regular winners of *coups de coeur* from *Guide Hachette,* and prove the need for a good team of independent winemakers in Buzet to give the *coopérative* a good run for their money and keep them on their toes. A comparison between their respective top wines is most instructive.

Patrice Sterlin makes an attractive **rosé** (**A), but has given up making white wine because he feels it is no use trying to compete with Bordeaux at their own game.

■ **DOMAINE DU PECH**
Magali Tissot and Ludovic Bonnelle
47310 Sainte-Colombe-en-Brulhois
Tel: 05-53-67-84-20 Fax: 05-53-67-88-99
Email: pechtis@club-internet.fr
www.domainedupech.net

Magali took over this domaine when her father, Daniel, died in 1997. Since then she and her partner, Ludovic, have made significant changes while at the same time maintaining the very high standards of wine-making which Daniel had set them. There are 20 hectares, of which only one is given over to white grapes. The entire vineyard is cultivated biodynamically, no fertilisers having been used for over 20 years. Even copper and sulphur are used to a minimum extent, preference being given to medicinal plants. Daily checks are made in the vineyard to confirm the health or otherwise of the vines, and there are weekly tastings when every wine is put to the test. The vineyards are worked almost entirely by hand, including the preparation of the soil, pruning, disbudding and the tending of the foliage in summer. There are no *vendanges en vert*, Ludovic believing that, with severe pruning and disbudding, they are not necessary; according to him they are a mutilation of the plant, to which the vines in due course will respond by finding their own ways of over-producing. Needless to say, harvesting is nowadays by hand too. By achieving the best balance between soil and vine, Magali and Ludovic can reduce to zero the use of any oenological products or processes in the *chais,* sulphuring having been abandoned in 2001. Artificial yeasts and enzymes are banned too; nothing but the grapes goes into the wines.

It would seem that the conversion to biodynamic practice has not commended itself to the local tasting committee, dominated by powerful voices within the *coopérative*. They have withheld the all-important *agrément* in respect of the 2003 and 2004 vintages on grounds which do not seem to correspond with reality. No one could objectively criticize these wines for lack of 'matter', or for containing 'vegetal flavours'. It is more likely that such perverse decisions reflect the desire in some quarters to force the handful of independent growers into the arms of the *Cave*. Any independent *syndicat* of growers should welcome and encourage growers of the quality of Magali and Ludovic rather than try to force them out of business. This pair will doubtless win through somehow, because their wines are excellent.

In the cellar, Daniel's splendid old *foudres* have been retained, and Magali and Ludovic have invested in four brand-new ones from Taransud in the Charente, the only ones of their kind I have seen in the South-West. All the wines here are raised in wood, the *foudres* being supplemented by 600-litre *demi-muids* in preference to the more usual 225-litre Bordeaux casks.

The one hectare of white grapes produces a small amount of **sauvignon blanc** (**B); the grapes are given 36 hours' preliminary maceration before being fermented in new *demi-muids,* where they also get a malolactic fermentation before being aged for a further twelve months. The result, being

somewhat atypical in terms of *sauvignon* style, is certainly different and interesting.

It is the red wines, however, on which the reputation of the domaine rests, and these may well be the best of the appellation. There are just two *cuvées*. **Le Domaine de Pech** (***B) is from the two *cabernets* and *merlot*, the proportions being governed by the yields harvested in any given year. The grapes are fermented and macerated in stainless steel for four or five weeks and then aged for two years in a mix of old and new *foudres*. Success seems assured in every vintage; in some years like 2000 and 2003 the accent is on concentrated matter and structure, while in 2001 there was more charm and finesse. Ludovic, unlike many other wine-makers in the South-West, believes that their wines from the 2003 vintage were the best they have made, perhaps because they delayed picking until there was a little rain to restore life to the parched vines.

The second red is called **La Badinerie du Pech** (***B) and is a blend of the best bunches of each year. The wine is vinified in Burgundy-type wooden *cuves* for four to five weeks with regular *pigeage*, by hand of course, before being transferred for their second fermentation into *demi-muids* about one-third of which will be new each year. This excellent wine seems to combine the best features of every vintage, power with elegance, structure with finesse and the finish is always soft and long.

The use of wood at this domaine is exemplary. The influence of oak has moderated over the years. Today none of the wines leaves any taste of it, but the *élevage* adds sumptuousness and complexity in a way which should be a lesson to all.

▌CHÂTEAU DE SALLES

Henry de Batz de Trenquelléon
47230 Feugarolles
Tel and fax: 05-53-95-27-49
Mobile: 06-83-42-69-93
Email: henrydebatz@wanadoo.fr
monsite.wanadoo.fr/buzetchateaudesalles/

There is nothing particularly swashbuckling about this charming descendant of the famous musketeer D'Artagnan, who, on leaving Gascony to go to court at Versailles, deemed the family name de Batz a trifle naff for the Hall of Mirrors, so changed it to his better-known alias. The wines have the same well-bred character as their maker, whose family have owned this beautiful property since the 18th century. There were 50 hectares of vines here before the phylloxera, and Henry de Batz, a passionate wine lover, was always determined to replant vines when he could, to add to the family's substantial estate of cereals and sunflowers. The present plants cover five hectares and date from 1989. The first vintage was in 1994, and the wines were first commercialized in 1998. *Merlot* accounts for two-thirds of the vineyard, the balance being made up by the two *cabernets* in equal proportion.

Élevage was in tank until 2004 when Henry de Batz made his first attempt at barrel-ageing to try and meet the demand of a changing market. He is wary about the effect of wood and prefers to use the larger 400-litre casks, where the proportion of wood area to volume of wine is lower than with the traditional *barrique bordelaise*.

To counteract the massive marketing power of the *Coopérative*, which he never cared to join, he has developed a loyal body of customers at the door who account for over a third of his sales. In May and August he opens his doors to a market of producers of country products. These events attract a wide public who have a chance to get to know the wines of the château.

There was no *cabernet* in the wines until 2002 because the *cabernets* were later plantings which had not matured. The first wine in 1998 (*B) was all *merlot* and a successful début. The 2000 (*B) is richer and longer, while the 2001 (*B) is floral and scented with nice acidity and grip. The 2002 (**B), the first year in which the *cabernets* appear, shows the effect of the changed *encépagement*, spicy and better structured. The atypical 2003 (*B) is forward, fruity, rich and easy to drink.

The wines here may not benefit from the sophisticated apparatus and techniques available at the *Cave Coopérative*, but they certainly have personality and a sense of style and passion, as befits a descendant of D'Artagnan.

▌CHÂTEAU SAUVAGNÈRES

Jacques Thérasse
47310 Sainte-Colombe-en-Brulhois
Tel: 05-53-67-20-23

Buried away like their neighbour Magali Tissot on a hillside near the little town of Sainte-Colombe, nowadays a dormitory suburb of Agen, the Thérasse family were inspired by friends to look for a small vineyard in the Bordelais. They found, not surprisingly, that the prices were too high, so settled in Buzet in the 1970's and planted 20 hectares with a typical mix of *merlot* and the two *cabernets*, more or less in equal proportions. There is also a little *sauvignon*. The family built the *chais* themselves, literally. The use of the word *château* is euphemistic; they do not live there, as there is no house at all.

At the beginning of the 1990's, Thérasse began producing wines which were rounder and softer than previously, anticipating a trend for fruitier and easier wines. Certainly the wines which he now makes are among the easiest and most approachable of Buzet wines, emphasizing a plummy roundness rather than austere tannins and huge structures. The *cuvaisons* are shorter than most, and there is little use of wood for *élevage*.

The **blanc sec** (*A) from *sauvignon* is attractive and refreshing and rather more in the style of northern wines than wines from the Midi made with this grape variety. In lighter years it has the unmistakeable gooseberry character, while in fatter, hotter vintages the wine can develop exotic fruit flavours and even a little honey.

Of the two reds, the principal **Classique** (**A) is raised in tanks after a conventional vinification and shows the soft ripe fruit characteristic of the property. The **Cuvée Prestige** (*B) has a similar character, but is given some time in oak, because, as Thérasse says, some like it that way.

Visitors may be treated to a harangue on wine politics. Thérasse is more than impatient with the wine authorities, who he says will not let growers make the kind of wine they could sell in a way the market would like to see. He has no time for INAO (Institut National des Appellations d'Origine) or local wine bodies. 'C'est un beau pays, mais peuplé d'imbéciles'. But then Thérasse's family is Belgian, so he can get away with such statements.

▌CHÂTEAU TOURNELLES
EARL Bertrand-Gabriel Vigouroux
47600 Calignac
Tel: 05-65-20-80-80 Fax: 05-65-20-80-81
www.g-vigouroux.fr

This is a Vigouroux (Cahors) enterprise in semi-disguise, a 15-hectare estate which the family bought from a young Belgian who decided to cash in his chips in Buzet. The vineyard is to the south of Calignac, looking over rolling countryside into Gascony. The *encépagement* consists of 10% *malbec*, the balance being made up equally by *merlot* and the two *cabernets*, all the vines being about 30 years old. Standards here are copybook: hand harvesting of the grapes, long macerations.

Bertrand-Gabriel Vigouroux believes the *malbec*, his native *cahors* grape, is the key to the character of this wine, though neither cahors nor bordeaux. There is just the one *cuvée*, **Château Tournelles** (**B), named after the property, found widely in restaurants, wine shops and deluxe food stores and the Vigouroux 'Atrium' in Cahors.

The wine is a worthy representative of the appellation, as well as of Vigouroux standards. It is surprising, therefore, that it has on occasion fallen foul of the opinion of the all-important local *comité d'agrément*. (See above under Domaine du Pech, page 243.)

OTHER GOOD BUZET PRODUCERS

▌**DOMAINE DE L'HERÈS**
(the wine is called Château Barada)
Jean-Louis Barada
47160 Buzet-sur-Baïse
distributed by Vignobles Arbeau
82370 Labastide-Saint-Pierre
Tel: 05-63-64-01-80

▌**CHÂTEAU PIERRON**
GFA de Château Pierron
Route de Mézin, 47600 Nérac
Tel: 05-53-65-05-52

▌**DOMAINE DE VERSAILLES**
Jean Ryckmann
47600 Montagnac-sur-Auvignon
Tel: 05-53-97-10-53

CÔTES DU BRULHOIS

AREA OF VDQS: Selected parcels covering 280 hectares.

DEPARTMENT OF GERS: communes of Flamarens, Gimbrède, Peyrecave and Saint-Antoine.

DEPARTMENT OF LOT-ET-GARONNE: communes of Astaffort, Aubiac, Caudecoste, Clermont-Soubiran, Cuq, Estillac, Fals, Fieux, Grayssas, Lamontjoie, Laplume, Layrac, Marmont-Pachas, Moirax, Nomdieu, Puymirol, Roquefort, Saint-Jean-de-Thurac, Saint-Pierre-de-Clairac, Saint-Romain-le-Noble, Saint-Urcisse, Saint-Vincent-de-Lamontjoie and Saumont.

DEPARTMENT OF TARN-ET-GARONNE: communes of Auvillar, Bardigues, Castelsagrat, Caumont, Donzac, Dunes, Gasques, Montjoi, Perville, Le Pin, Saint-Cirice, Saint-Clair, Saint-Loup, Saint-Michel and Sistels.

Red and rosé wines only.

PERMITTED GRAPE VARIETIES: cabernet sauvignon, cabernet franc, fer servadou, merlot, côt and tannat. Some tannat compulsory (amount not specified).

MINIMUM ALCOHOL LEVEL: 10%.

MAXIMUM YIELD: 50 hl/ha.

PLANTING DENSITY: min. 4000 plants/ha.

PRUNING: single Guyot only.

Grapes must be destalked. Rosé wines must all be *saigné*.

ANNUAL PRODUCTION: 13,500 hectolitres

Brulhois is the name given to a stretch of countryside in the shape of a sausage which faces Agen on the left bank of the Garonne, with a small annexe on the right bank east of the town. Nobody knows for sure why it is called Brulhois—perhaps because in the old days they *brulé* (burnt) the wine; perhaps because the wines are traditionally dark in colour and look burnt; perhaps the name has been adopted from the *occitan* word *brulhes,* meaning a wooded riverbank; or, more romantically, perhaps there was once an important feudal lord in the area with a name like that, which has been lost in the smoke of past revolutions and wars.

Wine-making here goes back to Roman days; today the district straddles the *départements* of Lot-et-Garonne (47) and Tarn-et-Garonne (82) with a small overflow into the Gers (32), the politicians who shuffled all the cards after 1789 having divided the local countryside into units which defy logical explanation. Until 2002, each *département* other than Gers had its own 'Brulhois' *Coopérative*, but common sense has prevailed and merger has produced a single entity, 'Les Vignerons du Brulhois.'

In pre-phylloxera days, the wines were famous and much prized for their colour and strength by the Bordeaux blenders. Production averaged 48,000 hectolitres a year, about four times the current volume. There was fierce competition with the vineyards upstream near Moissac, which disappeared after the plague when the vineyards were replanted with *chasselas* table grapes. Today these enjoy their own AOC Moissac. The local port was at a village today called La Magistère, in English 'The Mistress', named after a powerful lady who pocketed the dues she was able to extract from the growers who used her river frontage and sloping ramps to load their barrels onto the boats.

The development of wines of quality in the Brulhois is of fairly recent date; 1957 saw the creation of the first of the two *coopératives* at Goulens, and recognition of quality came in 1984 with the grant of VDQS status to vineyards in no fewer than 48 communes. The vineyards are thus fairly widespread, reflecting the polycultural nature of local farming. The strategy of the local growers has been to establish an identity which distinguishes their wines from those of, say, Buzet and Marmande. To this end the permitted grape varieties include not only *merlot*, the *cabernets* and *malbec*, but *tannat* and *fer servadou* too; the rules make compulsory the presence of *tannat*, which is particularly successful at the eastern end of the appellation, where there are a lot of pebbly *graves* in the soil as well as the friable soft sandy clay the French call *boulbènes*. Application has also been made for the inclusion of *abouriou* in the list of *cépages*. The introduction of rules regulating the permitted yield from the vines and also prescribing a high density of plantation has brought about an astonishing increase in quality, which has encouraged the local growers to apply for full AOC status. This may well have been granted by the time this book appears. The wines, deep ruby in colour, are today generous and full bodied, with plentiful tannins as well as good fruit.

PRODUCERS OF CÔTES DU BRULHOIS

■ **CAVE LES VIGNERONS DU BRULHOIS**
(two addresses)
82340 Donzac
Tel: 05-63-39-91-92 Fax: 05-63-39-82-83
Goulens, 47390 Layrac
Tel: 05-53-87-01-65 Fax: 05-53-87-03-31
Email: info@vigneronsdubrulhois.com
www.vigneronsdubrulhois.com

The *Cave* controls about 90% of the total production of côtes du brulhois, but it is not their policy, unlike some other *coopératives,* either to ignore the six private growers or to try and swallow them up; on the contrary, Christian Guérin, the director, stresses the importance of collaboration and fair competition, and the independent growers all confirm this. There are even combined tastings of the *Cave* and the independents, which give all parties the opportunity to exchange notes, pick up hints and generally promote the well-being of the *Côtes*. This is good news for the budding appellation, contrasting with other areas not far distant where bad relations between *coopérative* and private producer have sometimes stood in the way of progress.

The *Cave*, which has tasting and sales facilities at both its branches, offers wines which are at least as good and often better than other more famous ones downstream. They like to compare their wines with those of Cahors and Madiran, and with justification. Brulhois has more backbone and grip than many duras and buzets, a style which seems to go down well in the region of Agen. Not surprisingly, prunes and truffles are flavours which the fanciful have managed to find in the wines.

Brulhois wines are very good value. Everything from the *Cave* is price A, except for the flagship **Vin Noir** (**B), which is clearly intended to underline the difference between brulhois and other Garonne wines. It is made from roughly equal quantities of *merlot*, *tannat* and *cabernet franc*, the latter being much preferred locally to *cabernet sauvignon*. The Vin Noir enjoys long maceration but is raised in tank, not oak. Deep in colour, obviously, and with a nose that has been found by various tasters to include prunes, black fruits, leather, liquorice, violets, spices and truffles. In the mouth it has good structure, substantial but quality tannins and loads of fruit which gives softness and roundness.

There are two **rosés** (*), the one called **Grand Chêne** having more elegance than the basic one. Reds which can guarantee pleasure include **Carrelet des Amants** (*), a quaffable wine for everyday drinking; **Cuvée des Anciens Prieurés** (**), which has more *cabernet sauvignon* than some of the other wines; a **Cuvée Prestige** (**) raised for 10 months in barrel and showing some signs of that; and **Grand Chêne** (**), which comes in both oaked and unoaked versions and has lovely blackcurrants and blackberries on the nose, liquorice too.

INDEPENDENT PRODUCERS OF CÔTES DU BRULHOIS

▣ CHÂTEAU LA BASTIDE

Catherine and Isabelle Orliac

47270 Clermont-Soubiran

Tel and fax: 05-53-87-41-02

Email: chateau.orliac@wanadoo.fr

www.2soeurs.fr

Visitors will admire not only the good wines, but also the wonderful hilltop position, splendid view and traditional architecture of this venerable château, the only Brulhois independent property on the right bank of the Garonne. Isabelle was trained at Barton and Guestier in Bordeaux and later by the famous oenologist Emile Peynaud personally, so had little need to go to college. Wine-making here goes back many generations, the tasting room being adorned with evocative photographs of viticulture 80 years ago, when all the work was done by horse or oxen. Nowadays the grapes are machine-picked.

Nor is there anything old-fashioned about today's wines. A pretty middleweight **rosé** (**A) is a fitting prelude to the one **rouge** (*B), which has recently been rebaptised **La Réserve des Deux Soeurs en Aquitaine** with a smart new label and logo, and presented in tall-necked old-fashioned bottles. Nor is this sheer gimmickry, because the quality is good. Made from equal quantities of *merlot*, *cabernet franc* and *cabernet sauvignon*, the wine is aged for six months in a mixture of old and new oak. The wood is well used so as not to bring out woody flavours, or at least not too much so. Up to and including the 2002 vintage the wine was named simply after the château.

Much of the wine from the property is exported, and the owners are planning direct sales to the UK by website in quantities of not less than 60 bottles.

▣ DOMAINE DU BOIS DE SIMON

Christophe Avi

Laclède, 47310 Laplume

Tel and fax: 05-53-67-84-38

Mobile: 06-09-85-71-91

Email: avi6@orange.fr

www.domaineduboisdusimon.com

Christophe's great-grandfather fled from Italy during Mussolini's rise to power and got work in the mines of Northern France, but he didn't like the climate so moved south and set himself up at this domaine just west of Agen on the road to Nérac. To start with, grapes were grown for table and later for making basic wine for the farm, but towards the end of the 1960's the family started to plant noble grape varieties. Encouraged by the grant of VDQS to Brulhois in 1984, Christophe's father bought some vines in the Buzet appellation, since the family farm sits astride the boundary between the wine areas. Christophe himself, trained in viticulture and oenology, took over in 1992, and the first home-bottling was in 1998. He has to send his Buzet wines to the *coopérative*, because the rule is that Buzet wine must be bottled within the area of the appellation, and Christophe's *chais* is just outside it. The Brulhois wines are however all home-vinified and -bottled. The *encépagement* of the vineyard was completed with the plantation of a little *malbec* in 2003, and at present it is made up of 26% *merlot*, 22% *cabernet franc*, 35% *cabernet sauvignon*, 12% *tannat* and 5% *malbec* or *côt*. Christophe is, however, keen to plant some *abouriou* as and when that grape becomes authorized in Brulhois.

Christophe's first red wine which he made himself was, rather ambitiously, aged in wood, and has developed into the flagship wine of the domaine. It is called **Réserve Laclède** (***B) and in 2002 was made from roughly equal quantities of the four grapes Christophe then had, rather more *cabernet sauvignon* than *merlot*. Longish maceration of 30 days, after 25% was drawn off to make rosé, was followed by 12 months in used barrels. The wine is spicy as well as fruity, and has liquorice tones as well, with nice back-up tannins.

Christophe calls his more recently devised basic wine **Les Combes** (*A), the 50% *merlot* tank-raised content ensuring a fruity, easily quaffable bottle. The **rosé** (**A) is nearly all *cabernet sauvignon* with just a touch of *merlot*.

■ DOMAINE COUJÉTOU-PEYRET
Jean Hébrard
Peyret, 82340 Donzac
Tel: 05-53-39-90-89 Fax: 05-53-39-05-96
Mobile: 06-07-29-33-79

Jean Hébrard has taken over fully from his father and he now has just over 20 hectares of vines. The *terroir* here is rather sandy on the surface, but below there are layers of red sandstone which give the wines structure. Jean realizes that the tendency in modern times is to prefer wines which are fruity, more approachable than they used to be, so he has adapted his style, which, when he began, tended towards big, rather austere wines, reflecting the Brulhois appellation as it then was, but perhaps not easy to market.

He makes wines both in the Brulhois appellation and as *vins de pays de l'Agenais*. For the VDQS wines there are two reds: a nice easy-going **Tradition** (**A) which, even in big years, does not need more than three years ageing in tank. The red **Cuvée Mathilde** (**A) is given some time in barrels and has a good dose of both *tannat* and *malbec* to add muscle to the *merlot* and *cabernet* base. The charming **rosé** (**A) makes up the VDQS range, but visitors should not overlook a seductive **moëlleux** (**A) made from 100% *muscat* table grapes, light with only 11 degrees of alcohol and unique, at least commercially. For his *vrac* wines, Jean has a little *abouriou* and even *syrah,* which he uses to give something unusual to the blend.

There are always queues at his door, so Jean has no difficulty in selling his wines. Private customers are always the most faithful, and Jean gives them all a good welcome. He is a talented and much respected grower in the region.

■ DOMAINE DES THERMES
Dominique Jollet-Peraldi
La Garenne, 82340 Bardigues
Tel and fax: 05-63-39-62-09

Ask for directions at the *auberge* in the village of Bardigues, where Dominique's wine is served, otherwise he cannot be found by the light of nature or any map alone. Dominique says that he sells all his wine locally from his remotely situated vineyard, without the need to do any marketing whatsoever. The locals are on to a good thing, because Dominique makes excellent wine, some of the best in this fast-improving appellation. He used to send the grapes from the eight-hectare domaine to the *Coopérative*, but decided in 1990 to make and bottle his own wine, with a little help from an oenologist he shares with Clos des Jacobins in Saint-Emilion.

'Thermes' apparently refers to an old well on the property, where the *terroir* has a deal of pebbles above the impermeable subsoil. The *chais* is perfectly adequate without being glamorous, and the emphasis here is obviously on care of the vines rather than fancy techniques in the vinification. The **rosé** (**A), from *merlot* and *côt,* has all the right elements: good fruit, freshness and a dry finish. The *tradition* red, called simply **Domaine Des Thermes** (*A), is largely *merlot*, a mere quarter coming from small quantities of the two *cabernets* and *côt*. The wine he likes best is called **Cuvée Dothi** (***A/B), where the *encépagement* is reversed, a mere 25% *merlot* being balanced by a mix of *tannat* and *cabernet franc*; the wine has real structure and backbone, the tannins being quite soft and balancing the fruit well with just the right touch of acidity to keep the wine at peak for some years.

Dominique does not like new barrels, but you would not guess that from tasting his **Fût de Chêne** (**B), which he makes because some of his customers ask for it. He ages it in cask for upwards of a year and it is basically a blend of equal quantities of the other two reds.

■ **CLOS POUNTET**

Guillaume and Amanda Combes
La Simone, 82340 Saint-Cirice
Mobile: 06-23-84-82-45
Email: contact@pountet.com
www.pountet.com

A recently established grower who makes an unoaked red called **Eclats de Fruits** (*A) and an oaked version called **Horloge** (*B), well worth following up. The property is just south of Auvillar.

Max Dupin at **Domaine Vignobles Garlin**, 82340 Dunes, makes lovely old-fashioned wines but sells them all *en négoce* and does not bottle any himself. Pity.

VINS DE PAYS DE L'AGENAIS

The region known as Agenais corresponds with the modern department of Lot-et-Garonne, a bureaucratic mishmash created by government officials during the Revolution. It has no cultural specificity, reflecting the spirit of the Lot Valley in the north-east, Bordeaux influences in the west and Gascony in the south.

Outside the areas of *Appellation Contrôlée* and VDQS, three pockets of viticulture have earned the right to attach the name Vin de Pays de l'Agenais to their wines: the extension of the Cahors vineyards called Thézac-Perricard; a clutch of growers further downstream near Villeneuve-sur-Lot and Monflanquin; and the neo-Gascon *vignerons* based round Mézin, almost into the Landes, who are just as likely to use the Côtes de Gascogne name as Agenais. Those listed below make and bottle their own wine, although many others may either sell their grapes to one of the *coopératives* or, if they make their own wine, sell it *en vrac* to *négociants*. Agenais wines are also found at the Marmande, Buzet and Duras *coopératives*, and at domaines of some of the independent growers within those appellation areas.

SOME OF THE MOST INTERESTING OF THE INDEPENDENTS

DOMAINE DE CAMPET

Carole and Joël Buisson

47170 Sos

Tel: 05-53-65-61-47 Fax: 05-53-65-36-79

Email: domainecampet@club-internet.fr

www.domainedecampet-vin-floc-armanac
.over-blog.com

The village of Sos is in the very south-western corner of the *département,* almost on the edge of the forests of the Landes. Buisson is therefore very much a Gascon producer, and tending more and more to profit from the well-publicized image of the Côtes de Gascogne than the Agenais, which he finds people do not understand too well. His wines are, however, not what you might expect from a Gascon; the **dry white** (**A), largely from *ugni blanc*, with a little *gros manseng* and *colombard* (not a grape he likes), turns out to be unusually delicate and fresh, with absolutely no *bonbons anglais*. A gentle **moël-leux** (**A) is made entirely from *gros manseng*, delicious to drink with or without food; the **rosé** (**A) is flowery and perfumed while remaining perfectly dry; and the **Rouge Tradition** (*A), with just a touch of Gascon *tannat,* has a lot of blackberries on the nose and a spicy mustardy character, though it is rather light on the palate for today's taste perhaps.

Buisson does not like using barrels for his wine; that is his taste and he finds that, more and more, his customers are returning to a fruitier, lighter style of wine with less elaborate *élevage.* He does, however, make and mature his own armagnac as well as prize-winning floc de gascogne.

DOMAINE CÔTES DES OLIVIERS

Jean-Pierre Richarte

47140 Auradou

Tel: 05-53-41-28-59 Fax: 05-53-49-38-89

Email: cotes-des-oliviers@wanadoo.fr

Until 1977 Richarte made wine only for the family, but his friends and neighbours seemed to like it so he started to become a professional grower, planting four hectares with the Bordeaux grape varieties. He adopts many of the features of organic viticulture, which reduce the number of 'treatments' during the course of a season to a minimum. No machines are used, the harvest being picked by hand. There are **red** and **rosé** wines (*A) which are well made, and a red *cuvée* raised **en barriques** (*A) too. Richarte also makes a **moëlleux** (**A), deliciously fresh and light in style, and a **blanc sec** (*A) from a blend of *sauvignon* and *chenin,* with just a little *chardonnay* making a rare appearance in South-West France. Richarte has eight hectares of plum orchard too, whose fruit he converts to prunes in his own ovens, and six hectares of walnut trees. As someone passionately devoted to the excellence of local produce, he started a *marché à la ferme* down the road at Frespech, where on Fridays in July and August you can sample the wares of local producers: charcuterie, fruits and vegetables, bread, the local *tourtière,* cheeses, and of course wines and prunes. Chickens are roasted over wood fires, turning on their strings rather than on an electrical spit. A lovely day out for the family, with plenty of shade under the trees to enjoy your purchases, especially Monsieur Richarte's wines.

DOMAINE LOU GAILLOT
Gilles Pons
47440 Casseneuil
Tel: 05-53-41-04-66 Fax: 05-53-01-13-89
Email: lougaillot@wanadoo.fr

Gilles is the president of the growers of Vins de Pays de L'Agenais, and is himself a dedicated, oenologically trained and totally professional winemaker. He represents the seventh generation of producers at this domaine, where there are 16 hectares grown on a *terroir* with a lot of flint and pebbles in it. Nowadays grapes are the only crop.

In addition to the usual Bordeaux grapes, Gilles has a plantation of *egiodola*, a modern cross between *abouriou* and *fer servadou*, which he uses together with *merlot* to make his first **rosé** (**A), dry and especially good as an aperitif; the second, **Rosé Tendre** (*A), is mainly from *cabernet sauvignon* and is slightly off-dry, calling for food. The **blanc** (**B) is also off-dry, from a blend of *sémillon* and *sauvignon*, hand-picked from only the healthiest bunches. The wine is deliciously fruity after an *élevage sur lies* in the barrel.

Of the reds, the **Tradition** (*A) is aromatic, with all the tannin you would expect from its *cabernet sauvignon* base; the **Prestige** (**A) is largely *merlot*, half raised in tanks, the other half in barrels only 10% of which are new, the effect of the wood being barely discernible. The top red, **Excellence** (**B), is smoky and round, again mainly *merlot*, and aged for 15 months in barrels, half of which are new, half already used.

The wines from this property are regular medal winners and frequently cited in the French wine guides, deservedly too.

LES VIGNERONS DE THÉZAC-PERRICARD
Plaisance
47370 Thézac
Tel: 05-53-76-03-90 Fax: 05-53-64-35-61
Email: info@vin-du-tsar.tm.fr
www.vin-du-tsar.tm.fr

No doubt in the old days the vineyards of Cahors were not restricted to the *département* of the Lot, and would have spread over to what is now part of Lot-et-Garonne. However, the sages who determined the limits of the Cahors appellation called a halt when they came to the boundary. Administrative tidiness obviously got the better of them. Growers on the other side to the west were left in limbo—that is, until eight or so of them grouped together in 1980 to form their own *coopérative* and create what is today called **Le Vin du Tsar** at the *Cave Coopérative* of Thézac-Perricard. Thézac-Perricard was granted the right to its own *vin de pays* status in 1988.

Mechanical stone-crushers were required to break up the soil, enabling grapes to be replanted. Rocks brought to the surface were broken up in pieces and cleaned, and young vines were planted between the rows of stones. The plants were thus able to derive nourishment from deep down in the poor subsoil, while the stone on the surface reflected the heat of the sun back onto the grapes.

It was decided as a matter of policy to create for the new *Cave* an entirely different image from the conventional idea of Cahors. There would be no *vins de garde*; rather, a style of wine would be made suitable for drinking young, but with a true *goût du terroir*. For grapes they chose the traditional *auxerrois*, softening it with 20% *merlot*, and eschewing *tannat* altogether. The wines are made nowadays at Thézac in a fine new *chais*, though in the beginning the grapes were sent to the Brulhois *Coopérative* at Goulens.

There will be two or three *cuvées*, a **Tradition** (*A) as the *entrée de gamme*, and perhaps two others, **Bouquet** and **Cuvée de Millénaire**(**A), the latter being aged in barrel. There is also an attractive **rosé** (*A), a wine with which Cahors is forbidden by its own rules to compete.

Where did the name come from? One story is that the French president Fallières introduced the wines of Thézac to Emperor Napoleon III and, through him, to Tsar Nicholas II at a banquet in Paris. The tsar is said to have been so enchanted by the wine that he ordered 1000 bottles to be sent to Moscow, but sadly there was not enough stock. Another explanation for the Russian connection concerns a White Russian restaurateur in Paris, who invented the name Cuvée des Tsars and ordered in recent years a quantity of the wine to launch his restaurant. Sadly, it went bankrupt before it opened and the growers were left with a lot of stock on their hands, but the name stuck.

DOMAINE LANCEMENT
Sandrine Annibal
EARL Andel
Grands Champs, 47370 Thézac
Tel: 05-53-40-76-05
Email: contact@domainelancement.com
www.domainelancement.com

After working at Harvey Nicholls in London and then at William Pitters, the Bordeaux *négoçiants,* Sandrine Annibal returned to the family vineyard of four hectares and declared independence from the *Coopérative* at Thézac-Perricard in 2003 to become one of two independent domaines in this pocket-sized appellation, and very good the wines are too. Sandrine makes just the one *cuvée* in bottle of red (**A), from 70% or more *malbec*, the rest *auxerrois*, and the emphasis is on fruity intensity. Dark in colour and full in body without heaviness or astringency, the attack is good and the flavour very characterful. A thoroughly delicious and good-value alternative to Cahors proper, as is the bag-in-box wine, which Sandrine makes from pure **auxerrois** (**A). It would not be surprising to see this talented and determined grower make quite a stir in the local scene.

OTHER MAKERS OF
VINS DE PAYS DE L'AGENAIS

DOMAINE DE CANTELAUZE
Jean-Luc Aureille
67 Route de la Plaine, 47300 Bias
Mobile: 06-22-19-06-59
www.domainedecantelauze.com

DOMAINE DE CHALÈS
Les Frères Crozat
47300 Saint-Colombe-de-Villeneuve
Tel: 05-53-40-00-91 Fax: 05-53-40-08-09

DOMAINE DU CAZAL DU BOSC
Edmond Deffes
47600 Nérac
Tel: 05-53-65-14-90

DOMAINE DE CAZEAUX
Eric Kauffer
47170 Lannes
Tel: 05-53-65-73-03
Email: info@domaine-cazeaux.com
www.domaine-cazeaux.com

VINCENT DELMOTTE
Le Chai, 47700 Leyritz-Moncassin
Tel: 05-53-93-93-47

DOMAINE DE LIONS
Yannick Montel
47370 Thézac
Tel: 05-53-40-78-58 Fax: 05-53-40-78-65

DOMAINE DE MASSÉE
Jean-Michel Siquier
47310 Moirax
Tel and fax: 05-53-67-84-51

DOMAINE DE QUISSAT
Anne-Marie and Rémy Delouvrier
47130 Bazens
Tel and fax: 05-53-87-47-84
(on the way to organic production)

DOMAINE RHODES HAUTES
EARL Crozat et Fils
47150 Laussou
Tel and fax: 05-53-36-47-50

LA CAVE DES SEPT MONTS
(*Coopérative*)
Mondésir, 47150 Monflanquin
Tel: 05-53-36-33-40

DOMAINE DU SERBAT
CAT Lamothe Poulain
47340 Laroque-Timbaut
Tel: 05-53-95-71-07 Fax: 05-53-95-79-61

THE WINES OF GASCONY

GASCONY

All the wines so far described, except those consumed locally, used at one time to be carried by boat down one of the rivers of the Garonne basin to Bordeaux. But this was not always the case with the wines of Gascony and Béarn, which were more rarely seen in Bordeaux and less used for blending than the other wines of the *haut-pays*. Most were ferried down the river Adour and its tributaries to Bayonne, rather than transported overland to Bordeaux. None of the local tributaries of the Garonne were navigable.

The Adour has its own basin and river system. It rises in the high Pyrenees almost on the Spanish frontier and flows north until it starts a long bend towards the west, rather like the Loire further north. On the right bank are the wines of the Gers, and then on either side the wines of the Côtes de Saint-Mont. On the left bank are the vineyards of Madiran, its white sister Pacherenc and Tursan. Further towards the south a watershed separates the basin of the Adour from the Béarn and its capital, Pau, through which runs a river which flows northwest to join the Adour just short of Bayonne.

Until the 1960's, the vines which grew on the right bank of the Adour produced weak wines none of which were, at least in recent history, of any commercial interest in their own right. They were intended for distillation into Armagnac. The making of brandy calls for more acidity in the grape than most palates will accept.

On the left bank, the situation was different. Here red wines of quality had been made for centuries, historically based on the *fer servadou* grape but more recently on the *tannat,* which is sometimes locally called *moustroun. Tannat* wines have always been robust and often frankly rustic, so the modern taste for more supple wines, fruity and quicker-maturing, has resulted in the gradual introduction of the *cabernets*, which round out the rigours of the pure *tannat* juice.

The only white wine which acquired any fame beyond its region of production was jurançon, which until recently was always sweet in style. Until the Second World War, there was no local demand for dry wines locally. Nowadays dry jurançon must be sold under its own appellation, Jurançon Sec, to distinguish it from the traditional sweet style.

Today, Gascony and Béarn produce a complete range of wines of all colours and styles, each having its own local character. For example, in the area traditionally the home of Armagnac, dry white table wines have had a spectacular success, following a complete reorganization of the vineyard.

VINS DE PAYS DES CÔTES DE GASCOGNE

At the heart of the enormous province which was once Gascony are the vineyards devoted to Armagnac. They cover nearly all the Gers, spilling over in their north-west corner into the Landes. The soil, which has a deal of sand in it, favoured the grape varieties best suited to the making of brandy. For a long time the landlocked Gers was isolated, its poor roads and the barrier of the marshes of the Landes making access to Bordeaux difficult. The navigable rivers flowed to Bayonne rather than Bordeaux. The railway system seems to have skirted the Gers almost deliberately. Then there is the famously individual character of the Gascons, the adaptable character of the local terrain to produce a range of crops, and the emphasis on subsistence farming, which inhibited the production of anything surplus to the domestic needs of the farm. Given all this it is easy to understand why the production of wine and even brandy was destined almost exclusively for local consumption.

Today the Gers remains archetypal of what is called *La France Profonde*, a land of ducks and geese, hearty stews, seemingly ageless farms built of the local mud on a lath and plaster base, with red pantile roofs sometimes stained by the fumes of the Armagnac housed within—*la part des anges* (the angels' share), as the saying goes. And everywhere the passion for rugby and bull-fighting (or rather bull-teasing because the poor beasts are not killed).

Armagnac calls for high-yielding vines of little breeding; it seems that the poorer the *cépage,* the better the brandy. The vines traditional to the Gers were the lowly *ugni blanc* (confusingly also called *Saint Emilion*, though unconnected with that famous region); *baco 2*, of even more dubious quality and banned everywhere as a source of table wine; and *folle blanche*, also called *picpoul*, a variety which did not graft so well after the phyllloxera and largely yielded place to *ugni blanc*. *Listan* was another local grape, known better as *palomino* in Spain, where it is the basis of sherry. Although *colombard* too was grown, it was too good a variety for distillation. Today modern techniques have proved that *colombard* is more than capable of making wine which is lively and easy to drink, and the fashion for it has no doubt been fed by its success in California, where it is widely planted. We shall see that *colombard* became at first the principal and typical constituent of the white wines of the Gers, although more recently it has given ground to some extent to the more substantial *gros manseng*, the principal grape variety of the wine regions further south. *Gros manseng* lends itself to *élevage* in wood, and more and more producers are having a go at so-called modern wines aged in barrel. *Sauvignon* is sometimes also to be found, giving wines a touch of distinction and a zing they might otherwise have lacked.

White côtes de gascogne on a *colombard* base will have a bouquet of citrus fruits and apples. Typically they are completely dry and need to be served chilled. Often they are reminiscent of pear drops (*bonbons anglais)*. They are light, quaffable and very refreshing on a hot Gascon summer's day. Some find them full of charm, others baulk at the pear-drops-cum-nail-polish-remover style. The reds are generally not as interesting, sometimes being rough rather than ready. They tend to be *tannat*-based, with either or both of the *cabernets* added to modify the austerity of the *tannat*.

From being a newcomer to wine lists, Côtes de Gascogne has become in the UK the best known wine of the South-West, especially in wine bars. The total production is over 500,000 hectolitres. It is widely available in supermarkets all over the world. It would be unjust to countless growers, and particularly to the Grassa family whom we will meet presently, to pretend that the three-headed *coopérative* called **Producteurs Plaimont**, with wineries at Plaisance, Saint Aignan and Saint Mont, developed this wine on its own, though it is entitled to a large share of the credit. The *Coopérative* owes its success in no small measure to André Dubosc, who started it from scratch in the 1970's.

THE EMERGENCE OF PRODUCTEURS PLAIMONT

Dubosc was travelling in Germany in 1973 when he conceived the idea that the Gers could make wines of commercial quality. At first nobody believed him, seeing no reason to diversify their production. The trade in Armagnac was flourishing at the time. But when Armagnac sales slumped badly in the late 70's, local growers began to realize that there was a gap in the market for fresh fruity wines at a reasonable price, particularly dry whites. Côtes de gascogne may be a simple wine of variable quality, but it has become a benchmark for everyday-drinking wines offering value for money.

After the phylloxera many vineyards were allowed to deteriorate to the point where the plants were growing wild in the local fruit orchards. The first task of the *Coopérative* was therefore to rebuild the vineyard, adopting strict rules of viticulture for all members, and to market the wine in bottles so as to get away from the image of producers of wine fit only for distillation.

Today the *Cave* produces a range of other wines (see below), but it was their Côtes de Gascogne which initially made their reputation. They still use the flagship brand which they invented at the beginning, **Colombelle** (*A), which as its name suggests is based on the *colombard* grape (70%), with some *listan* (10%) and *ugni blanc* (20%). Dubosc claims for the wine notes of hawthorn and honeysuckle as well as the usual grapefruit and apple character. A modern style of presentation is given to another range of *vins de soif* with suitably jazzy labels, and Plaimont has recently absorbed the *Cave* at Condom, where similar wine is presented in waisted bottles. Some *merlot* is grown in the Condomois and goes into a fast-selling red blend with *tannat*. A pair of red and white quaffers go under the title of **Les Bastions** (A).

Plaimont products are variously called Vins de Pays du Gers, Comté Tolosan and Côtes du Condomois as well as Côtes de Gascogne, but essentially all are alike in style; as Dubosc says, 'We have kept our accent while burning our clogs.'

PRODUCERS OF CÔTES DE GASCOGNE

CHÂTEAU DU TARIQUET

La Famille Grassa

32800 Eauze

Tel: 05-62-09-87-82

Email: contact@tariquet.com

www.tariquet.com

Mention has already been made of the Grassa family, who are famous for their Armagnacs just as much as for their table wines. Pierre Grassa started out in life as a hairdresser in Bordeaux, leaving the family home at **Château du Tariquet** to seek fame and fortune. At that time there were only five hectares of vines, all of them the poor hybrid *noah*. Having returned home with his wife, Héléne, they and their son, Yves, and daughter, Maïté, have built a sizeable empire close to their home town, Éauze. Their holdings represent the largest independent wine-estate in the South-West; they now own or control 900 hectares. They used to market their wines from four different properties, but today all their wines bear the name Tariquet, which has in effect become their brand name and which they have used to launch their wines in English supermarkets. Until recently they concentrated on the local grapes, *colombard*, *ugni blanc* and, for their brandies, *folle blanche*, but now a large part of their production is from varietals such as *chenin*, *sauvignon, chardonnay*, and *gros* and *petit manseng*. Every table wine they make is sold as *vin de pays des côtes de gascogne*, and their hallmark is freshness, the result of meticulous vinification and an abundance of fruit.

For example, their basic **ugni blanc (70%)/ colombard (30%) blend** (**A) has nuances of exotic fruits as well as the more familiar citrus varieties. The **chenin** (**A) presents a characteristic white almond flavour to set off the spring flowers. The **sauvignon** (**A) combines vivacity with good structure, while the **chardonnay** (**B), fermented and matured in barrel, displays the expected vanilla and buttery characteristics one might expect, and there is a **tête de cuvée** version of this wine, similar but more so. The **chardonnay/sauvignon blend** (A**) is one of their best wines. The *gros manseng* grapes are used to make a **Premières Grives** (**B) in *moëlleux* style ideal as an aperitif or with foie gras, while the *petit manseng* becomes **Dernières Grives** (**B), a wholly sweet wine perhaps best drunk on its own in lieu of dessert.

A red *vin de pays* called **Le Grand Mage** (**A) is a blend of *syrah* and *tannat;* it is not sold under the Grassa banner, so as to avoid confusion with their predominantly white ranges.

OTHER *VINS DE PAYS* DES CÔTES DE GASCOGNE / TERROIRS LANDAIS

Wherever you go in the Gers you see signposts leading down rough country lanes and tracks to farms selling the local wines as well as home-reared ducks and foie gras. Nowadays côtes de gascogne has become so successful commercially that the name is used also to market wines from a part of the *département* of the Landes and even the southern part of the Agenais. A separate appellation for the Landes is fast disappearing in this part of Gascony, though it survives further west as we shall see. Thus wines from the whole of the Armagnac area are now produced and sold under the same Gascon umbrella, reducing the confusion for the consumer.

Wine merchants and private buyers, seeking refuge from the two all-powerful influences described above, have a wide choice of smaller independent growers of whom the following are among the most interesting. They will mostly be in price range A, some spilling over into B.

DOMAINE D'ARTON
Patrick de Montal
32700 Lectoure
Tel: 05-62-68-84-33 Fax: 05-62-68-73-09
Email: patrickdemontal@arton.fr
www.arton.fr

Interesting range includes an oaked red, **Victoire d'Arton** (**B), and an unusually domaine bottled Haut-Armagnac.

* DOMAINE DE BORDES
Christian Morel
47170 Saint-Maure-de-Peyriac
Tel: 05-53-65-62-16

Noted particularly for a *moëlleux*, whose apparent sweetness is countered by good citrus acidity.

** DOMAINE DES CASSAGNOLES
Gilles and Janine Baumann
32330 Gondrin
Tel: 05-62-28-40-57
www.domainedescassagnoles.com

Frequent prize winners throughout their range. The 100% *gros manseng* wine called **Medium** (**A) is a winner.

** DOMAINE DE CAZEAUX
Éric Kauffer
47170 Lannes
Tel: 05-53-65-73-03 Fax: 05-53-65-88-95
www.domaine-cazeaux.com

The red Tradition, raised in cask, generally has good spices and flowers, embellished by complex aromas. Good finish with suggestions of the forest floor. (See also under *Vin de pays* de l'Agenais.)

DOMAINE D'ESPÉRANCE
40240 Mauvezin d'Armagnac
Tel: 05-58-44-85-93
Email: info@esperance.fr
www.esperance.fr

DOMAINE DE LA HIGUIÈRE
Paul and David Esquiro
32390 Mirepoix
Tel: 05-62-65-18-05
www.esquiro.com

*** DOMAINE DE JÖY
Olivier and Roland Gessler
32100 Panjas
Tel: 05-62-09-03-20
Email: contact@domaine-joy.com
www.domaine-joy.com

** DOMAINE DE LABALLE

Noël Laudet

40310 Parleboscq

Tel: 05-58-44-33-39

Noël Laudet was formerly *régisseur* at Château Beychevelle in the Médoc.

** DOMAINE DE LAUROUX

Nicolas and Karen Kitchener

32370 Manciet

Tel: 05-62-08-56-76 Fax: 05-62-08-57-44

Email: nick@lauroux.com

or karen@lauroux.com

www.lauroux.dom

A 100-hectare estate recently taken over by a courageous English pair, who are attracting some attention.

** DOMAINE DE MAGNAUT

Jean-Marie Terraube

32250 Fourcès

Tel: 05-62-29-45-40 Fax: 05-62-29-58-42

www.domainedemagnaut.com

Notable especially for a *moëlleux*-style wine from *gros manseng* (**A).

* DOMAINE DE MENARD ET HAUT MARIN

Elisabeth Prataviera

32800 Bretagne d'Armagnac

Tel: 05-62-29-13-33

Email: contact@domainedemenard.com

Especially for the sweeter wines.

*** CHÂTEAU DE MILLET

Laurence Dèche

Avenue de Parleboscq, 32800 Eauze

Tel: 05-62-09-87-91

Email: chateaudemillet@wanadoo.fr

www.chateaudemillet.com

The family makes a full range of wines from their 50 hectares, including splendid artisanal armagnacs and floc. The table wines include a zesty and gooseberry-ish blend of *colombard* and *ugni blanc* and a just as vibrant pure *colombard*.

* DOMAINE DE MIRAIL

Charles Hochman

32700 Lectoure

Tel: 05-62-68-82-52 Fax: 05-62-68-53-96

www.domainedemirail.com

Wines of a heftier style than most.

* CHÂTEAU MONLUC
Noël Lassus
32310 Saint-Puy
Tel: 05-62-28-94-00
Email: commercial@monluc.com
www.monluc.fr

Notable also for their sparkling wine and the Pousse-Rapière to go with it.

** DOMAINE DE PAPOLLE
Bernard Piffard
32240 Mauléon d'Armagnac
Mobile: 06-71-60-93-23

** DOMAINE DE PELLEHAUT
Gaston, Martin and Mathieu Béraut
32250 Montréal-du-Gers
Tel: 05-62-29-48-79 Fax: 05-62-29-49-90
www.pellehaut.com

DOMAINE DE PUJO
Daniel Dubos
32150 Larée
Tel: 05-62-69-55-08

* DOMAINE DE SANCET
Alain Faget
32110 Saint-Martin d'Armagnac
Tel: 05-62-09-08-73
Email: domainedesancet@wanadoo.fr

*** DOMAINE DE SAN DE GUILHEM
Alain Lalanne
32800 Ramouzens
Tel: 05-62-06-57-02
Email: domaine@sandeguilhem.com

One of the most individual and consistent producers, with some *egiodola* in his reds.

** DOMAINE DU SÉDOUPRAT
Nick Patrick
32800 Eauze
Tel: 05-62-08-15-29
Email: nickpatrick@wanadoo.fr

It is hard to find red côtes de gascogne as good as these. Recommended are a fruity *merlot* perfect after three years; also a *cabernet sauvignon* and a blend of the two grapes. In addition a very agreeable 100% *colombard*.

VIGNOBLES FONTAN
Nadège Fontan
32800 Noulens
Tel: 05-62-08-55-28
Email: contact@vignobles-fontan.com
www.vignobles-fontan.com

Notable for a good 100% *gros manseng* called Domaine de Maubert in irritatingly sealed bottles.

CAVE DES COTEAUX DU MÉZINAIS
47170 Mézin
Tel: 05-53-65-53-55

CAVE DES VIGNERONS DU GERLAND
32110 Panjas
Tel: 05-62-09-07-11

CAVE VIVADOUR
32150 Cazaubon
Tel: 05-62-08-34-00

And many producers of Madiran (see page 284).

Working outside the Côtes de Gascogne circle but within the same area is an interesting grower producing wines as *vins de table:*

DOMAINE DE BOUSCAS
Floréal Roméro
32330 Gondrin
Tel: 05-62-29-11-87
Email: romero-floreal@wanadoo.fr

Roméro works biodynamically from his 12 hectares, a couple of kilometres south of the village of Gondrin. His wines, which he has succeeded in selling to Paris restaurants, include a pure **colombard** (*A), which he sometimes treats to a malolactic fermentation depending on the vintage. Better is his red **tannat** (**B), which after a few years softens its gentle tannins to back the abundant fruit. Better still is a wine which he would like to call *liquoreux* but is not allowed to, and to which he gives the name **Dulcinée** (***C), a late-picked *colombard* whose mango-like sweetness is set off beautifully by the underlying acidity of the grape variety. This wine would live happily in the company of some of the best sweet wines from the South-West. It is absurd that a producer like Roméro is prevented from calling such a wine either *liquoreux* or *doux* and instead is restricted to the term *moût partiellement fermenté issu des raisins passerillés*. What everyday consumer is going to understand that mouthful? Competition with other sweet wines becomes virtually impossible; a man with a wooden leg is unlikely to win the 100-metre hurdles.

SAINT-MONT

AREA OF VDQS: selected parcels in
DÉPARTEMENT OF GERS: Cantons of Aignan, Eauze, Marciac, Montesquiou, Plaisance and
Riscle.
DÉPARTEMENT OF LANDES: Aire-sur-Adour.

Red, rosé and white wines.
PERMITTED GRAPE VARIETIES:
REDS AND ROSÉS: tannat (at least 60% of grower's red wine vineyard), fer servadou
(at least 10%, rising to 20% by 2020). Also cabernet sauvignon, cabernet franc and
merlot (the last-named being phased out by 2020). All wines must include at least
some tannat and fer servadou.
WHITES: arrufiac (min. 20%), petit courbu (min. 20%) and petit manseng (min. 20%).
Also gros manseng. Clairette being phased out by 2020. The two mansengs together
should not exceed 60%, and whites should include at least three varieties.
ALCOHOL CONTENT: all wines 10% minimum, 13% maximum
MAXIMUM PERMITTED YIELD: 60 hl/ha.
PLANTING DENSITY: 3600 plants per hectare minimum with transitional relief to 2020.
Maximum 2.5 metres between rows.
PRUNING: Guyot single or double only.
Hand-harvesting is compulsory. Transporting vehicles cannot exceed 5 tonnes, and
must be emptied by gravity. Continuous presses are forbidden. Rosé wines must all be
saigné, and red grapes must be destalked. Wines must have finished their malolactic
fermentation before being presented for their *agrément*.

Even before the launch of the all-conquering Côtes de Gascogne, there had been tentative efforts to re-establish the reputation of a wine-growing area based round the abbey of Saint-Mont, founded by the Benedictines in the year 1050. Saint-Mont is on the left bank of the Adour River, halfway along the road from Aire to Madiran. In 1957, 30 or so growers clubbed together to determine which grape varieties would be best suited to a possible area of appellation, and which parcels of land and which communes should be included. The growers imposed a strict discipline that involved low yields, hand-harvesting and eventually an elaborate system whereby wine could be traced back to the growers who had contributed the grapes. The idea was to try to get themselves included in the Madiran appellation, but this idea was rejected by the authorities in Paris.

Not many men can be said to have developed an appellation single-handed, but André Dubosc, now formally retired but still very much in evidence, is certainly one of them. As founding director of Producteurs Plaimont, a merger of three *caves* at Saint-Mont, Plaisance and Aignan, he has taken the Saint-Mont enterprise under its wing and in the process made Saint-Mont more of a brand than an appellation, which is perhaps why INAO is reluctant to admit Saint-Mont to full AOC status, for which Saint-Mont has been knocking on the doors in Paris for 12 years or more. Maybe this does not upset André unduly, because he and his colleagues, not forgetting his members, have made Plaimont the most dynamic and successful of all the *coopératives* in the South-West. The list of practically every wine merchant in the UK seems certain to contain at least one Plaimont wine. Standards in the vineyard are as high as any you will find with any independent producer: state-of-the-art plant in the *chais*, every modern vinification technique in the book and an energetic marketing team, make Plaimont synonymous in the minds of many wine buyers with South-West France, perhaps too much so. In 1981, following a brilliant marketing operation culminating in a big show in the middle of Paris, and backed by willing sponsoring partners from the Gascony region, VDQS Côtes de Saint-Mont was born.

The area is spread over 49 communes in the south-west of the Gers, and today there are 850 hectares devoted to red wines and 250 to white. The red grape varieties are *tannat*, *pinenc* (the local name for our old favourite *fer servadou* and a grape which is highly favoured by Producteurs Plaimont) and the two *cabernets*. All these apart from the *pinenc* contribute to the making of pink wines. The whites are based on *gros manseng* and two varieties particular to the extreme south-west and which are commonly found in the wines of Pacherenc du Vic-Bilh and Jurançon: *petit courbu,* which adds zest and good acidity to a blend, as well as floral and ripe fruit aromas; and *arrufiac*, which gives pale juice, a delicate bouquet, suppleness and finesse, offsetting the more up-front character of the *gros manseng. Colombard* is *not* included in the list of authorized grapes, nor *ugni blanc, folle blanche, listan* etc. Thus a clear distinction is made between saint-mont and the *vins de pays des côtes de gascogne.*

PRODUCERS OF SAINT-MONT

PRODUCTEURS PLAIMONT
32400 Saint-Mont
Tel: 05-62-69-62-87 Fax: 05-62-69-61-68
www.plaimont.com

This cooperative dominates the appellation. Although there is a handful of independent growers, they account for a mere 7–8% of the total production.

Plaimont make four styles of blended wines, and five domaine wines. Of the former, **Les Vignes Retrouvées** (***A) is perhaps the best known, certainly in the United Kingdom, where it is widely available. It is exclusively white, deriving from 60% *gros manseng*, 20% *arrufiac* and 20% *petit courbu*, aged on their lees to give richness and balance. Citrus fruits dominate the bouquet, giving way to more exotic and mineral hints. Grapefruit carries through onto the palate, where the attack is powerful. **Les Hauts de Bergelles** (**A) come in all three colours, and the reds and whites are aged in wood for six months, while the exclusively red **Esprit des Vignes** (*B) is from old vines and is oak-matured for 12 months. Top of the range is **Le Faîte** (**C), red and white, representing a selction of the best barrels, from which blends are made in consultation with sommeliers and restaurateurs. The white in particular is very fine, made from *arrufiac, petit courbu, gros manseng,* and just a little oak-aged *petit manseng*. It has all the richness and aromatic power of a top dry jurançon, complete with the typical *agrumes,* while the small dose of *petit manseng* adds just a touch of richness to the blend.

Of the domaine wines, the flagship is **Château de Sabazan** (**B), the name taken from a historic monument in the hills north of Riscle going back to the 15th century. Yields are controlled by leaving only four or five bunches on the vine, and production is limited to 45,000 bottles a year. Closer to home in Saint-Mont, the red wine **Monastère** (**B) is even scarcer; seven growers have been selected to make this wine, which the cave describes as 'exclusive and *élitiste*', only 10,000 bottles of it being made each year. At **Château Saint-Go** (*A), six other *vignerons* took over the vineyards in 1998, and they make good red and white wines, most often to be found in French restaurants and supermarkets, while at **Château du Bascou** (**B) there are charming *gîtes* and *chambres d'hôte* as well as excellent wines to taste.

It should be mentioned that Plaimont also has members in the Madiran AOC area, and so they make red madiran and white pacherenc too (see page 293). They also use the title Vignobles de Gascogne on their wines in some supermarkets.

Producteurs Plaimont have developed initiatives intended to keep the organization in the vanguard of the cooperative movement. Because a cooperative by definition belongs to the growers, they believe it is not sufficient for members simply to grow their grapes and deliver them to the Plaimont cellars for vinification. Like independent growers, they are expected to become a part of the marketing and promotion of the *Cave's* wines. A number of them are learning English so as to be able to form direct relations between grower and customer; others have created *gîtes* to welcome visitors to the area, and, quite exceptionally for such a large cooperative, some of the members can offer Plaimont wines for sale at their own farms.

It would be a mistake to miss out on some of the small independent producers of saint-mont. The *Cave* recognizes that, despite the high quality levels which it has established, there has to be room in an area of appellation for independent competitors.

DOMAINE DE TURET
Jean-Luc Garroussia
Peyrusse Vieille, 32160 Plaisance
Tel: 05-62-70-92-57 Fax: 05-62-70-91-02
Email: jean-luc-et-lysiane.turet@wanadoo.fr
www.domaine-turet-nolimit.com

Jean-Luc Garroussia claims more or less to have given birth to the *Coopérative* of Saint-Mont,

but when they demanded that he send all his crop to them, he decided to regain his independence because he already had a wine-making plant on his farm that he wanted to go on using.

Garroussia was not made to fit into the French wine system; he will not make wines to suit other people's image, keeping very much to what he likes doing and what he knows he can make well. You might be surprised, for example, to be offered an 11-year-old **sauvignon sec** (*A), and you would be further surprised by its freshness and acidity after all that time. A *doux* called **La Turenière** (*A) is another wine with surprising acidity, providing a good counterbalance to the sweet flavour of melons and peaches. His **rouge** (**A) is quite southern and meaty in style, delicious and an excellent value. He sells his wines mainly to regular private customers, but he also takes them to market at Vic-de-Bigorre every Saturday.

Jean-Luc does not limit himself to table wines; he makes floc, of course, and has developed a good line in armagnac, which he distils and ages himself; he and his wife also have developed a surprising aperitif called **Belle de Nuit**, whose recipe is secret. Jean-Luc is a man of considerable resource; after an accident some years ago which prevented him from doing hard physical work on the farm, he taught music for two years, specializing in harmony. If you remember to bring your music, you might accompany him on his complete range of saxophones (he plays everything from soprano to baritone) in lyrical versions of 'Ave Maria' (Gounod's, of course), 'Take Five' etc. He has a purpose-built *salle de concerts* with a resounding bathroom acoustic. As a vineyard visit, this is far from conventional.

DOMAINE DE BARTAT
Pierre Fitan
32400 Maulichères
Tel and fax: 05-62-69-77-39

The Fitans have but five hectares of vines, but with beautiful exposure looking south over the valley of the Adour just outside the town of Riscle. They have other crops too, including 50 hectares of maize, which earns them as much as but no more than their wines. They sell their saint-mont dry white and red mostly *en vrac*, but their star wine which they put into bottle is undoubtedly a lovely **moëlleux** (**A), made wholly from *gros manseng*. It suggests but does not overstate exotic fruits, while retaining a vivacity, particularly on the finish, which redeems the sweetness of the fruit. This is definitely worth looking out for and rates a detour if you can find the way.

CHÂTEAU LA BERGALASSE
Didier Tonon
32400 Aurensan
Tel: 05-62-09-46-01 Fax: 05-62-08-40-64

With its 25 hectares, this is by far the largest property in Saint-Mont to remain outside the *Coopérative.* It is also one of the most beautifully situated in Gascony. Seen from the valley, the perfectly cultivated vines provide a complexly abstract and patterned landscape, the rows planted verti-cally contrasting with those whose lines follow the contours of the land. From the *chais* itself there are panoramic views over the whole of the Madiran-nais, with the Pyrenees providing a snow-spattered backdrop on mist-free days.

Tonon has the misfortune to be just a few metres away from the AOC Madiran boundary. But for this quirk of administrative perversity he would be a less worried grower. He makes floc from about two hectares of his vineyard, and of the rest about half aspires to appellation status, the other half being a source of *vins de pays des côtes de gas-cogne*. Both ranges are made in **all three colours** (*A). The wines make an agreeable counterpoint to the *Coopérative*'s own.

DOMAINE DE MAOURIES
Messieurs Dufau
32400 Labarthète
Tel: 05-62-69-63-84 Fax: 05-62-69-65-49
Email: domainemaouries@32.sideral.fr
www.domainedemaouries.com

A producer of good wines (**B) under both the Saint-Mont appellations and Madiran (see page 284).

TURSAN AND COTEAUX DE CHALOSSE

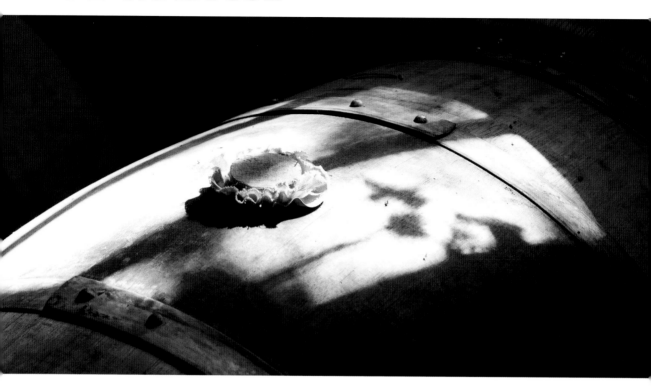

West of Saint-Mont, and stretching downstream from the Adour almost to the town of Dax, are the vineyards of Tursan, which enjoys VDQS status, and the Coteaux de Chalosse, still limited to making *vins de pays des terroirs landais*. Since the year 2000 the two principal producers, the *caves coopératives* of each region, have merged, so that their wines are vinified together at Geaune and marketed by the combined enterprise. The style of the wines is different, made in the case of the whites from quite different grape varieties. In addition to the merged *Coopérative*, there is a handful of independent growers whose wines are well worth seeking out. These again divide naturally into those clustered round Geaune and entitled to VDQS declaration (sometimes called Vignobles des Côtes de l'Adour) and those in the Chalosse restricted to *vin de pays* status (Vignobles des Coteaux de Chalosse).

The two districts adjoin and they share a similar kind of countryside, completely agricultural, gently sloping, undramatic. Tursan is home to famous chef Michel Guérard, while the beef from Chalosse is famous throughout France, and is at the heart of the repertoire of glorious stews to be found in the local kitchens during the cool wet winters. Farmers will usually keep a few hectares of pasture for cattle, despite the competing claims of the nationally cherished golden poultry and foie gras, for which the region is as celebrated as it is for its meat. Polyculture persists, so that vines are only one of a farmer's crops. He is generally happy to transfer the responsibility for the making of the wine to a *coopérative*, rather than invest himself in the expensive plant and buildings which he would need as an independent producer.

In days gone by, vines grew almost everywhere in the Landes, but Tursan, tiny as it is, is the largest source of production of wine in the region to have survived the phylloxera. The pest had almost everywhere the same disastrous effect as in other parts of France. Until then the wines had enjoyed a good reputation. The marriage of Eleanor of Aquitaine to the English Crown created a dynamic export market; pilgrims going to and from Compostelle were customers and enthusiastic ambassadors, opening markets for the wines in Spain and the Low Countries and thence to northern Germany. The Adour gave perfect access to the ocean from the port of Bayonne, where, although levies were imposed on the passage of wine through the harbour, the burden was not heavy, partly due to the influence of the Castelnau family from Tursan, who had friends in high places in Bayonne.

Most of the wines were almost certainly red, because there was little demand for whites. The *cépages* were most probably *tannat* and *cabernet franc*, the latter being known in the region as *sable rouge de Capbreton,* a reminder of the old vineyards which used to thrive close to the Atlantic. These two grape varieties, together with *cabernet sauvignon*, still dominate the vineyard, although *tannat* seems to be losing its place in the face of the demand for easier-drinking wines.

The white wines, such as they were, derived from a grape called *claverie*, also called locally *bouguieu*. After the phylloxera it was replaced by another variety called *baroque,* which was also to be found in Béarn and Irouléguy, suggesting it may have had a Spanish ancestry. Nobody knows for certain its history, some maintaining that it was brought back by the monks from the Crusades. Others suggest it is an old cross between *sauvignon* and *folle blanche*. Whatever the truth may be, it is odd that this grape has survived nowhere but in Tursan and the neighbouring vineyards of the Chalosse. Today it is the dominant white grape in use in the region. A little *sauvignon* and *gros manseng* are also grown. Some writers have been rude about the *baroque* grape, but when well handled it is perfumed, fine, fruity and rather lively, relatively low in alcohol and therefore delightfully easy to drink. It is somehow reassuring to find a purely local grape like the *baroque*, which is not only surviving but flourishing, giving to the wines a local and pronounced personality all their own. It represents more than 60% of the white grapes in Tursan.

The reds of Tursan have been slower to revive after the phylloxera. As recently as 1960 Morton Shand, in his excellent *Book of French Wines* (Jonathan Cape, London, 1960), describes the reds as 'of little importance', but now they, along with the rosés, have overtaken the whites. Today, Tursan has twice as many red-grape vines as white. Sadly, the *tannat* grape is gradually giving way to the *cabernets*, nowadays representing less than half of all the reds, and it would be a pity if red *tursan* became just another Bordeaux satellite red. The typicity which the grape gives to the local reds is well worth preserving.

Tursan achieved VDQS status in 1960, but the Coteaux de Chalosse have not progressed beyond *vins de pays,* despite the fact that some of their wines are just as attractive, sometimes more so, than those of their ennobled neighbours. The vineyard was once extensive and, as at Tursan, of great commercial importance. With easy access to the Adour, the region had one great advantage: the river upstream from Saint-Sever was not navigable, which meant that the wines of Tursan and Madiran were loaded onto boats there or further downstream at Mugron. The quality of the wines of Chalosse is confirmed by the fact that in 1800 they fetched prices comparable with those of Jurançon and Tursan. From then on, however, production went into decline, partly due to the plantation of *armagnac* grapes to meet the neighbouring demand. A trade grew up in the sale of local wines fortified with *armagnac,* which did nothing to maintain the reputation of the local traditional table wines.

The port of Mugron was in times past extremely busy, but the Adour is a capricious river. Floods at the end of the 18th century forced its closure, but the town remained an important warehousing centre for all the wines of the region. Today the river is silent, its clients having deserted it for the railways and the motorways. Phylloxera was slower to take root here than in some other areas, partly because of the sand in the soil and also because the vineyards were dispersed and in small parcels, which slowed down the advance of the aphid. In the end, however, Chalosse succumbed like the rest.

Wine-making continued in the hands of a few independent growers, and grapes were also grown as a crop by other farmers who sent them to the Chalosse *Coopérative.* Until the merger with Tursan, production was centred round the *chais* at Mugron, but the number of members fell from about 300 in 1990 to 160 as of 2005, which no doubt partly accounts for the merger. Tursan claims only 150 members, but the average holding of vines is higher than at Chalosse, the total land in Tursan under vine being about 400 hectares, compared with only 200 in Chalosse.

Chalosse boasts some virtually unique grape varieties. Apart from the *baroque* already mentioned, white wines are completed by *arriloba*, a grape not found anywhere else, it seems. For the reds, besides the two *cabernets* and *tannat,* winemakers also use some *egiodola*; sometimes found in red floc, this is otherwise a modern hybrid which has yet to catch on.

PRODUCERS OF TURSAN AND COTEAUX DE CHALOSSE

LES VIGNERONS LANDAIS TURSAN-CHALOSSE
40320 Geaune
Tel: 05-58-44-51-25 Fax: 05-58-44-40-22
www.tursan.fr/cave

With the merger so recently accomplished, it is hard to be confident about what range of products might be available in the near future. As a general guide, however, it is safe to say that the quality at both *caves* is more than fair and the prices low (all A).

Tursan produces a basic range called **Esprit de Tursan**, available in all three colours, the white based on *baroque* and *gros manseng*. In its more ambitious range, called **Impératrice**, the red is mainly *cabernet* with a touch of *tannat*. The dry white is from equal parts *sauvignon, gros manseng* and *baroque*. As of now there are three domaine wines, **Domaine de Peyssat, Domaine de Garledes** and **Château Bourda,** as well as summer red and pink wines called **Course Landais** and **Pierre de Castelnau.** Finally, from old vines there is a prestige wine called **Mémoire de Tursan.**

The chalosse range starts with an easy-to-drink collection called **Coteaux de Chalosse**: an interesting 100% dry *arriloba*, and red and pink wines from *cabernet franc*. The red single-domaine wine, called **Domaine de L'Hoste**, is a blend of *cabernet franc* and *tannat,* while **Soleil des Coteaux**, a seductive *moëlleux,* is from the two *manseng* varieties.

INDEPENDENT GROWERS IN TURSAN

CHÂTEAU DE BACHEN
Michel Guérard
Duhort-Bachen, 40800 Aire-sur-Adour
Tel: 05-58-71-76-76 Fax: 05-58-71-77-77

If you are a famous chef with a restaurant in a wine-growing region, it is no doubt tempting to make some of your own wine. Guérard is of course the apostle of *cuisine minceur*, his complex of hotel and restaurant facilities at Eugénie-les-Bains being a mecca for weight-watchers as well as hungrier folk. He does not live there himself: his home is at nearby Château de Bachen, a beautiful late-18th-century 'listed' building, built on the foundations of an old feudal castle demolished during the Revolution. The château is almost entirely surrounded by vines, which command extensive views over the Adour Valley.

The appellation in which he finds himself may not be the most prestigious in France, but, almost as if to underline that fact, Guérard's red, called **Rouge de Bachen** (**B), is not even a tursan, but a modest *vin de pays des terroirs landais,* no doubt because it is made almost entirely from *merlot*, a grape which is not allowed into red tursan. A delicious food wine, it is, like its companion **Rosa la Rose** (**B), an excellent accompaniment to the dishes which Guérard serves, particularly at La Ferme des Grives, his restaurant to which most purses can stretch.

Guérard's two white wines are both proper tursan. The grapes are 50% *baroque*, 25% mixed *mansengs*, the remainder equally divided between *sémillon* and *sauvignon*. The former has not hitherto been allowed in white tursan, but the French authorities recently adjusted the rules, which is fortunate for Guérard. In establishing his vineyard, Guérard was helped by Jean-Claude Berrouet, the distinguished wine-maker at Château Pétrus, and by Denis Dubourdieu, equally famous as an exponent of the making of white wines; no expertise is spared. Nor was expense spared in the creation of the *chais*, the barrels being stored underground in a cellar built rather like a romanesque chapel, with

casks replacing the pews and, instead of an altar at the eastern end, a tasting room in the shape of an apse, all of it contained in a palladian-style shell of great elegance. 'Scénographie virgilienne' is Michel Guérard's phrase.

Much of the wine is naturally destined for the Eugénie complex, the rest being marketed through Bordeaux dealers. Of the two whites, the **Château de Bachen** (**B) is raised in tanks, while the prestige **Baron de Bachen** (**C) is aged in wood. Both are of course of fine quality, even if hardly what one would expect of a typical tursan, and they are a splendid accompaniment to the dishes which Guérard serves with them.

CHÂTEAU DE PERCHADE

La Famille Dulucq (EARL Dulucq)
40320 Payros-Cazautets
Tel: 05-58-44-50-68 Fax: 05-58-44-57-75
Email: tursan-dulucq@wanadoo.fr
www.tursan-dulucq.com

Not to be outdone by the sheer marketing power of the *Cave Coopérative* or by the glamour of Michel Guérard, the Dulucq family combine traditional standards with modern wine-making techniques, and with their 20 hectares of south-facing vines produce wines more than a match for either of their competitors.

At one time there were only six hectares, all replanted after the phylloxera and paid for out of the sales of Madame Dulucq's foies gras and confits. But for a long time now the family has had no other crop but the vine. The grapes are all traditional tursan: *baroque*, *gros manseng* and a little *sauvignon* for the **dry whites** (**A); *tannat*, the two *cabernets* and a little *fer servadou* for the **reds** and **rosés** (all **A). Nowadays there is also a *moëlleux* called **Symphonie** (**B), made from the two *manseng* grapes. Delicious it is, particularly when you feel you should be on your way to lunch.

The standards here have risen enormously over the years, the family having hung up their clogs a long time ago. I asked Dulucq *père* why he had not thrown in his lot with the *Coopérative*. He told me that he had in fact founded it, but left when he was required to deliver them the whole of his crop, which he was not willing to do. Today most of the burden of the wine-making falls on the younger generation, which enables Alain, as father of the family, to devote more time to the wild orchids of the region, which are his second passion.

A visit here brings home forcibly that this is the only truly artisanal property in Tursan: the *Coopérative* is too large to bother about such a concept, and Michel Guérard is producing wine for a different public.

INDEPENDENT GROWERS IN CHALOSSE

Even in areas dominated by *coopératives*, one will usually find a sprinkling of growers who relish their independence. The decision whether to sell one's grapes for very little money but with relatively little outlay, or to aim for the bigger returns from bottled wine even if this means having one's own *chais de vinification*, sometimes depends on whether there are facilities which have been in the family for a long time. In an area like Chalosse, it would be a bold entrepreneur indeed who would set up from scratch a modern winery: the wines would not fetch enough in the marketplace to justify the considerable expense involved in current conditions.

It is refreshing to find in this remote and little-known region a handful of intrepid spirits who are making wine of their own from the traditional grapes of the region, and not fusty-dusty old-fashioned stuff either but wines of a good, even contemporary style.

DOMAINE DU TASTET

Jean-Claude Romain
40350 Pouillon
Tel: 05-58-98-28-27 Fax: 05-58-98-27-63
Email: domainetastet@voila.fr
www.domaine-du-tastet.com

When M. Romain started 30 and more years ago, he had but two hectares of a rather run-down vineyard, which he has restored and expanded to its present 13 hectares, three-quarters of which are devoted to red-wine grapes (42% *tannat*, 39% *cabernet franc*, 14% *cabernet sauvignon* and 5% *egiodola*), and the other quarter to white (44% *baroque*, 24% *gros manseng*, 24% *petit manseng*, 8% *chasan* and *arriloba* together). *Chasan,* incidentally is a modern cross between *listan*, which is traditional in Gascony, as we have seen, and *chardonnay*, which is not. This is my only sighting of *chasan* in the South-West, which is surprising because it likes the local cooler soils, in which the acidity does not fall away as sharply as say in Languedoc. It is also an early-maturing variety, and so well suited to this maritime climate where rain can be a problem in autumn.

Among the wines made by M. Romain, who has now been joined by his son, there is a good **100% tannat** (B*) wine, which he gives a long vinification and eight months in the barrel, a suitable partner for the local game birds which are so famous in the South-West. Or, with the oysters and other seafood from the nearby Atlantic, try his **blanc sec** (*A), wholly from *baroque*, which is dry, fresh and fruity.

DOMAINE DE LABAIGT
Dominique Lanot
40290 Mouscardès
Tel: 05-58-98-02-42 / 05-58-90-18-49
Fax: 05-58-98-80-75

M. Lanot manages to produce a full range of attractive wines with abundant local character. The **Domaine Fût Chêne** (*A) will appeal to those seeking lower rather than higher alcohol content in their wines; this one comes in at 11.5 degrees, even in a good year like 2000. Dark ruby in colour, it has a bouquet which is ripe, warm and inviting. Although well structured, the wine is gentle on the palate, well balanced and capable of ageing a few years. There is plenty of *arriloba* in the **blanc sec** (A*), judging by its typical aromatic bouquet; the wine is quite big but supple and well balanced on the palate. The **moëlleux** (*A) is based on *gros manseng*, as will be apparent from the exotic fruits on the nose; flowery too, it is full and satisfying on the palate. The wine I like best here is the **rosé** (**A), with the characteristic red fruits of *cabernet franc*. A fresh, aromatic wine with plenty of volume on the palate and a notable 13 degrees of alcohol. A wine for food, and it finishes absolutely dry.

OTHER CHALOSSE GROWERS

BERTRAND ABADIE
40180 Bénesse-lès-Dax
Tel: 05-58-98-71-67

DOMAINE DE LISÉ
40290 Habas
Tel: 05-58-98-03-30

VINEYARDS OF THE SANDY SHORE

It is generally believed that the endless pine forests of Les Landes, so familiar and well described in the novels of François Mauriac, go back to the beginning of time. Not so: almost incredibly, they are barely a century old. Until the end of the 19th century, the whole of the region south of Bordeaux, coloured green on the Michelin motoring maps, was a swamp, with here and there a few pockets of pasture for sheep. The shepherds needed stilts to get about, and these still feature on the more folkloric postcards of the region.

This used to be one of France's poorest regions, but small vineyards were planted here and there, especially on the coastal strip where the soil was sandy. The vines thrust their roots deep into the soil, which helped them for a long time avoid the worst of the phylloxera. The plants were pruned in such a way as to grow as close as possible to the soil, which reflected the heat of the summer sun onto the grapes. This in turn enabled the fruit to come to maturity before the October rains arrived over the nearby Atlantic.

Today a few growers are still making wines in this area and in this way. The vineyards are to be found in small parcels tucked in just behind the sand dunes which border the coastline. They are very widely spread, which perhaps explains why there is no real commercial development of them. Nor is there any *coopérative* or association of growers, just a handful—half a dozen or so—independents. Most of the production is of red wines, based on the *cabernets* (principally *franc*) and *tannat*, while a few whites come variously from *arriloba*, *baroque* and sometimes a little *gros manseng*.

PRODUCERS OF VINS DES SABLES

DOMAINE DU POINT DU JOUR
40170 Lit-et-Mixe
Tel: 05-58-42-83-02

DOMAINE MONTGRAND
40560 Vielle-Saint-Girons
Tel: 05-58-42-91-47

DOMAINE MALECARRE
40660 Messanges
Tel: 05-58-48-10-11

These wines are on the list of the Auberge des Pins just outside the village of Sabres, near the Landes Museum, and the *patron* may pull out some older vintages that have been tucked away if he thinks you will appreciate them.

SCEA VIGNES
Chemin Carmentron
40660 Messanges
Tel: 05-58-48-93-26

DOMAINE DE LA POINTE
40130 Capbreton
Mobile: 06-07-47-41-26

DUPRAT FRÈRES
Quai Pièce Noyée, Chemin Saint-Bernard
64100 Bayonne
Tel: 05-59-55-65-65

This last is notable particularly for a *cabernet/ tannat* red called Fleur des Landes.

FLOC DE GASCOGNE

The persistence of the polycultural tradition underlines the large number of *vignerons* in Gascony, and at the same time the tiny area of land which the average among them devotes to the vine. As well as the foie gras and farm-made confits, the wine and the armagnac, you will also discover a product called floc. The Gascon character being what it is, many of the locals claim to have invented floc.

C. E. Page, in his book *Armagnac, the Spirit of Gascony* (Bloomsbury, London, 1989), gives the credit to Henri Lamor of Sarclé near Nogaro, who he says launched floc in 1974. That, however, was the year of my first visit to Gascony and I seem to remember that it was already being commercialized at that time. Page may be right, however. Even so, it could still be that floc is an old country drink, based on a peasant recipe from the 16th century, a theory supported by the French expert on the region, Pierre Casamayor. Alternatively, perhaps Docteur Garreau, whose château-farm near Labastide d'Armagnac houses a museum devoted to all manner of regional products and whose publicity brochures claim that 'floc was born at Château Garreau', may have been the real inventor.

What is floc? It is a local version of pineau des charentes, an aperitif based on grape juice which is not allowed to ferment, and thus initially contains no alcohol. It is then blended with armagnac, usually 55 to 68 degrees in alcohol by volume, in the proportion of three parts grape juice to one of brandy. The spirit prevents the grape juice from fermenting.

Floc may be made from white or red juice, its colour varying accordingly. It is drunk chilled and sometimes on the rocks. If you like pineau you will surely like floc, particularly tempting as a drink in late summer when the weather locally can be quite torrid. White floc can be drunk either as an aperitif or with foie gras or dessert.

White floc is usually made from the juice of the same grapes as go into armagnac such as *ugni blanc* and *folle blanche*. In addition, *gros manseng*, *baroque* and *sauvignon* are sometimes used. At Domaine Boignères, a famous armagnac estate, they use an unconventional mix of *sauvignon*, *sémillon* and *gros manseng*. After the *assemblage*, they age their floc in locally made barrels and bottle it at between 16 and 18 degrees of alcohol by volume.

Merlot, cabernet sauvignon, cabernet franc, malbec, gamay and sometimes some *egiodola* go into the making of red floc. *Egiodola* has the merit of adding deep colour to the blend. To stop the juice from fermenting, red floc is macerated at low temperature. As well as being an aperitif, it goes well with hard ewes' milk cheese, strawberries and, especially, melon.

The producers of floc, nowadays numbering in the hundreds, have created their own *syndicat*, based at Éauze. An academy of ladies and troubadours has for their sole object the promotion of floc.

Just as floc is the local version of pineau des charentes (which is made with cognac), so Gascony has invented its own version of a champagne cocktail. Pousse-Rapière is the name of a branded mixer, based on armagnac of course, made at Château Monluc in the Gers. The name of the drink is no doubt intended to describe the effect. It is made from brandy infused with orange, a little like Benedictine. Only a small quantity needs to be added to a glass of sparkling wine. One glass is enough before a meal, especially if it is a Gascon meal, which will almost certainly not be a teetotal affair.

THE WINES
OF MADIRAN
AND PACHERENC

MADIRAN

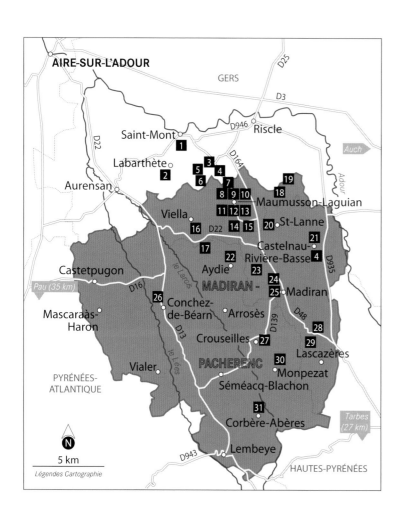

AIRE-SUR-L'ADOUR

GERS

D25

D3

D946 Riscle

Saint-Mont

D22

1

D164

Labarthète

3

5 **4**

2

Aurensan

6

7

19

18

8 **9** **10**

Maumusson-Laguian

Viella

11 **12** **13**

16 D22 **14** **15** **20** St-Lanne

21

17

Castelnau-

22

Rivière-Basse

Aydie

23

4

D935

MADIRAN –

24

Castetpugon

25 Madiran

Pau (35 km)

D16

26

Conchez-

D48

de-Béarn

Arrosès

Mascaraàs-

D13

28

Haron

Crouseilles

27

29

Lascazères

le Lées

PACHERENC

30

Vialer

Monpezat

Séméacq-Blachon

Tarbes
(27 km)

31

PYRÉNÉES-
ATLANTIQUE

le Larcis

Corbère-Abères

N

Lembeye

5 km

D943

HAUTES-PYRÉNÉES

Légendes Cartographie

Adour

Auch

AREA OF AOC: selected parcels totalling 1400 hectares.

IN THE GERS: communes of Cannet, Maumusson-Laguian and Viella.

IN PYRÉNÉES-ATLANTIQUES: communes of Arricau-Bordés, Arrosès, Aubous, Aurions-Idernes, Aydie, Bétracq, Burosse-Mendousse, Cadillon, Castetpugon, Castillon, Conchies-de-Béarn, Corbères-Abères, Crouseilles, Diusse, Escurès, Gayon, Lasserre, Lembeye, Mascaraàs-Haron, Mont-Disse, Monclar, Moncaup, Monpezat, Portet, Saint-Jean-Poudge, Séméac-Blachon, Tadousse-Ussau and Vialer.

IN HAUTE PYRÉNÉES: Castelnau-Rivière-Basse, Hagedet, Lascazères, Madiran, Saint-Lanne and Soublecause.

Some other parcels have appellation rights which will expire in 2022.

Red wines only.

GRAPE VARIETIES (BASED ON A GROWER'S TOTAL 'MADIRAN' VINEYARD): tannat (between 40% and 60%), cabernet franc (also called bouchy), fer (pinenc) and cabernet sauvignon.

MINIMUM PLANTING DENSITY: **4000 plants per hectare with transitional relief for nonqualifying plantations.**

MAXIMUM YIELD: **55 hl/ha.**

All grapes must be destalked before vinification; artificial concentration is forbidden. No continuous presses or self-emptying hoppers permitted in the chais.

Madiran may not be put on the market until the first November following the year in which it was made.

ANNUAL PRODUCTION: **approximately 67,000 hectolitres.**

Madiran is but a small village, but it has given its name to what is perhaps the most characteristic wine of the South-West, tough, sturdy, sometimes rustic and always macho in style. Pacherenc is a wine which was produced mostly in an area adjoining that of most madiran, but by a process of political and viticultural osmosis, both wines are today made in the same appellation region, madiran being wholly red and pacherenc white.

Straddling inconveniently the borders of three modern French *départements*, Gers, Pyrénées-Atlantiques and Hautes-Pyrénées, the northern and eastern limits of the appellation are bounded roughly by the river Adour; to the west it stretches to the main road to Pau, and to the south it ends at the small town of Lembeye.

Madiran village is at the heart of its eponymous appellation. Benedictine monks founded an abbey here in the Middle Ages on one of the principal routes to Saint-Jacques-de-Compostelle, and the abbey church survives to this day. A special Mass is celebrated there each year to open the local Fête des Vins, which is held in the park of the former abbey in the middle of August. The monks are thought to have come from Marcilhac in the Lot Valley, and although their foundation no doubt acted as a magnet for pilgrims seeking sustenance on the road, the actual vineyards were mostly in the hands of local growers, many of them peasants with tiny holdings.

The character of the wines of this area in those days is unguessable after so much time, but they were sufficiently good to attract the attention of the English occupying troops during the Hundred Years' War. Quantities were shipped back to England. The wines were appreciated also in the Low Countries, which bought 2,000 tonneaux on average during the latter part of the 17th century. The Baltic republics were also thirsty customers. The local market for the wines lay mostly in the Pyrenean towns to the south of the vineyards, such as Tarbes and Pau.

MORE GEOGRAPHY AND HISTORY

The river Adour flows north only a few kilometres to the east of Madiran. The river was navigable, however, only from further downstream. The local wines therefore were transported in ox-carts to the little ports of Saint-Séver, Mugron and Tartas before being sent on a three-day journey to Bayonne. Some wine also found its way overland, a difficult and perilous journey, to the Quai des Chartrons in Bordeaux, where, like the wines from other regions, it was mostly blended. The last Madiran wine-drover died only in 1992 at the age of 97.

The wine historian André Jullien, writing in 1816, tells us that the wines of Madiran came from only five communes, all situated in the then new *département* of Hautes-Pyrénées. This may have been strictly true if he was talking about wines sold under the Madiran name. But the production of wines in this area was by no means circumscribed by the county-boundary, wines being made at least in pre-phylloxera times all over the region, including the southern Gers and the Basses-Pyrénées, well beyond the limits of the modern appellation area.

Phylloxera came late to this region, which meant that the local growers were able to turn to their advantage the shortage of wine created by the destruction of vineyards further north. The region of Madiran and the adjoining growers still had wines to sell. Furthermore, when the plague did arrive, it was already established that the only remedy was grafting, as had already been practised in the other red-wine areas of the South-West. Much time and anguish were saved by this knowledge. Some replanting from the early 1890's was swift, but sadly most of the new vines were either poor hybrids or varieties introduced from Languedoc, which did not really suit the cooler *terroir* of Madiran. There was very little replanting of the varieties which had earlier made the renown of the region.

Until the turn of the 20th century, most of the white wines now called pacherenc came from the west of the river Larcis as well as from vines to the north in the commune of Viella. Those from Portets and Diusse were particularly prized. Viella made red wines of quality too, but most of the reds came from further south, from Madiran itself, Aydie and vineyards round Castelnau. Production of white wines declined markedly, local production shifting to the red wine–growing areas. The centre of gravity shifted east. Today by far the greater part of the production, and most but not all of the best wines, red and white, come from east of the Larcis.

THE EVOLUTION OF MADIRAN

Soon after 1900, a number of local growers, spurred on by moves elsewhere to combat fraud and debasement of quality, began to establish an official delimitation of the area of the Madiran vineyards. Progress was slow, and arguments bitter, not always about wine affairs but more between the clerical and *laïque* camps, between left and right political cliques, and among three *départements* concerned. A rearguard action was fought to keep Madiran itself as the centre of the appellation, and it was not until the eve of the grant of AOC status in 1948 that the communes of Maumusson and Cannet were included in the privileged area. Viella was inexplicably excluded until as late as 1965. Saint-Mont had also applied for admission to the Madiran appellation, but had been refused. It is significant that today Viella and Maumusson produce well over 50% of all madiran.

The grant of AOC status did not have the incentive effect on growers which might have been imagined. The conditions attached were so onerous that for some years only four or five growers declared their wines under AOC rules. For example, yields were restricted to 25 hectolitres per hectare, subsequently extended to 55; more significantly, wines were required to be aged in barrel for at least 33 months. This period was reduced to 24 months in 1959, 20 months in 1962, and finally in 1966 to 12 months, from which time onwards wine could be aged in tank as well as barrel. The gradual relaxation of the over-strict requirements of the original AOC statute no doubt was one of the spurs to the sudden increase of AOC production from the mid-60's onwards.

PACHERENC DU VIC-BILH

AREA OF AOC: as for madiran (see page 284).

Separate AOCs for traditional pacherenc (sweet) and pacherenc sec.

PERMITTED GRAPE VARIETIES: arrufiac petit courbu, gros manseng, petit manseng, also (rarely) sauvignon and sémillon.

Arrufiac must represent 30% of a grower's pacherenc vineyard. Courbu and petit manseng together must represent 60%. Sauvignon and sémillon together or singly must not exceed 10%.

PLANTING DENSITY: 4000 plants/ha. Max. 2.5 metres between rows, and plants must be min. 80 cm apart.

MAXIMUM YIELDS: 60 hl/ha for sec and 40 hl/ha for sweet.

ALCOHOL CONTENT: minimum 11% for dry and 12% for sweet wines.

The derivation of the name Pacherenc is uncertain. Some think it is a corruption of the phrase *piques en rang,* denoting what was in times gone by the exceptional practice of growing vines in rows rather than higgledy-piggledy all over the place—*en foule,* as the French say. Pacherenc was also undoubtedly an alternative name for the *arrufiac* grape, which we shall see is still an important component in pacherenc wines. If madiran was at one time known only to connoisseurs, the production of pacherenc was infinitesimal. It had fallen largely because in the west of the appellation region, which was the heartland of pacherenc, scarcely any wine of either colour was declared to conform under the rules. In 1985, nearly 30 years after the grant of AOC, only six growers made pacherenc, and although today there are 45, they share a total of only 235 hectares of white grapes. Production is at a rate of only 20% that of madiran. Pacherenc can be either dry or sweet and may be vinified traditionally or in oak barrels. It was once barely known outside its region of production, and even today is not easy to find away from the far South-West. Its modern AOC area corresponds exactly to that of the red madiran, the two applications for grant having been lodged and considered together. Many madiran producers make pacherenc, but there are no independent producers of pacherenc who do not at the same time make madiran. The full name of the wine is Pacherenc du Vic-Bilh, Vic-Bilh meaning simply 'old district'.

THE LIE OF THE LAND

The vineyards of Madiran and Pacherenc are cradled in a long, slow bend of the river Adour, with adjacent valleys running in parallel. The hillsides in between are occasionally interspersed with small, steep gaps, whose south-facing slopes, usually quite small parcels of land, are among the most favoured spots for growing grapes.

Such a topography tends also to display extraordinary geological variety, and the landscape of Madiran lends itself to division into three broad categories of terrain. On the western slopes there is a deal of clay, which retains moisture well. It is here that the grapes are grown for the white pacherenc wines. The eastern slopes are heavily endowed with iron and magnesium. A thick layer called *greppe* has built up which neither rain nor the roots of the vine can easily penetrate. This is the home of the most intense, dark and tannic madiran reds.

Elsewhere, the soil can be a blend of sand and clay, mixed with tiny stones. The drainage system allows the development of roots that can penetrate deep into the subsoil and extract moisture, however hot and dry the summer. But when the summer is wet and stormy, the surplus water drains away. Here the red wines, while firmly structured and still quite tannic, are rounder and more supple.

A MILD CLIMATE

The influence of the Adour is also responsible for a micro-climate which lends itself to the late harvesting of grapes. Although the proximity of the ocean and the mountains provides a moist and mild climate overall, rainfall in the summer and autumn is generally small, particularly in the northern and eastern communes of the appellation, which perhaps explains why so many good wines are made there.

The temperatures are mild too, corresponding broadly with other wine-growing areas of the South-West, despite fewer total hours of sunshine in Madiran. Frost is rarely a danger when the grapes are forming, but spring is wet, the month of May particularly so. Summer arrives generally towards the middle of June, after which the weather is hot, often stormy, with the danger of hail. But above all, the long autumns help the grower, the weather in September and October often being more stable than in the high summer. Picking begins here normally in the first fortnight of October and, for the white grapes, can continue well into November and even December. This corner of France seems to have a weather cycle which lags about a month behind that of the rest of the region.

THE MADIRAN GRAPES

The climate has favoured the development of grape varieties which respond to a late Indian summer. As with Cahors, Gaillac and Fronton, the character of the wines of Vic-Bilh derives principally from the adoption of these varieties. *Tannat* today, though not in years gone by, represents over half of the total vines planted. It is thought that in pre-phylloxera times the *fer servadou*, here called *pinenc,* dominated the better vineyards, although it is today fairly rarely seen. André Dubosc from Plaimont believes that, if *tannat* is to be blended at all, he would rather see *pinenc* used than the *cabernets* which have crept in during modern times.

Tannat is a tough, sturdy vine, high in tannins, as its name implies, but also in alcohol and acidity, so that the wines made from it tend to be slow-maturing and require long ageing. When the wines are young, the bouquet of fresh red and black fruits contrasts with the weight of the tannins, which can come as a shock to the uninitiated. With time the tannins soften, developing a range of spicy aromas and flavours of toast and vanilla. The complexity of the wine is often heightened by the use of wooden barrels, some new, some one or more years old, which many producers today consider essential if the wine is to show off its full potential.

Under the rules of the appellation, a grower's madiran vineyard must contain between 40% and 60% *tannat*, the balance being made up of the two *cabernets* and sometimes a little *pinenc*. These auxiliary grapes help to soften the toughness of the *tannat*. The *cabernet franc* does not like too much humidity, but there are years when its fruity freshness serves as a better foil to the *tannat* than the more structured and austere *cabernet sauvignon*. The *cabernets* were probably introduced into the madiran *encépagement* at the behest of INAO, just as *merlot* became authorized in Cahors. Thus, wine can be made of pure *tannat*, leaving the grower to find other uses for the remaining *cépages*.

The problem for madiran producers is how to preserve the typicity of the wine which can still be marketed within a reasonably commercial time-scale. The authorities have helped by reducing the length of time which a wine must be aged before release to the market from three years to one. They may then be given their *agrément* (the necessary permission to label and market wines under the AOC). Some growers have helped themselves by reducing the proportion of *tannat* to the legal minimum or by reducing the period during which the juice remains in contact with the skins and pips. Other growers have gone to the other extreme, making wines deriving entirely from the *tannat* grape and giving the wines an enormously long period of maceration and *élevage* in new wood.

THE PACHERENC GRAPES

The variety of pacherenc styles is even more pronounced than that of the red madiran, the climate varying from one vintage to the next. Nowadays most *vignerons* like to produce both dry and sweet styles by balancing the proportions of the grape varieties they grow and also by going over the same vines several times, picking on each occasion only those grapes which will suit the desired style. This selective harvesting is called *tries successives* by the growers, as it is in Bergerac and further south in Jurançon.

Traditionally, *arrufiac* was the hallmark ingredient of pacherenc. It is, however, not obligatory, although there is a movement to ensure its survival or even a return to its former preeminence. In practice most producers have some, but the proportion can vary from 80% (Château Viella's *sec*) to nil (Domaine Berthoumieu and Château de Fitère, for example). One of the reasons *arrufiac* has been tending to give way to other varieties is that it is not suitable for making really sweet pacherenc, a style which is becoming more and more popular, along with foie gras and the local hard Pyrenean cheese, for both of which it is such a good partner.

The balance of the *encépagement* for pacherenc comes from the *gros* and *petit manseng* grapes, though, especially for really dry wines, some growers (e.g., Alain Brumont) like to have some *petit courbu*; indeed, his Montus Sec is 100% *petit courbu*. Its drawback, however, is that it ripens early, thus disrupting the cycle of work in the vineyards and *chais*. Fans of *petit courbu* like it for the perfume and freshness that it gives to young wines in particular. This grape, less often seen today in Jurançon, hangs on in Pacherenc because the rainfall is substantially less than further south in the mountains and so rot is less of a danger.

The *gros manseng* grape is giving way to *petit manseng*, the principal ingredient in the sweet wines which are now all the rage. It has a thick skin and can remain on the vine late into the season, even over the New Year, without rotting. It does not attract the noble rot, but its evaporated extract is enormously rich, the sugar being balanced by fine acidity. It is the balance between sugar and acidity that determines the quality of a sweet pacherenc. The range of aromas detected by expert tasters is amazing, starting with pineapple and grapefruit and taking in spiced bread, roasting coffee, mango, elderflower and mint.

In Vic-Bilh, the grapes are grown, as in Jurançon, fairly high off the ground to protect the young shoots against the possibility of frost. The madiran vines are cultivated rather like a half-standard rose, while the pacherenc vines are grown with the shoots at eye-level along wire. The density of plantation is unusually low in the older vineyards.

NO VINS ROSÉS?

Neither appellation covers pink wines, which must be sold as *vins de pays* de Béarn, Pyrénées-Atlantiques, Gers, Côtes de Gascogne or Comté Tolosan. The production is less important than the AOC reds and whites, but such rosés as can be found are attractive all the same despite their humble labels.

DEVELOPMENT SINCE THE GRANT OF AOC STATUS

Because of the original stringent requirements of the AOC, the development of madiran was very slow to take off. At Aydie, Frédéric Laplace had been keeping the flame alive for years, as had the Vigneau family at Domaine Pichard (the first estate to bottle its own wines). Jean Dartigue at Domaine Taillerguet, his friend Maurice Capmartin at Château Barréjat and the Robillauds at Château Peyros were others at that time. The *cave coopérative* at Crouseilles, founded in 1950, quickly subsumed the earlier *cave* at Diusse, where business had fallen off badly as it was no longer a centre. The old building at Diusse still stands, although there is a melancholy air of better days about the place.

Crouseilles was in very large part responsible for the renaissance of madiran, facilitating the maintenance of the vines of the smallest growers and encouraging those who wished to remain independent to follow in the *Cave*'s footsteps by restructuring their vineyards and improving their methods of vinification. Hence, in the ten years following 1965, production of AOC madiran doubled. Today it is approaching 70,000 hectolitres. The last quarter of the last century saw a frenzied increase in planting, especially in the area of Maumusson. Today there are over 50 independent growers making and bottling their own wines.

THREE COOPERATIVES

■ **PRODUCTEURS PLAIMONT**

(see also page 268)

32400 Saint-Mont

Tel: 05-62-69-62-87 Fax: 05-62-69-61-68

www.plaimont.com

Although specializing in the wines of Saint-Mont and the Côtes de Gascogne, there are some members of the Plaimont *Cave* who grow grapes within the Madiran AOC, which are then vinified at Saint-Mont. These growers account for a little over 10% of the total production of madiran. Many from Viella in particular are loyal to Saint-Mont, even though that village is outside the Madiran AOC (it was deliberately excluded in 1948, along with Viella itself). Indeed, their forebears were responsible for setting up the *Cave* in the first place.

It is good to see that Plaimont and Madiran's own cooperative at Crouseilles is now working for the better marketing of both madiran and pacherenc. Plaimont has always been an innovative enterprise, and with their madiran they are seeking a more popular style of wine which can be enjoyed young. **Maestria** (*A) is meant to be drunk with grilled or roasted meat, so has good body but less harshness and softer tannins than many more traditional madirans. Plaimont also produces a range of more or less oak-aged madiran, varying in price as in quality (e.g. **Plenitude**, *B). Their recent *tête de cuvée*, called from 2002 onwards **Viella Ricaut** (**B), is particularly interesting. In due course it will be made from four hectares of grapes planted in 2002 in the area of Viella. These are planted to a density of no

less than 9000 plants to the hectare, the rows being only a metre apart. While these vines are maturing, the wine is being made from grapes grown nearby, 60% *tannat* and 40% *cabernet sauvignon*, but as time goes by, fruit from the new vines will be increasingly added to the blend, until by 2014 the transfer will be complete and all the wine will come from the new grapes. According to Fabien Olaiz, who is in charge of marketing at Plaimont, the problem with madiran is not the *tannat* grape but the *cabernet*, which they therefore allow to overripen on the vine, usually until the end of October, in order to secure maximum natural sweetness. The *tannat* is accordingly vinified at 32 degrees for quick extraction and thus the minimum of rough tannins, while the *cabernet* is made at only 23 degrees to soften the fruit. The wine is aged for 12 months in French barrels, and experiments are being made with putting the wine in the wood for its malolactic fermentation.

Plaimont also makes some sweet pacherenc, but no dry. The **Collection Plaimont** (*B) is a medium-sweet rather than honeyed pacherenc, while the sweeter **Saint Albert** (*B) is made from later pickings. **Saint-Sylvestre** (**B), as its name implies, is made from grapes picked on New Year's Eve, a highly concentrated and ultra-sweet, exotically perfumed wine of excellent quality. In some years an apples-and-pears character helps to distinguish it from a jurançon.

Recently at Plaimont there has been a collaboration between a score or so of independent growers, including many of the best, to produce a madiran designed to appeal to the young market and to overseas drinkers, both somewhat intimidated by the traditional madiran style. Under the bilingual title of **Fruit and Passion 1907**—being the year when the first selection of madiran *terroir* was established—and a jazzy label lurks a wine shamelessly devoted to fruit and little else; with no tannins and only minimum acidity, it leaves an overall impression of sweetness. This is a wine on which Plaimont pins a great deal of hope. It will obviously hit the spot at which it is aimed, but it is not likely to wow the lovers of true madiran.

■ **CAVE DE CROUSEILLES**
(Les Vignerons du Vic-Bilh-Madiran)
64350 Crouseilles
Tel: 05-59-68-10-93 Fax: 05-59-68-14-33
Email: contact@aapra.aquitaine.fr

The *Cave* was founded in 1950 and was immediately joined by growers who had neither the capital nor the inclination to set themselves up as wine-makers. Soon the *Cave* accounted for 90% of madiran production. As the years have gone by, some have left to make their own wine after all, others have joined; meanwhile, the ranks of independent growers have been swollen by newcomers, so that today the *Cave* at Crouseilles makes just over one-third of the total output. This figure, however, masks the increase in volume actually produced for members. There are over 200 of these, with vines covering about 450 hectares, so an average holding would not justify a grower in setting up on his own.

The *Cave* has a staff of over 20, many needed to oversee the production of a range of *vins de pays* as well as AOC madiran and pacherenc. Of the red wines, the two most likely to be found as continuing brands are the **Folie du Roi** (*A), a lightly oaked *vin de garde* with a real *terroir* character. In good years this wine will keep for up to 10 years. The wine called **Château de Crouseilles** (**B) is even better, the *Cave*'s flagship product. The château is a real one; it was bought by the *Cave* in 1981 as a tasting and sales venue. Vines were then planted there and the first wine came on stream in 1988.

The *Cave* itself is just a few hundred yards away down the hill. This wine competes on its own terms with the best of the independents, and because of the *Cave*'s marketing clout, it is one of the madirans mostly likely to be found on a restaurant wine list. It must have long cellaring, however, to give time for the new wood to do its work.

The *Cave* also makes wine for the owners of two private domaines, the Château de Gayon and Domaine Mourchette, and they are entrusted with the marketing of some of the wines of **Château d'Arricau Bordès** (*B) and **Château de Mascaraàs** (**B), this last a very promising newcomer to the ranks of single-domaine wines and a worthy counterpart to Château de Crouseilles. The *Cave*'s pacherencs include both dry and sweet, sold under the brand **Folie du Roi** (*A), and some extra-sweet ones under the names **Hivernal** (*B) and **Prélude à l'Hivernal** (*B).

■ **CAVE COOPERATIVE DU MADIRANNAIS**
65700 Castelnau-Rivière-Basse
Tel: 05-62-31-96-21

This *Cave* exists to serve the few growers in the *département* of Hautes-Pyrénées who do not make and bottle their own wine. In the early days it refused to cooperate with Crouseilles because of local political rivalry. Until the new millennium it was making very disappointing stuff, a shame because its strategic position on the main road south from Bordeaux to Tarbes may have given passers-by a poor idea of madiran and pacherenc.

However, the *chais* is only a few hundred yards up the road from Alain Brumont's Château Montus, and he has lent the *Cave* the services of his oenologist and taken over the front-of-house sales operation with a marked improvement, which one hopes will continue. Generic wines are sold under the *Cave*'s names and there are a handful of single-domaine bottlings, including **Domaine Rengouer** (*A). This *Cave* showed its wines for the first time at the Madiran *Fête des Vins* in 2004.

INDEPENDENT GROWERS

■ VIGNOBLES LAPLACE

Famille Laplace

Château d'Aydie, 64330 Aydie

Tel: 05-59-04-08-00 Fax: 05-59-04-08-08

Email: pierre.laplace@wanadoo.fr

Frédéric Laplace, a legendary hero of madiran, was one of the few local growers to keep the torch of Vic-Bilh shining during the dark post-phylloxera years. In his time, the Laplace family farm was indeed just that, a charming rustic assembly of buildings, presided over by this genial countryman who was as passionate about *la chasse* as he was about his wine. The trophies above his fireplace attested to his marksmanship as much as his skill as a wine-maker. Without removing his beret, which remained in place at all times except for intimate family occasions, he would seat you at his dining-room table and give you generous tastings of his red and white wines before posing for photographs in his traditional *chais,* his new *remontage* pump proudly in hand. Alain Brumont was at that time still a schoolboy.

Much has changed. The grandchildren have taken over since Frédéric's death and that of their father Pierre, and they have bought the imposing Château d'Aydie, over the road from the family farm. The *chais* has been modernized and is now equipped with immaculate 400-litre barrels, although the old *foudres* of which Frédéric was so proud have been kept as decoration. Modern machines now do the work of the oxen, and commercial imperative as much as the rules of the appellation have brought

about the installation of shiny new stainless steel tanks and other state-of-the-art equipment.

The family have expanded the vineyard too. They have 55 hectares of vines, three times as many as old Frédéric had. Most are at Aydie, but some are a few kilometres away at Saint-Lanne and Moncaup. An increasing amount of space is given to white grapes, the family having as much if not more faith in the future of pacherenc as of madiran. Ten hectares are given over to pacherenc production.

The quality of the wines has not changed, even if the style has. The planting of *cabernet franc* and *cabernet sauvignon* has enabled the present generation to develop three distinct styles of red wine, whose names change from time to time. Frédéric bothered only with one. The *entrée de gamme* is currently called **Madiran Laplace** (**A), an agreeably light and gently oaked red which needs really ripe grapes if the fruit is to shine through. **Odé d'Aydie** (**B) has rather more *tannat* (80%) and riper, softer fruit. The wine is aged in barrels, where it has undergone its second fermentation, but the effect of the wood is not as noticeable as with the top red, **Château d'Aydie** (C***). This wine seems rather less tough than it did a few years back and reflects a house style which is moving towards what they call the 'civilization' of Madiran; the wine is aged in barrels for two years before bottling and should keep another 10 years after that. By then the tannins will have melted and the effect of the oak will have merged with the fruit, giving an extraordinary complexity and satisfying finish. Sadly, most wine from the château will have been drunk before it has had a chance to express itself.

The Laplaces believe in long macerations to achieve maximum extraction from the must. The lees are reincorporated with the wine as a matter of course, and the technique called *microbullage*, which the Laplaces pioneered with their cousin Patrick Ducournau (see page 306), is much used. Neither of the two top wines is filtered or fined, so decanting, preferably three hours before consumption, is highly recommended.

Because the wines of this property generally need considerable cellaring and the Laplaces are fully conscious that their house style tends towards the heavyweight, they have been experimenting jointly with Ducournau with a more wine-bar style of madiran, in which the *tannat* grapes are given a quick hot maceration to extract their colour and their fruit, but with fewer tannins. The *tannat* is then vinified cold, as for a white wine. The other grapes are vinified traditionally, after which all the juices are blended and aged mostly in tanks, a small proportion going into barrels. The result is a fruity, cassis-cum-redcurrant style of wine, appropriately called simply **Autour du Fruit** (*B), sometimes marketed as **Les Serps**.

Pacherencs are a speciality at this domaine; the dry version, **Cuvée Frédéric Laplace** (**B), is made from 40% *gros manseng*, 25% *arrufiac*, 25% *petit courbu* and 10% *petit manseng*. The grapes are picked by hand and sorted in the vineyard, before the two *mansengs* are given a preliminary maceration overnight. Part of the wine is raised in oak with frequent *bâtonnage*, while the rest is matured in tank at low temperature. Grapefruit and pineapple are noticeable on the bouquet of this long-finishing and rather atypical wine. There are two sweet pacherencs (called *moëlleux* here to distinguish from the use of the word *doux* in Jurançon), one, **Fleury Laplace** (**B), almost entirely from *gros manseng* with just a touch of the *petit*, the other, **Château d'Aydie** (**C), entirely from the *petit*. The first has the same grapefruity acidity as the dry wine, though it is balanced by the extra sweetness.

The second is richer with more exotic fruits, the vanilla from the oak showing on the finish.

In 1999 the Laplaces bought 20 hectares of vines away to the east near Fleurance, where they are making red and white *vins de pays* which they sell under the name **Aramis** (*A). The red is mainly from the two *cabernets,* the white from *colombard* and a little *gros manseng*.

The Laplaces have recently taken over the management of the Ducournau vineyards and the making and marketing of the wines there (see page 306).

DOMAINE DE BARBAZAN
Thierry Casse
65700 Soublecause
Tel and fax: 05-62-96-35-77
Email: domaine.barbazan@tele2.fr

In the south-east corner of the appellation, Thierry Casse, a native of Alsace, has a mere 2.5 hectares of vines but is showing good promise as a newcomer to AOC production. Until recently he did not have any grapes other than *tannat*, and that disqualified him from using the Madiran name. Until 2004, therefore, his wines had to be sold as *vins de pays*, a ludicrous result of bureaucratic rigidity when so many of his colleagues are producing 100% *tannat* wines which qualify as AOC only because they have some *cabernet* in their vineyards. Thierry's solution was to rent some *cabernet franc* vines from another grower; he has now joined the ranks of AOC producers.

Casse is a bio grower, and on his tiny vineyard he has no less than three types of soil: the usual chalky clay, some more of the same with quartz fragments and a third plot on higher ground with a lot of *galets* where he grows his *cabernet*. In his functional but primitive *chais*, part of an 18th-century farm, he makes a wine fruity in style, but with firm tannins. The AOC **madiran** (**B), nearly all *tannat*, is dark ruby in colour, with a bouquet of sweet spices and ripe cherries. It is aged half in tanks and half in barrels already used previously. Surprisingly

But in his time Maurice was as much an innovator as any of the young Turks. He was the first grower in modern times to plant *tannat* in the commune of Maumusson, but at the time did not espouse the idea of a wine made exclusively from that grape. Nor until recently did his son Denis, who has been in charge for more than 10 years. Denis believes that his faithful customers want something rounder and softer than pure *tannat* can offer. It has also taken Denis a long time to come round to the idea of ageing his wines in new wood, and perhaps he does this too as a gesture to the market, because it is surely no coincidence that the wines which he puts in barrel are not generally as attractive as those which he ages in tank.

The **Pacherenc Sec** (***A) is one of the best you can find; a preliminary maceration brings out the crispness in the fruit (90% *gros manseng* and 10% *arrufiac*) and rigorous selection of grapes in the vineyard ensures a top quality and rather delicate wine with just a touch of *bonbons anglais*. There are two sweet wines. One, simply called **Pacherenc du Vic-Bilh** (***A), is a model of the older style of pacherenc, which does not aim for ultra strength or extreme sweetness. This is a gentle *moëlleux* of real class. The **Cuvée de la Passion** (**B) is like many of its oaked rivals, but rather better made. The all–*petit manseng* juice is fermented and aged for 18 months in new barrels.

Like Denis's dry white, the **Madiran Tradition** (***A) is one of the best, and a wonderful value. Though only 60% *tannat*, it can sometimes suggest cigar smoke, certainly freshly made toast; the fruit is abundant and very fresh, the attack on the palate is excellent and the tannins are silky. The **Madiran Séduction** (*A) is basically the same wine, but it is questionable whether its ageing in oak, part new, part old, does anything for it but mask some of the freshness. With the **Cuvée des Vieux Ceps** (*B) the *tannat* content rises to 80% and the wine is given its fermentation in new barrels, in which the wine is then aged.

tender on the palate, the wine is elegant rather than forceful and has a good finish. A more ambitious wine from **vieilles vignes** (**B) is all *tannat* and is correspondingly more in need of ageing. Casse deserves encouragement, because he is perched on a knife-edge; on the one hand there is his obvious talent, on the other the tiny size of his domaine, the fact that he is working alone and the difficulty of making way in an appellation whose cliquiness may be hard to break into. His holding of *cabernet franc* enables him to make a béarn which he sells in bag-in-box format to help his cash flow, but the result is variable and should not be allowed to divert attention from the real madiran.

▌CHÂTEAU BARRÉJAT
Denis Capmartin
32400 Maumusson
Tel: 05-62-69-74-92 Fax: 05-62-69-77-54

Before Denis's father, Maurice, took over this property in 1964, the wines were all sold *en négoce*.

■ **CLOS BASTÉ**

Philippe and Chantal Mur

6, Chemin Deviau, 64350 Moncaup

Tel: 05-59-68-27-37

This property near the southern border of the region is noted for its consistency, year in and year out, and is improving rapidly, clearly aiming for the top of the appellation. The equivalent of the Tradition style is called **L'Esprit de Basté** (**B) and has 60% *tannat*. This is a very madiran madiran. The *tête de cuvée* is called simply **Clos Basté** (***B) and is a pure *tannat* wine given 12 to 15 months in new oak barrels. It needs time for the oak to blend in with the wine. This is clearly an estate to watch.

■ **DOMAINE BERTHOUMIEU**

Didier Barré

32400 Viella

Tel: 05-62-69-74-05 Fax: 05-62-69-80-64

Email: contact@domaine-berthoumieu.com

www.domaine-berthoumieu.com

The Barré family has been growing vines at Viella since 1850, and Didier represents the sixth generation. While still a young man it was decided that Didier would concentrate on the wine-making while his father looked after the vines. His roguish and teasing manner conceals a deep seriousness for his wines, which are regularly cited as among the best of the region. The vineyard covers about 24 hectares, partly on a pebbly-clay plateau to the west of the village and partly on a south-eastern slope over to the east where Didier grows his grapes for pacherenc. Some of his vines go back 100 years.

Like many other growers, Didier makes an easy fruit-based wine for quick drinking at cool temperature; it is called **Cadet** (**A) and it has only 50% *tannat*, but balanced with 20% *pinenc* and the rest a mix of the *cabernets*. It is easily approachable and most attractive.

Didier makes two mainstream reds. His **Haute Tradition** (**B), a wine which softens earlier than many other madirans, comes generally from 55% *tannat*, 20% *cabernet sauvignon*, 15% *cabernet franc* and 10% *pinenc*. The *tannat* is given 14 days on the skins, the other grapes 10, and the wine is aged partly in tanks and partly in old barrels. It is then bottled during the spring following the vintage. In the glass the wine shows good red fruits, a good structure and plenty of substance.

The other red is called **Cuvée Charles de Batz** (***B). This was the real-life name of the famous D'Artagnan, whose descendant we met in Buzet. The wine has all the swagger and heartiness of the man it is named after. It also has 80% or more *tannat*, the rest *cabernet sauvignon*. The *tannat* is given three weeks on the skins for a higher extraction, and the finished wine is matured in new barrels for a year. The oak is very well handled. This wine is known for its bouquet of woodland aromas, spices and toast, as well as good red fruits. Suggestions of liquorice envelop the tannins on the palate.

For his **Pacherenc Sec** (**B), Didier picks the grapes fairly early to secure the maximum freshness of style. Half *gros manseng*, 30% *petit courbu* and 20% *petit manseng* make up the blend. Two-thirds of the juice is fermented in tank, the rest in barrel. The *petit courbu* gives the wine a touch of gun-flint and an attractive thirst-quenching acidity. The *moëlleux* is called **Symphonie d'Automne** (***B) and is mostly from *petit manseng* with just a touch of *petit courbu* to give the wine freshness and prevent it from seeming heavy. The *manseng* grapes are picked late in November and December. The juice is barrel-fermented and the wine aged thereafter in wood for six months with regular *bâtonnage*. Didier describes this wine as 'amber-gold in colour, with preserved fruits especially medlar on the nose, almonds and white peach too; well constructed and elegant on the palate with a hint of acid drops on the finish'. This is generally held to be just about the best pacherenc of this ultra-sweet style.

Didier also makes (in the name of his wife, Marie-Line) a small quantity of a kind of *vin doux naturel*, a late-picked *tannat* wine whose sugar is kept from fully fermenting by the addition of neu-

trally favoured alcohol. He calls this **Tanatis** (**C). This might be termed Madiran's answer to Banyuls, being inspired by Didier's friendship with one of the port-makers in the Douro. It is thus made in the vintage rather than the oxidized style. Like banyuls, it is recommended as an accompaniment to chocolate and also to blue cheeses.

▌ **CHÂTEAU BOUSCASSÉ (SEE MONTUS)**

▌ **DOMAINE CAPMARTIN**

Guy Capmartin

Le Couvent de Maumusson, 32400 Maumusson

Tel: 05-62-69-87-88 Fax: 05-62-69-83-07

Email: gcapmart@terre-net

At an early age, when he was still learning the skills of wine-making from his father, Guy Capmartin, brother to Denis at Château Barréjat, was convinced that the future of madiran lay in the qualities of the *tannat* grape. Here was a clear divergence of views within the family. Guy was more in tune with the *nouvelle vague* of madiran growers than his father or brother, though the family has always remained close and for many years Guy made his wine at Barréjat. He decided, though, to buy his own domaine and make wine in his own style. In 1987 he acquired the old convent on the western edge of Maumusson village, starting with barely 1.5 hectares. Today he has expanded to 15, including some vines which he rents from an uncle.

There is a relatively small production of red *vin de pays* des côtes de gascogne, not qualifying for AOC because there is not enough *tannat* in it; and some rosé de Béarn, mainly from *cabernet franc* and *pinenc*, with just a touch of *tannat*. These go some way to help his cash flow, which must be strained because of the long ageing which his other wines require. It is his range of madiran and pacherenc wines which have made his reputation as one of the most consistent quality producers in the area.

All the grapes, even for the *vin de pays* and pink wines, are hand-picked; fertilizers are mainly from home-produced compost, and spraying is kept to a minimum. As Guy has developed as a wine-maker, he has grown more and more into a devotion to the *tannat* grape, long macerations and oak ageing; but his mastery of cutting-edge technique is such as never to interfere with the expression of the *terroir* or concentration on elegance and class rather than power. The use of wood is exemplary too.

The **Madiran Tradition** (***A) may have as little as 45% *tannat*, the *cabernets* dominating the formula but not the style; it is a supple and fruity wine, raised in tank after a 20-day fermentation. The **Vieilles Vignes** (***A) enjoys 70% *tannat*, a rather longer fermentation and ageing in second-hand oak barrels; this wine is well built, with ripe fruits and elegant tannins. The **Cuvée du Couvent** (***B) is an all-*tannat* wine from the very best parcels of vines, vinified for 32 days and aged in new barrels. These wines are all of the best that madiran can offer. In exceptional years like 2001, Guy also makes an ultra-premium wine which he calls **Esprit du Couvent** (***C) in the style of a *cuvée de concours,* a Formula One kind of wine, perhaps more likely to appeal to professional tasters and media professionals than the average wine-drinker, although it is not as tough as it used to be.

The pacherencs are equally distinguished; the **sec** (***A), from 80% *gros manseng* and 10% each *arrufiac* and *petit manseng,* is matured on its lees and a small proportion is given some oak ageing, but the wine retains a predominantly unoaked character. There are three sweet pacherencs: the basic **doux** (***A), aged in tank on its lees for six months and made with only 20% *gros manseng*, the rest *petit*—a wine which has the character of exotic fruits but which is for drinking young; the **Pacherenc du Couvent** (***B), all *petit manseng* picked in three separate *tries*, barrel-fermented and -matured, sweet but lively with a honeyed character; and in the best vintages, **Pacherenc Confidence** (***C), from *petit manseng* grapes picked in December and bottled in 50-centilitre format. This is ultra-concentrated, complex and conjures up flavours of fruits bottled in *eau-de-vie.*

■ **DOMAINE DU CRAMPILH**
Bruno and Marie Oulié
64350 Aurions-Idernes
Tel: 05-59-04-00-63 Fax: 05-59-04-04-97
Email: madirancrampilh@aol.com

This domaine is over to the west of the appellation in the heart of the old Vic-Bilh area, where the vines are on lower and less hilly ground and can thus be machine-harvested. The family prefer to pick grapes from the older vines by hand, not out of respect or romantic attachment, but because old *tannat* fruit needs careful handling.

The Ouliés have been making wine here for many generations, although during the period when madiran as a name had almost disappeared, they grew other crops as well. They kept some of their old vines, and these are still producing to this day, but in the 1960s they replanted a lot more until today they have 23 hectares.

Bruno Oulié gives the impression of being a traditionalist. His father has the quiet reserve of the peasant farmer, but also a disarming smile. He enthusiastically embraced the best of old and new techniques. Bruno keeps to long macerations of his red grapes, but sees the merits of oak barrels, even if he prefers to use them for some of his *cuvées* only.

There are two red AOC wines. There used to be three, but Oulié seems to have discontinued the hefty new-oak Cuvée Baron, which was excellent of its kind if you liked that sort of thing. Nowadays his first red, called **L'Originel** (***B), is one of the best of all the traditional unoaked madirans; about 60% *tannat* to 40% *cabernet* (mostly *franc*), it combines deep fruit with solid structure, the two together demonstrating perfectly the true style of madiran. No less good is the wine from the **Vieilles Vignes** (***B/C, depending on vintage), made wholly from *tannat* and aged mostly in wood, some barrels new, others having already been used. Both these wines benefit from long cellarage, so as to allow the tannins to melt into the fruit and develop the full phenolic potential in the wine.

The Ouliés are no less renowned for their pacherencs. Until 1988 they made only one, leaving the nature of the vintage to determine whether it turned out dry or sweet. This was how pacherenc was made in the old days, but the customers wanted the domaine to make both a dry and a sweet wine, although they say it is difficult to make anything but a dry wine in bad years. The **Sec Cuvée du Domaine de Crampilh** (***B), raised wholly in tank, is outstanding, always very dry in style, even flinty and needing some chilling. Of the two sweet whites, one is *moëlleux* rather than *doux*, with more *gros manseng* than *petit* in the blend. Called simply **Domaine du Crampilh** (***B), it is made in a style which was almost universal in the south-west before the fashion for dry white wines developed after the Second World War. In fact, this old style of three-fourths sweet wine is a better accompaniment to most foods than the heavyweight *liquoreux* style. Which is not to downgrade the excellent **Vendanges Tardives** (***B), which Oulié makes exclusively from *petit manseng* grapes in small quantity and oak barrels. The wood lends exuberance without managing to affect the taste of the wine.

To meet the modern demand for something easier to tackle than a traditional madiran, the domaine now makes a **vin de pays** (**A) from *cabernet sauvignon* which is very attractive and full of fresh fruit.

■ CLOS FARDET
Pascal Savoret
3 Chemin Beller, 65700 Madiran
Tel and fax: 05-62-31-91-37
Email: closfardet-madiran@libertysurf.fr

Pascal's father sent the grapes from his tiny holding of just over one hectare to the *Coopérative*, but Pascal, who trained in agriculture at Bordeaux, was determined to make over the family vineyard to top-quality home-made and -bottled wine. His first vintage was in 1998, and since then he has expanded the vineyard to a more realistic 10 hectares. Since the *terroir* is rich in manganese, all south-facing and very poor, he makes no white wine, just two reds.

The vineyard is almost entirely *tannat*, with just a little *cabernet franc*, and as a wine-maker Pascal places extraction as being more important than concentration. The grapes are hand-picked and brought in in the now fashionable small *cagettes* to avoid damaging the fruit with resulting oxidization of the juice. The *chais* is temporarily rather basic; he is proud of a wonderfully traditional old hand press which sits in a sunken trough, thereby enabling the juice to remain in contact with the skins. Fermentation is in fibre-glass, which Pascal says allows the wine to 'breathe', and in December the wine is put into barrels for its second fermentation; it is aged there for 12 months, after which it yields place to the then-current vintage and is bottled. The proportion of new wood 'follows the availability of cash', but he prefers the larger 400-litre barrels to the more usual *barriques bordelaises* of 225 litres, because the ratio of wood area to wine volume is lower and thus less likely to give the wine unwanted floorboard flavours. The wines are neither filtered nor fined.

Now that Pascal with his enlarged vineyard has stopped being a *vin de garage* producer, he will no doubt evolve his own house style. In the past he has been the victim of wildly fluctuating vintages, some being rather too endowed with alcohol, others having amazing elegance and finesse and much better balance. The two *cuvées* are called respectively **Beller** (**B), with 20% *cabernet franc* to balance the *tannat*, raised in older barrels; and **Moutoué Fardet** (***B), named after his grandfather, all *tannat* and given whatever new wood is available. These wines are not for the faint-hearted, but will appeal to devotees of the New World style.

Pascal's father is proud that his son and no one else other than the Laplaces have managed to woo the wine buyers at Galéries Lafayette in Paris. Pascal has abundant talent: *c'est un vigneron à suivre,* as they say in France.

■ CHÂTEAU DE FITÈRE
René Castets
32400 Cannet
Tel: 05-62-69-82-36 Fax: 05-62-69-78-90

At the age of 19 René was thrown in the deep end when his father was taken ill and had to hand over this old domaine to René. It had been in René's mother's family for many generations. Undaunted, René promptly decided to expand the vineyard, and today it covers 23 hectares. The vines enjoy magnificent exposure to the south and south-west, with views over the valley where the growers of Maumusson have their vineyards.

René used to make just one red wine, his traditional **Château de Fitère** (**A), with an unusually high percentage of *pinenc* in the blend; it is an outstandingly good wine, as well as a good value. It is given but ten days' maceration in concrete, and then aged partly in fibro-cement, partly in ordinary lined concrete. In good years René also makes a separate wine from his **vieilles vignes** (** B), which is given a much longer maceration but no *élevage* in wood. This wine has greater depth and structure without being soupy or tough. There are also two special *cuvées* named after ancestors, **Cuvées Darius** and **Marius** (both **B), which are usually surprisingly forward.

René makes no dry pacherenc, but the first of

his sweet ones is named after his daughter. **Cuvée Karine** (**B) is consistently of high quality. It manages to evoke exotic fruits such as mango without the assistance of oak barrels, whereas the **Château Fitère** (*B), despite, or perhaps because of, all its medals, seems rather exaggerated and over the top. It is well made, though, and a typical example of the modern style of these oaked sweet wines.

■ **DOMAINE LABRANCHE-LAFFONT**
Christine Dupuy
32400 Maumusson
Tel: 05-62-69-74-90 Fax: 05-62-69-76-03
Email: labranchelaffont@aol.com

In a macho appellation where rugby football is just as important as wine-making, young Christine Dupuy is even more conspicuous than she would be elsewhere. She needs to stand up to her male colleagues, and this she does with a vengeance. In her first year at the Madiran wine fair she walked off with first prize for her top red, and she has consistently proved herself one of the most talented of the local growers.

Christine and her mother inherited the vines at Maumusson from M. Dupuy *père,* and since she took over Christine has acquired some more at Saint-Lanne, alongside the second vineyard of the Laplace family. There she plans to increase the density of plantation by introducing new rows between the existing ones. Back at Maumusson, Christine has a few pre-phylloxera vines whose juice goes into her top red. She now has 18 hectares in all. When she takes you on a visit to her vineyard, she has an almost personal relationship with each vine, which she treats as lovingly as she does her two charming daughters.

Her **Rouge Tradition** (***A) is made from 60% *tannat*, with a generous balance of *cabernet franc,* which ensures good fresh fruit (prunes particularly), hints of liquorice and an acceptable level of soft and well-integrated tannins. The **Vieilles Vignes** (***B) needs some ageing, but patience is well rewarded to do justice to the firm, complex structure of a wine which shows quite fierce tannins in its youth. When mature (seven or eight years), the wine is quite simply magnificent, the gentle *élevage* in wood having had time to do its work.

Christine used to put more *arrufiac* in her dry pacherenc than she does nowadays. At present

it accounts for a mere 10% of the *encépagement*. The balance is made up of 20% *petit manseng* and 70% *gros*. Half the wine is raised in barrel, which contributes plenty of citric fruit richness without detracting from its natural vivacity. This is very fine **Pacherenc Sec** (**A). Her sweet wine, called simply **Pacherenc du Vic-Bilh** (**B/C), has all the technicoloured richness of the modern-style 100% *petit manseng* wines.

▌ CHÂTEAU LAFFITTE-TESTON

Jean-Marc Laffitte
32400 Maumusson
Tel: 05-62-69-74-58 Fax: 05-62-69-76-57
Email: contact@chateau-laffitte-teston.com
www.chateau-laffitte-teston.com

Jean-Marc has the stentorian voice of a Chaliapin and the appearance of a tough second-row rugby forward. He is a charming, generous and very informative guide to his domaine. He is also a fast driver and enjoys the long straight road from his vineyard to Madiran village. The domaine is just to the north of Bouscassé (see page 304), and here he has built a splendid underground cellar, not in imitation of his neighbour Alain Brumont (that would be *lèse-majesté)*, but because during the torrid summer months his wines can only achieve their potential in such a perpetually cool atmosphere.

Jean-Marc succeeded his father in 1975, taking over the 12 hectares of vines. He recalls his grandfather telling him that in the 1920's the white pacherenc wines were the favourite apéritifs served in the bars of the nearby town of Riscle, which in those days could boast 12 bistros. Anise drinks still lay in the future, let alone the fashion for whisky.

The Laffitte-Teston vineyard still retains 3.5 hectares of genuine 85-year-old *tannat*, the grape without which, in Jean-Marc's view, madiran would not exist. Nevertheless, in the dark ages of the post-phylloxera period, the family planted all manner of poor hybrids. These have today been ripped out, giving place to more *tannat* and some *cabernet*, along with *manseng* grapes for making pacherenc.

The first Laffitte red is named after Jean-Marc's son, **Joris** (**A), and is a highly agreeable quaffing wine, though it is said to keep well. More 'serious' is the red **Reflets du Terroir** (**B), which despite its name is raised partly in barrels; it contains 70% *tannat*, the balance being a mix of the two *cabernets*. Macerations can vary between 15 and 20 days, depending on the vintage, and the wines are aged for six months in tanks before being transferred to the wood. The attack on the palate is bigger and the fruit is sweeter than in Joris, but the tannins are somewhat tougher. The middle of the wine is soft and plummy. The **Vieilles Vignes** (**B) is for oak-lovers, the wine being exceptionally well made, even if a little exaggerated in style.

If the red wines are generally good, the pacherencs are tremendous. The standard of the dry **Erika** (***B), named after his daughter, never seems to vary. It is the finest of all the oaked dry pacherencs, lively and fresh, floral and perfumed and usually with fine acidity to balance the fatness resulting from the *élevage*. To achieve this dry style with 60% *petit manseng* in the blend is somewhat unusual. The *moëlleux,* which is called **Rêve d'Automne** (***B), is from *petit manseng*. It is the quintessence of sweet madiran raised in barrels, and here one should expect the oak to be quite prominent.

Both Erika and Joris are helping their father on the domaine, so the succession, still hopefully some ways off, looks assured.

▌ DOMAINE LAFFONT

Pierre Speyer
32400 Maumusson
Tel: 05-62-69-75-23 Fax: 05-62-69-80-27

Pierre Speyer is a Belgian and obviously passionate about wine. He is a serious wine-maker, but does not share the same roots as other madiran producers, who all, without exception, are native Gascons. He started looking for a vineyard in 1989 and chose Madiran because he likes gutsy wines and the climate is rather kinder than it is back home. The domaine is small, just four hectares in one parcel round the house, which is not elaborate. Nor is the *chais*, though the rows of barrels are impressive for such a small estate. All the wines here are raised in oak.

Speyer is entirely self-taught, though he had useful advice from friends he made locally. He is a respectful grower; no weedkillers are used on the vines. The grapes are picked by hand and destalked by vibration before being hand-sorted. They go into the tanks by gravity without pumping, and eventually into 500-litre barrels.

The red **Tradition** (*A) is largely from *cabernet franc* beefed up with some of the *vin de presse* from his *tannat*. It is raised in barrels which have already seen two or three wines. Next there is **Erigone** (**B), named after a sultry beauty seduced by the Greek god Dionyius. It is 80% *tannat* and made in concrete *cuves*, where it gets regular *pigeage*; after 30 days half is transferred into barrels for the malolactic fermentation, the other half left in tank. After the malo the wine is aged in oak on its lees for 18 months. Its colour is opaque. Black fruits, coconut, vanilla and coffee mingle in the bouquet, while cassis, blackberry and spice feature on the fleshy palate. **Hécate** (**B) is all *tannat*, vinified in new 500-litre barrels, kept there for its second fermentation and then aged for 18 months on its lees. It is altogether a tougher proposition.

As may be imagined, these wines need plenty of time for the oak to be absorbed into the wines, which have very good fruit, a firm structure and substantial but well-controlled tannins.

Pierre's sweet **pacherenc** (**B) is particularly striking, but made only in small quantities entirely from *petit manseng*. The grapes are picked in two or three *tries*, fermented and raised in the barrel without sulphur and with frequent *bâtonnage*.

▌ **CHÂTEAU MONTUS AND CHÂTEAU BOUSCASSÉ**
Alain Brumont
32400 Maumusson
Tel: 05-62-69-74-67 Fax: 05-62-69-70-46
Email: brumont.commercial@wanadoo.fr
www.brumont.fr

If madiran owes its survival to the Laplace family and a handful of other enthusiasts, it owes its renaissance in no small measure to the extraordinary genius of Alain Brumont. The farm at Bouscassé had been the family home for many generations, but Alain's father had no real interest in madiran wine, nor any confidence in its future. Alain, however, had the vision to see that, by concentrating on the *tannat* grape and by adopting modern methods, madiran could have a great future. So in desperation he went off on his own and bought the then run-down and abandoned Château Montus. Here, where there was already a magnificent *chais*, he replanted the derelict vineyards.

His rapid rise to fame no doubt helped a family reconciliation, and he turned his attention to Bouscassé, where he rebuilt the family home and constructed a state-of-the-art winery and an underground storage facility worthy of the most prestigious Bordeaux châteaux. Bouscassé is the centre of his business, even though he has spent a fortune restoring Montus and opening it briefly as a luxury hotel.

Brumont is happy to boast that he is entirely self-taught. He insists that he is not an innovator and that what he is doing is to restore the style and techniques of madiran to what they were before the AOC rules were invented. He thinks that all other grapes than *tannat* should be outlawed. Some may agree, but many others need the softening influence of other grape varieties in order to make wine which does not need cellaring for 10 or more years. It is not surprising that Brumont has made waves in the region. This does not seem to bother him; he even stands aloof from his fellow growers, going his own way and leaving the others to get on as best they can. In spite of the respect in which he is held by his fellow Madirannais, he is not always loved by them.

Brumont owes his success to his amazing talent for self-promotion and for charming the media, just as much as to his wines. 'Maumusson will be the Napa Valley of the South-West', he proclaims, and the French press laps it up. He has projected his own wines, even if not those of other Maumusson producers, to a position of equal status with the *crus classés* of Bordeaux, and he prices them accordingly. On average they fetch double the price of his colleagues' wines, and his boutique top-of-the-range wine costs a small fortune.

How much of this is hype, or is his position as the pope of Madiran justified? Much stems from the fact that he has enlarged his landholdings to a point where he owns just about 10% of the AOC vineyard, but it is also true that, during the 1980's and early 90's he built up such a commanding superiority over other growers that they only started to catch up rather later. But catch up they have, and in some areas there are *vignerons* that are making wines which are just as good as and perhaps better than Brumont's. It is hard, perhaps impossible in the long term, to lead from the front.

At Montus there are 85 hectares of vines, all on very stony, gravelly soil with plenty of the large round pebbles called *galets*. *Tannat* represents 80% of the vineyard, *cabernet sauvignon* 20%. Several years of financial roller-coastering have obliged him to trim the number of different wines which he now offers. Apart from his boutique wine La Tyre, there is but one red, **Montus Prestige** (**C), all *tannat* and the wood is all new. The *élevage* of **La Tyre** (*D), also all *tannat* can last as long as 40 months. This last is a *vin de dégustation*, that is, destined for professional assessment rather than general consumption, calculated to attract medals at *salons* rather than admiration at table. Quantities are in inverse proportion to the price. The Montus Prestige tends to follow the same road, with increasing oak character, long extractions and fierce tannins requiring long ageing. It is arguable that the wines of Montus in earlier years were more approachable and attractive.

There are no boutique wines made at Bouscassé, but the **Bouscassé Vieilles Vignes** (**C) is no less formidable, largely because the soil is mostly *argilo-calcaire* with a lot of the characteristic iron and manganese, called locally *grepp*. The wine is all *tannat* and aged for upwards of a year in new wood.

Mention should also be made of an unoaked wine called **Torus** (**B), which is in effect the second wine of the combined estate, made also with grapes grown from vines which are less than eight years old. While not pretending to the same class as the single-domaine wines, it is undeniably attractive and much more approachable than its prestigious fellows. It is the equivalent of other growers' 'Tradition' wines.

Brumont's pacherencs are as famous as his madirans. He is well known for his love of the *petit courbu* grape; in his dry whites he uses nothing else. The **Montus** (***B) is the archetypal oak-aged dry pacherenc, but many other growers attempt this style with unconvincing results. The **Bouscassé** version (**B) is nearly in the same class, but made for drinking earlier than the Montus, which will keep well and improve with age. Brumont's sweet pacherencs are sold not under the name of either property but according to the lateness in which the grapes were picked. Thus there is **Vendemiaire** (**B), picked in October; **Brumaire** (**C), picked in November; and **Frimaire** (***C), picked in December. For these Brumont uses only grapes which have respectively a minimum potential of 18, 19 and 20 degrees before harvesting.

Brumont also makes a range of varietal *vins de pays*, of which the most successful is the **gros manseng** (**B).

▐ **DOMAINE MOURÉOU ET CHAPELLE LENCLOS**
Patrick Ducournau
Tel: 05-62-69-78-11 Fax: 05-62-69-75-87

Patrick's family are cousins of the Laplaces at Château d'Aydie. His father bought their farm at Maumusson as recently as 1968, and he concentrated on the cereals while Patrick went off to study oenology at Montpellier and then Bordeaux. Being of an inquisitive and inventive turn of mind, Patrick has experimented for many years with a method of saving money on the buying of new barrels: the most expensive part of a barrel is the curved area which gives the barrel its characteristic shape.

Instead of buying a few whole new barrels each year, why not simply replace the cheaper flat ends of all the barrels?

More famously, Patrick is the inventor, along with his Laplace kinsmen, of the technique known as *microbullage*, or micro-oxygenation. Normally a wine is transferred from one container to another while it is ageing in the *chais*, in order to expose it to oxygen, a process called racking. Believing that the less a wine is disturbed once its fermentation is finished, the better, Patrick evolved the technique whereby the wine is left in situ and is oxygenated by the injection of tiny quantities of air into the container. Apart from avoiding the disturbance to the wine, Patrick believes that the wine gains a better structure this way; its appearance is clarified and excess filtration is avoided. In addition, and very importantly in the case of madiran, the ageing process is speeded up.

Patrick has recently branched out into the marketing of oak chips. These are not yet allowed in the maturing of AOC wines in France, but Patrick must have a flourishing business in them as he has a large staff to help him. He has therefore asked the Laplace family to look after his vineyard, and they are currently making and marketing the wines too.

Patrick has 14 hectares of vines on two very different *terroirs*; the wines from one are called **Domaine Mouréou** (***B), the soil on which the grapes are grown containing much chalk with an impenetrable subsoil which slows down drainage. The black grapes are 70% *tannat* and 30% cabernet *franc*. The other *terroir,* said to be superior, is called **Chapelle Lenclos** (***B), and here the red vineyard is all *tannat*. The Mouréou wines always have good fruit, sometimes gamey; they have good acidity; and the tannins are firm but needing less time to soften nowadays than the Chapelle Lenclos, which is more complex and requires long ageing. Both are at the top of their appellation.

There is no white wine production from Patrick's vineyards these days, which is a pity, because his pacherencs were always first class.

■ **DOMAINE SERGENT**
La Famille Dousseau
32400 Maumusson
Tel: 05-62-69-74-93 Fax: 05-62-69-75-85

When I asked Gilbert Dousseau many years ago what ambition he still had in life, he said it was to retire. He is still there, though he has handed over much of his responsibility to his two daughters. His grandfather bought the property just before the First World War. Today there are touching on 14 hectares of vines, of which two are given over to white-wine grapes, just a little *arrufiac*, the rest divided between the two *mansengs*. His 12 hectares of black grapes include a little *pinenc*, to give some rusticity to his *assemblages*.

Dousseau sold all his wine in bulk until 1975, when he began to bottle and market it himself. He still makes up a special *cuvée* for *la chasse*, containing rather more *cabernet* than usual. It seems that no self-respecting *chasseur* goes off shooting without a good bottle of quaffing wine in his knapsack. The Dousseau **Rouge Tradition** (**A) is given a relatively short fermentation and aged in stainless steel. It is one of the most attractive in this style as well as being a very good value. There is always delicious fresh sweet fruit, plenty of alcoholic strength too, and the tannins are gentle.

All the other wines here, including the red **Vieilles Vignes** (**B), are nowadays aged in oak, some of it new, some of it not so new. This superior red is sometimes rather dry, perhaps a shade over-tannic, but the quality, especially in more difficult years, is there for all to taste. The **Pacherenc Sec** (**B), which seems much harder to make than the sweet version, is representative of the style and will not disappoint, but the **Vendanges Tardives** (**B) is in a different class, the grapes being picked in several *tries* and the wine given 10 months in the barrel.

OTHER GOOD GROWERS OF MADIRAN AND PACHERENC

▎DOMAINE BERNET

Yves Dousseau

32400 Viella

Tel: 05-62-69-71-99 Fax: 05-62-69-75-08

A domaine which improves with each year that passes.

▎DOMAINE BRANA

Pierre and Gisèle Delle-Vedove

32400 Maumusson

Tel: 05-62-69-77-70 Fax: 05-62-69-85-52

Email: delle.vedove@hotmail.fr

www.domainebrana.com

A reliable and good-value estate.

▎DOMAINE DAMIENS

La Famille Béheity

64330 Aydie

Tel: 05-59-04-03-13 Fax: 05-59-04-02-74

A long-established property making wines of real character and often of great distinction. The sweet pacherencs are particularly noteworthy.

▎DOMAINE DE GRABIÉOU

René and Frédéric Dessans

32400 Maumusson

Tel: 05-62-69-74-62 Fax: 05-62-69-73-08

Email: dessans@wanadoo.fr

Another successful Maumusson vineyard.

▎DOMAINE DE LACAVE

Patrick Ponsolle

32400 Cannet

Tel: 05-62-69-77-38 Fax: 05-62-69-83-10

The wines from Cannet are often a little less severe and more approachable than those from other communes.

▎DOMAINE LAOUGUÉ

EARL Dabadie

32400 Viella

Tel: 05-62-69-90-05 Fax: 05-62-69-71-41

Email: earldabadiepierre@32.sideral.fr

www.domaine-laougue.fr

Notable for an excellent-value Tradition, which seems regularly to mature earlier than most.

▎DOMAINE LARROQUE

Raymond Galbardi-Larroque

65700 Madiran

Tel: 05-62-96-35-46 Mobile: 06-84-53-62-82

A fairly recent débutant who shows good promise.

▎DOMAINE DE MAOURIES

Dufau Père et Fils

32400 Labarthète

Tel: 05-62-69-63-84 Fax: 05-62-69-65-49

Email: domainemaouries@32.sideral.fr

www.domainedemaouries.com

A consistent property on the northern side of the appellation, not far from Saint-Mont. The domaine produces wines under the Côtes de Saint-Mont appellation as well as Madiran.

▎CHÂTEAU PEYROS

Eric Saignes (manager)

64350 Lembeye

Tel and fax: 05-59-68-10-51

Email: contact@leda-sa.com

A founding Madiran estate in the far south of the appellation. Peyros is having a rebirth after some time in the critical wilderness.

▎CHÂTEAU DE PIARRINE

Patrick Achilli

32400 Cannet

Tel: 05-62-69-77-66 Fax: 05-62-69-70-80

Notable for its substantial stocks of older vintages.

■ DOMAINE PICHARD

Rod Cork and Jean Sentilles
65700 Soublecause
Tel: 05-62-96-35-73 Fax: 05-62-96-96-72
New proprietors are giving new life to this long-established domaine, with assistance from former owner Bernard Tachouères. A feature is the good stock of old vintages in the cellar.

■ DOMAINE TAILLERGUET

François and Christine Bouby
32400 Maumusson
Tel: 05-62-69-73-92 Fax: 05-62-69-83-69
A traditional estate, where the older generation are experts in Madiran history and folklore.

■ CHÂTEAU VIELLA

Alain Bortholussi
32400 Viella
Tel: 05-62-69-75-81
Email: chateauviella@32.sideral.fr
www.chateauviella.com
A successful property which produces wines commanding media attention and considerable respect from its neighbours and rivals.

One of the problems in Madiran is that there are a few growers who excel in all styles of wine, but many who are are brilliant in perhaps one or two. Some Madiran growers make less good pacherencs than madirans, and vice versa. Some make lovely traditional wines, while others succeed better at more concentrated and extracted styles. The following table, extracted from the above chapter, may help to make selection easier. The initials NM indicate that the named grower does not make wine of that style.

DOMAINE	ROUGE TRADITIONNEL	ROUGE FÛTS	PACHERENC SEC	PACHERENC SEC FÛT	PACHERENC DOUX	PAECHERENC DOUX FÛT
AYDIE	★ ★ ★	★ ★	NM	★ ★	NM	★ ★
BARRÉJAT	★ ★ ★	★	★ ★ ★	NM	★ ★ ★	★ ★
BERNET	★ ★	★	NM	NM	NM	
BERTHOUMIEU	★ ★	★ ★ ★	★ ★	NM	NM	★ ★ ★
BOUSCASSÉ	NM	★ ★	★ ★ ★	★ ★	NM	See Montus
BRANA	★ ★	★ ★	NM	★ ★	★ ★	NM
CAPMARTIN	★ ★ ★	★ ★ ★	NM	★ ★ ★	NM	★ ★ ★
CH. L'ENCLOS	NM	★ ★ ★	NM	NM	NM	NM
CRAMPILH	★ ★ ★	★ ★	★ ★ ★	NM	★ ★ ★	★ ★ ★
DAMIENS	★		★ ★	NM	★ ★ ★	NM
FARDET	NM	★ ★ ★	NM	NM	NM	NM
FITÈRE	★ ★	★ ★	NM	NM	★ ★	★
GRABIÉOU	★		★ ★	NM	★	NM
LABRANCHE-LAFFONT	★ ★ ★	★ ★ ★	NM	★ ★ ★	NM	★ ★ ★
LACAVE	★ ★	★	NM	NM	NM	NM
LAFFITTE-TESTON	★ ★	★ ★	NM	★ ★ ★	NM	★ ★ ★
LAFFONT	★	★ ★	NM	NM	NM	★ ★
LAOUGUÉ	★ ★ ★	★			★	
LARROQUE	★	★	NM	NM	NM	★
MONTUS	NM	★ ★	NM	★ ★ ★	★ ★	★ ★ ★
SERGENT	★ ★	★ ★	NM	★ ★	★ ★	★ ★
VIELLA		★ ★	NM	★ ★	★ ★	★ ★

INTERESTING *VINS DE PAYS*

It must not be forgotten that, all over the South-West, the description *Vin de Pays du Comté Tolosan* is available to growers who for one reason or another do not fall within any other category. Similarly, *Vin de Pays des Pyrénées Atlantiques* covers many of the non-appellation wines from growers mentioned in this chapter.

Two properties not so far mentioned, and which are not in any known area of production, are very worthy of attention.

CHÂTEAU DE CABIDOS
Édouard and Vivien Nazelles
64410 Cabidos
Tel: 04-67-24-19-16
www.vin-de-cabidos.com

A few kilometres to the west of the main road leading from Aire-sur-l'Adour to Pau, and lost deep in the Béarn countryside, is this beautiful manor house bought by the present owners' mother in 1992. There was at the time a tiny parcel of vines, 0.1 hectare in all, which Madame Isabelle replanted with some *petit manseng* and some *chardonnay*. Today her sons have a total of seven hectares under vine, which they plan to expand to 12. *Chardonnay* features on the list of grape varieties, as well as a little *syrah*.

The Nazelles, whose home is in the Hérault, have a resident *maître de chais*, to remind one that this is no amateur enterprise. The vineyards are tended and the grapes picked by hand with loving care, and the wine made in state-of-the-art style with the help of a celebrated Swiss wine-maker, Jean-Christophe Novelle. Although the addition of *syrah* to the repertoire suggests plans to make red wines, the wines so far are all white, both dry and sweet, all barrel-fermented and aged for 12 months on their lees. The **Cuvée Comte Philippe** (**C) is made in both styles, while the **Cuvée Saint-Clément** (**C) is a sweet wine of model balance and showing considerable finesse, sometimes developing hints of white truffles, so some say.

DOMAINE BORDÈS-LUBAT
Francis Lubat
64330 Taron
www.bordes-lubat.com

The village of Taron is between the western boundary of the Madiran appellation and the main road south to Pau, not far from the Château de Mascaraàs. At this domaine, a typical family farm in the Béarnais style, Frances Lubat makes a wine which is a madiran in all but name, **100% tannat** (**A), but soft with plenty of dark berry fruit and good backbone. Furthermore, the tannins are quite silky and soft. Lubat dispenses with oak-ageing. The property takes some finding but is worth the detour, as *Michelin* would say.

THE WINES
OF BÉARN
AND THE PYRÉNÉES

BÉARN

AREA OF AOC: corresponds with the area of Madiran and Jurançon. Also 209 hectares in the communes of Bellocq, Lahontan, Orthez and Salies, these having the right to the suffix 'Bellocq'.

Red and rosé wines from tannat (maximum 60%), cabernet sauvignon, cabernet franc (bouchy), fer servadou (pinenc), manseng noir and courbu noir.
White wines from gros manseng, petit manseng, courbu, ruffiat, lauzet, camaralet and sauvignon.
MINIMUM ALCOHOL CONTENT: 10.5% for all colours.
ANNUAL PRODUCTION: 16,000 hectolitres, equally divided between red and rosé (very little white).
MAXIMUM YIELD: 50 hl/ha.
PLANTING DENSITY: minimum 2000 plants per hectare, 10,000 buds maximum.

Béarn is an old French county which separates the Basque country from Gascony. Like the *pays basque*, it was once part of the kingdom of Navarre.

The wines of Béarn go back a long while, how long is hard to say for certain. The vineyard may, according to some, have been planted even before the coming of the Romans. In 1587 the port of Bayonne had been opened to river traffic, making it possible for flat-bottomed boats to navigate the river called Gave de Pau, albeit with some difficulty and much risk to life and limb. From Bayonne, wine could be exported to England and Holland in rather greater safety than from Bordeaux, where the constant wars between French and English made transport intermittently difficult and dangerous. Béarn also enjoyed easy access to Spain over the Somport pass.

Following the Peninsular Wars in 1814, many of Wellington's troops stayed behind in Pau to found a substantial English colony there, and they left their imprint on the town by taking a special interest in its infrastructure, engineering good clean drainage, plumbing and drinking water. As recently as the 1930's Dornford Yates was setting nostalgic novels in Pau, and it was an English lady from Pau who became the wife of Alfred de Vigny. A special version of *sauce béarnaise,* called *paloise,* is today flavoured with mint rather than tarragon, no doubt to reflect the English way of enjoying roast lamb. The lasting legacy of the English is the splendid Boulevard des Pyrénées whose construction they inspired, with its magnificent views—on a clear day—of the snow-capped mountains.

Today, the wines of Béarn can be made by those who also make wine in Jurançon and Madiran, though the facility has fallen somewhat into disuse. However, there is no such thing as red or pink jurançon, a name which is allowed only for white wines; nor is there a white madiran, though many of the growers there make their white wines as pacherenc, as we have seen. Outside and between the Jurançon and Madiran vineyards, there is a specific area called AOC Béarn-Bellocq, centred in practice on the *coopérative* at Bellocq, a small village on the south side of the Gave de Pau, just west of Orthez. The area of this inner appellation is small, covering just the communes of Bellocq, Lahontan, Orthez and Salies. Altogether there are 160 hectares of vines, and annual production is at the rate of 8000 hectolitres. The inspiration of an oenologist called Henri Meyer, the *cave coopérative* at Bellocq was created in 1947 and instantly achieved a remarkable success from the fashion in Paris at the time for *vins rosés*. An instant hit, *the rosé de Béarn* was no doubt the reason for the region's quick promotion to VDQS in 1951 for all three colours of wine; full AOC status followed in 1975. The growers may have been lucky to achieve such rapid recognition, but at that time the quality of modern jurançon and madiran had not yet established itself and many growers from those areas were only too happy to profit from membership in the Bellocq *Cave*.

The Béarn AOC area round Bellocq is particularly attractive; the red tiled roofs of Salies recall those of the Dordogne. Salies is also the centre of production of a particularly valued variety of salt, which is largely used for the curing of *jambon de Bayonne*; in fact, no ham is worthy of that name if it has been cured in any other salt.

The grape varieties for the red wines are the same as already encountered in Madiran. There is an upper limit of 60% for the amount of *tannat* which a grower may have in his vineyard, otherwise there are no rules about the proportion of grape varieties; indeed, some growers use no *tannat* at all. Black varieties of the *courbu* and *manseng* are also permitted but rarely seen in practice. The pink wines come of course from the same grapes, and the whites from those which will be found in Jurançon, though there is a particular local grape called *raffiat de moncade* which does not seem to crop up anywhere else. It is sometimes called *rousselet de Béarn*. It was once thought this was the same grape as the *arrufiac* of pacherenc, but comparison between the plants shows that this is obviously not correct. There are only about 30 hectares of this grape in the whole of Béarn, but it is holding its own among growers who value it.

Apart from the *coopératives* at Bellocq, Crouseilles (Madiran) and Gan (Jurançon), only a few independent growers in Madiran and Jurançon also produce béarn. It will be pink in Madiran and either pink or red in Jurançon. Within the inner Béarn-Bellocq area, there seems to be only one independent property, but very good it is.

PRODUCERS OF BÉARN

DOMAINES GUILHÉMAS ET LAPEYRE
Pascal Lapeyre
52 Avenue des Pyrénées
64270 Salies-de-Béarn
Tel: 05-59-38-10-02 Fax: 05-59-38-03-98

The Lapeyres have been making wine here for nearly 100 years. Pascal is a fourth-generation *vigneron,* but only the first to have trained in oenology. Better still, he did a *stage* at Château Cheval Blanc in Saint-Emilion. The Lapeyre wines have always had a loyal local following, but have been overwhelmed by the size of the Bellocq *Coopérative*. Their rosé was the first to be produced in fluted bottles, which aroused the wrath of the growers in Alsace. The Lapeyres won the ensuing court case, and fluted bottles are still the norm for pink béarn and some of the dry white jurançon.

Pascal has ratchetted up the reputation of the family wines; they are today much praised in the French press. Although there appear to be two domaines, the names are used to distinguish between the lighter Guilhémas, aged in tanks, and the more ambitious range, Lapeyre, where the whites and the reds are given some oak-ageing.

The vineyards, planted on a fairly steep *terroir* of *argilo-calcaire,* some of which is more chalk than clay, are a little way away from the *chais,* which is on the outskirts of Salies. The gradient makes hand-harvesting a desirable necessity. The **Guilhémas** wines come in all three colours. The **Blanc** (**A) is particularly interesting, as it is made entirely from raffiat de moncade, which yields a light wine with a very attractive fruity perfume and dry finish. The **Rosé** (*A) has the much sought after combination of fruit on the palate with dryness at the end, while the **Rouge** (*A) derives its dark colour from the 50% *tannat* in the *assemblage,* its soft black fruits from *cabernet franc* and its structure from an equal quantity of *cabernet sauvignon.*

The **Lapeyre** range is wholly different. The **Blanc** (**B) has more than an affinity with dry jurançon, but with a little less acidity; it is made mostly from *gros manseng* with a good dose of *petit,* the latter giving a richness and modern style. The wine is aged in new casks for about six months. As one might expect, there is plenty of evidence of exotic fruits and perfumes and the finish is quite nutty. The **Rosé** (**B) is a blend of *cabernet franc* and *tannat* and is altogether a much bigger affair than the Guilhémas, quite intense on the palate; a rosé to accompany food. The **Rouge** (**B), with 60% *tannat,* 30% *cabernet sauvignon* and 10% *cabernet franc* in a typical year, is given regular *pigeage,* though the extraction is not overdone, and depending on the vintage, sometimes a little *vin de presse* will go into the ultimate blend. The wine is aged in cask, but the barrels are not all new, being renewed on a five-year cycle. The wine is lightly filtered after fining with egg yolks. This is a big wine with distinctly modern tendencies, although it will mature faster than some of its neighbours from Madiran.

LE CHAIS DES VIGNERONS DE BELLOCQ
64270 Bellocq
Tel: 05-59-65-10-71 Fax: 05-59-65-12-34

The excellence of Lapeyre's wines should not deter visitors to the Béarn from trying the wines of this local cooperative or those of the cooperative at Crouseilles mentioned above. The Bellocq *Cave* has been taken over by the *Cave des Producteurs de Jurançon*, and one of the results of the merger has been that the AOC Béarn which used to be made at Gan is now made at Bellocq, so that Gan can concentrate on their majority production of white wines. Gan also vinifies and bottles the rosé wines which used to be made at Bellocq. The Bellocq production accounts for 90% of the total AOC output.

IROULÉGUY

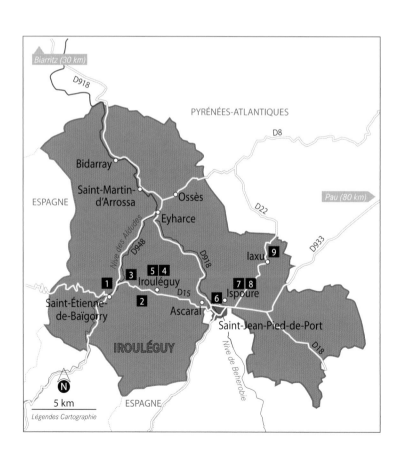

Biarritz (30 km)

D918

PYRÉNÉES-ATLANTIQUES

D8

Bidarray

Saint-Martin-
d'Arrossa

Ossès

ESPAGNE

Eyharce

Pau (80 km)

D22

Nive des Aldudes

D948

D918

Iaxu

9

D933

3

5 **4**

Irouléguy

7 **8**

Saint-Étienne-
de-Baïgorry

1

D15

6

Ispoure

2

Ascarat

Saint-Jean-Pied-de-Port

IROULÉGUY

Nive de Béhérobie

D18

N

5 km

ESPAGNE

Légendes Cartographie

AREA OF AOC: selected parcels covering **200** hectares in the communes of Aincille, Anhaux, Ascarat, Bidarray, Bustince-Iriberry, Irouléguy, Ispoure, Jaxu, Lasse, Lecumberry, Ossès, Saint-Etienne-de-Baïgorry, Saint-Jean-le-Vieux and Saint-Martin d'Arossa.

White wines from petit courbu, gros manseng and petit manseng.
Reds and rosés from tannat (maximum 50%) and cabernet sauvignon and cabernet franc (minimum 50% either together or singly).
MINIMUM ALCOHOL CONTENT: reds and rosés 10%, whites 10.5%.
MAXIMUM YIELDS: reds and rosés 50 hl/ha; whites 55 hl/ha.
PLANTING DENSITY: no limits.
PRUNING: *méthode* Guyot (double or single).
ANNUAL PRODUCTION: **7250** hectolitres.

WINE FOR THE PILGRIMS

We are in the Basque country, the larger part of which lies over the mountains in Spain. Irouléguy is the only official Basque wine made on the French side of the Pyrenees.

Today the attractive town of Saint-Jean-Pied-du-Port is a tourist centre, and in the Middle Ages it served a similar purpose as the last staging post for pilgrims before they crossed the Pyrenees on their long haul to Saint-Jacques-de-Compostelle. Pied-du-Port means literally 'the foot of the pass', the pass in question being the Ibanéta. On the far side of it the Church built the Abbey of Roncevaux to give pilgrims refreshment both spiritual and temporal. For both of these the monks needed wine, but the abbey was too high in the mountains to sustain a vineyard, so they planted instead in the valley of the river Nive which runs through Saint-Jean. The vines were centred round two priories dependent on Roncevaux, one in the village of Irouléguy and the other in nearby Anhaux.

In the 17th century the Treaty of the Pyrenees between France and Spain ceded to France all the Basque lands to the north of the Pyrenees. The monks of Roncevaux, deprived of easy access to their vineyards, left them in the hands of the local farmers. The wines have since been known by the name of Irouléguy.

A FAMILIAR TALE

At the end of the 19th century, Irouléguy enjoyed a high local reputation, some people saying that there were nearly 500 hectares of vineyards extending downstream as far as Itxassou. However, successive plagues of mildew almost destroyed the vines and the phylloxera delivered the coup de grâce, even though it did not reach this far south until 1912. Most farmers dug up their old vines and replanted with other crops. The vineyard shrank, retaining only a token presence in the villages of Saint-Etienne-de-Baïgorry, Irouléguy and Anhaux. Here, a handful of quality producers kept going, starting a movement for recognition as an appellation. VDQS status was achieved in 1952 (a year which saw the formation of the *cave coopérative* at Saint-Etienne-de-Baïgorry). Initially the statute covered only the wines of the three traditional communes, but three more were added in 1962. Full AOC status was achieved in 1970 and now extends to selected parcels in 14 communes.

VITICULTURE IN IROULÉGUY

Today there are about 200 hectares of vines, grown mostly on a reddish sandstone, but here and there on a mixture of alluvia washed down from the Pyrenees. The sandstone is porous but still manages to retain good humidity. It seems to suit the *cabernet* grapes in particular, and to give wines which are softer and quicker to mature than those grown on the chalky clay.

About two-thirds of the vines are planted on terraces, some rising 600 metres or so above sea level. Here the yields are much lower than in most other conventional vineyards. Everywhere the plants are grown high off the soil, as at Jurançon, to protect the budding shoots from the spring frosts. To add to the producer's burdens, all picking and work in the vineyard has to be done by hand because of the extreme gradients. One compensation is the gentle climate. As in Jurançon there are often long Indian summers which last well into November and even December. Another is the spectacularly beautiful landscape with its views of the Pyrenees and the lush green sheep and cattle pastures. This is still a land of polyculture.

Irouléguy remains a small appellation, so the vines sometimes are hardly noticeable as a feature of the countryside, except, that is, on the hill called Arradoy which rises behind Ispoure, a northern suburb of Saint-Jean. Here the bold terraces, baring themselves to the full force of the southern sun, are unmissable.

As in Madiran, the grape varieties are *tannat* and the two *cabernets*. Jean Brana maintains that *tannat* was never the preponderant grape in the *pays basque.* He argues that the *cabernet franc* was born here before spreading to the Landes, Bordeaux and the Loire. He contends that *tannat* originated in the Gers and the Mediterranean. As may be imagined, the higher the proportion of *tannat* in a blend, the more robust the wine and the greater its keeping potential. The style is roughly comparable to that of madiran, partnering well the local enthusiasm for *pelota*, tug-of-war and rugby football, as well as the local cuisine, which is liberally sprinkled with the native red pepper of Espelette.

Traditionally, the production of irouléguy was almost exclusively of red wine, but nowadays there is a growing thirst among the holiday makers on the coast around Biarritz for *vins rosés*. These represent a substantial proportion of the local growers' output. White irouléguy was once a rarity, but production of this too is growing. It is made mainly from the *gros* and *petit manseng* grapes for their rich fruit, with a little *courbu* sometimes giving the wine some extra zing.

A LOCAL GLOSSARY

The Basque language being an almost total mystery to outsiders, the following list of terms may be useful in interpreting wine labels and literature:

Izkiriota	*Gros manseng*
Izkiriota ttipia	*Petit manseng*
Zerratia	*Courbu*
Bordolesa Beltza	*Tannat*
Axeria	*Cabernet franc*
Axedria haundia	*Cabernet sauvignon*
Xuri	White
Gorri	Red
Argi	Pink
Ansa	The name of a small area of cultivation
Mignaberry	Old vines
Ilarria	Heathland
Lehengoä	From olden times
Haitza	Oak
Harri	Stone

Basque spellings are as quixotic as the people themselves and can vary quite a lot.

IROULÉGUY PRODUCERS

LES VIGNERONS DU PAYS BASQUE
64430 Saint-Etienne-de-Baïgorry
Tel: 05-59-37-41-33 Fax: 05-59-37-47-76
Email: irouleguy@hotmail.com
www.cave-irouleguy.com

In South-West France it has so often been the cooperative movement which has launched the renaissance of dormant wine-making areas. The *Cave* at Irouléguy is no exception. Founded in 1952, its pioneers constructed a fine *chais* and tasting room in the following few years. Although it boasts 50 or so members, a mere 18 of them account for 80% of the production. The average area of vines belonging to the others is less than one hectare each. Its founding director, Michel de Berguignan, is today president of the *syndicat* of growers, his executive successor being Xavier Pierre. The *Cave* is responsible for about two-thirds of the total production of Irouléguy.

In recent years substantial investment by the *Cave* has yielded spectacular results. The large older tanks have been replaced by smaller ones, and new modern presses installed; there is temperature control throughout the *chais,* and a full-time oenologue is employed. They make a full range of wine. An inexpensive quaffable and very-good-value white is called **Andéréna** (*A/B), based on *gros manseng* (80%); pale yellow with greenish tinges, fresh and fruity on the palate, it is ideal with Basque shellfish. More ambitious is the **Xuri d'Ansa** (***B), its 30% *petit manseng* giving the wine extra richness, ripeness and roundness, with exotic fruits and flowers on the nose and elegance as well as fullness on the palate. This is one of the best of the irouléguy whites, and comparable in quality with the better dry jurançons.

Nearly half the output of the *Cave* is of *vin rosé*, perhaps not surprisingly following the huge popularity of nearby béarn not so many years back. The *Cave* makes two: **Argi d'Ansa** (*A), from a surprising 85% *tannat*, deep coral in colour, quite strong (13 degrees) and with a bouquet of strawberries and raspberries; and **Axeridoy** (*B), from 60% *cabernet sauvignon,* having rather more finesse and suggesting redcurrants. Both wines should be drunk within the year following the vintage.

Axeridoy (*B) is also the name of one of the reds, this time based on both *cabernets* with just 20% *tannat*. Here again the bouquet suggests red fruits with some spice. On the palate the wine shows quite good balance. Less ambitious is their **Prémia** (*A), round, fruity and reminiscent of cherries. One stage up from here is **Gorri d'Ansa** (*B), much darker in colour with about 55% *tannat*. The fruits here are black, and the wine has rich tannins to back up the spices.

None of the wines above has been aged in wood. **Domaine de Mignaberry** (**B), however, is, its 60% *tannat* and 30% *cabernet sauvignon* ensuring a good structure worthy of oak-ageing, which is well handled. The *soi-disant* top wine, called **Omenaldi** (C), gives more than a nod in the direction of Robert Parker. It has up to 85% *tannat* and is given up to six weeks' maceration before being transferred into oak barrels which are 90% new; the wine is left for

15 months before bottling. Perhaps the ten years' ageing which the *Cave* say will bring it to maturity will soften this monster? We shall see.

▌DOMAINE BORDATHIO

Pascale and Bixintzo Aphaule

64220 Jaxu

Tel and fax: 05-59-49-18-22

Here is a newcomer, although M. Aphaule has been making cider from his apple crop *en biologique* for many years. There are just two hectares of vines, all *tannat,* some of the vines being more than 50 years old. From these he makes just one wine from partly destalked grapes, which he ages in barrels 25 years old. No oaky flavours, just the use of casks as ideal containers for the maturing of wine with slow oxygenation. Aphaule was trained by Pascale Labasse in Jurançon and should know a thing or two about quality wine-making. His **Lur Umea** (**B), which means 'the newborn', is, not surprisingly, rather madiranlike, a little dumb on the nose but with enormous promise on the palate and with tannins which soften quite quickly. Not a typical irouléguy but none the worse for that. Clearly this is a domaine to follow.

▌DOMAINE BRANA

Jean and Martine Brana

BP 20, 64220 Saint-Jean-Pied-du-Port

Tel: 05-59-37-00-44 Fax: 05-59-37-14-28

Email: brana.etienne@wanadoo.fr

www.brana.fr

The Brana family were *négociants* in the wine trade as far back as 1897. They moved from Ustaritz to Saint-Jean in 1970. When his father died soon after, Etienne Brana faced the agonizing choice of becoming a professional saxophonist or going into the family business. Music lost out. In 1974 Etienne founded a distillery for making *eaux-de-vie* not only from grapes but from other fruits as well. He established a reputation in this field so successfully that the family brandies and liqueurs are held to this day to be among the best produced in France.

But Etienne also nursed a passion to be a wine-maker, something which soon infected his son Jean, one of whose early friends was Jean-Claude Berrouet, now famous as the wine-maker at Château Pétrus in Pomerol. They bought some ground on the side of the Arradoy mountain, now extended to 22 hectares with some more round the corner of the mountain where today Jean grows the grapes for his pink and white wines. The gradient of the slopes is at least 65%. Etienne visited the Valais in Switzerland to study the techniques of preparing and maintaining the soil for this kind of vineyard. He went to Marcillac too, where the gradients are similar. The site at Ispoure was perfect; with maximum exposure to the sun and views across to the Pyrenees, the grapes benefit from the soft southern wind blowing in the autumn from Spain, which disperses the morning mists and minimizes the risk of rot. Yields were tiny, not more than 12 hectolitres per hectare.

To crown this pioneering enterprise, the Branas built a splendid winery—no other word will do. Part of it is underground, built into the flank of the mountain. It was designed by the same architects who created Michel Guérard's installation at Tursan. Above the principal door is a Basque inscription which translates as 'Taste this good wine and you will have a good life'.

The first wines came on stream in 1989. Etienne lived but three years to enjoy the fruits of his hard work. Today Jean and Martine make and market wine of all three colours. There are at least three whites; they include **Ilori** (*B), roughly two-thirds *gros manseng* and one-third *petit courbu*, which is given a short preliminary maceration before pressing and not quite such a cold fermentation as **Domaine Brana Blanc** (**B), which has about 20% *petit manseng* for extra richness. Brana was largely responsible for the revival of white wine-making in Irouléguy. The **Harri Gorri Rosé** (**A) is three-quarters *cabernet franc* and has all the charm of red summer fruits.

Of the three reds, I liked the basic **Ohitza** (**A) best, not because it is spared oak, but because it has more *tannat* than the more ambitious **Harri Gorri Rouge** (**B), which remains in tank for its malo before being aged for a year in twice-used barrels; and **Domaine Brana Rouge** (**B), which is given some new wood on a five-year cycle. There will soon be an all-*cabernet franc* red in production to add to the present range.

Jean's friend Berrouet has planted a few vines of his own adjoining the Brana vineyards. Brana makes the wine. A white, **Herri-Mina** (**B), is bone dry and quite minerally but with good freshness and fruit too; it has quite a long finish, but despite its distinguished pedigree, it does not seem any better than the Branas' own whites. Berrouet also has some black grapes from which 2006 will have been the first vintage.

The Brana tasting rooms are, it should be noted, on the main road connecting Ispoure with Saint-Jean and not at the *chais*. Before leaving, try their aperitif **Txapa**, an infusion of herbs in wine, as well as their range of *eaux-de-vie,* in the making and selling of which Jean's sister Martine is the presiding genius.

▌ DOMAINE ABOTIA

Jean-Claude Errecart
64220 Ispoure
Tel: 05-59-37-03-99 Fax: 05-59-37-23-57
www.irouleguy-abotia.com

The empathy between the red sandstone of Ispoure and the *cabernet franc* grape is certainly reflected in the style of Brana's neighbour, former *coopérateur* Jean-Claude Errecart, whose rather smaller eight-hectare vineyard is to be found on the way up to the Brana eyrie close to Ispoure church. A maximum of 65% *tannat* and relatively short macerations of 12 days or so are the order of the day here, resulting in an **Abotia Rouge** (*A) which is lighter in style than most, but which Errecart thinks will keep well nevertheless. The oak calls for food to balance the strong vanilla flavours.

As at *chez* Brana, the harvesting here is all done by hand, and Errecart too went to Switzerland to find out how to create and look after terraces on steep gradients such as his. For his eight hectares, he needs 20 people for six days to pick the grapes. It is little wonder that irouléguy wines are not as cheap to buy as madiran, which is made from grapes grown on much more manageable terrain.

Errecart's red is not unlike a ripe claret, strong on black fruits with tea-like tannins, robust but elegant at the same time.

▌ DOMAINE MOURGUY

Florence and Pierre Mourguy
64220 Ispoure
Tel: 05-59-37-06-23
Email: domainemourguy@hotmail.com
www.domainemourguy.com

This brother-and-sister partnership inherited 10 hectares from their *coopérateur* father. Instead of splitting the domaine into unviable units, they decided to set up in partnership as independents, something which Florence always wanted to do. She has done *stages* with Laougué at Madiran and Dalle at Château de Campuget in the Costières de Nîmes. Florence looks after the *chais*, while Pierre runs the vineyard. They work *en douceur,* which means they avoid disturbing the wine as much as possible, by *pigeage* for example.

Their first vintage was 2003, and only the **rosé** (**A) was available when they launched the following year, the red not having been assembled let alone bottled. This good pink wine is one of the vinous kind, a good full colour, though not as dark as some, with good fruit and plenty of character.

Meanwhile the 2003 **rouge** (**B) has been marketed, and excellent it is. Lovely soft fruit, good acidity even in 2003, a year when it was difficult to achieve this kind of balance, soft tannins, all heralding a wine which you do not need to keep for years but which still has the characteristic Basque taste. They have quite an up-to-date *chais* with small stainless steel *cuves*, but they have kept two old-fashioned presses and even their grandfather's very ancient one. They are using barrels, but are determined not to develop a heavy oak style.

On his 10 hectares of vines, which immediately adjoin Berrouet's on the Arradoy, Pierre does two *tries* and picks by hand in small *cagettes*. He intends to dig up some old and unproductive vines and replant with *cabernet franc*, *de haut en bas* and not *en terrasse* as an experiment. Pierre and Florence are a serious-minded duo, who have already impacted on the local scene.

▌DOMAINE ETXEGARAYA
Marianne Hillau
64430 Saint-Etienne-de-Baïgorry
Tel and fax: 05-59-37-23-76

Joseph Hillau was tragically killed in a tractor accident early in 2006, having built a fine reputation for his excellent irouléguy. After years of switching from independence to membership in the *Coopérative* and back again, he had finally opted for independence in 1994 and had been making and bottling excellent wines ever since. His widow and his two daughters are carrying on the good work.

Of the nearly eight hectares there are no vine producing white grapes, though there has always been a fresh **rosé** (*B) in which raspberries are suggested by the colour in the glass and on the nose and palate too. There were two reds, the first from 60% *tannat* and 40% *cabernet franc* called simply **Rouge Etxegaraya** (**B), an open, inviting style of wine with plenty of red fruits and spices, and the **Rouge Cuvée Lehengoa** (**B), containing 80% *tannat* from vines said to be more than 100 years old. If this claim is true, the vines may well be pre-phylloxera, because that disease did not arrive here until 1912. It also would suggest that the *tannat* grape is not, as claimed by Brana, all that recent an introduction into the region. In any event, this wine had fairly stiff tannins but masses of fruit to balance, some roundness as well on the palate, and the wine was always the better for keeping a few years. Neither of these reds was ever aged in anything but old wood or in tank.

▌DOMAINE ILARRIA
Peio Espil
64220 Irouléguy
Tel: 05-59-37-23-38

Until 1990 Peio (Pierre in French) was one of only two independent irouléguy producers. He has a particularly attractive house in the centre of Irouléguy village. The front door opens directly to a large ground-floor open-plan space, which serves partly as a tasting room. An old pony-trap furnishes one of the corners, while the long refectory table used to be the centre of family life for 13 hungry eaters. Peio has but eight hectares, all of them nowadays organically farmed as is so often the case with the irouléguy independents, and part of the vineyard is on the site of the old priory which once belonged to the monks of Roncevaux. He has no ambitions to extend the vineyard much, though he would like to grow a little *petit manseng*, being fully aware of the potential of this grape to produce fabulous sweet white wines.

The domaine has been in the ownership of Peio's relations for hundreds of years, and they have all been devoted to Basque tradition. The family still speak the strange language among themselves at home. Peio has some very old vintages of Irouléguy tucked away and he is proud of the longevity of the local wine. He told me that some centenarian bottles were found in the cellar of President Poincaré after the latter's death.

Apart from a little *cabernet sauvignon*, Peio's vines are divided equally between *tannat* and *cabernet franc*. He gives the former 15 days in tank and the latter 20. Peio prefers to plant up and down the gradient of the hill (*de haut en bas*) rather than on terraces, the maintenance of which he believes disturbs the soil too much. Both his red wines (he makes some rosé too) are robust and quite austere when they are young, the **entrée de gamme** (**B) rather less so than the **Cuvée Bixintzo** (***B), which is the Basque name for Saint Vincent, the patron saint of *vignerons*. The latter wine is pure *tannat*, rather after the style of the more macho madiran producers, by whom he is much admired. Peio ages his wines for six months in tank before transferring them to barrels, some newer than others, where they will remain for 18 months. They

need at least four years to shed their purple colour, though they remain dark and dense as they age.

▌ DOMAINE ARRETXEA
Michel Riouspeyrous
64220 Irouléguy
Tel and fax: 05-59-37-33-67

Michel and his wife, Thérèse, near neighbours of Peio Espil, took over this small domaine from Michel's father in 1989. Previously the grapes had gone to the *Coopérative,* but Michel was determined to make his own wine. He replanted much of the vineyard, particularly the terraces on the higher ground. At the same time he built his own *chais*.

Today there are eight hectares on the slopes of the Jarra mountain, all cultivated to biodynamic standards, without fertilizers other than sheep manure and vegetal concoctions of Michel's own making, fenugreek, nettles, willow-bark, bracken, peppers and horsetail being just some of the ingredients. Only copper and sulphur are used as a defence against rot and disease. The vines are sheltered by the mountain from the north wind and Atlantic humidity, while their south-facing exposure

guarantees the optimum benefit from the warm autumn winds coming from Spain. The soil is largely red sandstone with some schist, the *terroir* yielding calcium, magnesium, potassium, iron and manganese. Together these account for the very particular style of Michel's wines; sometimes they have a hint of astringency which is not at all disagreeable and which makes one yearn for another glass. None of his wines, except occasionally part of his white and pink, is filtered or fined.

Vinification proceeds after destalking, but with no further crushing, in small steel tanks, which are fed by gravity without pumping. The **rosé** (**B) is pressed directly rather than *saigné*, intended to accompany food rather than as a thirst-quenching aperitif. The bouquet is fresh, curranty with cherries. The cool fruit carries through on the palate to give a lively wine which keeps surprisingly well.

Michel's **white** (***C), 60% *gros manseng* and 40% *petit* with just a touch of *courbu,* is a surprisingly original wine, dry but quite exotic, on a par in terms of quality with the reds which have really made his reputation. The wine has a great deal of *gras*. In 2004, a particularly fine year for whites in this south-western corner of the country, it exceeded the statutory limit for residual sugar by just 0.002 degrees, so the wine was refused its *agrément*. As a gesture of defiance, Michel and Thérèse christened it 'Désagrément' and labelled it as *vin de table*.

The first of the reds, which simply bears the domaine's name, **Arretxea Rouge** (***B), is described by Michel as *style primeur*, but this hardly does justice to its powerful fruits, with even a hint of bitter cherries on the nose. Supple but at the same time well backed up by tannins, it needs three or four years to come to its best, though it can be drunk young. Then there is the **Cuvée Haitza** (***C), from grapes (80% *tannat*) grown in the best parcels, which even those who baulk at the use of oak will unhesitatingly place in the same top league, a wine which has established Michel and Thérèse as the cult-growers in Irouléguy. The wood is scarcely discernible apart from the richness and complexity which it adds to the wine. This is incidentally the only wine to which they accord wooden barrels. It will be at its best between seven and 10 years after the vintage.

▌**DOMAINE AMEZTIA**
Jean-Louis Costéra
Germieta, 64430 Saint-Etienne-de-Baïgorry
Tel and fax: 05-59-37-93-68
Mobile: 06-83-23-19-70
Email: ameztia@wanadoo.fr

Until recently Jean-Louis's principal revenue came from raising sheep, whose milk went into the making of the delicious cheese of Ossau-Iraty. Today he has not only joined the small ranks of producers of irouléguy, but is already producing a red of such quality as to ensure him a place at the top of the tree. But he is still for some of his time a shepherd, with pastures up in the hills and a dog of supreme intelligence as well as great charm.

Germieta is on the south flank of the valley, but Jean-Louis's vines are on an opposite slope, all south-facing. He started off with only three hectares, but he planted a further two (nearly) in April 2004 and has some more in hand. His total plantings will cover 6.5 hectares, but it will be some time before the new plantings produce grapes to the same standard as his original vines, some of which are 40 years old. Plans include the planting of *gros* and *petit manseng* to make some whites.

Jean-Louis is almost self-taught but acknowledges great debts to Alain Bortolussi (Château Viella in Madiran) and to Michel Riouspeyrous, his neighbour across the valley. He spent some time learning from both of them. His first vintage was his 2001, which he started to market in 2003 with such success that his wine features on the wine list of the best local restaurants, including the popular Hôtel Arcé in Saint-Etienne itself. Not the least of its advantages is an eye-catching label in the contemporary style, the top of which is cut to show the gradient of his wine terraces.

To help his cash flow, as well as to meet an almost insatiable demand for the fashionable pink wines, Jean-Louis makes a **rosé** (**A) as good as any you will find locally, which has 45% of each of the two *cabernets* and thus less *tannat* than his **red** (**B), which averages about two-thirds *tannat*. He has learnt from his mentors the virtues of *vendanges vertes* and the need to remove surplus leaves in summer, as well as the benefits of using small containers for harvesting. His yields are on the low side too, never more than 30 hl/ha. The grapes are fermented in tank where they spend about 30 days, each variety being vinified separately. They will have two *pigeages* and a *délestage* as well as the usual pumpings-over. The wine is left to undergo its malolactic fermentation in tank before one-third of the *tannat* is transferred to barrels, where it will be aged for up to a year. The *assemblage* will bring all together for three months before bottling.

Jean-Louis is careful not to exaggerate the Irouléguy style. He is careful too with his extractions and skilful in his use of wood. Plans include the making of a special *cuvée,* perhaps to be called 'Artzaina', the Basque for shepherd. His wines should have a great future.

JURANÇON

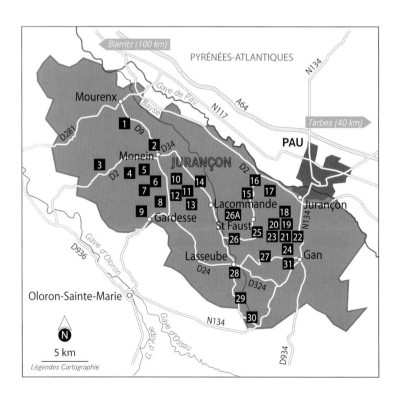

PYRÉNÉES-ATLANTIQUES

Biarritz (100 km)

N134

Mourenx

Gave de Pau

N117   A64

Tarbes (40 km)

PAU

D281   D9

1

2 D34

Monein

JURANÇON

D2

3

4 **5**

D2

10   **14**

16

6

7 **11**

12

15   **17**

8

13

Lacommande

Jurançon

9

Gardesse

26A

18

N134

St Faust

20 **19**

26   **25**

23 **21** **22**

Gave d'Oloron

D936

27

24

Lasseube

28

Gan

31

D24

D324

29

Oloron-Sainte-Marie

N134

30

G. d'Aspe

Gave d'Ossau

D934

N

5 km

Légendes Cartographie

AREA OF AOC: selected parcels in communes of Abos, Arbus, Artiguelouve, Aubertin, Bosdarros, Cardesse, Cuqueron, Estialescq, Gan, Gelos, Haut de Bosdarros, Jurançon, Lacommande, Lahourcade, Laroin, Lasseube , Lasseubetat, Lucq-de-Béarn, Mazères-Lezons, Monein, Narcastet, Parbayse, Rontignon, Saint-Faust and Uzos.

WHITE WINES ONLY: two appellations: jurançon and jurançon sec.
Description 'vendanges tardives' limited to wines deriving from gros manseng and petit manseng and subject to two jury tastings and from grapes picked not earlier than five weeks following the beginning of the jurançon harvest.
GRAPE VARIETIES: gros manseng, petit manseng, petit courbu, lauzet and camarelet (the last two being rarely found and not permitted to exceed together or singly 15% in any one wine).
MAXIMUM YIELD: 40 hl/ha (moëlleux), 65 hl/ha (sec).

PLANTING DENSITY: **2.8 metres between rows maximum (except on terraces), 1.3 metres between plants.**
AREA UNDER VINE: **820 hectares.**
HARVESTING BY HAND OBLIGATORY.
ANNUAL PRODUCTION: **55,000 hectolitres (60% sweet, 40% dry).**
MINIMUM ALCOHOL CONTENT: **11% (sec), 12.5% (moëlleux)**
RESIDUAL SUGAR: **4 grams per litre max. (sec), 35 grams per litre min. (moëlleux).**

'Bi dou rey, rey dous bis' (wine of kings, king of wines): so goes the local slogan and football song. The future King Henry IV of France, whose lips are said to have been moistened at birth with the good wine of Jurançon, bequeathed to the advertising agents of the next millennium a powerful marketing story. But it was his grandfather Henri d'Albret, king of Navarre, who had already put the wines of Jurançon on the map some years earlier when he left Paris to establish his own court at Pau. D'Albret gave a lead by planting a substantial vineyard himself, and his courtiers followed the royal example. As Pau became a rich and prosperous city with a new merchant class, the ownership of vines became an important status symbol; and so the Jurançon vineyard multiplied in size and renown. It was this period which saw the reputation of Jurançon made, a fame which survived the little-publicized abandonment of Pau by Henri IV once he became king of France in 1598. He frequently sent home demands for hams and cheeses from the region, but never the wines, perhaps because his mother had allowed the vineyard to revert to nature.

The earlier history of jurançon is, like the Pyrenees in the distance, often shrouded in mist. Thousands of years before Henri d'Albret came to Pau, the country between the mountains and the Gave de Pau (rivers are called *gaves* in Béarn) was covered in forest, wonderful hunting country for wild boar and deer. The Château de Rousse, today a well-known vineyard, was once the site of a hunting lodge used by Henri IV himself. But before him, little of any certainty is known. Mosaics from buried Roman villas contain vinous motifs, but such motifs were commonplace in Roman culture and prove little. More certain is that the church at Lacommande was a resting place for pilgrims to Saint-Jacques-de-Compostelle.

In the 13th century the rulers of Béarn had introduced the concept of 'cru', based on the value of the parcels of vine. This was a first attempt at wine classification in France. Henri d'Albret therefore must have planted his vines with every expectation that they would produce good-quality wine.

Until the late 19th century, the rich burghers of Pau had their vineyards just across the *gave* on ground which has today become a virtual suburb of Pau and has arrogated to itself the name of Jurançon. The vines here have all but disappeared, the combined result of the phylloxera and the greed of property-developers; in the town of Jurançon itself and to the east of the main road south to Gan there is no commercially worked vineyard. West of the highway, on the south-facing slopes of successive ridges running in a south-east to north-west direction, are most of the present-day vines, while others extend west and south of Gan into the foothills of the Pyrenees themselves.

TERROIR

Not even the panorama from the Boulevard des Pyrénées in Pau with its romantic views across to the snow-capped mountains gives any hint that there are vineyards just a few miles away. They are totally invisible; indeed, it is easy to go through the whole of the Jurançon district without actually seeing any vines at all. This is because the vineyards are scattered over a wide area and are mostly to be found on steeply sloping ground, often away from the heavily wooded roads.

For us today it is impossible to imagine the effect of the sudden eruption from Earth's centre of the Pyrenean mountain chain, causing as it did a geological upheaval which is fundamental to the landscape. On many varieties of bedrock, successive erosions have created soils in which stones of all sorts are mixed in with clay, and everywhere there are round pebbles the size of cricket balls embedded in the soil. Thus the nature of the *terroir* tends to change as you pass from one ridge and valley to the next. For this reason, and also because visitors to the region will find it impossible to cross from one of the vine-ridges to the next, but must travel by one of the main roads round either end if they wish to go either east or west, it is convenient to divide Jurançon into four areas, corresponding with different *terroirs*.

Furthest to the west and a good half-hour's drive out of Pau, Monein is the centre of what is today the most important area of production. The land is much more gentle and pastoral here. Varied crops apart from the vine are possible, and many growers have only small holdings of vines, preferring to hedge their bets in the familiar pattern of polyculture. The relatively moist climate ensures good grazing for cattle too. It is not surprising that so many of the members of the *Coopérative* at Gan come from the Monein area, growers for whom it is not worth their while to create wine-making facilities of their own.

Monein is a rather sprawling wine region, stretching from Cardesse in the south almost as far as the gas fields of Mourenx and Lacq to the north. From the centre of the village of Monein itself, roads reach out like spiders' legs to distinct *quartiers*, which separate the more remote growers from each other. It used to be thought that this *terroir* was inferior to the others further east, but pioneers like Alfred Barrère and later Georges Bru-Baché showed how false this was. They helped to keep jurançon alive during the difficult post-phylloxera period, establishing Monein as the *terroir* from which some of the finest and most elegant jurançons come.

The lower ground in the valleys is not suitable for vine-growing, and some vineyards there were declassified in 2001. On the middle slopes the clay is mixed with crushed particles of various minerals and the ubiquitous *galets*, which combine to form a soil which is not too rich, fairly well drained but retaining moisture well in a hot summer. Higher up, thick coverings of *galets* make for a more arid terrain, ideal for the production of low yields from late-maturing grapes. The climate at Monein is also milder than elsewhere in the Jurançonnais, because the altitude is lower. Grapes ripen here two or three weeks earlier than they do in vineyards further east, which are on much higher ground.

Over the hills east of Monein the village of Lacommande, sadly decaying but housing the Commanderie des Vins du Jurançon as well as the church much frequented by the Compostelle pilgrims, leads across its stream to a complete change in *terroir*. Here begins the so-called *poudingue,* a cement-like crushed chalk mixed with *galets* which forms the subsoil right through to the east of the appellation. On top of this is clay mixed with chalk, crushed pebbles and more big *galets*. You find these huge pebbles everywhere, washed down from the mountains millions of years ago. The growers here at Aubertin and Saint-Faust think their *terroir* is distinct from that further east at La Chapelle de Rousse, which has the same *poudingue* base, but the distinction is not nearly as noticeable as at Monein.

La Chapelle de Rousse takes its name from a chapel on the crest of a ridge which runs almost from Jurançon itself to the town of Gan further south. The terrain here has sometimes been sculpted by nature into amphitheatres called *conques* (literally, 'sea-shells'), where growers are obliged because of the steepness of the slopes to grow their vines on terraces. This kind of cultivation lends itself well to *passerillage* because it ensures maximum exposure to the sun, which at the important late-ripening season is low in the sky. The wines here are said to be more minerally and lively, to have what the French call *toupet*, real nerve.

At the southernmost part of the appellation, the *terroir* changes yet again. The subsoil is *flysch*, a sediment left behind during the formation of the mountain chain in alternating layers, as if streams had run over the land one after another: chalk, schist, and sandstone in separate strata, each compacted so as to form a *millefeuille* of soft and hard rock. The long-term effect of frost and vegetation causes these layers to fragment, leaving a *terroir* which is poor but well drained and easy to work. This type of soil makes for fruitiness in the wines, accentuated by the late maturing of the grapes at this southern altitude, where the nights are much cooler than in the other *terroirs*.

CLIMATE

Another factor determining the character of jurançon wines is the unusual climate. Growers will claim that there are in fact any number of micro-climates. Overall, the annual rainfall is higher than in other southern vineyards, although here and at Irouléguy the vines are grown in a landscape where the surrounding countryside gets more rain than the vineyards themselves. The spring and early summer are wet, allowing the water table to store up supplies and so help the vines through periods of drought. From the flowering season onwards the weather is usually warmer and drier, though there is danger of hail and frost far into the early summer. The autumn continues warm, and the early winter is sunny and mild. The wind from over the Pyrenees has the same effect as the *foehn* in Switzerland or the *vent d'autan* in Gaillac. In the best vintage-years the grapes can be left on the vine until Christmas or beyond, some growers today picking the last of their crop as late as mid-January in the following year if weather permits.

THE GRAPE VARIETIES

The *terroir* and climate have determined the choice of grape varieties. The heavier than usual rainfall and the more than usually impermeable soil call for plants which can withstand more humidity underground than most. The Indian summers also suit *cépages* which mature late. The dry ripening season also means that there are no mists or humid weather to encourage botrytis, so grapes with thick skins have the advantage of remaining entire during late ripening.

The *manseng* varieties fit the bill admirably. Historically it is likely that the *petit manseng* is a development of the *gros*. They look exactly alike except that, as their names suggest, the bunches and the individual grapes of the *gros manseng* are bigger than those of the *petit*. The *gros manseng* is historically the principal grape variety of jurançon, but with the spread of ultra-sweet wines in recent years, the *petit manseng* has come into its own. It would be an over-simplification to say that the *gros manseng* is better suited to drier wines and the *petit manseng* to the sweeter style. In practice one finds wholly sweet wines made from the *gros*, and some dry wines made wholly or in part from the *petit*. The *gros manseng*, if left long enough on the vine (as at Château Jolys, for example), can yield a fully *vendanges tardives* kind of wine, while Henri Ramonteu makes one of his finest dry wines wholly from early-picked *petit manseng*.

The picking season may extend over four months, so the range of bouquets and flavours which can be obtained from these grapes seems never-ending. When picked early, there is an apple-and-pears aroma which is unmissable, lemons and grapefruit also being sometimes prominent. Mid-season pickings yield wines which will develop notes of apricot, almonds, figs, mandarines and dried fruit, while the latest-picked grapes will give the richest juice, recalling honey, mangoes, guavas and caramel.

Apart from the *manseng* varieties, there is the *petit courbu*, sometimes called just *courbu*, a grape which many growers love to hate, because it matures much earlier than the *mansengs* and so complicates the vineyard cycle; it is also fragile, being liable to disease in the spring and rot in wet weather. Some *vignerons*, however, value it for its vivacity, which helps to counteract the sweetness of the *manseng* wines.

Two near-rarities complete the range. *Camaralet* is still occasionally to be found, for example at Domaine Nigri, where it is prized for its spicy character, a good partner for the *gros manseng* in dry wines. Other growers are thinking of experimenting with it, but as of 2006 there was little evidence on the ground of their having done so. *Lauzet* is the other curiosity, hardly ever seen, though it is thought to add minerality to both dry and sweet wines. It is also the only grape in the region which allows the development of *pourriture noble*, unique in *passerillage* country.

Because of the danger of spring frosts, all the vines in this region are grown high off the ground, *en hautain* as they say, as in the Madirannais. You will find no growth whatever for the first 70 centimetres or so above the ground. Because the vegetation of the *manseng* varieties is extremely rampant, and it is necessary to preserve this in order to feed the underground root system, the vine rows are usually a full 2.5 metres apart, roughly the distance to which some of the plants climb. This is the case even where the vines are planted in conventional rows rather than in terraces, where obviously the distance between rows must be greater in order to support the structure of the terraces themselves against erosion. The vines also need this much space between rows so as to allow the sun, much lower in the sky during the autumn ripening season, to get through to the grapes.

THE JURANÇON STYLE

Although there are two kinds of wine, *sec* and *moëlleux*, the styles of each are surprisingly homogeneous throughout the region despite the pronounced differences in *terroir*. Dry jurançon is regarded by some as a heresy. Traditionally the wine had always been more or less sweet, according to the climatic conditions of the vintage. Some growers, including the late Didier Daguenau, consider that neither of the two *manseng* grapes is suited to making a dry wine and it is a distortion of their nature to try and do so. The dry style emerged because of the switch in consumer taste away from sweet wines during the 1960's and 70's; sweet wines required *tries successives,* which were tiresome for polycultural growers if the maize harvest was ready and waiting to be picked; also the dry style was quick maturing and the producers, especially the *Coopérative,* which commands two-thirds of the market, could turn it round faster. Concentration on making a dry wine also avoided the potential risk in leaving the harvesting of the grapes until late autumn. Jurançon sec was granted its own appellation in 1975. It represents about two-thirds of the production of the *Coopérative*, but on average only about a third of that of the average independent grower.

Wines of each style can range from the basic and simple to the ultra-sophisticated. Dry jurançon can be fresh and fruity, to drink within the year, or it can be more structured. It can also be matured, even fermented in barrel, when it will offer great ageing potential, deep concentration and a complex variety of aromas.

A basic dry jurançon will have quite a special body and hints often of citrus fruits. It will be lively and refreshing, an ideal partner for *fruits de mer*. Older dry jurançon will acquire nutty overtones, a certain richness though remaining completely dry, perhaps hints of spice and dried fruits. Those raised in barrel will be more complex still, displaying vanilla and ripe exotic fruits.

The more traditional sweet jurançon can range from a basic *demi-sec* to the ultra-sweet, the *entrée-de-gamme* wines being perfect as an aperitif or as an accompaniment to fish or white meat cooked in sauce. Still reasonably light in texture, they will be easy to follow with a red wine during the rest of a meal, hence they are perfect with foie gras served as an entrée; too sweet a wine would unbalance the choice of a red wine to drink with the rest of the meal. The range gets sweeter and sweeter the later the grapes are picked. A middle-of-the-road wine, from grapes picked say in mid-November, would be lovely with blue cheeses or the hard ewes' milk cheese from the Pyrenees, or with patisseries or fruit-based desserts. The *vendanges tardives* style is best enjoyed on its own without food. An old jurançon *doux* will have lost some of its sugar, but will have gained a complexity and a variety of perfectly blended aromas which will be lacking in the younger wine. The finest vintage wines sometimes develop an unmistakeable aroma of black truffles.

The unique factor of all sweet jurançon wines is that they never cloy because of the element of acidity in the wines both young and old. They remain fresh and vital, and this is what distinguishes them from the other great *liquoreux* of France, where the accent is more on honeyed rich sweetness. Pierre-Yves Latrille told me that, with most grape varieties, there comes an ideal harvesting moment when the rise in sugar is balanced by a fall in acidity and that beyond this point other sweet wines can start to become heavy and unbalanced. With the *manseng* grapes, he maintains that the acidity will fall very little after that moment, which means that the grapes can be left to ripen further without fear that the sugar they produce will become cloying.

Would-be buyers of jurançon should note that if a bottle is labelled simply *jurançon,* it will be *moëlleux*; it cannot be dry because it must by law retain a substantial amount of residual sugar. Dry jurançon must be labelled *jurançon sec,* and may not contain more than a small maximum of unfermented sugar. The two wines are regarded as quite distinct from each other.

LA CAVE COOPÉRATIVE

The phylloxera came later to Jurançon than to most other vineyards in France, its full effect not being felt until the early years of the 20th century. It was just as devastating as elsewhere, although there are still a few vines surviving which were not killed off by the plague. Only a small band of determined growers kept up the standards of their forebears, most of their colleagues either giving up altogether or making an inferior type of wine. Sometimes they replanted with hybrid varieties, or they openly used industrial sugar to beef up the sweetness of rather flaccid juice. Most of the resulting product was sold off *en négoce*, and few growers practised the old-style *passerillage*.

Nevertheless, no doubt because of its long historical reputation, Jurançon was one of the first wine-growing areas in France to be granted AOC status, in 1936 and for its sweet wines only, at the time there being no such thing as dry jurançon. As in many other appellations the modern commercial revival was kick-started by the formation of the *cave coopérative* at Gan in 1949 under the stimulus of a man called Frédéric Miramon, following the example of Henri Meyer at Bellocq. With its impressive wine-making facilities and dazzling storage and display premises at Gan, this *cave* has become one of the most important in the South-West, its wines, particularly the dry ones, reaching far-flung export markets. They make a most impressive range of wines.

Today the *Cave* has around 272 members. The 550 hectares of Jurançon AOC vines they control include a handful of private domaines which the *Cave* either owns or runs itself, so the average holding of each *coopérateur* must be rather less than two hectares. The majority come from the Monein and Lasseube sectors.

PRODUCERS OF JURANÇON

■ **LA CAVE DES PRODUCTEURS DE JURANÇON**
53 Avenue Henri IV, 64290 Gan
Tel: 05-59-21-57-03 Fax: 05-59-21-72-06
cave@cavedejurancon.com
www.cavedejurancon.com

The *Cave*'s best-selling lines, just two out of a huge and ever-changing number, are both from *gros manseng*: **Grain Sauvage** (*A), which is dry, and **L'Apéritif Henri IV** (*A), which is *moëlleux* and from a second *trie* of the same vines made three weeks after the first. These are both excellent in their class and extremely good values for the money. Other rather more personalized wines in the dry category include the **Château de Navailles Sec** (*A), quite exotic and an interesting example of a dry wine wholly from *petit manseng*; and **Peyre d'Or** (**B), a step up in character as well as quality, a wine quite capable of holding its own with many dry whites produced by top independent growers. Depending on the vintage it can have quite a honeyed character suggesting some Caribbean fruits, while remaining completely dry.

Of the sweet wines, try the **Château de Navailles** (*B), raised in oak and having quite a roasted coffee style, or perhaps the **Château Les Astous** (*B), from a handsome domaine halfway out from Pau on the road to Gan. This property is also the source of a **sec** (*A), made entirely from *petit manseng* and accordingly somewhat richer in style than one might expect from a dry jurançon. There is also a *vendanges tardives* wine called **La Croix Du Prince** (**C), a good-value introduction to this technicolour style.

The *Cave* makes a small quantity of unremarkable *rosé de béarn*, and sends the *cabernet franc* and *tannat* grapes for red wine to Bellocq to be vinified and aged there.

Alongside the *Cave* there are about 100 independent growers, some of whom sell their wines *en négoce*, while 60 or so of them bottle and market their own wines. The standard is uniformly high and it is really hard to find a poor example of jurançon.

NOTABLE INDEPENDENT GROWERS

MONEIN

■ **DOMAINE BELLEGARDE**
Pascal Labasse
Quartier Coos, 64360 Monein
Tel: 05-59-21-33-17 Fax: 05-59-21-44-40
Email: contact@domainebellegarde-
  jurancon.com
www.domainebellegarde-jurancon.com

The catastrophe of the phylloxera plague persuaded Pascal's ancestors to emigrate to the United States where they settled in New Orleans. Eventually his grandfather decided to come back to France where he bought 6.5 hectares of land which were to form the nucleus of today's Domaine Bellegarde. He farmed them for other crops as well as the grape, but by the time Pascal took over from his own father, he had converted the whole to a vineyard, and today it has been extended to 16 hectares, on which Pascal grows half as much again *petit manseng* as *gros*.

Pascal was one of the young innovators to emerge during the 1980's. His first vintage was 1984, and he immediately made a stir. He still makes the premium sweet wine which he named after his baby son in 1990. Thibault is now grown up and no doubt enjoying his father's christening present.

In his early days Pascal kept an open mind on the merit of ageing wine in new or newish wood, but today all his wines except his *entrée-de-gamme sec* are matured in barrels. One-third of the *barriques* are renewed each year. The house style tends towards finesse and delicacy rather than overstatement, although there is nothing restrained about his super-*cuvée* **Sélection DB** (***D), a pure *petit manseng* wine from grapes which are so shrunken that they yield a mere nine hectolitres per hectare. The bouquet sometimes suggesting black truffles, a feature of some of the best wines from this appellation, the wine explodes aromatically on the palate, calling up flavours of candied fruits, honey and apricots. The wine is made for a specialist market.

The high price is in inverse proportion to the quantities made, and it comes as no surprise to learn that this was the one wine from this property to receive praise from Robert Parker.

Other mortals in search of something to enjoy more often will be very happy with the two dry whites. The **Blanc Sec Tradition** (**B) is wholly from *gros manseng* and vinified and aged *en cuve*; vividly evoking grapefruit, wildflowers and peaches, it is a charmingly light and delicate sec. The **Cuvée Pierre Blanche** (**B) has many of the same characteristics, but, being largely from the *petit manseng* grape, it has more depth and complexity, though without any hint of sweetness.

There are two sweet jurançons to balance the secs. The **Moëlleux Tradition** (**B) is surprisingly lively, being from 60% *gros manseng*, the fruit nicely balancing the freshness. Vinified in tanks but aged in barrels, the wine shows great style, thanks to the 40% *petit manseng* in its make-up. Finally, the **Cuvée Thibault** (***B), wholly from *petit manseng* grapes which may be harvested late into November, has great depth of colour, aromas of oranges and lemons and candied fruits and an attractive smokiness. The beautiful balance suggests great ageing potential.

This domaine is one of the benchmarks from which to assess a jurançon wine, whether dry or sweet. Visitors should make a point of visiting Pascal's belvedere, which overlooks his *chais* and affords awe-inspiring views across the vines to the mountains.

▌ DOMAINE BORDENAVE

Gisèle Bordenave
Quartier Ucha, 64360 Monein
Tel: 05-59-21-34-83 Fax: 05-59-21-37-32
Email: domaine.bordenave@wanadoo.fr
www.domaine-bordenave.com

There is a confusing number of growers in Jurançon with the name Bordenave. They may or may not be related to each other, depending on whom you ask. *Bordenave* means 'new barn', which could explain the frequency with which the name occurs, but Gisèle does not need to rely on any family connection there might be with her namesakes.

Her earliest memories are of the family vineyard, framed in the majestic setting of the mountains and their snowy peaks. As a young girl she trotted after her parents through the vines and the cellar, fascinated even at that age by the magic world of wine. Later she learned that the enjoyment of wine was at once an art and a way of life, which sits well with her love of paintings and photography; she gets artist-friends to design and sign her labels. She has also created a little wine museum, which is a must for visitors. Gisèle is a delightful host, as well as being one of the region's most talented *vignerons*. She describes her work as a love affair with nature, whose whims you simply have to put up with.

Her vineyard and *chais,* whose history goes back to the 17th century, are three kilometres or so down a road which leads eastwards into the *quartier* of Monein called Ucha. She has gradually assumed the reins from her father, having entirely restructured the vineyard during the 1990's so that today only the *manseng* varieties are planted.

Her three dry white jurançons are all 100% *gros manseng* wines, given a preliminary skin contact before being fermented in stainless steel and aged for some months on the lees. Of the three grades, **Souvenirs d'Enfance** (**B) is fresh, powerful and elegant all at the same time, and tremendous value for the money as well, while **Terre de Mémoire** (**B) has more exotic fruits and weight, a sense of importance which suggests that it would benefit from a few years' keeping. **Les Copains d'Abord** (**B) is matured a little longer, aged partly in tank and partly in old barrels.

There is a range of no fewer than six *moëlleux* wines, of which the first three, all made from *gros manseng*, correspond to the three dry wines. **Harmonie** (**B), picked from the end of October through to the end of November, is a fine introduction to the range, a wine which will be offered to you as an aperitif in Pau's busiest bistro quite simply as *une Bordenave.* What better compliment to the wine-maker than that? **Terre de Mémoire** (**B) and **Les Copains d'Abord** (**B) follow the same ascending ladder as their dry namesakes, but of course from much later picked grapes.

The top three sweet wines are all made exclusively from *petit manseng.* In fact, it seems that Gisèle does not make any blend from the two varieties. **Cuvée des Dames** (**C), from vines yielding but 20 hectolitres per hectare, is raised in tank, spending one year on its lees. The lovely golden colour introduces pineapple, early summer flowers and spice on the bouquet, leading to honey and exotic fruits on the palate. With **Cuvée Savin** (***C) the yields are almost halved and the wine is fermented in barrel, the proportion of new wood being determined by the character of the vintage and the quality of the crop. Straw yellow in colour, the wine exhibits candied fruits, grilled almonds and a little oaky vanilla, although the wood is well absorbed and does not mask the fruit. With age the wine can develop hints of black truffle. Top-of-the-range **Cercle des Amis** (***D) is more exclusive still, 8 hl/ha being the average yield from very late picked fruit. The wine may well wait nearly four years before being bottled, after spending its life on its lees in barrels which are all new. An almost copper-coloured wine, with all the richness and exoticism one might expect from a top late-harvested jurançon.

▌ **DOMAINE BRU-BACHÉ**
Claude Loustalot
Rue Barada, 64360 Monein
Tel: 05-59-21-36-34 Fax: 05-59-21-32-67
Email: domaine.bru-bache@wanadoo.fr

Claude's uncle Georges Bru-Baché was of the time when today's stars were just beginners, and in many respects he showed them the way, bringing jurançon into the modern age by the adoption of burgundian techniques, including the introduction of *élevage* in new rather than old wood. A native of Monein, where he was born in 1933, Georges was for some years a polycultural farmer, the vines being but a small and dutiful part of the family domaine, more of a burden than a source of revenue. Most of the family income came from strawberries.

Georges died in 1992 and two years later Claude took over from Georges's heirs. The 10 hectares of vines overlook the huge church of Monein, with a fine panoramic view of the montains beyond. Like his uncle, Claude drew his inspiration from Burgundy, where he did a *stage* in Meursault before moving on to other wine-making areas for self-instruction. His *chais* is on the village street and his home close by. Visitors can easily feel that they are at the epicentre of this sector of jurançon.

The range of wines which he makes is much in line with that of his colleagues, two dry, representing about a third of his production, and four sweet. He grows only the two *manseng* grape varieties. His first **sec** (*A), made and aged in tank, has a certain richness deriving from six months spent on its lees, while the other, called **Cuvée des Casterasses Sec** (**B), named after a castle which once dominated the terraces here, benefits from barrel-ageing in casks which have already been used twice or three times, with regular *bâtonnage* for six months and regular racking thereafter. It is a complex and delicious wine which will benefit from keeping for several years, because the wood sometimes shows on the nose when the wine is young, though not on the palate.

The first of Claude's sweet wines, which I have a feeling he has more time for than his dry wines, is an orthodox **moëlleux** (**B), wholly from *gros manseng*, picked as the grapes are just beginning to shrivel. Ageing is in tank and the wine is bottled in the early summer following the vintage. This is a fine example of the basic style of sweet jurançon. The **Cuvée des Casterasses Doux** (**B) is three-quarters *petit manseng*, picked mid-November usually and fermented and aged in old barrels. It is much more ambitious. The wine has a certain

voluptuousness and concentration, redeemed from vulgarity by a superb balance of acidity with the sugar. One step further along the path of sweetness and sophistication is **Quintessence** (**C), all *petit manseng* vinified and aged in a mix of new and one-year-old barrels. This is fat and rich indeed, the presence of oak well held in check, a wine which Claude says will last 20 or 30 years. If this be the case, his **Éminence** (***D) must be destined for immortality, its *petit manseng* grapes picked sometimes as late as the middle of December, and fermented and aged in new oak for 18 months. The wine features the typically *jurançonnais* candied orange flavours, apricots and dried fruits, and is really best drunk on its own; at the price you can expect pure gold, and you get it.

▌ CLOS CANCAILLAU
Anne-Marie Barrère
64150 Lahourcade
Tel: 05-59-60-08-15 Fax: 05-59-60-07-38

Arriving at this dignified old house in the centre of the village, you may be greeted by three charming ladies, and if you ask which of them is Madame Barrère, they will reply in unison, 'We are all Madame Barrère'. As indeed they are, mother and daughters. The father, whose name was Alfred, was one of the longest-established growers in Jurançon, and he earned a formidable reputation for his *moëlleux* wine, which he called Cancaillau after the name of the parcel where the vines for it grew. The name is still preserved in the classic sweet wines of this property. It means, incidentally, *champ de caillou*, or 'field of pebbles'.

The *chais* adjoins the pretty *maison bourgeoise*, a town farmhouse which dates back to the 17th century. The equipment is housed just across the courtyard within the former barn, which is faced, like many buildings in the regions, with large round *galets*. There are three separate vineyards: the Cancaillau; the Clos de la Vierge, so called because of its proximity to a statue of the Virgin on the high ground beyond the village, where the grapes for the dry wines are grown on a rather pebbly soil; a few hectares at Cuqueron, some ways away to the east, the other side of Monein.

As so often, there are two jurançons secs. The one, called **Clos de la Vierge** (*A) after its parcel of vines, is wholly from *gros manseng* and matured in tank, a wine with aromas of flowers and acacia and a distinctly peachy character. The **Confidences du Clos** (*B) is fermented in all old barrels. The wine is given eight months in the oak on its lees. The nose is complex, and in the mouth the wine is round. The effect of the wood is not to add oaky flavours at all, but to make the wine seem less mineral than the inox version, but more spicy. It will improve with bottle age.

The sweet wines, which represent about two-thirds of the total production at this property, are three in number. First, a *cuvée* called simply **Cancaillau** (*B), made from the first picking of *gros manseng* and raised wholly in stainless steel, a delicious *entrée-de-gamme* medium-sweet wine, fruity and elegant, easy to drink and excellent as an aperitif. **Cancaillau Crême de Tête** (**B) is made from equal quantities of the two *manseng* varieties, the *gros* being the second picking about three weeks after the first. The wine is again raised in tank, is sweeter and more concentrated than the first *moëlleux,* but still has the indispensable freshness of a well-balanced jurançon. It manages to be both old-fashioned and modern at the same time.

Despite the united front of the three ladies, it is one of the daughters, Anne-Marie, who is in sole charge of the wine-making, and she has ensured that the family wines, for long regarded as ultra-traditional, have made the transition into the 21st century. She is careful about the use of new wood, but with her top *cuvée,* **Cancaillau Gourmandise** (**C), made wholly from the last picking of *petit manseng*, she makes a very fine sweet wine indeed, but free from exaggeration. The wine, like its dry counterpart, is vinified and aged in barrel for eight months.

▌**DOMAINE CAPDEVIELLE**
Didier Capdevielle
Quartier Coos
64360 Monein
Tel and fax: 05-59-21-30-25
Email: domaine.capdevielle@wanadoo.fr
www.domainecapdevielle.com

Casimir Capdevielle handed over the reins at what was then a very traditional property to his nephew Didier in 1995. It is one of the oldest domaines in Jurançon, having survived the lean years of the first half of the 20th century. Didier has basically continued his uncle's philosophy and methods, although he has doubled the vineyard slightly to cover its present total of 11 hectares. Didier is the sixth generation of Capdevielles to make wine here, but his uncle, though strictly speaking retired, still has much help to contribute, and likes to share in greeting visitors with his jovial laughter and raucous jokes.

Didier, like his uncle, believes in harvesting his grapes only from midday onwards; by that time any dew has been dried off them by the warm southern wind from Spain. The wines remain very traditional at this estate, reflecting the glow of the sunshine on the hillsides, the serious constancy of the family's work in the vineyard and their love of their *terroir.*

When he took over from his uncle, Didier built a new *chais* and an impressive landscaped terrace overlooking the countryside to the south-east. There is also a spanking new tasting room. Didier still has one hectare of *gros manseng* which predates the phylloxera and managed to survive, so those vines are not grafted. The **jurançon sec** (**A), all *gros manseng*, is a lively wine made in gleaming new stainless steel and aged there for a year on its lees, which give it exotic undertones as well as the usual citrus fruit character of dry jurançon. The first *moëlleux* is called **Vent du Sud** (***B); a fifth of the grapes only are *petit manseng,* which add a richness and structure to the vivacity of the juice from the *gros.* This provides a wonderful balance which makes this the most attractive wine from the property. Which is not to detract from the quality of the **Noblesse d'Automne** (**B), all *petit manseng*, vinified and aged in tank for three years, with pronounced flavours of preserved and very ripe fruits. There is an oaked version of this which Didier makes only in really good years, called **Rêve de Pyrène** (**C); it is given 10 months in barrel, the only wine of this property to be matured in wood.

One gets the feeling that Didier is only now finding his own feet. His talent is clear to see and the domaine surely has a bright future.

▪ DOMAINE CASTÉRA
Christian Lihour
Quartier Ucha, 64360 Monein
Tel: 05-59-21-34-98 Fax: 05-59-21-46-32
Email: christian.lihour @wanadoo.fr

Castéra itself goes back to the 18th century, but the Lihour family bought it as 'recently' as 1895. It is quite remotely situated, a few kilometres south-east of Monein, some way beyond Gisèle Bordenave's vines. The modesty with which it hides itself matches the reticence of the wines here and the discreet charm of their maker.

Christian's great-grandfather was a farmer devoted to polyculture, and it was only in the early 1990's that the stables were converted to a *chais* and Christian, who took over from his father in 1985, confined his energies exclusively to wine-making. He may miss the benefit of having his home-produced fertilizer from their cattle, but the wine does not seem to have suffered. Indeed, Christian has made this property into one of the stars of the appellation.

Christian's father had only six hectares of vines, all of them *gros manseng,* which for many years had been regarded as the basic *cépage* for jurançon. Christian maintains that *petit manseng* was mainly introduced to lend an extra dimension of quality to the top c*uvées* of jurançon. In the old days the two varieties would be grown intermingled with each other, *en foule*, and vinified together. Christian has acquired a further four hectares of land which he has planted exclusively with *petit manseng*, so that this variety now accounts for 60% of the vineyard, *gros manseng* the other 40%. Christian grows no other varieties.

The family always considered that *gros manseng* should be used entirely in the dry white wine of the house and also in the first of the sweet wines, only the top sweet *cuvée* being made wholly from *petit manseng*. Christian, having so much more *petit manseng* these days, makes his *entrée-de-gamme doux* from equal quantities of both. He has, however, continued to exercise the family's doubts about barrel-ageing by raising only the top *vin doux* in wood, and then with only part of the *assemblage.*

The general style of the wines at Castéra is one of delicacy and subtlety, without any effort to achieve technicolour sweetness for its own sake. The **jurançon sec** (***A), for example, is beautifully pale and translucent, lightish in the mouth but with exceptional length and excellent balance, even if, as in 2004, the bottled wine managed 14 degrees of alcohol by volume. This is textbook dry jurançon, which can rival the wines of any other domaine, and it is better value for the money than most. The first **doux** (**B) is equally good to look at, quite pale again and delicate rather than powerful, a delicious apéritif wine. **The Cuvée Privilège** (***B) is another matter, although its mixed *élevage*, partly in tank and partly in wood, continues the impression of elegance and finesse. It is rich but not exaggerated in style, and is particularly successful in lighter years such as 2002.

This is a domaine which has not attracted quite the attention it deserves, but nevertheless is much admired by true lovers of jurançon. The range of wines on offer may be small, but the quality is top class, rivalling many others which are no better but often more expensive.

▌DOMAINE CAUHAPÉ
Henri Ramonteu
64360 Monein
Tel: 05-59-21-33-02 Fax: 05-59-21-41-82
Email: contact@cauhape.com
www.cauhape.com

In the early 1980's many of the country people in the Béarn flocked to Lacq, where natural gas installations had recently been constructed. Ramonteu travelled against the tide, moving *from* Lacq to buy four hectares of vines on the western fringe of the Jurançon vineyards. The vines were in pitiful condition and were mostly nasty hybrid varieties, except for a few 90-year-old *gros manseng* plants. Saving these, Ramonteu dug up all the rest and replanted. He has also gradually increased his holding of vines to a present-day total of 40 hectares, which makes his the largest property in the appellation, recently overtaking the Latrilles' 36 hectares at Château Jolys.

Cauhapé is a few kilometres to the west of Monein, where the height of the vineyards above sea level is about half that of Jolys at La Chapelle de Rousse. The landscape is less hilly, and the slopes easier to work; indeed, at Cauhapé all the vines are grown in traditional rows, without the need for terracing. The *terroir* has a mixture of clay, crushed bits of quartz and round pebbles. Ramonteu has been to jurançon what Brumont has been to madiran. Apart from some vineyard training at Bordeaux, he is virtually self-taught. He shares Brumont's passion, has the same phenomenal energy, self-confidence, powers of persuasion and talent for marketing. He also enjoys the same kind of respect from colleagues, who may be tinged with jealousy and resentment at his success. He is also a magnificent wine-maker, his influence on the younger generation of jurançon makers being as important and profound as Brumont's in the Vic-Bilh.

His talent for self-promotion has gained him a reputation which puts his wines at the upper end of the market, his best *cuvées* selling for prices which transcend the position of this appellation generally. Nevertheless, his *entrée-de-gamme* wines not only sell well, but are affordable and offer fair value for the money. The dry **Chant des Vignes** (**B), for example, is made from *gros manseng* picked early in September before the grapes have fully ripened; the bouquet is fresh and powerful, with aromas of apple, peach and pears as well as citrus fruits and hints of something more exotic; on the palate the wine is clean and fresh, with good minerality and acidity. The **Sève d'Automne** (**C) is from grapes picked rather later and is fermented and aged in old barrels for eight months. Citrus fruits mingle with vanilla, butter and minerals on the nose, while in the mouth the wine is quite spicy. A third dry white, formerly called **Noblesse** (***D), and renamed **La Canopée**, is without doubt more ambitious, with a much smaller production and made from *passerille petit manseng*.

The first of the sweet wines is called **Ballet d'Octobre** (**C), from *gros manseng* grapes which Ramonteu planted himself: a delicate and elegant *moëlleux* recalling mangoes and passion fruit, with apricots and peaches on the palate, the whole backed by the typical jurançon minerality. **Symphonie de Novembre** (***D) is all *petit manseng,* fermented in new wood and aged there for 10 months before transfer to tank for further refinement; the wine is bottled two years after the first winter. **Noblesse du Temps** (***D) takes us into the realm of the ultra-sweet, with candied fruits, honey and hazelnuts featuring on the bouquet, medlars and fruit pickled in brandy on the palate. An extraordinary exotic wine. Not as exotic, though, as the two micro-*cuvées*, **Quintessence du Petit Manseng** (***D+), from yields of only 9 hectolitres per hectare and two years in new wood, let alone the **Folie de Janvier** (***D+), made only in the very best and driest winters from a tiny production of four hectolitres per hectare. No wonder the prices are stratospheric. These last two wines are in the style of *vendanges tardives* without being presented as such, and are surely best appreciated on their own without food. They seem made for the benefit of professional tasters rather than amateur wine-lovers. Extraordinary *tours de force,* perhaps somewhat over the top for all but a few devotees, they should be tried, even if only just once.

▌ DOMAINE NIGRI
Jean-Louis Lacoste
Candeloup, 64360 Monein
Tel: 05-59-21-42-01 Fax: 05-59-21-42-59
Email: domaine.nigri@wanadoo.fr

Jean Lacoste was for many years the archetypal traditional jurançon producer, who didn't want to know about skin contact, thermoregulation or new oak barrels. Nowadays he is more likely to be found enjoying his retirement by a comfortable fireside in the delightful family farmhouse a few kilometres due south of Monein. It is built round a courtyard, many of the old farm-buildings serving as *chais*, and one of the lintels proudly and authentically bearing the date 1625.

In 1993 Lacoste handed over the domaine to his son Jean-Louis, who had trained professionally as an oenologist and is very much of the new school of wine-makers. He is experimenting with specially commissioned 400-litre barrels and using *camaralet* and *lauzet* in his blends as well as the traditional *mansengs* and *petit courbu* grapes. Jean-Louis particularly likes the *camaralet* with *gros manseng*, a mix which he says frequently comes in top in blind tastings locally. He says it has good apple and pear qualities, is not too alcoholic or acidic, and gives a spicy character to the wines. From 2005 onwards he is using some *lauzet* in his sweet wines, because it gives minerality to balance the sugar.

Another novelty is a brand-new *chais de stockage* which he has built a few hundred yards away on the hillside overlooking the farm. I asked him why he had painted the timbers green and he explained that he had used the fungicide *bouillie bordelaise* and this was its natural colour: in commerce it is coloured blue artificially so that the spray stands out better against the green of the vines' foliage. Another novelty is the insulation in the roof: compacted duck feathers, which he says do not absorb humidity like fibre-glass.

The wines here are novel too. His first jurançon sec, **Le Domaine Nigri** (**A), is raised in steel. This is where you find his *camaralet* and some *lauzet* as well, in a wine for drinking young, to be enjoyed for its flowery and fruity character, with notes of acacia, honeysuckle and passionfruit. The sec **Réserve du Domaine Nigri** (**B) is altogether more complex, fermented as it is in barrel and aged there on its lees for the best part of a year. Although dry, the wine has some of the characteristics, derived no doubt from the wood, which you might find in a sweet jurançon, including dried fruits, orange peel and brioche; but the wine has splendid minerality, just perhaps a touch too much of the oak.

There are two sweet wines to match the dry; first the **Jurançon Domaine** (*B), quite barleysugary, but not too sweet and with nice acidity to balance the honey and candied fruits. **Réserve du Domaine Nigri** (***B) is in a different class, made expressly for lovers of the exotic rather than the discreet, but with terrific tropical fruits, especially mangoes and guavas on the palate.

I asked him whether, in this appellation which is devoted exclusively to *passerillage*, botrytis ever occurred. He told me that perhaps it did occasionally in a wet autumn, but that many growers in the region were so unaccustomed to it that they did not distinguish between the good *Botrytis cinerea* and the bad *pourriture grise*, so they would destroy any grapes affected by it! In Jurançon, rot is rot.

Jean-Louis is one of the few jurançon producers today to make a **red béarn** (*A) from just a few *tannat*, *cabernet* and *fer servadou* grapes, which he is reluctant to dig up. Good it is, too.

■ CLOS UROULAT

Charles and Marie Hours

Quartier Trouilh, 64360 Monein

Tel: 05-59-21-46-19 Fax: 05-59-21-46-90

Email: charleshours@wanadoo.fr

www.uroulat.com

Charles Hours bought this domaine in 1983, when there were only 3.5 hectares of vines. Today there are a little over 14 if you include a few hectares from which he buys the grapes from outsiders.

Hours started his life as a business administrator but soon decided to abandon that and take up wine-making. He already had two distant cousins in the Jurançon region, and their vineyards were not far away from Charles's present estate. To learn his new career, Hours went to study oenology at Talence before installing himself at Uroulat.

A visit here is always a joy. Good Béarnais that he is, Charles enjoys a chat; he says life is a bit lonely spending all one's day in the vines, so he likes to engage in lively conversation with potential clients in his tasting room. As a new arrival at a young age in an established appellation, he probably found it easier than an old-stager would have done to set up the first of the local *syndicats* of growers, leading the way by establishing in this very confusing countryside a system of signposts to vineyards without which a comprehensive tour would be infuriatingly impossible.

Charles Hours started off with rather more *petit courbu* in his vineyard than he has today. He has kept just a little to give finesse and vivacity to his **Cuvée Marie** (***B), one of the finest of all dry jurançons. It has a depth and richness uncommon in a dry wine. Apart from the *petit courbu*, this wine is 90% *gros manseng*. In the vineyard the vines are grown extremely high off the ground to protect against spring frosts; the vegetation can reach three metres in height. Early picking in mid-October allows generous yields of 50 hl/ha. Picking is by hand, of course; the bunches are not then destalked but pressed immediately, slowly and gently. The debris is then removed by gravity. Hours is not in favour of prior skin-contact because he says he prefers wines which do not show the hand of the wine-maker behind the wine. This explains why his wines show less evidence of being messed about with than those of some others.

His dry wine is fermented in barrel for 11 months, only a small percentage (about 10%) of the casks being new. In the glass, spring flowers and exotic fruits vie with the wood flavours, while on the palate the balance between acidity and weight of matter is perfectly calculated.

Just as there is only one dry jurançon, so there is only one *moëlleux*. But with wines of such excellence, who needs a multiplicity of *cuvées* to choose from? Hours's sweet **Uroulat** (***C) is wholly from *petit manseng*, the yield from the vines being somewhat lower than for his dry wine. The grapes are picked as late as Hours dares, and the wine is raised in barrel for 11 months. On average about a quarter of the barrels are new each year. The resulting wine is richly perfumed, though the presence of wood is very discreet. On the palate the wine has ample concentration, but the keynote is the finesse reflected in the elegant acidity. The wine has an amazingly long finish.

Hours speaks nostalgically of the late Madame Migné and her mythic Clos Joliette, where the wines were raised in very old barrels for 10 years before being bottled. He describes her as 'L'Arlésienne' of the appellation, meaning a character who made herself felt rather than heard in Jurançon. (In the play of that name, the eponymous heroine was the main character but never appeared on stage.) Hours was one of the fans in the queue to buy Clos Joliette when Madame Migné died, but he had to content himself with buying a few bottles of her wine, one of which he was generous enough to give me on my first visit to him in 1992. It was a 1974 sec and fabulous. Everyone still talks of this lady; evidently she is still L'Arlésienne of Jurançon. Will someone one day please undertake the rebuilding of her vineyard, today sadly abandoned?

GROWERS ON THE CENTRAL COTEAUX

■ LES JARDINS DE BABYLONE
Guy Pautrat and the heirs of Didier Daguenau
Chemin Cassioula, 64290 Aubertin

Another of the hopeful aspirants in the market for the famous Clos Joliette of Madame Migné was a young man from the Loire, Didier Daguenau, who created a big reputation for himself. Foiled by the refusal of Madame Migné's heirs to sell Clos Joliette, Didier had to wait a decade before he discovered in 2002 a small parcel of *petit manseng* grapes three kilometres south of the village of Aubertin and down a tiny road now signposted simply 'Babylone'. The vineyard is in a perfectly formed amphitheatre of its own with a dress-circle view of the mountains, and used to belong to a grower who sent his grapes to the *coopérative* at Gan. Daguenau could not believe his eyes when he first saw this gem, which he called a *vignoble de rêve*. With his typical dash, he bought it on sight and built himself a tiny *chais,* which houses in miniature the customary equipment for bottling and labelling and just a few oak barrels, three of them six hectolitres in size, the other four of them just under four.

In September 2008 Didier Daguenau died tragically in an aeroplane accident and the wine world went into mourning. As in his native Pouilly, his legacy was to turn upside down the work practices of Jurançon. Les Jardins de Babylon will from now on be run by his colleague Guy Pautrat, who will, it is hoped, produce a wine which does not seek the ultimate in sweetness, but instead a fine balance, subtle and elegant, a style doubtless influenced by Didier's work in the Loire.

The house style is not to leave the grapes on the vine until the last possible moment, nor to pick by *tries successives*, inasmuch as the vineyard is small enough to justify the picking of the grapes at one session. Harvesting can take place as early as October 20, while some other growers might be picking six weeks later. Didier Daguenau believed the tendency in recent years to try and beat sauternes and monbazillac at their own game was a mistake, just as he believed that the *gros manseng* grape is not really suited to making dry wine.

Madame Hégoburu (see p. 347) told me that

she thought her wine could hold its own against all comers in Jurançon, but that she had to make an exception in favour of Didier's. The **Cuvée Jardins de Babylone** (***D+) has a beautiful balance between acid and sweet fruits, grapefruits and oranges balanced by mangoes and quinces. The wine should keep forever. Delicate but long, subtle but rich, Daguenau's jurançon will be fascinating to taste down the years. It will also be interesting to see what his impact will be on the style of other producers' wines.

■ DOMAINE VIGNAU-LA-JUSCLE
Michel Valton
64290 Aubertin
Tel: 05-59-83-03-66 Fax: 05-59-83-03-71
Email: domaine-vignaulajuscle@vins-jurancon.com
www.vignaulajuscle.com

Michel Valton is almost as much an eccentric as Didier Daguenau. He and his wife both work full-time in the medical profession, but manage to find time to make wine in their tiny three-hectare vineyard, which is, like Didier's, lost in the depths of the Aubertin countryside. If you express surprise at the small size of his domaine, Michel will remind you that, in the old days, one hectare was considered a lot of vines.

It would be condescending to suggest that Valton makes wine for a hobby, because he is in fact very professional about what he is doing. Having such a small vineyard, he has no difficulty in selling his wine. He has, rather to his surprise, established a certain reputation and buzz in the media for the quality of his product. Now fully converted to organic production, he uses no artifical yeasts, nor any mechanical pumping. He makes just the one jurançon, and that is all from *petit manseng*, a *vendange tardive* at that. He is interested only in making wine in that style. To protect his shrivelling grapes, loaded with sugar, from thrushes, he completely covers his vines in netting for the last few weeks of the ripening season. His three hectares require 25 kilometres of net.

Michel is a fourth-generation Béarnais, and he and his wife moved here in 1996. They planted all their vines themselves, using riparia *porte-greffes*. He says he can get as much as 20 hectolitres per hectare in a good year, but in 2005 he suffered badly from hail, so the yield was only six. For many this would have been a complete disaster, but Michel was able to take it in his stride. Lucky man indeed.

Vendanges tardives for Michel involves replacing one-third of his barrels each year, although he vinifies part of the crop in tanks. The rest is fermented in the wood and left on its lees for 18 months. He explained to me that, in order to qualify for the right to use the expression *vendange tardive* on the label, you have to declare your intention in advance to INAO and you cannot pick the grapes until at least five weeks after the *ban de vendange* has been announced. In practice he picks a lot later than the earliest legal date, usually in mid-December, though only at weekends. To get the *agrément*, that is to say the right to use the appellation on the label, he has to undergo two special tastings by independent experts.

As might be expected, the wine **Vignau-la-Juscle** (**C) is extremely rich, a completely successful realization of Michel's intentions, but he still manages to retain the essential freshness which is the hallmark of the *petit manseng* grape, even when it has been reduced almost to the state of a sultana. His wine is therefore perfectly balanced. He is a colourful addition to the ranks of Jurançon growers, but it may be wondered whether the old-stagers in Jurançon view this semi-amateur with the same fraternal admiration as they do Didier Daguenau. Or does Michel mind if they do or not?

GROWERS AT LA CHAPELLE-DE-ROUSSE

■ CLOS LAPEYRE
Jean-Bernard Larrieu and Frédéric Borde
La Chapelle-de-Rousse, 64110 Jurançon
Tel: 05-59-21-50-80
Email: jean-bernard.larrieu@wanadoo.fr
www.jurancon-lapeyre.fr

The Larrieu family goes back several generations at this domaine; Jean-Bernard's forefathers used to grow a variety of crops, including strawberries, as well as vines whose fruit went to the *coopérative* at Gan. Jean-Bernard, however, struck out on his own in 1985, with the first vintage which he made and bottled himself from his 10 hectares of vines. At 330 metres above sea level, he occupies a privileged site towards the northern end of the ridge called La Chapelle-de-Rousse. The hillsides are very steep, so the vines are grown on terraces. Jean-Bernard, a very proud Béarnais, combines much of traditional wine-making with modern techniques. Following the practice he learnt from the *coopérative*, he vinifies at relatively high temperatures and does not necessarily give all his grapes a prelimi-

nary cold maceration; but he is now wholly organic, avoiding herbicides and fertilizers of course, but also working the soil by hand to encourage the vines to plunge as deep as possible into the soil.

The vineyard is roughly equally divided between the two *manseng* varieties, with just a little *petit courbu*. Jean-Bernard's basic **jurançon sec** (*B), aged six months on its lees after vinification in tank, is all *gros manseng*, showing the typical steeliness of this *terroir* and some herbs as well as the usual citrus fruits on the palate. The concentration is balanced by good acidity, and the structure is firm and deep.

If the first *sec* is good, the second is outstanding, made from old vines, which are called in the local language **Vitage Vielh** (***B). The 10% *petit courbu* is complemented more or less equally by the two *mansengs*, at least 60 years old. The grapes are usually harvested at the end of October and fermented in barrels, some new and some having been used once. The wine is aged for 10 months on its lees in the wood, with frequent *bâtonnage*. Jean-Bernard likes to mature this wine as long as possible, sometimes up to four years, before he markets it. It has plenty of grip, a lovely flowery nose touched off by herbs and spices. It is big on the palate, intense with a touch of the cornfield, quite one of the most successful and characterful dry jurançons.

The first **jurançon moëlleux** (**B) is mostly *gros manseng,* usually harvested by two successive *tries* in November. Half is barrel-fermented, the rest made in vat. Jean-Bernard sometimes uses *microbullage* to enhance the fruit. The sweetness is if anything understated, with just a little honey and plenty of herbs on the nose. It is rich on the palate, with excellent balance and appropriate acidity. The **Sélection Petit Manseng** (***C) is harvested even later, perhaps with three visits to the vines. It is only partly fermented in the barrel but to an exotic golden colour. Again there are herbs to balance the tropical fruits, which show an extraordinary fullness in the mouth, with plenty of ripe apricots and mangoes, for example. The wine has a *vendanges tar-*

dives character even if Jean-Bernard does not call it that. It recalls some of the richer wines of Henri Ramonteu, whom Jean-Bernard much admires and who served as his role model in earlier years.

The range of wines ends with two *micro-cuvées*, both from *petit manseng*. One is called **Magendia** (***C) and is only a medium greenish gold in colour, not nearly as dark as you might expect. The wine is a delicious mixture of honey and lemon flavours, seeming to bypass the usual exotic fruits altogether. A bitter-sweet wine indeed, with superb delicacy and refinement.

The other is called **Vent Balaguèr** (***C). Balaguèr is the local name for the warm wind from Spain. In this case Jean-Bernard may stop the plant system from feeding the fruit by picking the grapes earlier than he might otherwise have done and leaving the grapes out on trays to dry in the sun and the wind. If rain threatens, he brings them indoors under cover. This process results in an extraordinary concentration. In the wine you may discover flavours of candied fruits, figs, oranges, currants or apricots, or any combination of these. Despite the opulence, there is the essential underlay of delicate acidity, which continues long into the finish.

■ CAMIN LARREDYA
Jean-Marc Grussaute
La Chapelle de Rousse, 64110 Jurançon
Tel: 05-59-21-74-42 Fax: 05-59-21-76-72
Email: jm.grussaute@wanadoo.fr
www.caminlarredya.fr

Grussaute and Larrieu are neighbours, their boundaries at one point dividing the same amphitheatre. They are also close friends and work regularly together. There is some similarity in the style of the wines as well, though none in the appearance or personality of the wine-makers. Grussaute is big, stocky and very much the second-row forward, while Larrieu is wiry, bearded and more the quiet thinker. Their two domaines, at both of which the vines are all *en terrasse*, share the same sharp

gradients, the same kind of sandy clay soil with large pebbles, and the *poudingue* underground. Grussaute too was once a *coopérateur* but left in 1988 to take charge of the family vines and produce his own wine from them. He had meanwhile trained as an oenologist at Blanquefort.

Larredya is a romantic name, having two meanings in the béarnais tongue; 'twilight' is one, but it also signifies the kind of wooden tiles which were used in times gone by to cover the roofs of the houses in the region. Jean-Marc owns about 8.5 hectares of vines himself, and he buys in grapes from a neighbour who has a further 1.5 hectares. Although he has expanded the vineyard during his cultivation of it, he is not producing any more than he used to because he has disciplined himself to much lower yields than when he began. He allows only one leader per vine, and prunes very hard.

Jean-Marc makes different wines from different parcels of vines. His **jurançon sec** (**B) is also called **L'Esguit**, meaning 'daybreak' in the local tongue, because the plants are on lower and cooler ground but, facing east, more sheltered than most from the midday sun. A blend of the two *mansengs*, picked in mid-October, with a little *petit courbu*, the wine is made like Larrieu's partly in barrel, partly in tank. It is dry and very minerally, firm and full of character. He calls this a *vin de bouche* because of its fruit and volume in the mouth.

Of his three *moëlleux*, the first, **Tradition** (**B), is also called **Costat Darrer**, meaning 'in the back', i.e behind his house. It is beautifully balanced, with just the right freshness to cut through a foie gras. It is made typically from two-thirds *gros* and one-third *petit manseng*, picked towards the end of October or sometimes early in November. **Les Terrasses** (**B), also called **Capseu**, meaning 'high sun' in Béarnais, sometimes displays figs, apricots and mandarines in a year like 2003, though the 2004 was rather finer and more restrained, more a pineapple and quince vintage. The sweetness is accentuated by pinching the stalks of the vine to cut off the supply of sap from the earth, thereby concentrating the juice already in the grapes while retaining the natural acidity (cf. Patrice Lescarret in Gaillac). Jean-Marc's wine is matured in barrels for a year and then a further six months in tanks.

The top *cuvée* is called **Simon** (***C) (also **Sòlhevat** or 'sunrise' because from grapes on east-facing slopes) and is not as heavyweight as one might expect from a top-of-the-range jurançon. The grapes, all *petit manseng*, produce a wine which is fragrant, bright with acidity and 'as multi-layered as the Pyrenean earth from which it derives' (in Jean-Marc's own words).

■ DOMAINE DE SOUCH

Yvonne Hégoburu
805 Chemin de Souch, 64110 Laroin
Tel: 05-59-06-27-22 Fax: 05-59-06-51-55
Email: boyrie.jeanne@neuf.fr

Star of the film *Mondovino,* along with Marguérite, one of her three Pyrenean mountain dogs, Madame Hégoburu is at once the *doyenne* of the appellation and one of its newest recruits. She lives just six kilometres outside Pau, but her pretty *gentilhommière* is completely hidden in the woods south of the city, with magnificent views across the countryside to the Pic du Midi d'Ossau. Although she was born not far from Monein and is thus a daughter of the *pays*, it was not until 1987 that, at the age of 60, she planted vines round her lovely country home. She wanted, she says, to perpetuate the memory of her beloved late husband, who was incidentally a champion *pelota* player.

She describes her venture as a bet with nature, a challenge which she has triumphantly won. She converted to biodynamic production in 1994, out of respect for her husband's belief in natural production. He had played a prominent role in fighting the introduction in the region of industrialized pig-farming because it polluted the rivers and streams. Nor is she exactly a fan of Total and their natural gas excavation at the foot of the hills behind her, though there is little she can do about it. Neigh-

bourhood feeling is so strong on these matters that, according to Madame, one local peasant hanged himself in protest.

Yvonne Hégoburu has a modest six hectares of vines, half of them planted classically in rows, the other half, where the slopes are steep, on terraces. Apart from 15% *gros manseng* and 10% *petit courbu*, the vines are all *petit manseng*. The subsoil is the local *poudingue,* which she translates as pebbles set in crushed rock with the strength and texture of concrete; on top of this is a mix of clay and small stones, allowing the vines to find their way deep into the earth to find moisture.

Madame says the locals call her *la Vieille Folle*; she says she doesn't mind the *folle* bit but doesn't like to be reminded about the *vieille*, and indeed, she carries her years well and elegantly. Her son, Jean-René, so far shows little interest in the vineyard, though officially he is joint owner of the estate. Madame must hope that one day, like so many sons of *vignerons,* he will want to take over the reins.

Meanwhile, her wines are outstanding. The **sec** (**B), from *gros manseng* and *petit courbu,* is pale and fresh, straight and honest; the attack is lively, mineral and lemony. It is made in stainless steel and is aged on its lees for six months. There are two sweet wines, one aged in tank, the other in barrel. The **moëlleux** (**B), from equal quantities of the *mansengs,* has the same liveliness and citrus fruits as the dry wine, but the grapes are of course picked later and the result is half-sweet and delicately balanced, a great aperitif wine. Even in a hot year like 2003 the wine shows lovely acidity. The **Cuvée Marie Kattalin** (***C) derives great complexity from its oak-ageing; it has wonderful barley-sugar, but with a fine grip that keeps the wine from cloying. If you are lucky enough to sample a mature version of this wine, say 10 years on from the vintage, the aromas of Périgord truffle are unmistakeable.

■ **CHÂTEAU JOLYS**
Pierre-Yves Latrille and Marion Latrille-Henry
64290 Gan
Tel: 05-59-21-72-79 Fax: 05-59-21-55-61
www.chateau-jolys.com

It was Monsieur Latrille's mother who decided to buy this property as a residence when the family felt obliged to leave Algeria in 1959. There were no vines whatsoever at the château then, which in fact is more of an attractive manor house, mostly from the 18th century, though the cellars go back to the 15th. The roof is covered with pretty tiles in the old béarnais style.

If he had remained in Algeria, Monsieur Latrille would no doubt have continued with his already successful business career. When he arrived at Jurançon he knew nothing about white wines, but this did not deter him from planting a vineyard—and not an experimental parcel, but 36 hectares of land, by far the largest area under vine in the whole district. The locals thought he was mad. He is no peasant-*vigneron,* but an astute commercial operator, and this is how he conducts his vineyard. He is almost proud of the fact that he has never sat on a tractor: he has staff to do that sort of thing. All the same, he likes to get away from his paperwork, and nothing gives him greater pleasure than to escape

at weekends and spend a few hours on his own, talking to his vines. Today he works in partnership with his daughter Marion, who has pushed further even than her father in the direction of the *vendanges tardives* style.

M. Latrille will not mind if I describe him as a prototypical Frenchman of the old school, with his *belle époque* courtesy and a style of flattery left over from that more elegant age. His voice is loud and clear, and when he starts talking about his beloved vines, he might be rehearsing a speech from Racine, or perhaps from General de Gaulle. He is a great admirer of Henry IV, so much so that, in designing his tasting room, he demanded that its panoramic window should have a view not over the mountains but over the Château of Pau, the birthplace of his hero.

The vineyard at Jolys is divided into three parcels of just about equal size, but some of the vines are planted on north-facing slopes, something which caused local eyebrows to go up and fingers to be wagged back in 1959. M. Latrille is pleased with the results from this eccentricity, except when there are severe spring frosts. The fact that these vines have a later cycle than those more conventionally planted enables him to manage more easily his considerable task of harvesting. He grows only the two *mansengs*, having no time for the *petit courbu* despite recommendations from local experts. 'Advisers don't pay the bills', he says, and there speaks the businessman, fearing the effect of *coulure* in the spring or rot in the autumn on a notoriously fragile grape variety.

The Château Jolys **jurançon sec** (*A) is one of the domaine's best-sellers. It is their only dry wine. Almost all *gros manseng*, the fruit receives the usual destalking and preliminary maceration, but it is also given a malolactic fermentation after the alcoholic fermentation has finished. This is almost unheard of in Jurançon, and his experiment is being watched by others with interest. Perhaps the 'malo' detracts from the fresh fruitiness of the young wine, but it adds instead a depth and con-

centration more often found in the sweeter wines. This is more of a wine for drinking with food.

When he began, Latrille did not believe in *tries successives,* not even for his sweetest wines. Today, perhaps in view of the fact that the domaine now offers four sweet wines, perhaps also because of Marion's innovative contribution, and perhaps also because the law so requires, both *petit* and *gros manseng* grapes are picked in several sessions between the end of October and the new year. For the basic **doux** (*B) the juice, half each *petit* and *gros manseng*, is vinified in tanks and aged there until bottling in the spring of the succeeding year. A fine aperitif, it can also accompany foie gras, smoked salmon, food in a creamy sauce and fresh fruit desserts. The **Cuvée Jean** (**B) is all *petit manseng,* and from the free-run juice of the grapes without addition of any *vin de presse*. The grapes will usually be picked in the middle of November after at least three *tries*; vinified in the tank, the wine is aged in barrel. This is perhaps the best as well as the best-selling wine of the property. The **vendanges tardives** (*D) is from a still later *trie* of *petit manseng*, picked in December, and is made and raised in oak, while the wine called **Epiphanie** (**D+), Marion's creation, is to be much admired by those who love the ultra-rich style, made as it is from grapes picked in January and, for obvious reasons, only in the best years. It is barrel-fermented and aged in the oak for 14 months. Almost orange in colour, the wine has a bouquet of jammy fruit, medlars perhaps, and in the mouth the wine has a plasma-screen power which will be to the taste of many, while contrasting vividly with some of the more delicately styled jurançons produced by Lihour or Daguenau, for example.

One of the great successes of this property is that father and daughter have established a worldwide market for their wines, doing much on the way to put Jurançon as an appellation on the map; the wines continue after many years to be fine examples of the appellation.

■ CLOS THOU

Henri Lapouble Laplace

Chemin Larrédya, 64110 Jurançon

Tel: 05-59-06-08-60 Fax: 05-59-06-87-81

Mobile: 06-80-63-79-58

Email: clos.thou@wanadoo.fr

www.clos-thou.fr

Underlying this seven-hectare vineyard on the eastern side of the Rousse ridge is the charcteristic base of *poudingue*, overlaid with pebbly clay, rich in iron and manganese. The vines face full south, and are made up of 75% *petit manseng*, 20% *gros manseng* and the rest divided between *petit courbu, gros courbu* and *camaralet*. Now well on the way to official organic certification, Henri has for many years insisted on alternation of weed-free and weeded rows, without artificial weedkillers, and fertilized only with natural compost and liquids.

The **jurançon sec** (***B) here is where Henri puts his *petit courbu* and *camaralet,* and they give a lovely balance of freshness and individual character to the more usual grape varieties. This wine will last easily for five years. After a slow pressing, one-third is fermented and aged in wood, the other two-thirds in tank. The sweet jurançons include a tremendous unoaked **100% petit manseng** wine (***C) as well as more conventional blends from the two *manseng* varieties (**B/C). Although it is hard to find poor jurançons anywhere, there are few properties with such individual style as this.

GROWERS IN THE LASSEUBE DISTRICT

■ DOMAINE DE CABARROUY

Freya Skoda and Patrice Limousin

64290 Lasseube

Tel: 05-59-04-23-08

Email: freyskoda@hotmail.com

www.domaine-cabarrouy.oloron-ste-marie.com

These two enterprising adventurers moved here in 1988, having previously been making wine in Muscadet. They lost no time in making their mark in the south, particularly with their refreshing style of dry wine. When they arrived, Freya and Patrice had to give the vineyard priority, and it is only recently that they have found a little time to spare to make their pretty farmhouse a warm and welcoming home.

Clean fruitiness is the hallmark of the wines of this sector of Jurançon. The cooler nights in proximity to the mountains cause the ripening of the grapes to be slower and more balanced. They also explain why the leaves here are still green when picking has almost finished in Monein and the foliage there is all an autumnal brown. The snag at Lasseube is the danger of frost in springtime, so here in the deep south at Cabarrouy the system of growing vines *en hautain* is exaggerated by attaching the plants to stakes two metres high; the vines are then trained to the stakes in espalier style so as to keep the vegetation safely away from the ground. There is still, however, plenty of hot sun just when it is needed in the late autumn, and at Cabarrouy the vines are gently exposed in rows running from north-west to southeast on gently rolling slopes close to the house.

The vineyard covers but 5.5 hectares, which Freya and Patrice planted from scratch. Although tradition has it that the *petit courbu* grape is well suited to this *terroir,* Cabarrouy is devoted entirely to the two *mansengs*. The *gros* is on its own in the **sec** (**A), which is full on the palate but quite sharp and dry in a muscadet kind of way. It is strange how growers who arrive in a new region from another bring with them a style of wine-making which speaks of their first home just as much as it does of their new-found *terroir*.

Eighty percent of the production here is, however, of sweet wines, of which there may be as many as four. A **moëlleux** (**A) from *gros manseng* really is *moëlleux* and not *doux,* delicate, fine and very much a mid-morning refresher. Or there may be a **petit manseng** (**B) raised in tank, marmaladey but still very fresh and lively, a real foie gras partner. Another *doux* is called **Sainte-Catherine** (**B) from late-picked *petit manseng*, which is raised in old barrels. Finally, in bottles the colour of Bristol blue, the top *cuvée,* called **Extrème** (**C), is an all-*petit manseng* wine raised in barrels, half of them new. This is another original wine in the ultra-sweet style, rich in candied fruits and best drunk on its own after dinner, or perhaps in place of a dessert.

■ CLOS GUIROUILH
Jean Guirouilh
Route de Belair, 64290 Lasseube
Tel: 05-59-04-21-45 Fax: 05-59-04-22-73

Clos Guirouilh is towards the southern extremity of the appellation. Following a country road south from Lasseube, you will see signposts now and then to this remote domaine, which can be found after several kilometres of sharp bends that wiggle their way through a lovely countryside, more up and down than at Monein but without the panoramic views that are such a feature at La Chapelle-de-Rousse. This is quiet, really rural Béarn. Jean Guirouilh has a gentle charm and a welcoming smile as well as an impish humour. His beret remains firmly in place, concealing a head whose hair is somewhat in retreat. In the old days his farming forebears used to grow and make a bit of everything, including wine, although the vines were mostly poor hybrids, apart from a parcel of old *gros manseng* which went back to pre-phylloxera times.

Today Jean Guirouilh devotes himself entirely to wine-making, and somehow, from his 10-hectare base in the remotest part of the Jurançonnais, he has managed to secure a place among the great. The family farm may be austere, but the wines are rich; his *vendanges tardives* style is among the most admired of the region. This is all the more remarkable because he keeps himself rather apart from the mainstream of Jurançon life, apparently finding no need to belong to the s*yndicat* of growers or to benefit from their publicity or maps or from being included in the so-called Route des Vins. He combines old and new techniques: he is devoted to his old *foudres,* which he still uses for vinification, but is also wedded to experimentation with newer barrels both for making and ageing his wines.

Guirouilh likes his dry jurançon to be light and fresh, but he dispenses with a preliminary maceration. The **sec** (**A) has a touch of *petit courbu* but is otherwise *gros manseng*; it is flowery and quite grassy, big and with individual character. A second dry wine called **La Peïerine** (**B), meaning 'small stone', is raised in old barrels which have seen perhaps five wines made in them. The wine suggests just the faintest touch of oak, and is quite attractively smokey in character.

With his sweet wines, Guirouilh believes that the optimum maturity of his grapes should coincide with the end of the vine's cycle. So he picks later than most others. The basic **jurançon doux** (**B) is aged partly in barrel and partly in tank. The fruit is deliciously ripe, and this is an outstanding example of a 'first' sweet wine, unpretentious and very drinkable. The **Vendanges Tardives** (***C) is much more serious, the majority *petit manseng* yielding plenty of currants and dates on the palate. The wine is quite viscous, and there is even a touch of Alsatian-style kerosene on the finish; indeed, the wine is quite riesling-ish. The top-of-the-range **Petit Cuyalàa** (**D) is made from the oldest parcels of *petit manseng* and has amazing concentration. Curiously, it is not as big as the Vendanges Tardives. In this world of ultra-sweet wines it is hard to compare one with another with any meaningful accuracy, especially when the general standard is so high. Here, as so often in Jurançon, the difference between two and three stars is marginal.

OTHER GOOD JURANÇON GROWERS IN THE MONEIN DISTRICT

CLOS BELLEVUE
Olivier and Jean Muchada
64360 Cuqueron
Tel: 05-59-21-34-82
Email: closbellevue@club-internet.fr

CLOS CASTET
Alain Labourdette
64360 Cardesse
Tel: 05-59-21-33-09

DOMAINE GAILLOT
Francis Gaillot
64360 Monein
Tel: 05-59-21-31-69
Email: contact@jurancon-gaillot.fr
www.jurancon-gaillot.fr

DOMAINE LARROUDÉ
Christiane and Julien Estoueigt
64360 Lucq-de-Béarn
Tel: 05-59-34-35-40
Email: domaine.larroude@wanadoo.fr
www.domaine-larroude.fr

DOMAINE BORDENAVE BAYARD
Sébastien and Fabrice Bordenave-Montesquiou
Domaine de Montesquiou
64360 Monein
Tel: 05-59-21-31-36

ON THE CENTRAL COTEAUX

DOMAINE BOUSQUET
Jean-Pierre Bousquet
64110 Saint-Faust
Tel: 05-59-83-05-56

DOMAINE DE CINQUAU
Pierre Saubot
64230 Artiguelouve
Tel: 05-59-83-10-41
Email: p.saubot@jurancon.com

AT LA CHAPELLE-DE-ROUSSE

DOMAINE BAZAILLACQ
Alexis and Jean-Luc Bazaillacq
La Chapelle-de-Rousse
64110 Jurançon
Tel: 05-59-83-06-30

CLOS LABRÉE
Michel and Bernard Pissondes
La Chapelle-de-Rousse
64110 Jurançon
Tel: 05-59-21-74-45

CHÂTEAU DE ROUSSE
Marc Labat
La Chapelle-de-Rousse
64110 Jurançon
Tel: 05-59-21-75-08
Email: chateauderousse@wanadoo.fr

CRU LAMOUROUX
R. H. and P. Y. Ziemek-Chigé
La Chapelle-de-Rousse
64100 Jurançon
Tel: 05-59-21-74-41
www.crulamouroux.com

IN THE LASSEUBE SECTOR

DOMAINE BORDENAVE-COUSTARRET
Isabelle and Sébastien Bordenave-Coustarret
64290 Lasseube
Tel: 05-59-21-72-66
Email: domainecoustarret@wanadoo.fr

DOMAINE LATAPY
Irène Guilhendou
64290 Gan
Tel: 05-59-21-71-84
Email: contact@domaine-latapy.com
www.domaine-latapy.com

GRAPE VARIETIES OF SOUTH-WEST FRANCE

Those wines for which a given grape variety is an important element, sometimes a mono-cépage or varietal, are written in capital letters. Grape varieties written in italics are falling out of use.

ABOURIOU	CÔTES DU MARMANDAIS, vdp Saint-Sardos
ALICANTE	vdp Agenais
ARRILOBA	vdp COTEAUX DE CHALOSSE, Vineyards of the Sandy Shore
ARRUFIAC	PACHERENC, CÔTES DE SAINT-MONT, vdp Côtes de Gascogne
AUXERROIS	CAHORS, COTEAUX DU QUERCY, vdp THÉZAC-PERRICARD, Côtes de Millau, Fronton, Bergerac, Pécharmant, Côtes de Duras, Côtes du Marmandais, Côtes du Brulhois, Floc, Ariégeois
BAR(R)OQUE	TURSAN, Floc
BOUCHALÈS	vdp Agenais
BRAUCO	(see Fer Servadou)
CABERNET FRANC	Entraygues, ESTAING, Côtes de Millau, Gaillac, BERGERAC, PÉCHARMANT, CÔTES DE DURAS, CÔTES DU MARMANDAIS, BUZET, CÔTES-DU-BRULHOIS, Fronton, LAVILLEDIEU-DU-TEMPLE, vdp MONTAUBAN, vdp SAINT-SARDOS,TURSAN, vdp COTEAUX-DE-CHALOSSE, BÉARN, Madiran, Iroulèguy, Ariégeois
CABERNET SAUVIGNON	Entraygues, ESTAING, Gaillac, BERGERAC, PÉCHAR-MANT, CÔTES-DE-DURAS, CÔTES DU MARMANDAIS, BUZET, CÔTES DU BRULHOIS, Floc, CÔTES DE SAINT-MONT, Tursan, Béarn, Madiran, Fronton, Ariégeois
CAMARALET	Jurançon
CHASAN	Coteaux de Chalosse
CHENIN BLANC	ENTRAYGUES, ESTAING, CÔTES DE MILLAU, Saussignac
COLOMBARD	vdp CÔTES DE GASCOGNE, Floc
CÔT	(see Auxerrois)
COURBU NOIR	Béarn
COURBU (PETIT)	Côtes de Saint-Mont, Pacherenc, Jurançon, IROULÉGUY
DURAS	GAILLAC, Côtes de Millau
EGIODOLA	Floc, Coteaux de Chalosse
FER SERVADO	(aka fer, mansois, braucol and pinenc) MARCILLAC, ENTRAYGUES, GAILLAC, CÔTES-DU-BRULHOIS, BÉARN, Côtes de Saint-Mont, Madiran, vdp Agenais
FOLLE BLANCHE	vdp Côtes de Gascogne, Floc
GAMAY	Entraygues, GAILLAC, CÔTES DE MILLAU, COTEAUX DE GLANES, Fronton, LAVILLEDIEU-DU-TEMPLE, vdp Montauban, vdp Saint-Sardos, Floc
GAMAY SAINT-LAURENT	(see Abouriou)
JURANÇON À JUS BLANC	vdp Montauban
JURANÇON NOIR	vdp Côtes-du-Tarn, vdp Agenais, Coteaux-du-Quercy

LAUZET	Jurançon
LEN DE L'EL	GAILLAC
LISTAN	vdp Côtes de Gascogne
MALBEC	(see Auxerrois)
MANSENG, GROS	vdp Côtes de Gascogne, Floc, CÔTES DE SAINT-MONT, Tursan, PACHERENC, JURANÇON, Irouléguy
MANSENG NOIR	Béarn
MANSENG, PETIT	CÔTES DE SAINT-MONT, PACHERENC, JURANÇON
MANSOIS	(see Fer Servadou)
MAUZAC	GAILLAC, Estaing, Côtes de Millau, vdp Comté-Tolosan
MÉRILLE	Fronton, vdp Agenais, vdp Comté-Tolosan
MERLOT	Cahors, Gaillac, vdp Thézac-Perricard,Estaing, vdp Montauban, BERGERAC, MONTRAVEL, PÉCHARMANT, CÔTES DE DURAS, CÔTES DU MARMANDAIS, BUZET, CÔTES DU BRULHOIS, Coteaux de Glanes, vdp Thézac-Perricard
MOUSTROUN	(see Tannat)
MUSCADELL	Bergerac, MONBAZILLAC, Saussignac, Rosette, Montravel, Gaillac, Côtes de Duras
NÉGRET DE BANHARS	Estaing
NÉGRETTE	FRONTON, Lavilledieu-du-Temple
ONDENC	Gaillac
PINENC	(see Fer Servadou)
PINOTOUS D'ESTAING	Estaing
PRUNELAR(D)(T)	Gaillac, Lavilledieu-du-Temple
RAFFIAT DE MONCADE	Béarn
ROUSSELET DE BÉARN	BÉARN
SAUVIGNON	Gaillac, BERGERAC, Monbazillac, Saussignac, MONTRAVEL, CÔTES DE DURAS, CÔTES DU MARMANDAIS, BUZET, Floc, Tursan, Pacherenc
SÉGALIN	Coteaux de Glanes
SÉMILLON	Gaillac, BERGERAC, MONBAZILLAC, SAUSSIGNAC, ROSETTE, MONTRAVEL, CÔTES DE DURAS, Buzet, Floc
SYRAH	CÔTES DE MILLAU, GAILLAC, Fronton, LAVILLEDIEU-DU-TEMPLE, vdp Montauban, vdp Saint-Sardos, Coteaux du Quercy
TANNAT	Cahors, Côtes de Millau, Lavilledieu-du-Temple, vdp Montauban, vdp Saint-Sardos, Floc, CÔTES DE SAINT-MONT, TURSAN, vdp Coteaux de Chalosse, MADIRAN, BÉARN, IROULÉGUY
UGNI BLANC	vdp CÔTES DE GASCOGNE, Floc

WINE AND FOOD PAIRINGS

The wines of the South-West are ideal partners for the food of the region, itself as idiosyncratic as the wines.

For those not familiar with the wines, the following table may be of help in buying wines, ordering them in a restaurant or trying to organize a party on the spot or back home.

	Shellfish Other fish, grilled or fried	Fish with sauce	Garbures, potées, pot-au-feu, etc.	Foie gras	Charcuterie	Salades composées	Mushroom dishes
Dry white (1) Entraygues, Estaing, Millau, Gaillac, Landes, C. de Gascogne, mousseux brut	🍷	🍷	🍷	🍷	🍷	🍷	🍷
Dry white (2) Bergerac, Montravel, Duras, Marmande, Buzet, Brulhois, St.-Mont, Tursan	🍷	🍷	🍷	🍷	🍷	🍷	🍷
Dry White (3) Pacherenc, Jurançon Sec, Irouléguy, all oaked dry whites	🍷	🍷	🍷	🍷	🍷	🍷	🍷
Medium White Bergerac moëlleux, Rosette, C. de Montravel, Gaillac moëlleux, mousseux demi-sec	🍷	🍷	🍷	🍷	🍷	🍷	🍷
Sweet White (1) Gaillac doux, Haut-Montravel, Pacherenc sec (all unoaked)	🍷	🍷	🍷	🍷	🍷	🍷	🍷
Sweet White (2) Mousseux doux, Monbazillac, Saussignac, Jurançon, all other oaked whites	🍷	🍷	🍷	🍷	🍷	🍷	🍷
Vins Rosés	🍷	🍷	🍷	🍷	🍷	🍷	🍷
Red (1) Fronton, Tursan, Primeurs	🍷	🍷	🍷	🍷	🍷	🍷	🍷
Red (2) Marmande, Landes vins de pays	🍷	🍷	🍷	🍷	🍷	🍷	🍷
Red (3) Brulhois, Gaillac, Duras, unoaked Bergerac, St.-Mont, Béarn	🍷	🍷	🍷	🍷	🍷	🍷	🍷
Red (4) Buzet, Cahors (unoaked), Pécharmant	🍷	🍷	🍷	🍷	🍷	🍷	🍷
Red (5) Madiran, Irouléguy	🍷	🍷	🍷	🍷	🍷	🍷	🍷

Four categories of matching are proposed:

ideal   good   possible   bad

These suggestions are conventional rather than original. Particular dishes or recipes may suggest unusual wine partners. In restaurants where there is a wine waiter who looks as if he knows his job, take his advice if in doubt.

Light entrées, chicken, veal	Offal, poultry, roasted or in sauce	Cassoulet	Grills, roasts	Stews, game	Soft cows' cheeses	Hard cows' cheeses	Roquefort, hard ewes' cheeses	Fruity desserts	Sweeter desserts
bad	bad	bad	bad	bad	possible	possible	bad	bad	bad
possible	possible	bad	bad	bad	good	good	possible	bad	bad
possible	possible	bad	bad	bad	good	good	good	possible	possible
good	possible	bad	bad	bad	good	good	ideal	ideal	good
possible	bad	bad	bad	bad	possible	possible	ideal	ideal	ideal
bad	bad	bad	bad	bad	possible	possible	ideal	good	ideal
good	bad	possible	bad	bad	possible	good	possible	possible	bad
good	good	ideal	good	bad	ideal	ideal	good	good	bad
ideal	good	good	good	good	ideal	ideal	good	possible	bad
ideal	good	good	ideal	good	ideal	ideal	good	bad	bad
good	possible	bad	ideal	ideal	good	ideal	bad	bad	bad
possible	good	possible	ideal	ideal	possible	good	possible	bad	bad

GLOSSARY

GLOSSARY

agrément the formal licence from INAO to use the name of an appellation on the label of a wine

agrumes citrus fruits, such as lemon and grapefruit, whose aroma is commonly recalled on the bouquet of white wines

appellation d'origine contrôlée (AOC) a top area of wine production, strictly controlled by statute

argileux consisting of clay

argilo-calcaire clay mixed with chalk or lime-stone

argilo-limoneux clay mixed with ground quartz and similar elements

argilo-sableux clay mixed with sand

assemblage a blend of wines from different grape varieties or containers

ban de vendange an official announcement authorizing the beginning of the grape harvest

barrique a wooden barrel or cask normally containing 225 litres (about 300 bottles)

bâtonnage the breaking up, usually with a stout wooden stick or sometimes by mechanical means, of the solid matter which falls to the bottom of a cask during fermentation or during the ageing of wine in the barrel, and reincorporating it into the wine

bidon a portable wine container, usually made of plastic

bonbonne a demi-john, a glass container often clothed in wicker

botrytis a fungus which attacks the skins of grapes. A variety of it called *cinerea* is a pre-condition of many fine sweet wines and is thus called 'noble rot'.

bourru rough, unsophisticated, still fermenting (said of newly made wine)

cagette a small, usually perforated container for carrying the grapes from the vineyard to the *chais*

calcaire chalk or limestone

cassis blackcurrants

cave cellar

caviste a wine merchant

cayrou a walled enclosure (also *clos*)

cépage grape variety

chais a building for the making or storing of wine

chapeau the solid mass made up of grape skins, pips etc., thrown to the surface of wine during fermentation

clos see *cayrou*

collage the fining of wine, causing the lees to sink to the bottom of a container, achieved by pouring egg whites or bentonite on the surface of the wine

coulure a disease of the vine halting the development of young grapes and ultimately causing them to rot and fall from the plant

culture raisonnée the voluntary adoption of some neo-organic practices

cuvaison the period of time, including that following the end of fermentation, during which the wine remains on its skins, stalks and pips

cuve a vat, usually of concrete, steel or fibre-glass

cuvée wine drawn off one or more vats

dans un seul tenant an unbroken expanse of vineyard all in one parcel

débourbage the drawing off of grape juice from its *débris* prior to fermentation

délestage the draining of a vat during vinification, the re-homogenization of the must and its return to the vat for further fermenting

demi-muid a wooden barrel of varying volume, usually about twice the size of a *barrique*

effeuillage the removal from the vine of leaves tending to prevent exposure of the grapes to the sun

égrappage the stripping of stalks from the bunches of grapes prior to vinification

élevage the maturing or ageing of wine after vinification

encépagement the proportion of various different grape varieties either in a vineyard or in a particular wine

entrée de gamme a grower's first, basic, least sophisticated wine

finesse a quality of subtlety, elegance and softness as opposed to rough strength

floraison the flowering of the vine

foudre a large old-fashioned vat, often of huge proportions

fouloir a machine for crushing grapes often combined with an *égrappoir* for removing the stalks, when it is called an *égrappoir-fouloir*

fût a cask, usually denoting a new or nearly new oak barrel

galet a large round pebble-like stone of the kind often found beside or in rivers

gouleyant quaffable, more-ish, easy to drink

goût du terroir the taste of wine deriving from a combination of soil, locality, grape variety and climate which is characteristic of a particular wine

gras fat, rich, buttery

grave (of the soil); gravelly, composed of small stones

greffe a vine graft

gris a very pale pink colour (not grey)

guyot the training of vines on wire, limited to one (*guyot simple*) or two (*guyot double*) long shoots

hectare an area of 10,000 square metres, the equivalent of just under 2.5 acres

hectolitre 100 litres, about 22 gallons

INAO Institut National des Appellations d'Origine: French national regulator for wines

liquoreux the sweetest grade of wines, nothing to do with liqueurs

macération the leaving of skins, stalks, pulp, fruit and juice in contact with each other

macération carbonique a technique of vinification where the grapes go into the vats whole and are allowed to disintegrate on their own under a protective layer of carbonic gas

macération pelliculaire maceration at a cool temperature before the commencement of vinification, also called 'skin-contact'

maître de chais cellar-master, in charge of the wine-making and the ageing of the wines

malolactic fermentation a second fermentation of wine after the first alcoholic fermentation has finished. It converts malic (sour) acids into softer malic acids. Sometimes called 'malo' for short.

méthode gaillacoise (or **ancestrale**) the original pre-champagne method of making sparkling wine, as in Gaillac

méthode traditionelle the Champagne way of making sparkling wine, where the words *méthode champenoise* are not allowed to be used

microbullage micro-oxygenation: the introduction of tiny quantities of oxygen into a maturing wine, so as to avoid the necessity of racking the wine and so disturbing its lees

millerandage uneven swelling of the grapes, a problem usually associated with a cool summer

moëlleux mellow and full, usually denoting a degree of sweetness

mono-cépage a wine that is made exclusively from one grape variety, otherwise called a varietal

must the contents of a *cuve*, both liquid and solid, during fermentation

négociant a dealer in wine, often a blender too

nerveux lively and vigorous, as applied to wines

oxidization the effect of the exposure of wine to oxygen

pain grillé an element in the bouquet of some wines, recalling toasted bread

passerillage over-ripeness of grapes attained by leaving them to shrivel and partly evaporate in the sun

perlé containing tiny bubbles, giving a tingly rather than fizzy sensation on the tongue

phylloxera a rapidly multiplying aphid which feeds on and destroys the roots of vines

pierre à fusil the smell or taste of gun-flint, a steeliness on the bouquet of wine

pigeage the breaking up of the crust which forms on the top of fermenting wine, so as to ensure that the juice has maximum access to the solids

porte-greffe a rootstock on to which grape-bearing varieties are grafted

primeur a wine made for drinking within a year from the vintage, and certainly before the next one

racking transferring the wine from one container to another to aerate it, and then returning it to its original container

rafle the wood and fibre, as opposed to the fruit, in a bunch of grapes

récolte harvest or crop

régisseur the overall manager of a vineyard, the owner being often absentee

remontage the circulation of the wine in a fermentation container, by pumping it back into the top of the container so as to keep the crust on the top of the wine moist, preferably submerged

rendement the yield in terms of quantity of a vineyard, usually expressed in hectolitres per hectare

robe the colour or appearance of a wine

saignage the bleeding off of pink juice from fermenting black grapes to prevent full colouring of the wine. A method of making *vins rosés*.

schiste a flaky, brittle soil; shale

soutirage *see* racking

tête de cuvée a producer's top wine

tonneau a large cask, a hogshead

tonnelier a cooper or barrel-maker

torréfaction the smell of hot, dry roasting, as of the coffee bean

trie the selective picking of well-ripened grapes, either on the vine or in the *chais*

typicité the individual character of a wine or vineyard, distinguishing it from another's

vendange the grape harvest

vendange tardive the late harvesting of over-ripe grapes, usually well into the early winter

vendange verte the removal of whole bunches of unripe grapes in midsummer to promote concentration and quality in the bunches remaining

vigneron a grower of vines, or a wine-maker, often both at the same time

vin de garage wine, usually from a small grower, made in tiny quantities, to the highest specification, and usually sold at inexplicably high prices

vin de garde a wine that needs ageing

vin de pays a wine from a recognized area, but not within a district of AOC or VDQS. Also, a wine made within an AOC or VDQS which does not comply with their rules.

vin de presse the wine that results from the pressing of the solid matter at the bottom of a container, after the free-run juice has been drawn off

vin de table a wine which conforms to no known rules, because it need not by law do so

vin délimité de qualité supérieure (VDQS) statutory, legally controlled area of wine production, not so highly rated as AOC areas

vrac (en) in bulk; in large containers other than bottles

BIBLIOGRAPHY

ENGLISH TITLES

Brown, Michael, and Sybil Brown. *Food and Wine of South-West France.* London: B.T. Batsford, 1980.

Duijker, Hubrecht, and Hugh Johnson. *The Wine Atlas of France.* London: Mitchell Beazley, 1997.

George, Rosemary. *French Country Wines.* London: Faber & Faber, 1990.

Page, C. E. *Armagnac: The Spirit of Gascony.* London: Bloomsbury, 1989.

Penning-Rowsell, Edmund. *The Wines of Bordeaux.* 4th ed. London: Penguin, 1979.

Robinson, Jancis. *Vines, Grapes and Wines.* London: Mitchell Beazley, 1986.

Shand, P. Morton. *A Book of French Wines.* London: Jonathan Cape, 1960 (also revised by Cyril Ray, London, 1964).

Simon, André. *The History of the Wine Trade in England.* London: Holland Press, 1964.

FRENCH TITLES

Baudel, José. *Le Vin de Cahors.* 2d ed. Parnac: Les Producteurs des Côtes d'Olt, 1977.

Baynac. *La Crise Phyolloxérique et ses Conséquences dans le Canton de Luzech.* 1884.

Blanc, René. *Histoire du Pays de Duras.* Bayac: Éditions du Roc de Bourzac, 1987.

Bosc, Zéfir. *La Vigne et le Vin du Fel et d'Entraygues.* Rodez, 1992.

Brumont, François. *Madiran et Saint-Mont.* Biarritz: Atlantica, 1999.

Capdevielle, Pierre. *Le Vin de Cahors des Origines à Nos Jours.* Toulouse: Éditions Milan, 1983.

Casamayor, Pierre. *Vins du Sud-Ouest et des Pyrénées.* Toulouse: Éditions Daniel Briand/Robert Laffont, 1983.

Catalogue des Variétés et Clones de Vignes Cultivées en France. Le Grau-du-Roi: Etablissement National Technique pour l'Amélioration de la Viticulture (Entav), 1997.

Delfaud, Jean, and Jean-François Dutilh. *Vignobles du Piémont Pyrénéen.* Pau: Les Feuilles du Pin à Crochets, 2003.

Dufor, Henri. *Armagnac, Eaux-de-Vie et Terroir.* Toulouse: privately printed, 1982.

Duquoc, Emmanuel. *Guide des Vins de Cahors.* Castelnaud-la-Chapelle: L'Hydre Éditions , 2003.

Dutilh, Jean-François, and Dominique Julien. *Le Jurançon en Lumière.* Pau: Éditions Gypaète, 2005.

Escudier, Adrien. *Histoire de Fronton et du Frontonnais.* Toulouse: APAMP: 1982.

Féret, Edouard, and Marc-Henry Lemay. *Bergerac et Ses Vins.* Bordeaux, 1994.

Ginestet, Bernard, and Jean-Pierre Déroudille. *Bergerac/Monbazillac.* Paris: Jacques Legrand, 1987.

Gombert, Pierre. *Le Vallon de Marcillac.* Rodez: Éditions B. J. Photo, 1990.

Guyot, Jules. *Rapport sur la Viticulture Comparée du Sud-Ouest et la France.* 1863.

Guyot, Jules. *Etude des Vignobles de France Région Sud-Ouest.* Paris 1876 (reprinted by Jeanne Laffitte, Marseille, 1982).

Jouffreau, Jean. *La Passion Faite Vin . . . de Cahors.* Cahors: privately printed, 1993.

Jullien, André. *Topographie de Tous les Vignobles Connus.* Paris/Geneva: Champion-Slatkine, 1985.

Loubergé, Jean. *Jurançon, Un Vin d'Hier Pour Aujourd'hui.* Biarritz: J. & D. Éditions, 1993.

Monteil, Alexis. *Déscription du Département de l'Aveyron.* Rodez: Éditions pour le Pays d'Oc, 1816.

Rézeau, Pierre. *Le Dictionnaire des Noms de Cépages de France.* Paris: CNRS, 1997.

Séguier, Philippe. *Le Vignoble de Gaillac.* Toulouse: Éditions Daniel Briand, 1991.

INDEX

ACKNOWLEDGMENTS

My deepest thanks to the countless winemakers of South-West France who have been so generous to me with their time and their wines; and to my wife, Jeanne, for her eagle-eyed proofreading of my text.

My greatest pleasure has been the co-edition of this book by my friends at Éditions du Rouergue in Rodez, France, and the University of California Press in Berkeley, USA. My warmest thanks to those who have made this possible and to the teams in both firms who have worked to produce this book. Its availability in the French and English languages will serve to make the wines of South-West France known to an ever-widening public.